LEARNING

DISORDERS

Volume 4
Reading

BARBARA BATEMAN, Editor

Special Child Publications, Inc.

© 1971 SPECIAL CHILD PUBLICATIONS, INC.
4535 Union Bay Place N.E.
Seattle, Washington 98105

3 7 /. 9
H 3 6 L
9 9 9 / 6
Feb. 1977

Standard Book Number: 87562-023-X
Library of Congress Catalog Card Number: 68-85

Printed in the United States of America

The editor thanks

The authors who generously, competently, and efficiently shared their ideas,

The readers who care enough about helping children learn to read, to read one more book of readings on reading,

Jeanne Carlson who assisted mightily and outstandingly in preparing the manuscript, and

Hope Yee who knows why.

Barbara Bateman
Eugene, Oregon

CONTENTS

PART I. PREVENTING READING FAILURE

PART II. DIAGNOSIS AND REMEDIATION—
PSYCHOEDUCATIONAL VIEWS

PART IV. THE FUTURE

THE PLAN OF THIS BOOK

This book, Volume 4 in the LEARNING DISORDERS series, differs from the first three volumes in that it has a single theme—reading and its disorders. Part I presents papers on initial reading instruction. If reading instruction were improved significantly, it is reasonable to hope and believe that the incidence of reading failure and disability could be decreased. These first papers constitute promising approaches to "doing it right the first time," i.e., preventing reading failure, and are of special interest to all those concerned with developmental reading programs and their implementation—regular classroom teachers, administrators, and reading specialists.

However fervently we might hope or believe that much reading failure is preventable, nonetheless, at this point in time there are millions of children in our schools who are handicapped by inadequate reading skills. Parts II and III of this volume present papers on the diagnosis and remediation of disabled readers from psychoeducational and medical-educational views. The controversial concept of dyslexia is presented in Part III in two papers which we believe offer educationally useful and constructive implications. Many believe that the confusion surrounding the term dyslexia is so great that the best alternative is to abandon it completely. Another position is that greater efforts should be spent in clarifying the concept, rather than in giving it up. The papers in Parts II and III are of direct interest and concern to those involved in reading pathology, including remedial reading specialists, psychologists, pediatricians and others.

The final section, Part IV, highlights issues and trends, particularly as they effect future directions in reading instruction and research. Researchers, curriculum planners, and all thoughtful, concerned citizens will find food for thought in these papers dealing with evaluating reading instruction, future reading research, status of reading in our inner city schools, and the examination of the importance and relevance of reading to the electronic age.

Each Part is introduced by a brief integrative overview of the papers and issues in the section. We hope and believe this form of a summary and abstract will be useful to our readers.

Barbara Bateman, Ph.D.
Professor of Education
Department of Special Education
University of Oregon
Eugene, Oregon

PART I. PREVENTING READING FAILURE

Editor's Introduction

We can no longer hide our heads or our inadequate reading instruction in platitudinal sands. Reading failure is a large and regrettable reality. It will not go away by criticizing reading achievement tests a bit louder or longer; it will not go away by counting the number of children who, fifty years ago, went to work on the farms and did not have to be taught in the classroom; it will not go away by shaking (or nodding) our heads in rhythm with the phonics versus whole word pendulum; it will not go away by listing once again the multiplicity of causal culprits said to be responsible; it might not even go away with the publication of one more volume of papers on the problem and possible solutions. The report of the Secretary's (HEW) National Advisory Committee on Dyslexia and Related Reading Disorders, READING DISORDERS IN THE UNITED STATES, published in August 1969, begins with the statement that "Eight million children in America's elementary and secondary schools today will not learn to read adequately."

The purpose of this present collection of papers is to provide a degree of educational direction and assistance and moral support to those committed to reducing the magnitude and severity of reading failure. The papers range in tone from angry to optimistic; in style from anecdotal to scholarly; and in terminological preference from dyslexia to dyspedagogia. One of the apparent controversies highlighted by contrasting papers in Parts I and III is whether the source of reading failure lies in teaching or in the child. Another controversy, more alluded to than presented directly, is that of how reading should initially be taught. The value of various approaches to diagnosis and remediation is another source of disagreement among the authors represented. Expressed opinions on the appropriateness of conventional multidisciplinary kinds of diagnoses range from essential to irrelevant.

The genuine resolution of controversy and disagreement is usually preceded by finding areas of agreement and followed by changes in behavior. We offer the following points as a possible beginning to constructive reconciliation and the shedding of light rather than heat on the complex and frustrating area of reading failure:

1. Improved initial reading instruction could substantially reduce, if not virtually eliminate, reading failure. The papers in Part I share this emphasis, which includes a shifting of responsibility for adequate reading performance from the child, his parents, his language background, etc., and onto the teacher and the reading program used.

2. The possibility exists that even if reading instruction were better, some children would fail to learn adequately because of differences or deficiencies within their own makeup (dyslexia). Although the Secretary's (HEW) National Advisory Committee declared that the term "dyslexia" serves no useful purpose, two papers selected for this volume use it and, in our opinion, need in no way apologize for so doing. Both papers describe the term sufficiently to be communicated clearly to most readers. Even if different reading teaching might have prevented or alleviated most severe disabilities, the fact is that we now have hundreds of thousands of severely disabled readers. To say they need not have been reading failures is not helpful to these children. Careful reading of the two papers which constitute Part II suggests that our abandonment of the term dyslexia may have been premature.

3. The evidence to date clearly suggests that decoding and comprehension are separable and it almost as clearly dictates a strong initial emphasis on teaching decoding skills. Schiffman and Daniels caution us against a total turning away from comprehension, however, as it will always remain the purpose for which we decode.

A child who is successfully taught to read will not, by definition, be a failure in reading. The papers by Bruner, O'Keefe, Glass, Vail, Deverell, and Schiffman and Daniels compellingly suggest that excellent initial reading instruction is possible and will probably reduce the number of reading disabilities in children. The papers by Bruner, O'Keefe, Glass and Vail present specific and detailed teaching suggestions. All four methods or programs—Distar, STARTER/101, Perceptual Conditioning, and Formula Phonics—have been used with very encouraging results. The programs all appear to have both developmental and remedial applications. Programs or techniques which work well with exceptional children or "difficult-to-teach" (for whatever reason) children frequently are even more effective with the bulk of ordinary children whose incidental learning capabilities are so intact the children seem to need but little systematic teaching.

A new and laudable emphasis on educational accountability pervades the philosophy of these programs. It is as though the authors have heard too many excuses for our schools' failure to teach reading well. They seem weary of the blame for reading failure being placed on the child because of some esoteric disability (dyslexia, perceptual dysfunction, etc.); on the family because of an absent father, aggressive sister, alcoholic mother, or on low achievement motivation; or on any other set of factors outside the school and the reading program. Now is the time, they seem to be saying, to look squarely at the nature of the skills to be taught and to build programs which efficiently teach these skills to all children.

The responsibility for successful reading is placed squarely on the reading instruction. If a child fails to learn to read it is because, to these authors, he was inadequately taught. Yes, of course; but isn't that just playing with words, some might ask. No, it is much more than that. The teacher who has specific, successful ways to teach all the essential skills of reading (and who is fully committed to the premise that all children will learn if she teaches well enough) may behave quite differently from the teacher who truly believes that factors such dyslexia, low IQ, immaturity, minimal cerebral dysfunction, or others, do prevent successful responses to reading teaching.

But, one might ask, are there not real, if rare, factors outside the teacher's control which make it all but impossible for some children to learn to read even with excellent instruction? Let us suppose for the sake of discussion there are. Even so, we cannot predict which children, if any, will fail to respond to adequate instruction. The authors in this section would probably agree it is better for the teacher to behave as if 100 per cent of the children can be taught and to fail with 1 per cent than to assume only 90 per cent will learn and thereby fail with at least 10 per cent and probably many more. During the school day the accountable teacher believes it is his responsibility to teach all his children and behaves accordingly; during the evening he may occasionally wonder if Rupert will ever remember the short vowel sounds.

Decoding has emerged from the shadows into its proper place as the essential prerequisite for reading to obtain meaning. Each of the reading programs described in this section systematically teaches children to unlock the printed word—to convert visual symbols into spoken words. Deverell's discussion of the feasibility and necessity of this conversion prior to comprehension is highly persuasive.

In the final paper of the section, Schiffman and Daniels examine the many splendored skills called comprehension. They acknowledge a rapid swing of the educational pendulum toward decoding and express some concern at the current neglect of comprehension. This section contains five papers on decoding and only one on comprehension—a division and emphasis which reflects the very focus of their concern. This emphasis on adequate teaching of decoding also reflects, obviously, the editor's conviction that reading failure will not be substantially reduced until teachers are more skilled in teaching decoding. These programs—Distar, STARTER/101, Perceptual Conditioning and Formula Phonics—represent the application of task analysis and principles of learning to the teaching of reading. We know the outcome of forty years of reading instructional techniques which were not so derived. Now is the "Right to Read" era; it seems an excellent time to explore new and promising programs.

Teaching Disorders

Elaine C. Bruner
Educational Specialist
Bureau of Educational Research
University of Illinois
Urbana, Illinois

Let us stop talking in terms of what children have learned. Let us not say that this child learned to discriminate configurations. Let us say that he was taught to discriminate configurations. Let us not say that a child learned to rhyme. Let us say that he was taught to rhyme. Let us not say that a child learned good listening skills. Let us say that he was taught good listening skills. Let us say further that if a child does not know something, he has not been taught. That means we cannot say that a child did not learn to discriminate between long vowels and short vowels. It means we must say that he was not taught to discriminate between long vowels and short vowels. We cannot say that a child does not remember sounds from one day to the next. It means we must say that he was not taught to remember sounds. We cannot say that a child did not learn how to read. It means that we did not teach him how to read.

If it sounds like I am asking you to reconsider what we have called the child's learning disorders and to relabel them teaching disorders, that is the message. In place of the word learning we will substitute the word teaching. In place of the phrase "he knows," we will substitute "he has been taught." The description of the child as "he knows or he has learned his letters" is now changed to "he has been taught his letters." This means that somehow through teaching he knows his letters. The teaching was accomplished either by teaching materials provided the child so he could teach himself, or by a teaching machine, or by a human teacher. Now we are talking in concrete terms. In place of saying "the child does not know his letters," we can say, "he needs materials, a machine, or a teacher to teach him his letters." We have to recast the problem this way in order to take action. This recasting or relabeling is urgent. When a teacher starts thinking in terms of teaching, she is automatically accepting the responsibility. Now she can examine her materials, machines, or herself.

Once the teacher has agreed to try to think in these terms, she can say to herself, "I accept the fact that learning is a by-product of teaching. If my student hasn't learned, I haven't taught him. I can't blame the student. I must blame the teaching — the teaching techniques, the teaching materials, or the teaching situation. If my student has learning problems, I have to translate them into my teaching problems."

I was taught (learned) this point of view in my recent years as a member of the University of Illinois research and teaching team presently headed by Siegfried Engelmann and Wesley Becker.[1] One day I faced the children I was teaching, children with labeled learning disorders ranging from "mentally handicapped" to "culturally disadvantaged" to "emotionally disturbed." I told myself that they could learn if I could teach them, and that if they could not learn it was because I could not teach them. Later that morning I faced the college students I was training to teach. Some of them were not learning. I told myself that if they were not learning, there was something wrong with what or how I was teaching or with me. That afternoon I went to a class where I was the student. The teacher could not understand why I was not absorbing a certain concept he had so carefully explained. I told him, "If I can't learn, it's because you can't teach me."

This paper will attempt to discuss the process of translating learning disorders into teaching disorders. I will try to teach the teacher how to start analyzing her teaching techniques, teaching materials and teaching situation to be a more effective teacher especially for those children who have been unable to learn to read, who are termed "not ready" or those reading below grade level.

PROBLEM AREAS

As a teacher who has been teaching for over ten years, I like to read papers such as this and be able to identify myself in the paper, recognize problems I have been faced with, and to abstract some ideas which I can translate into immediate action in the classroom. I will try to do this in the present essay, but first, we must delineate some specific prob-

[1]My debt to Engelmann is especially great. The reader is referred primarily to his books CONCEPTUAL LEARNING and PREVENTING FAILURE IN THE PRIMARY GRADES.

lems. After we have spelled out these problems, then we can suggest teaching techniques and materials to remediate them.

We are faced with the problem of teaching children who have been tested and labeled. But the label does not tell us what to do. This child now qualifies for special education classes. That child failed to pass reading readiness tests. Another child has perceptual problems. Still another is reading at the 1.4 grade level and he should be reading at 4.3 level. We have children with labels. Before we can begin to teach children, we have to pinpoint the specific deficits. What do we know about child one's ability to be taught the letter names? His label does not pinpoint his problem. Child two is not ready. Not ready for what? Not ready to be taught to rhyme? The child with perceptual problems — can he or can he not be taught to discriminate between one symbol and another? The child reading below grade level is a real challenge. Do we return him to where he would be working during the third month of the first grade?

One solution to the problem is to reason that reading is a skill with an absolute standard and that standard must apply to everybody. Either the child can read or he cannot read. The fact that he has been tested and has a label does not alter the standard, it alters the teaching method. If he cannot read, which subskills must he be taught? Driving a car is a skill with an absolute standard that applies to everybody. Think of yourself. Either you can drive a car or you cannot drive a car. If you cannot drive a car, which subskills must you be taught? Do you have to be taught to change a tire or clean the carburetor? If the latter two skills can be postponed because they would be nice to know but are not essential to being taught to drive, let us hope your teacher omits them and teaches them later.

Which subskills, for the absolute standard, must a child be taught so he can read? Are there some skills which we are trying to teach now that could be omitted or be taught after the child started to read? And, how do we define beginning reading?

We are going to start to examine what we have been teaching and how we have been teaching it. Then we are going to analyze these materials and techniques because the children with reading disorder labels need to have teachers who can analyze and criticize themselves. These children need teachers like that because, for a variety of reasons, they were not taught (did not learn) reading subskills initially and now have some failure and a poor psychological outlook compounded with their other problems. I know what a challenge this can be to analyze and criticize yourself and your materials, because I have done it and I am doing it every day. I am thinking now as I write that if you are not learning what I am presenting it is because I am not teaching you well enough. There is nothing wrong with your learning — it is with my teaching. A helpful attitude to have as you read the remainder of this paper is to say to yourself that for many of the children you are teaching this may be their last chance for success. If they experience another set of failures in reading they may never again trust another teacher.

Let us choose a few critical problem areas to discuss and see if we can then decide which skills we must teach, which are essential. Let us discuss various types of reading readiness, pupil performance level, and subskills.

Reading Readiness

A teacher holds up a large card with a red apple in the center. At the top are a capital *A* and a circle stick α. The teacher asks, "Who knows what this is?" This is a familiar readiness-type task. Some children must fail to learn from this presentation. Why? You play children for a moment and picture that card with the α and the apple. Can you think of a dozen answers to the question, "Who knows what this is?" What were some of your answers? Here are some:

"apple"
"card"

"fruit"
"red"
"round"
"my name — Anthony"
"I know"
"A" (as in ape)
"picture"
"letters"
"A-B-C's"
"eat it"

If you were a child who got the "wrong" answer, you would not feel good. If this happened often enough, you might get turned off on sound-symbol-picture cards. Look at the cards you are using and see how many contain capital and lower case letters as well as a picture representing the long vowel and/or the short vowel. Do you have an *E* card with an elephant and an eagle? Could the child think the pictures represented animal and bird? Would that help him remember the vowels, or could he be getting the wrong message? Does your *U* card contain an umbrella and a violin-looking instrument or a military-looking suit of clothes or a map? Does your *C* card have a cat? Could a child think he was wrong because when he looked at it he thought of animal, kitty, pussycat, Thumbelina?

We discussed earlier about teachers learning to analyze their materials and how they were teaching those materials. This teacher could analyze the number of possible answers to her presentation question, "Who knows what this is?" and conclude that the problem is improving her method of presentation. A more fruitful analysis would be to ask what we are trying to teach (what do we want the child to learn)? If we are trying to help him associate a sound with a letter symbol, we might consider presenting the letter symbol and then teaching the sound. We could hold up a card with either the upper or lower case *A* on it and pointing to the symbol say, "The sound for this is *A* (as in *at*)." And then we could ask the children, "What sound is this?"

If we say that the apple-*A* card teaches that, see what the child would have to know to associate properly. He would have to identify the fruit, listen to the word *apple,* hear the *A* sound in it and focus on *A* sound temporarily disregarding the other sounds he hears in the word and then to know that the sound he hears from naming the picture he sees has something to do with the upper and lower case letters on the card.

This kind of analysis would show us that no matter how well presented, the task should still be teaching more than one thing. It is difficult to teach a concept when there is more than a single possible interpretation in the series of examples. (Engelmann, 1969a) From the child's point of view, it was difficult to discover what the teacher was trying to teach because there were so many possible interpretations on the apple-*A* card. If he were presented with a card with a single letter symbol on it and zeroed in on the letter where all he had to remember was configuration and sound, his task would be more simple.

Let's look at another reading readiness task where children might have problems. The teacher passes out a sheet containing pictures in boxes of a dog, a cat, a table, and a horse. Either she says or the children hear on a tape recorder something like, "Make a circle around the one that is not the same." Most of us have taught children who would fail because of the language concepts involved in understanding that instruction. (Osborn, 1968) Of course a child would have to understand *make, circle, around, one, not, same.* Suppose he did understand that language. Could a child with excellent concept language still be confused and not feel good? Yes, because they *are* all the same. Why are they all the same? Can you think like children and list several reasons why the pictures of a dog, a cat, a table and a horse *are* all the same?

> they are all pictures
> they are all in boxes
> they are all on paper

they all have four legs
they all represent real objects
they are all familiar

Why are discrimination tasks with a, b, d, g, p all the same? Good answer. Yes, they are all symbols, letters, they all have circles and sticks. Can you identify a child you have taught who might not have a positive attitude toward reading because he could not feel good about or could not understand such a readiness activity?

Let us analyze the problem. Why do we teach discrimination tasks? We want the child to be able to focus on the characteristics of letters that distinguish one letter from another. Of course readers must learn this. But would improving the teaching method help with this kind of readiness material? It would be more beneficial to examine the material. Can we design some other materials to teach the letter symbols so that the children could more readily discriminate p and d and b and q and g; One way might be to teach one "circle-stick" until it was well identified and only then proceed to teaching another "circle-stick." Things that are too similar have a way of confusing the learner unless one was learned well before the second was introduced. Many adults still do not have an instant image when they hear the words *stalactite* (*t* shows it hangs from the *t*op) and *stalagmite* (*m* shows it forms from the botto*m*), because the two words were taught at the same time.

We might consider teaching one "circle-stick" like d, then teaching some letters that look different, such as *m, e, f* and others, and then teaching *b.* If we were taught *stalactite* first and then many days later were taught *stalagmite* we would have a better chance to discriminate. Our first remembering discrimination when learning *stalagmite* might be "It's the one that is *not* stalactite." Similarly if we teach *d*, then teach many other non "circle-sticks," then many days later teach *b* a child might first remember, "It's the one that is not *d.*"

Let us look at a last readiness activity. The child has to be taught to rhyme. The teacher takes out the rhyme chart with pictures alone or with pictures and words below them. The pictures represent fan, man, pan, can. The teacher says, "Look at the pictures. These words rhyme with *fan: man, pan, can.*" The teacher has the child repeat the series. Then she asks him if he can hear how these words rhyme. He does not feel comfortable answering "yes," because those pictures surely looked like Daddy, skillet, and Campbell's soup to him.

Once again analysis tells us that the teaching technique could be improved. But multiple interpretations are still possible with the materials. One suggested method for teaching rhyming, using no pictures, follows.

Subskills. Reading readiness activities of the type we have used for years could be the root of many reading disorders. The child associates the failure to understand with the reading process and decides it will at best not be easy for him and at worst he will not want any part of it. When I started examining the materials that I had been using, and relabeling the child's learning problem as my teaching problem, I had to face a serious fact. Perhaps I had not only not been teaching the child so that he would succeed, but perhaps I had been teaching him so that he would fail.

Pupils Performance Level

A teacher is teaching ten children in a homogeneous reading group. A child makes a mistake. The teacher corrects him. He repeats the correct word. The teacher says, "Everybody, look at that word. It has a *b* in it and not a *p*. So the word is *cab* not *cap*. Do you understand?" In a group of ten children we can usually find some combination of the following:
  "Yes"
  some shake heads affirmatively
  "cab"
  some look for the word
  no response
Then the teacher continues with the lesson.

I know you are analyzing what the teacher said. You can see that the teacher did not analyze what she said because her statement implied four things for the children to do at one time — look at the word, find the *b* and focus on it, differentiate the word *cab* on the page from the word *cap* not on the page, and answer a question. But here we are concerned with the pupils' performance level. Whatever the teacher did try to teach, she did not check to see whether every child understood. Teachers usually expect 100% pupil performance, but that teacher did not know what performance level she achieved because she did not check out each child. Perhaps because the first child repeated the correct word after her, she might have gotten 10% performance. But she can't be sure whether he was taught the word or whether he just copied her.

The teacher, still in a small group setting, has face down on her lap a letter card with the letter *s* on it. The children have been taught the letter. She says, "When I hold up this card, tell me the letter name." She holds up the card. Some of the children, watching her carefully, start to respond before the card is off her lap. Some chime in when the card is held up. Some respond at the tail end. Unless the teacher is aware of the possibilities, she may think she received 100% performance. I know you have analyzed the problem. Unlike the previous example, here the teacher's statement implied only one instruction. And unlike the previous example, here all the children did respond. But did she get 100% performance? Unless she was aware that the children who answered first might be cueing some of the late responders, she might think all the children demonstrated remembering the letter. This teacher, by the way, was me. I was unaware of the late responders cueing until I saw this segment on video tape. By watching the children's lips, I saw that some had their mouths open in the position for the beginning of the *s* letter name, and that some children responded with teeth showing on the last part of the letter name.

Why is this important? It is important because all the children in the group did not get a fair chance to demonstrate whether they knew or did not know the letter name. Some of the late responders may have known the name and some may not, but the teacher had no way of knowing who did and who did not because she let some children start to respond before the letter card was held up.

The less than 100% performance level from the children in the last two examples, if continued for any length of time, could lead to trouble for some of the children in the group. They could receive the message that an absolute performance was not important. When a tester administers a reading test 100% performance is demanded from each child because there is an absolute standard. It would help these children to have been taught in class that the teacher was only going to be satisfied with 100% performance. Maybe they do not understand everything correctly in class; maybe they have to be taught over again. At least they have learned that the teacher demands their participation, and further, that she is not going on in the lesson until they do participate. Unless she has feedback from each child, she cannot know what it is that she needs to reteach.

Children who cue from each other or who are not tested in the small group reading scene to a 100% criterion of performance feel lost in a standardized testing situation because there is no early responder from whom to cue, nor can they wait for the answer from the teacher. This argument might imply an individualized teaching situation. I will discuss this further in the section on *Levels of Teaching.*

Subskills. Teachers usually feel frustrated when the set of subskills used to prepare children to read does not automatically lead to the children being able to begin to read. By beginning to read we mean decoding. In beginning reading the children decode by sounding out the words in the primer. After identifying the word in his book, the child can understand (comprehend) what he has read. But the first step is the decoding by sounding out, the translating of the symbols on the page into words. The child who read the word *cap* in an earlier example might be able to demonstrate to the teacher his comprehension of that word. The problem is that what was called for was his comprehension of the word *cab* and until he could derive the word *cab* from his page he could not demonstrate his comprehension of it.

We have found that children often fail to read because they cannot take the first step. They cannot break the code. (Engelmann and Bruner, 1969) Many of us differ in delineating the subskills necessary to break the code. I will discuss in a later section the subskills we teach. But here I will deal with the one subskill which we all agree is essential; that is, the letter symbols. I will discuss some of the problems the child faces when he must deal with the letter symbols.

From the child's point of view he has to know too many symbols before he begins to read. Be a child now. You have to know at least 96 identifications. This number includes 26 names for upper case letters, 26 names for lower case letters, and 44 different visual symbols. Fortunately, except for size, eight letters are the same in upper and lower case (c, k, o, s, v, w, x, z), but you still must know 96. In some programs, this is only the beginning. In addition, you must learn the sound for each consonant plus one extra sound for *c* and *g*. This adds 21 to the total. Add the long and short vowel sounds and *y* (approximately 6) and the total is near 123. Furthermore, you are learning to write the letters and some of the ones you are writing, such as ɑ and 𝓰 , are not found in the printed reader. Instead you will see things like a, 𝓰, h .

This is the child's quandary. When he begins to decode, which of the possibilities for a letter symbol he encounters in a word shall he choose? Shall it be the name of the letter, or its sound? If a vowel, shall he choose the long or short sound? What if he tries the long or short *o* when he sees words like *do, done, women, woman*? What should he do with *th, sh, ch,* and *ing*? The child is facing the dilemma of the beginning reader: too many choices. We discussed this for rhyming and for reading readiness tasks, but nowhere is he in more trouble than with the letter symbols. As you analyze the problem of too many choices, you may conclude, as we did, that perhaps for a beginner the fewer the choices the more chance he has to master that small set.

In summary, the problem areas we have discussed concern the need to delineate critical subskills to be taught so that the child can begin to read. We have to be certain that we are teaching one and only one subskill at a time so that the child can focus on what we are trying to teach. We can see that the beginning reader has been faced with too many choices and that this has in some cases contributed to his failure. We have discussed the need for an absolute criterion for being able to read, regardless of which label the child has been given, and we have mentioned that there should be an absolute standard of performance. If the child does not respond or responds incorrectly, he must be corrected. In the remaining sections of this paper we will delineate some reading readiness subskills, some teaching techniques for teaching these subskills, and some correction procedures.

READING READINESS SUBSKILLS

We have found that if the child can perform certain critical operations he can begin to read, to decode on the beginning level. This section will outline the subskills in the Distar Instructional System. For detailed explanation on the rationale for the choice of these particular subskills, the reader is referred to the Distar Teacher's Guide. (Engelmann and Bruner, 1969)

Which specific subskills do we need to decode the word *mad?*

Subskill (1)—Sequencing

We have to know where to start, then where to go, and where to end.

We have to start with *m,* then *a,* then *d.* This is sequencing. Before the child starts to sequence using letter symbols, he needs to know how sequencing works, that is, one thing comes first, then another, then another. We start by teaching the child a series of actions like clapping his hands and slapping his lap. We label this sequence "the right way". Then we see if he can discriminate the right way, the reversal, and the wrong way.

Subskill (2)—Sound-Symbols

If we know where to start reading the word *mad,* that is at the first symbol, we are then ready to utter a sound. To facilitate the sounding out we teach the letter sounds, one sound for each symbol until the child reads well and then, the letter names, and then the alphabet. The reason for teaching sounds first is that the spoken word *mad* is easier to derive from the sequencing of sounds *m a d* than it is from the letter names *em ā dēē.* If the child sequences the sounds *m a d* and then accelerates the sequencing, he comes out with a close approximation of the spoken word *mad.* Using the letter names, the word comes out something like *emādēē.*

To make the sound-symbol association automatic in the early decoding days, we limit the choices, teaching a small set of sounds, one sound per symbol. The sounds that were chosen to be taught had to fulfill certain criteria if we were to eliminate the types of readiness described earlier in this paper.

the symbols for sounds should not look alike

the sounds for the symbols should not sound alike

the mouth, teeth, lip positions for the sounds should not be alike

and, most important,

30

the sounds taught must combine well into real words.

The latter criterion is most important because we believe that the best payoff for learning a skill is being able to perform that skill. Reading is a skill. The best payoff for learning to read is being able to read. And if you are going to keep psychological motivation high, it is important that the child begin to read early after starting his readiness. In Distar, using the sound-symbols below, the children start to sound out and decode real words within a month of beginning their readiness. These are the sounds taught, approximately one every three days, which are the baseline for reading the first words:

m, a(as in *at*), s, ē(as in *eat*), f, d, r, i, th(as in *this*).
We can use such real words as *me, am, is, feed, seed, rid, ram, sam, mad, the, this, sad* to make little stories. As new sounds are gradually introduced the vocabulary expands accordingly.

Subskill (3)—Blending

Before a child reads a word he has to be taught the basic principles of how sequencing operates, a baseline of sounds, and what to do with those sounds once he starts sequencing them. The subskills that teach what to do after he sequences the sounds deal with blending. When you sequence the sounds *m a d* you know that if you accelerate your sounding out, you will end up with an approximation of the spoken word *mad*. What you are really doing is to say those sounds faster and faster until you end up with *mad.*

Before a child reads any words at all in Distar, he is taught how to say fast words that are presented orally to him in parts. For example, "*Motor* (pause) *cycle.* Say it fast." When the child responds with the said-fast word *motorcycle,* he is shown a picture of a motorcycle. The message is that when you put the parts together and say them fast, you will end up with an approximation of the spoken word. The picture is a reinforcement.

Subskill (4)—Unblending

If blending is saying the parts fast, then the child must be familiar with the process of unblending or saying the word slowly. He must be familiar with what a word will sound like if it is in its parts before being put together. A reader, for example, must know that the spoken word *mad* is another version of the sounded-out word in its parts *m a d.* Before the child starts to decode any words in Distar, he is presented with a series of spoken words and taught to sound them out orally, and put them back together.

You be the child. I will give you the instruction. *"Mad.* Say it slowly." You'll say "mmmmaaaad." Then I will ask, "What did you say slowly?" You'll respond *"mad."* You can perform the same process if I give you the instruction, *"Mad.* Sound it out," or *"Mad.* Pull the word apart." Nonreaders cannot do this because they were not taught.

Subskill (5)—Rhyming

This is another oral activity the child is taught before he is ever presented with a written word. We want to prepare the child for encountering words that will have parts that look the same, so we teach him that words can have parts that sound the same. We do this without pictures. We teach him a convergent rhyming whereby we give a rhyme word and teach him to supply the ending for a number of words. For example, "Rhymes with *mad,* sssss." The child responds *sad.* "Rhymes with *mad*, lll..., ffff, b."

The above are the subskills which we found that most nonreaders could not perform — sequencing, sounds, blending, unblending, convergent rhyming. The next time you are teaching you might want to test this. Give a child some of the tasks to do and see if he can do them or if he must be taught. Our research indicated that without these critical readiness subskills a child was not ready to read — decode

32

by sounding out — words. We also found that mastery of these critical subskills was necessary regardless of the age of the nonreader or the below-grade-level reader. The same subskills for attacking new words had to be performed by preschoolers or junior high students, gifted or retarded children. This makes me conclude that readiness for reading is not an age or an IQ, it is mastery of critical subskills. A child is not ready to read because he has not been taught the subskills that enable him to begin to read.

PSYCHOLOGICAL MOTIVATION

Several times in this paper I have referred to the psychological motivation for wanting to learn to read. Reading is a skill like driving a car or any other skill. Motivation for learning to drive is wanting to learn to drive. You want to do it because it has a payoff. The big payoff is being able to perform the skill, whether it is driving or reading. In the car analogy, the teacher usually accompanies the student in a dual control car. The student has an idea of what the skill looks like. You make the car go. The teacher knows what the skill looks like. Making the car go is just one step. The student will also have to learn road signs, regulations, law, safety factors, minimal car maintenance, and so forth. The teacher has many choices about devising a teaching program. He knows which subskills lead to the driving skill. Now he must devise a program, spacing the necessary subskills over a certain continuum. If it is a good program, he lets the student get the feel of making the car go. This looks like a good teaching situation. There is a dual control car so the teacher can help. The teacher has a list of subskills which will culminate in the final skill of good driving. Now the teacher sets out to teach.

He puts the student behind the wheel. He lets him turn the wheel. He gives him a key and lets him put it in the ignition. He lets him turn the key. He lets him put his foot on the gas pedal. Then he stops. He has the student accompany him out of the car. The teacher opens the hood. He has the student examine the engine and feel the sparkplugs. He has the student watch him change a tire. He takes out a chart showing stop and yield signs. How does the student feel? He is tolerant, but he is probably disappointed. He came so close to one moment when (in the dual control situation) he could make the car move and feel the power of having achieved the skill.

What happens in many learning to read situations? The child sees a book. This is his goal, read the book. The teacher points to a word. The child gets the idea that reading deals with words. To prepare for reading words the teacher teaches a few letters, then more letters, then sounds, and so on. Then there are readiness and discrimination tasks. Then she stops for comprehension and building oral skills and appreciation of reading. In short, she has done what the driving teacher did. She started giving the student bits and pieces of many subskills, but never let him feel the power of accomplishing the skill, of the big payoff of reading words.

A better program would be to sequence the skills over a continuum, to say that a good reader must be able to do this and this. But the first step is the decoding of words, then the comprehension of the decoded word. The teacher knows that she will be in a "dual control" situation, she can help the child to get the feel of reading on his own. The child will want to continue to read if he gets the power and reinforcement of being able to read.

In Distar we program all the skills that a child will need to read independently, with comprehension, appreciation of reading, and so on, into a 340 teacher presentation continuum. The child begins to decode with the set of reading readiness subskills on the 30th presentation day of that continuum. There is an absolute standard for all children. They differ in the amount of time it takes them to reach a certain presentation, but when they reach a certain teaching presentation, they will have demonstrated mastery of what was taught in all the preceding presentations. The high performers may reach that teaching presentation in half the number of days and the slow performers may need twice that number of days to reach the same teaching presentation, but at that presentation the performance is the same.

Each teaching presentation consists of a half-hour lesson composed of several subskill segments taught by the teacher. As rewards for responding the children receive papers after each presentation. In the prereading presentations the focus is on the subskills necessary to decode and the paper rewards consist of sound-symbol sheets. When decoding starts, the focus in the presentations taught by the teacher is on reading and the children receive paper booklets as rewards. They receive one booklet after each presentation. They keep the booklets. The message is, if a child can read the booklet, he may keep it and take it home. It is his. The psychological motivation is enhanced by the materials reward, the proof that the reward for reading is owning what you can read.

THE TEACHING SITUATION

This section will discuss four levels of teaching that seem to be present in most teaching situations. Note that I refer to the teaching situation and I do not differentiate the most effective teaching situation from the least effective teaching situation because I believe that in a classroom all four levels are operating regardless of how good or poor the teaching situation is.

These levels are the
- (P) *Program* or the materials being taught
- (T) *Teacher* or the agent teaching the materials
- (G) *Group* consisting of a number of children
- (I) *Individual,* each individual child within that group

You be the individual child (I). You are in a reading group of ten children with performance similar to yours. Because the others in the group perform similarly, you have a good chance to feel success. You don't stop trying as you might if there were always so many super-

ior to you. Something new is being presented. In the subkills outlined above, the teacher is teaching a sequencing series. The Program
(P) contains statements for the teacher to read aloud (here in capital
letters) and procedures for her to follow (here in italics).

(P): *Say:* Everybody, look at me.
(T): "EVERYBODY, LOOK AT ME."
(G): Some look up, some do not.
(P): *Praise the children who look.*
(T): "GOOD FOR TOMMY AND JOHNNY. THEY ARE LOOK-
ING AT ME."
(I): Looks at Tommy and Johnny. Perhaps thinks it was nice
they got praised.
(P): *Clap your hands once; pause; slap your lap once with both
hands.*
Say: This is the right way.
(T): Claps her hands once; pauses; slaps her lap once with both
hands.
"THIS IS THE RIGHT WAY."
(G): Look at the teacher because of the noise and movement or
because it looks interesting.
(P): *Do the sequence four times. Go slowly.*
Before each sequence, say: Again.
After each sequence, say: I did it the right way.
(T): Claps hands, pauses, slaps lap. "I DID IT THE RIGHT
WAY."
"AGAIN." Claps hands, pauses, slaps lap. "I DID IT THE
RIGHT WAY."
(G): Some children try to do a part of the series.
(T): "I DID IT THE RIGHT WAY."
"AGAIN." Claps hands, pauses, slaps lap. "I DID IT THE
RIGHT WAY."
(I): Looks around. Some children (G) participating. He tries it.
(T): "I DID IT THE RIGHT WAY."
"AGAIN." Claps hands, pauses, slaps lap. "I DID IT THE

RIGHT WAY.''

(P): *Have the children do the sequence with you eight times.*
Go slowly. Say: Do it with me.
Before each sequence, say: Again.
After each correct sequence, say: We did it the right way.

(T): ''DO IT WITH ME.''

(T & G): Clap hands, pause, slap laps.

(T): ''WE DID IT THE RIGHT WAY. AGAIN.''

(T & G): Continue as above for eight trials. (Note that the teacher did not stop to correct the group.)

(I): Perhaps feels good that the teacher is continuing to demonstrate the right way and that he has other children to cue from.

(P): *Give each child a turn. Say:* Let's see you do it the right way.
Praise the children for correct responses.
To correct: *Do the sequence with the child. Say:*
Do it with me.
Before each sequence, say: Again.
After each correct sequence, say: We did it the right way.
If a child does not do it correctly after several tries, praise him for trying and go to another child.

(T): ''RALPH, YOUR TURN. LET'S SEE YOU DO IT THE RIGHT WAY.''

(I): Does the sequence incorrectly, partly correct, or nothing at all.

(T): ''DO IT WITH ME.''

(T & I): Clap hands, pause, slap laps.

(T): ''WE DID IT THE RIGHT WAY. EVERYBODY, WASN'T THAT GOOD?''

(T): ''RALPH, LET'S DO IT AGAIN.''

(T & I): Clap hands, pause, slap laps.

(T): ''WE DID IT THE RIGHT WAY.''
''NOW LET'S SEE YOU DO IT THE RIGHT WAY ALL BY YOURSELF'''

(I): Claps hands, slaps lap.
(T): "GOOD. MARY, NOW IT'S YOUR TURN."

The above is about half of a five minute teaching segment from Sequencing Presentation 1. It continues with the teacher doing the series the right way and asking the children if it is the right way; then doing it the wrong way and asking the children if it is the right way; then reversing the series and asking the children if it is the right way. This order changes daily.

We can only conjecture how (I) feels. Teachers using this program over the past few years report that the children see immediately that the teacher will demonstrate, the group will try together, the teacher will help the individual if he is in trouble, and the children feel an enormous confidence in the teaching situation. The three levels in this effective teaching situation are helping (I) on the fourth level. So he gets taught. We teachers who have been teaching for some time agree with the Coleman report finding that children (I) learn from each other (G), both academically and behaviorally. By the time (I) has to perform, he has had the benefit of three prior levels of teaching.

Why did level one (P) contribute to the effective teaching situation? The Program (P) was designed so that the teacher in the few minutes she spent on this activity would not have to analyze her materials and teaching techniques as she was teaching. We know how much easier it is to analyze either before or after we teach. Somehow with ten youngsters in front of us, there become more pressing problems in the teaching situation itself than analysis of what we are teaching at the moment.

As you can see if you acted the teacher's part in the above segment, this program is preanalyzed. A teacher should study the rationale of a particular program such as this, and if she likes it and trusts it, she should try the program. If she distrusts the rationale and theory, she should not use this type of direct teaching program. Teachers should

38

be able to study a program before teaching it to see whether they can find their style in it. Administrators should provide teachers with the opportunity to try a program before they are told to use it. Administrators are very aware of individual differences in children. But why, since they are aware of them, do not administrators take into account individual differences among teachers when suggesting possible teaching programs? The more I teach teachers the more convinced I am that the individual differences among teachers are greater than among children. After all, adults have lived longer and have had more time to become individually different. If a teacher is not comfortable with a program, with its rationale and theory, and does not want to try it, she should be given an option of refusal.

The Program segment above also suggested correction procedures. We know how we tend to panic when a child makes a mistake. We could tell him the answer, but then how do we know he can do it on his own? We don't want to respond "No, no, no," when he errs, but that is what often pops out. After we've said it, we know he won't feel happy, because there's not much information for improvement when he just hears "No." But with a correction procedure such as above, the teacher feels good. She demonstrates that she will help the child do it with her. Then she lets him have another turn. Teachers feel that is *teaching.* And teachers in their personal as well as their professional roles like instant feedback that they are "doing it the right way."

On level two (T) the teacher was free from analyzing her materials and could think of how to praise a particular child so it would be most effective for him. She had time to spend relating to each child both within the group and as an individual.

On the third or group (G) level, it can be seen that the group learns from the strengths and weaknesses of its members. There is a good feeling for a learner to be part of a group. Most of us like to learn new skills in a group. We enjoy the camaraderie. We as individuals enjoy showing that we can perform well when we are tested, but first we like to learn in a group. Very soon with children, as well as adults, in a teaching situation the group acquires an identity. The better performers reach out to the slower performers. The members of the group discipline each other because they are sometimes operating as a group and sometimes as individuals.

The individual (I) is benefited. He learns because he is taught. The program teaches him. The teacher teaches him. The group teaches him.

I believe that a teaching situation where four levels of teaching are occurring is effective. It is, of course, most effective when all the levels are superior. Excellent materials, superb teachers, perfectly matched groups of very intelligent children would be quite an operation. But in reality, many of us are teaching the kind of children we are teaching because we are stimulated by their need to be taught.

Some teachers enjoy teaching in the tutorial one child to one teacher situation. I have found this less effective because I feel the child is missing out on the security and excitement of learning in a group. I feel the same way about the one child-one teaching machine or one programmed reader situation for beginners. I believe that children who have not mastered basic skills need the group and the teacher reinforcement to boost their motivation. But I have seen many effective three level teaching situations with teacher, materials and one individual. I have seen many teaching situations that were effective on a two level basis, that is a teacher without materials teaching a single child. Parents, of course, do this all the time.

I have also observed effective teaching situations where there were 55 children in each first grade. (Bruner and Bruner, 1969) The children sat on wooden benches, shared books and pencils, had no artificial light in the schoolroom. Yet all the children were reading. There were no nonreaders. These were effective teaching situations because the teacher said her goal was to teach every child to read. As such every child read a passage until he read it perfectly every class day. The teachers did not move to the next part of the lesson until the lowest performing child in the room could read the passage. In other words, the teachers taught to the "low man in the group."

I could not teach in that situation. Most American teachers and American children would get bored. We would be intolerant of the teaching materials and school equipment. But those teachers taught those children in what was for them an effective teaching situation.

The experience I related above demonstrated to me again the need for teachers to teach to the lowest man in the group and to test each child individually to see who needs reteaching. The last section of this paper will deal with a suggestion for criterion referenced testing.

CRITERION REFERENCED TESTING

To determine which children did not learn in a teaching situation from the four levels of teaching, tests must be administered. In the teaching segment on sequencing, the program contained the teaching statements, the teacher demonstrated, praised, and helped the children, the group helped the individual by providing even more examples and practice. Yet the chance that even that amount of teaching was insufficient exists. The teacher tested each child after each teaching step, yet perhaps several days later a child has not retained what he learned.

At that point there must be a test. The test would be administered to each individual within the group setting in that part of the lesson devoted to, for example, teaching the sequencing subskill. This is an example of a criterion referenced test to be administered on the sixth sequencing presentation.

Test each child individually. If more than one child cannot do the following test correctly, repeat Sequencing 1 — 5, taking one lesson each day. Otherwise do Sequencing 6.

41

Now the criterion is clear. A test is to be administered to individuals within the group of perhaps ten children. If two cannot pass the test, the group is to repeat certain sequencing presentations. If the group passes, they move to the next presentation. The teacher then has a number of decisions about the children who did not pass. Either she has misgrouped them — they belong in another teaching group so she regroups her children — or certain children need reteaching, or she has not taught correctly. Whichever alternative she decides upon, she knows where to return and what to repeat. The test has provided specific information. Perhaps the teacher thought a certain child was a slow performer. Yet he was one of the children who passed the test. Perhaps he should be put in a higher group. At least she will consider this. Or, a child failed who the teacher thought was a high performer. She can now observe him for several days and consider regrouping him. Teachers like this specific pinpointing.

In a Distar 30 minute presentation, there might be five daily segments. One segment would be a sequencing activity (part of which was illustrated above), then there would be a blending say-it-fast segment, then a symbol identification segment. In addition the children would receive several sheets of paper as reward and reinforcement. On a certain day the sequencing segment would be tested, on another day the blending segment, on another day the symbol segment. Rather than repeat the entire lesson the teacher reteaches just the segment needing reteaching. The group then proceeds to where they should be in the other segments.

The profile of a particular homogeneous group at any point in the program ought to tell us something about how that group is proceeding. What can we surmise about the following group from its profile on the 16th presentation day? Completing one segment in each subskill would put the group at presentation 16 in each subskill. Yet they are being taught
    Sequencing 8
    Sound-symbols 12
    Say it fast blending 16

We assume that this homogeneous group is adept at oral blending skills because they are at presentation 16, less adept in retaining symbols because they have failed some tests and are repeating certain presentations, and slow in sequencing because they are repeating.

What do we assume about the following group on the 50th presentation day?

Sequencing	completed
Rhyming	completed
Sound-symbols	65
Blending	completed
Reading story	65

If this group has passed all its tests, the profile shows that the group has completed the reading readiness subskills, has skipped certain lessons in symbols and certain reading stories and is proceeding through the program at an above average rate. A different group on segment 50 in sound-symbols and reading story 50 on the 50th day would presumably be proceeding at one presentation per day.

Why are we describing groups instead of individuals? Because we are discussing the teaching situation comprising four levels of teaching. In the early mastery days the children are taught in groups, but of course each child reads independently. The instructional materials for the 340 teacher presentation continuum are all taught in the group setting because we are committed to the belief that the teacher is the best teaching agent. As each child progresses he completes his workbook materials, his writing exercises and comprehension on his reading books at his own rate, but he is still benefitting from being taught in a group setting.

I have been trying to teach the readers of this paper my point of view in a three level teaching situation without the benefit of group feedback. I hope that you will communicate such feedback to me.

REFERENCES

Bruner, Edward M., & Bruner, Elaine C. **Anthropological perspectives on primary education in Indonesia.** (Submitted for publication) 1969.

Engelmann, Siegfried. Conceptual learning. In K. E. Berry and B. D. Bateman (Eds.), **The dimensions in early learning series.** San Raphael, California: Dimensions Publishing Co. 1969. (a)

Engelmann, Siegfried. **Preventing failure in the primary grades.** Chicago: Science Research Associates. 1969. (b)

Engelmann, Siegfried, & Bruner, Elaine C. **Distar reading, an instructional system.** Teacher's guide. Chicago: Science Research Associates. 1969.

Osborn, Jean, Teaching a teaching language to disadvantaged children. In M. C. Templin, **Monographs of the society for research in child development.** Minneapolis: Institute of Child Development, University of Minnesota. 1968.

STARTER/101: A System for Structuring the Teaching of Reading

Ruth Ann O'Keefe, Ed.D.
Educational Studies Department
Washington School of Psychiatry
Washington, D.C.

Each year a large number of American first grade children do not learn to read. They are eventually promoted to the second and third grades, and again they do not learn to read. Indeed, many of these children maintain their illiteracy for a lifetime.

Yet, each of these nonreaders has learned to talk; each has assimilated from his own native environment the complex and often arbitrary vocabulary, syntax, and appropriate intonation necessary to understand and orally convey both concrete and abstract wants, needs, feelings and ideas.[1] The learning of oral language — surely the most complex cognitive learning any of us masters during our lifetime — is accomplished at an early age without benefit of a formal, organized educational system, and without benefit of an educational staff who have undergone extensive preservice training for their task! Surely learning to read the printed word is not a more complex or arbitrary skill than learning to talk. It seems an irony of the first order that modern educators are unable to successfully teach this simpler skill to many children who, at a tender age, have already demonstrated their ability to master highly complex language skills.

Of course, it is true that we do not know exactly how children learn to talk.[2] If we did, perhaps we could adapt the learn-to-talk model to a learn-to-read model, and we would have as many readers as we have speakers. However, just as we do know a great deal about the necessary *conditions* for learning to talk (Stevens and Orem, 1968), we also know a great deal about the requirements or conditions for learning to read.

In fact, as reading instruction is currently carried out, many children

[1]For an exceptionally competent and readable discussion of early language development and its relevance to reading, see Stevens, George, and Orem, R. C. THE CASE FOR EARLY READING, Warren Green Co., St. Louis, 1968. (Especially note Capters 2 and 3: "Language, Man, and the Child," and "The Nature of Language Learning in the Child.")

[2]For a significant discussion of the relationship between language and maturation, see Lenneberg, Eric H. BIOLOGICAL FOUNDATIONS OF LANGUAGE, John Wiley & Sons, Inc., New York, 1967.

do learn to read. Perhaps they could read earlier (Stevens and Orem, 1968), or better, or faster, or with more understanding, but they do learn the basic fundamentals of reading English, and they thus have the foundation upon which to build and develop further if and when they so desire. They have a choice of whether to read and what to read, because they *can* read. My concern here is for the children who do not easily learn the basic reading skills — the children who have no choice of whether or what to read, because they cannot read — the children whom every teacher encounters daily in her classroom — the children the school calls "reading failures." The abundance of existing reading materials is of little or no benefit to these children because they have not learned the skills required to make use of even the simplest of such materials. They may be six, or sixteen, or sixty. They cannot read.

Why have they not learned to read? The reasons are legion and may include excessive absence in the early grades, physical problems, environmental or cultural factors, psychological factors, and even problems associated with having an incompetent teacher. Edward Vaile (1969) presents an excellent discussion of possible reasons some children do not learn to read. But he also comments that, for practical purposes, it is often not especially important *why* children have failed to learn to read. I agree. Certainly children with physical problems should have problems identified, diagnosed, and treated. But too often we let the circumstances of the child's history of failure become our "cop out" — our explanation or rationale for why the child *will continue to fail.* On the contrary, these circumstances should provide our starting points or design requirements for developing systems that cannot fail our educational responsibilities to the child. It is no longer enough to say that we are striving to provide equal educational *opportunities* for all children; we must firmly decide that it is both desirable and possible to provide *all* children with at least fundamental reading competency.

As educators we must intensify our efforts and even more actively confirm and support U. S. Commissioner of Education Allen in his proposal for a new national educational goal, a goal of "assuring that by the end of the 1970's the *right* to read [italics mine] shall be a reality for all — that no one shall be leaving our schools without the skill and desire necessary to read to the full limits of his capability." (Allen, 1969)

In order to plan for the children who do not read, we must ask what it is about them — besides their inability to read — that distinguishes them from other more academically successful children.[3] There is substantial literature concerning the special attributes of the child with learning problems. For our purposes here, it is enough to say that almost all regular classroom teachers can point to several children in their classes who fit one or more of the following descriptions:

he often does not perceive shapes as they are — he cannot discriminate between some letters and words (for example, *saw* and *was* look the same to him, as do *p, b* and *d*.

he often does not perceive sounds as they are — he cannot discriminate between sounds such as *f* and *v* for example.

he cannot integrate information or generalize well; for example, he may be able to memorize or read *can*, but even if he knows *f*, he cannot read *fan*.

he has a poor facility in oral language (especially standard English), relative to other children.

he sees no relationship between the spoken language and the written language.

he cannot handle a pencil or crayon well, and has difficulty printing or making letters or simple shapes.

[3]Children who are severely physically handicapped, malnourished, hungry, or the victim of some other extraordinary circumstance are very much the concern of the author, but they are not the subject of this paper. No program, approach, or teacher can successfully serve these children until their basic needs are met.

The characteristics of the children who have not learned to read are well known. Of course, not all nonreaders exhibit all characteristics—there is probably a unique pattern of circumstances and characteristics associated with each individual nonreader.

So perhaps it makes more sense to look at the characteristics or skills that *are* required in order for a child to read.

What must the child be able to do in order to begin to read?

he must be able to see and perceive similarities and differences among letter shapes and words

he must be able to hear and perceive similarities and differences among letter sounds and words

he must be able to associate appropriate sounds to the 26 letters of our alphabet

he must be able to combine letters to form words, phrases, sentences, and meanings

he must above all relate the printed word to the spoken word, understanding that written language is only a representation of the spoken language with which he is familiar

If the child can somehow learn these skills or tasks, he can begin to develop the ability to decode the written language into the spoken language, and he will be on his way in reading.

Will the child always be constrained to a one-to-one relationship between a spoken word and a printed word? No. Someday he will be able to read much faster than he can talk, and he will be able to derive meanings from the printed page while only skimming quickly over the words. But, *in the beginning* it is necessary for the educator to emphasize the relationship between reading and speaking and to provide careful, detailed, structured and consistent assistance for the large number of children who do not learn this basic relationship easily or on their own.

After one decides on the requirements for success, the next step in developing an approach or a strategy for teaching reading is to ask, "What program design will enable children to develop the characteristics of children who do read?" Three of today's more rigorously designed and sequenced beginning reading programs are Sullivan's READING READINESS and READING (Sullivan, 1968a, 1968b), Woolman's LIFT-OFF TO READING (Woolman, 1966), and Engelmann's DISTAR (Engelmann, 1969).

These are programs in which the authors have courageously specified program objectives and insisted on the child's mastery of lower level skills and concepts before he may progress to higher level skills and concepts. They are programs with materials which carefully sequence skills to be learned — skills which are intended to lead toward developing the child's ability to read.

STARTER/101

Another approach, related in some respects to those mentioned above, is one we have recently developed (and have pilot-tested in the Washington, D. C., public schools) at the Educational Studies Department of the Washington School of Psychiatry. (O'Keefe, 1969) As a structured program for young non-readers, its underlying assumption is that all children who can learn to speak have the potential to master all basic skills and concepts that are required for reasonable and adequate reading ability and enjoyment. The program does not purport to be a comprehensive reading program but is intended to *prepare* children — many of whom come to school with a rich background of skills, but skills which are not basic to school success — to learn to use, enjoy and benefit from some of the excellent reading materials and programs commercially available. Currently, such materials are out of reach to many children until certain fundamental skills have been accepted and mastered. The new program, then, is a "starter" program and, as such, has been titled STARTER/101. The remainder of this chapter describes this program because it is the operational correlate of our philosophical and theoretical approach to helping children learn to read.

First, why do we call it *101*? It is our belief that children with learning problems need materials that are especially geared to them. As it happened, the first opportunity to translate our theoretical approach into a tangible program came in conjunction with a study involving primary grade disadvantaged urban children. The next STARTER program will probably be geared to preschool age children; and indeed, there may eventually be a series for functionally illiterate adults, or high school age nonreaders, or children for whom English is not their natural or first language, or deaf children, or whatever other group seems to warrant separate consideration.

It is clear to us that while a particular *approach* to teaching may be appropriate across many age, interest, and even cultural levels, materials must be differentiated to some extent to meet the needs of the children participating in the learning experience. A reading program is, after all, simply a series of planned learning events aimed at teaching some particular skills, tasks, or concepts. Common sense joins hands with research in telling us that these learning events, or experiences, must be relevant,[4] exciting, and fun for the intended learners, if they are to achieve the desired end. (Leonard, 1968; Glasser, 1969) Thus, STARTER/101 is the first of several programs, and it is aimed at a specific "target"—young, urban children.

---

[4]"Relevant" is sometimes interpreted as "realistic about the child's socio-economic or cultural environment." There is a "child culture," too, which crosses neighborhood boundaries. For example, Dr. Seuss books are often as appealing to Head Start children as to middle-class children.

The design of STARTER/101 takes into account three large and difficult problem areas in its effort to make the ability to read a reality. These three areas, discussed below, are:

teacher preparation to use the material;

enjoyment for children using the material;

mobility, or high turnover, of school children.

Teacher Preparation

First, STARTER/101 is designed for easy use by teachers. Two of the realities of modern, particularly urban, education, are the high turnover rate among teachers and the staggering work load often placed upon them. They often have large classes, unattractive working conditions, an abundance of clerical work, little or no assistance in planning or developing materials for their students, and inexperience in their task. If instructional materials are to be useful to teachers, they must be easy to understand and use. STARTER/101 is designed so that both the teacher and the child learn the pattern of the tasks to be learned. Once the teacher (experienced or inexperienced) works through a small portion of the program with a few students, she no longer needs an elaborate, explanatory teachers' manual — she is truly free to work flexibly and creatively with her students. The program tries not to make excessive demands upon the teacher — for, in reality, the teacher cannot and will not meet such demands.

Enjoyment for Children

The program is designed to be interesting to the children for whom it is intended. The importance of this program characteristic — for any program — cannot be overestimated. The educator who desires to "hook" young children on learning must do so on the children's own terms. Everyone knows that, while illustrations in and of themselves may not be able to make a program successful, they can certainly make it unsuccessful. If drawings, or learning activities, are dull and "no fun," the children will lose interest. STARTER/101 makes considerable use of Seuss-like drawings, comic book and coloring book format, and paper and pencil games.

Incidentally, the "fun" consideration, so vital to the success of children's educational experiences, is by no means confined to children. Adults make every effort to make their own work, surroundings, and activities as pleasant as possible. The astronauts on the moon mission ate the foods of their choice to the extent possible, talked by phone with their families, and enjoyed every comfort that could be provided. Adults selectively attend plays, watch TV, and read books — they seek whatever makes them feel good, just as children do.

Mobility

The program takes into account the fact that many children do not remain in one school for an entire school year. This real-life problem is one of the worst facing children, particularly in their early years. Many of the available reading approaches or programs (basal, programmed, language experience, and so forth) are developed and initiated on the premise that the child will be using them for an entire school year or preferably two or three years. Yet, in Washington, D. C.'s Model School Division (which includes 14 elementary schools), 60% of a sample of first grade children who started school in September, 1968, ended the school year in a different school. (Sherburne and Gannon, 1969) It is not only migrant children who are mobile during the school year — the turnover rate among urban children is very high and is often disastrous to their beginning education. Indeed, one of the strongest reasons often cited for urban children not learning to read is that they missed the opportunity for a continuous educational experience.

I do not deny nor dismiss the problem of intra- or inter-school-year mobility. The mobility is a reality and must be accepted as such. It must not be used as the reason for failure, but must be squarely faced, accepted, and *planned* for. In STARTER/101 we have attempted to cope with the mobility problem. The program is geared to equip the youngster to adapt to subsequent reading programs, even if he must leave STARTER/101 before he completes it. To this end, we carefully examined several different types of reading programs and included in the starter program the teaching of a number of skills which are intended to help the child move more smoothly into other programs. For example, some programmed materials teach only lower case letters, and some only upper case, at the beginning. If a child must go through all the letters in one case before being exposed to the other case, he is not prepared for the reality he will face if he is uprooted and placed in some other school. In STARTER/101, upper and lower case letters are presented concurrently — but the first letters in the program are letters which have the same (or nearly the same) form for both upper and lower case (U, P, C, and O). By choosing these letters, (or other letters which have the same upper-lower case forms), the teacher is circumventing the problem because, in his initial instruction, the child is not faced with the complexity of different-forms-with-the-same-meaning. (After all, children do not naturally know that *H* and *h, D* and *d,* or *A* and *a,* are the same letters!)

Three of the important general design considerations, then, have to do with making the program easy for teachers to use, fun for children, and feasible for both teachers and children even on a short-term basis.

Other Design Considerations

Other vital general design considerations relate directly to the characteristics of nonreaders mentioned previously. These characteristics, or problems, become a mandate for action, a starting point (rather than a barrier) for certain aspects of the program. Since oral language facility in nonreaders is often quite different from the style of language used in school and in books, oral language experiences are specifically provided — experiences that relate directly to the reading that will be done later in the program. Since many nonreaders have difficulties in visual and auditory perception, experiences are provided that develop these perceptions. For each of the characteristics known to be often associated with the nonreader (or poor reader), the program provides palatable experiences that are intended to lessen that characteristic.

The program is essentially the product of our task analysis of the process and potential problem of learning to read. (Gibson, 1966) We have delineated, sequenced, and integrated hundreds of specific objectives which, if achieved, we believe will develop in a child in a relatively short time period, the ability to read simple written material. In the process by which these objectives are achieved, learning proceeds on a step-by-step basis. The child learns only one new thing at a time, and he then combines the new learning with previously learned (review) activities or skills. Our procedure or method of organizing the specific program objectives was influenced by the work of Myron Woolman in programming for conceptual understanding. I have freely adapted his progressive choice model (Edward, 1966; Davy, 1962) to STARTER/101 because it is a model which, when properly developed and used by the educator, can help the child to journey from the spoken language to the written language in an orderly fashion. (Davy, 1963) The entire thrust of STARTER/101 is to attract and hold the child's attention and provide him with a carefully planned sequence of experiences that will contribute to the successful and continual development of his language and reading skills.

STARTER/101 is developed around a series of four-step cycles which repeat anew throughout the program. Each little cycle introduces a new letter, digraph, sight word, or other simple concept. Each cycle (and there are dozens of individual cycles in the program) is designed to lead the child from specific oral words (language) to their specific printed counterparts. The four steps in each cycle, which are described below, are:

language development

perceptual motor development

combining

reading development

Language development. The first of the four steps in each cycle of the teaching-learning process is the *language development* step, which provides opportunities for the child to speak and understand the specific words he will be reading in the fourth and final step (reading development) of the cycles. For the two cycles that teach the very first letters presented in the program, U and P, the only words in language development are UP and PUP. The aim of language development for the U and P cycles, then, is simply to make sure the child can understand and orally (and meaningfully) use the words *up* and *pup.* The program presents pictures (such as those shown in Illustrations 1 - A and 1 - B) to stimulate conversation leading to the use of whatever words are being taught in a particular cycle.[5]

In general, language development serves merely as vocabulary reinforcement rather than an introduction of new vocabulary, because the words used in STARTER/101 are usually familiar concepts to most children. This seems appropriate, for one of the concerns of the reading program is to make it necessary for the child to have to learn only the barest minimum in order to be able to read. If the educator includes unfamiliar language concepts, he is increasing the extraneous amount to be learned and hindering the accomplishment of the task at hand. A *beginning* reading program should rest on oral language that has already presumably been acquired by the child, but should include a Language Development phase to assure that the program de-

[5]The artist for the program was Mr. William Handel.

signer (author) and the child are in accord as to what language is indeed familiar to the child!

Perceptual motor development. The second step of each separate cycle is called *perceptual motor development* and speaks to the problems or immaturities some nonreaders have in the areas of perceptual and motor processes. Since many of the children have difficulty in discriminating among visual shapes (letters) and auditory sounds, the program includes specific experiences to develop these abilities. In perceptual motor development, the child learns to recognize, sound (not name)[6], and print *one* new letter (or digraph) in both its upper and lower case form. (Illustrations 2 - A—D) As mentioned earlier, the first four letters in the program — u, p, c, o — were selected partly because their upper and lower case forms are nearly identical except for size and placement on the page.

How the letters are sequenced is important when developing perceptual motor skills prerequisite to reading. The major considerations in sequencing letters — considerations which were of necessity given different weights at different times — were the letter shapes and the letter sounds. In general, letters that are similar in shape (for example P, B, D, and M, N, W) are kept far apart in the program. Thus, since the letter P (p) is introduced very early in the program, B (b) and D (d) are not introduced until much later, giving the child the opportunity to master P before being confronted with the two confusing letters. The intention is that he will become so familiar with P (p) that he will focus on the differences, not the similarities, of D (d) and later, B (b).

(The principle of shape-dissimilarity was occasionally overruled by other considerations. For example, three of the first four letters are essentially curved in shape — U, C, and O — and, as such, might be considered too confusing to the child. Pilot testing indicated that

---

[6]The thrust of the program is always to keep to a bare minimum what the child *must* learn in order to read. Letter *names* do not directly aid in reading, so letter *sounds* are the only required learning initially.

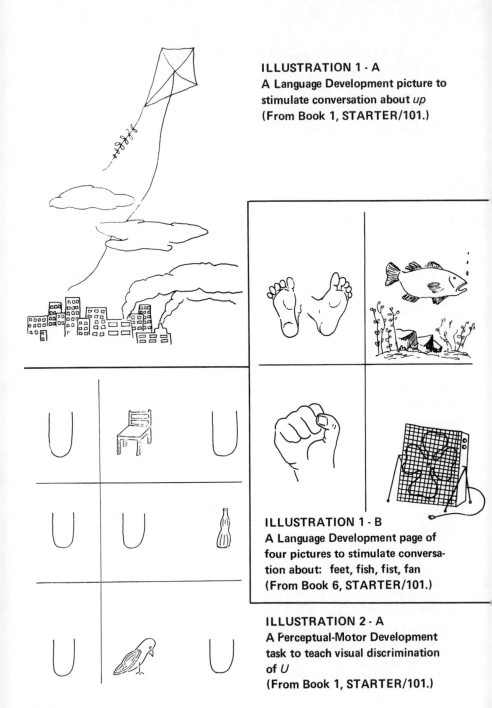

ILLUSTRATION 1 - A
A Language Development picture to stimulate conversation about *up*
(From Book 1, STARTER/101.)

ILLUSTRATION 1 - B
A Language Development page of four pictures to stimulate conversation about: feet, fish, fist, fan
(From Book 6, STARTER/101.)

ILLUSTRATION 2 - A
A Perceptual-Motor Development task to teach visual discrimination of *U*
(From Book 1, STARTER/101.)

58

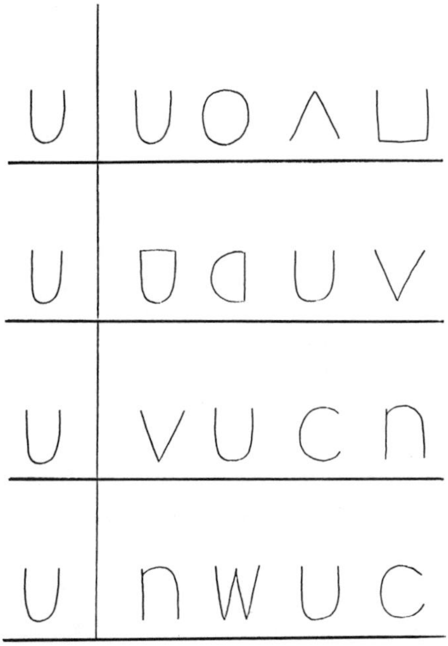

U	U O ∧ ⊔

ILLUSTRATION 2 - B
A Perceptual-Motor task to teach
visual discrimination of *U*
(From Book 1, STARTER/101.)

U	⊓ ⊐ U V
U	V U ⊂ ⊓
U	⊓ W U C

ILLUSTRATION 2 - C
Perceptual-Motor Development
task to teach printing of *U*
(From Book 1, STARTER/101.)

F	M	F	H	T
F	N	P	E	F
F	F	Ⴕ	⊦	E
f	s	p	d	f
f	Ⴕ	f	h	t
f	d	f	p	Ⴉ

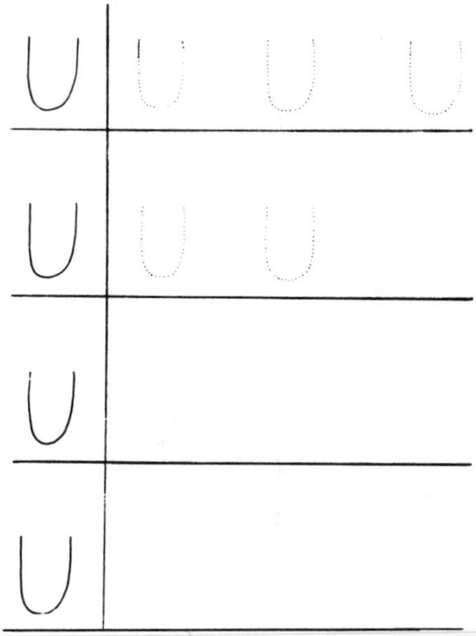

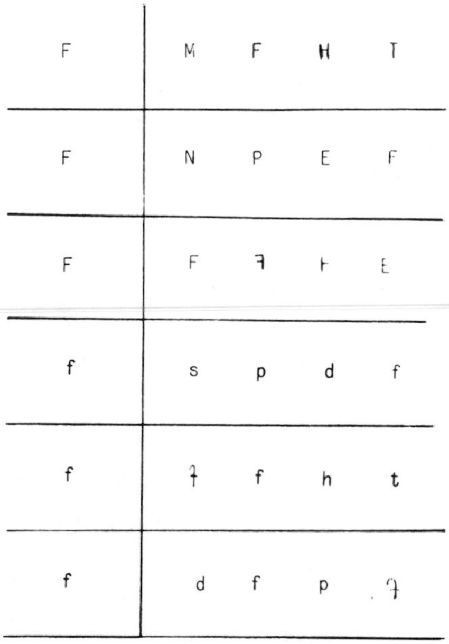

ILLUSTRATION 2 - D
Perceptual-Motor Development task
to teach visual discrimination of *F*
and *f*
(From Book 6, STARTER/101.)

the U, C and O shapes can be taught so that the child can readily recognize and distinguish between them. Thus, in this instance the
consideration of having letters which were both similar in upper/
lower case form and could be used to make familiar words, outweigh-
ed the consideration of consecutively sequencing visually dissimilar
letters.)

Letters were also sequenced according to their sound; an attempt was
made to separate letters with similar or confusing sounds. For example, since it is difficult for many children to distinguish between the
f and *v* sounds, these letters are kept well apart in the program.

It should be noted that, although the sounds of letters are of great
importance in the program, since the program is primarily a phonic
one, sounds are not all-important. For example, children who begin
the program saying *baf* for **bath** are likely to end the program with
the same pronunciation — and this seems appropriate to us. A phonics
program should not strive to obtain some sort of standard pronunciation from children — it should serve only as a guide to the child in discovering the relationship between the spoken and the printed word.
The crux of the reading task is to hear or perceive the **meaning** of the
printed word, and context clues and illustrations will assist the child
when a series of letter-sound relationships (i.e., a word) does not perfectly correspond. We cannot stress this point too much. As Vail
says, "There is justice in suggesting that many English words do not
sound out exactly. They don't have to. Close is good enough! Time
after time you will hear your pupil sound out a word incorrectly and
then immediately afterward pronounce it correctly." (Vail, 1969)

A final major consideration in deciding how to sequence the letters in
the program was the number of relevant words those letters would
make. For example, two letters that are visually very dissimilar are *O*
and *X*. They fulfill the requirements of having the same upper and
lower case shape and of having dissimilar sounds. But once the child
has learned O and X, the only possible word is *ox*. There is not much

basis for building many new words or for using X as the beginning sound in a word. On the other hand, some teachers might prefer to use O and X as first letters, adding B and F, to make *box* and *fox* — two nouns which are picturable. However, the upper and lower case forms of B (b) and F (f) differ, so there is a level of complexity added in the early instructional phase. Of course, for some children, there might be other considerations which, when evaluated, would lead to the conclusion that O and X (or another set of letters) are a better choice to begin reading instruction. At any rate, in STARTER/101, an attempt was made to sequence the presentation of the twenty-six letters so that letters near each other in the sequence a) are dissimilar in shape, b) are dissimilar in sound, and c) can be used to make words relevant to young children.

Combining. After the child has learned the shape and sound of a new letter in isolation, he arrives at the third step in the cycle which teaches the new letter. This step, *combining,* calls for the child to combine the new letter-sound with previously learned letter sounds to make a unified sound composed of two (and sometimes three) letters. The required sound is usually a meaningless sound, providing no meaning or contextual clue; the child must figure out the combining tasks solely on the basis of his sound-symbol association skill. (See Illustrations 3 - A—C.)[7]

This step of combining sounds is by no means new with STARTER/101. For example, Woolman's LIFT-OFF TO READING places great emphasis on *compounding*, to the extent of including many compounds (meaningless but pronounceable nonwords) which rarely or never appear as word parts — compounds such as *omo* and *opo*. (Woolman, 1966) Margaret McCathron's (1952) valuable and concise handbook for parents, YOUR CHILD CAN LEARN TO READ, stresses the learning of word parts or word families which appear frequently in English words. If the child is very familiar with these much used word parts,

---

[7]U + P, the child's introduction to the combining task (in Book 1), is an exception and *does* yield a real word, *UP.*

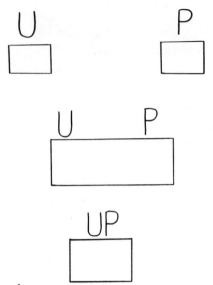

ILLUSTRATION 3 - A
A Combining page, aimed at helping the child combine *U* and *P* into a unified sound. The result, in Book 1, is the meaningful word, *UP*.[1]
(From Book 1, STARTER/101.)

[1]With teacher's help in sounding the letters, child prints letters in boxes and sounds what he prints. Child sounds more rapidly as letters move together in boxes.

A __	F	P	T
I __	n	f	p
f __	o	a	i
f __	ee	i	a
d __	i	a	u
__ D	A	O	I

[1]For example, in line one, the teacher says, "af," so the child would select *F* and print it on the line following *A* (A*F*).

ILLUSTRATION 3 - B
A Combining page; child sounds and matches word parts.
(From Book 6, STARTER/101.)

af	uf	if	af
IF	IF	OP	UF
uf	fu	uf	ip
FI	FO	IF	FI
fa	fu	fa	af
fee	kee	eet	fee

ILLUSTRATION 3 - C
A Combining page. The teacher dictates the word part, and the child chooses a letter that, when printed in the blank, will make the dictated word part.[1]
(From Book 6, STARTER/101.)

UP O□

ILLUSTRATION 4 - A
A Reading Development task
(The first reading page, Book 1,
STARTER/101; see Illustration
1 - A.)

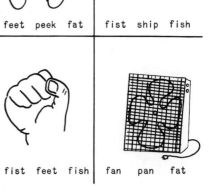

| | feet | peek | fat | fist | ship | fish |
| | fist | feet | fish | fan | pan | fat |

ILLUSTRATION 4 - B
A Reading Development task
(From Book 6, STARTER/101; see
Illustration 1 - B.)

	sand	sun	nut	skin
	fast	fog	fist	fan
	fins	din	fans	fun
	sing	fin	dish	ship

ILLUSTRATION 4 - C
A Reading Development page
(From Book 6, STARTER/101)

63

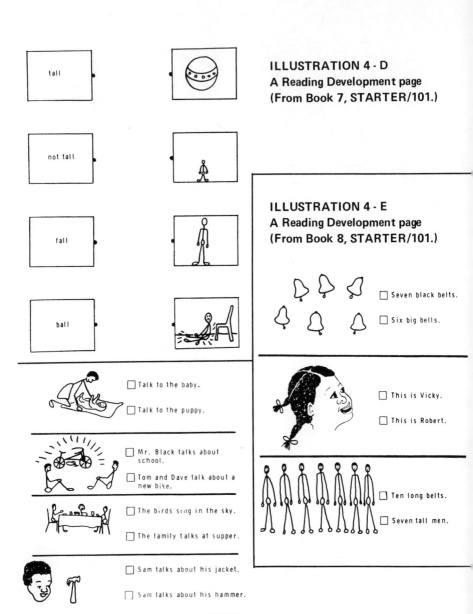

tall

not tall

fall

ball

ILLUSTRATION 4 - D
A Reading Development page
(From Book 7, STARTER/101.)

ILLUSTRATION 4 - E
A Reading Development page
(From Book 8, STARTER/101.)

☐ Seven black belts.

☐ Six big bells.

☐ Talk to the baby.

☐ Talk to the puppy.

☐ Mr. Black talks about school.

☐ Tom and Dave talk about a new bike.

☐ The birds sing in the sky.

☐ The family talks at supper.

☐ Sam talks about his jacket.

☐ Sam talks about his hammer.

☐ Jill talks to her school.

☐ Jill talks to her teacher.

☐ This is Vicky.

☐ This is Robert.

☐ Ten long belts.

☐ Seven tall men.

ILLUSTRATION 4 - F
A Reading Development page
(From Book 10, STARTER/101.)

You are <u>beautiful.</u>

beautiful	beaut	beautiful	beauful
beautiful	been	beautilul	beautiful
beautiful	beautiful	beutful	butfell

PRINT

beautiful _____ _____ _____

beautiful _____ _____ _____

☐ She is beautiful.

☐ She is buntful.

John gets a hammer.
John is happy. It is
his first hammer.

First, John hammers his finger.
"I hurt my finger," yells John.

Then, John hammers the wall.
CRACK. John hammers a crack
in the wall.

Then Dad gets a 🔨 and a ✏️
Dad tells John, "Hammering will
not hurt a 🔨 ."

John sits on the curb and hammers.
He will not hammer his finger.
He will not hammer the wall.
He hammers his 🔨 .

ILLUSTRATION 4 - H
A Reading Development page
(Story from Book 9, STARTER/101.)

[ ] John hurt his finger with a hammer.
[ ] John hurt a worm with a hammer.

65

or phonograms, he can more easily decode new words. In STARTER/ 101, almost all of the compounds or word parts included in the combining step are those which occur frequently in common English words. (Gibson, 1965) In general, we do not require the child to decode unusual or "unnatural" sound combinations — that is, compounds or sounds that do not occur often in the English printed language.

Reading development. As soon as the child has successfully learned the first three steps, which of course are really reading readiness skills, and has thus gained familiarity with several word parts or letter combinations using the newly learned letter, he begins *reading development.* This is the fourth and final step in each of the many learning cycles. In reading development, the child uses the new letter in words — words the meaning of which he learned (or had called to his attention) during the Language Development step for the given cycle. In reading development he progresses from simple two-, three-, and four-letter words to phrases and sentences and, during the latter part of the program, stories. (See Illustrations 4 - A—H.) After the child has completed the Reading Development section of instruction for learning the new letter, he is ready to begin a new cycle for another letter (or digraph, or sight word). The process begins once again, with the child moving from spoken to written language in an orderly and carefully sequenced fashion, aided by materials designed to appeal to him.

Program effect. Is the approach used in STARTER/101 foolproof? Of course not! Jeanne Chall, in her fine book, LEARNING TO READ: THE GREAT DEBATE, reaffirmed our belief that no one approach (method or material) is appropriate for all children. (Chall, 1967) In the early 1960's, Richard Bloomer (1961) conducted several research studies of the progressive choice model of organizing the teaching of reading skills. (As mentioned earlier, this model was influential in shaping the organization of STARTER/101.) He found that 6% of the first grade children using his version of a phonics program (organized along progressive-choice lines) did *not* achieve a second grade reading proficiency level at the end of first grade. Although this 6%

is considerably less than the 29% of control children who also did not achieve second grade proficiency, it is indicative that the approach is not successful for all. Further, in Bloomer's studies, almost exactly the same percentage of experimental and control children (52% and 53% respectively) reached second grade proficiency level by the end of first grade. Thus, for about one-half of all children in Bloomer's studies, a normal or expected reading achievement level was attained, regardless of method used. The remaining children progressed beyond grade level expectancy for end-of-first-grade. Thus, the effect of method appeared most apparent for the poor-achievers and the exceptionally high achievers: 42% of the experimental children (as contrasted with 18% control children) attained a proficiency above third grade level, and only 6%, as noted earlier, did not attain normally expected proficiency, at the end of first grade.

Some years ago, when I was teaching "trainable mentally retarded" children, I undertook to teach reading, with the goal that each child be able to read at the same level that he could speak. My rationale at that time was similar to that discussed at the beginning of this chapter — that if children could learn the most complex of skills, meaningful speech, they could learn to read. Since most of my pupils could use speech meaningfully to some extent, I felt each had a chance to learn to read. Did all children learn to read? No. After two years of approximately 20-30 minutes daily of fun-but-formal reading instruction (organized in accordance with Woolman's progressive choice model), all children continued to be much more fluent speakers than readers - but almost all did learn to read to some extent. (Davy, 1961, 1962)

How effective is the STARTER/101 program?[8] This critical question can be approached in two ways. First, a logical analysis of the mater-

[8]It should be noted that program development for STARTER/101 has only recently been completed. Field-testing is underway in the metropolitan Washington, D. C. area. Feedback from teachers with regard to their ease and the children's pleasure in using the program has been encouraging to date. We must wait until June 1970 to determine measurable reading skill development.

ials indicates that, in theory, children who successfully complete STARTER/101 will have acquired, in a systematic, step-wise fashion, all of the skills prerequisite to beginning reading. Specifically, they will be able to:

recognize, print, and correctly associate *at least* one sound to all letters, both upper and lower case

recognize, sound, and print combinations of letters (word parts)

recognize, sound, and print the most commonly used English digraphs and phonograms[9]

read and, to some extent, spell words containing the linguistic elements included in the program

read simple phrases, sentences, and stories using the linguistic and phonetic elements taught

read sight words drawn from the Dolch basic word list and other selected word lists (words such as "you" and "beautiful" — words whose spelling is not easily derivable from the taught linguistic skills but that are frequently used in materials written for young children)

Beyond the theoretical sufficiency of the STARTER/101 approach is the question of its empirical effectiveness. The first steps toward dealing with this global question were taken during a seven-month pilot study in cooperation with the Reading Center of the District of Col-

---

[9]These were generally selected according to whether or not they appear as most frequently used words on standard word lists, such as the Dolch basic word list. Thus, for example, "ow" and "ea" are taught because they appear in Dolch words such as "down" and "eat," but "oi" is not specifically taught because there is no "most frequent" word that uses the "oi" compound.

umbia Public Schools.[10] Pre- and posttest data were obtained on 98 children taught by a total of eight reading specialists and seven regular classroom teachers in nine different public elementary schools. The children selected for inclusion in the study were children who had shown little or no school achievement, and for whom there was a very guarded prognosis in terms of school progress in general, and reading achievement in particular. Most of the children were in the second and third grades, but there were some children from all elementary grades (1 — 6). The average chronological age was 8 years, 8 months, and the average IQ estimate (from the Peabody Picture Vocabulary Test) was 85.

Reading gains for this low-achieving, problem-ridden group were substantial. On the Wide Range Achievement Test (Reading), administered at the beginning and end of the program (an interval of seven calendar months, with a range of 22 to 55 hours of instruction), the children showed a mean gain of seven months — well over the expected gain for such a group. On the Sheldon Informal Reading Inventory, pre-post scores were available for 49 children. In the beginning, 48 of these children were reading below the primer level (with many at the readiness level); at the time of the posttest, 32 children were reading *beyond* the primer level. On the Botel Word Opposites Test (a post-only measure), only 14 children were unable to take the test; 66% of the children scored at or above the 1^2 grade level.

The results, both objective and subjective, indicate that the STARTER/101 approach can be effective in teaching beginning reading. Further research is planned to determine more precisely for which kinds of children (and teachers) and under what conditions STARTER/101 is most appropriate and effective in helping children learn to read.

Teacher's role. Does the teacher or instructor have a significant role in a system such as STARTER/101? Very definitely. It is true that the

[10]O'Keefe, Ruth Ann. "Report on the STARTER/101 Pilot Project in the Reading Center of the D. C. Public Schools," Washington School of Psychiatry, June, 1970. (Reprint available from Silver Burdett Company, Morristown, New Jersey 07960.)

workbooks, like those prepared for most reading programs, are designed for a great deal of independent work on the part of the child. But the nature of a program such as STARTER/101 *requires* the assistance of a reader (teacher, aide, tutor, or other) periodically throughout the program. The main *educational* function of this instructor is to provide the sounds associated with the symbols, but in fact, I believe a warm, responsive, constructive adult leader is vital in the educational lives of young children. Many children become discouraged while trying to learn to read, and the teacher can provide a human and crucial service to the child by setting up reasonable guidelines, rules, and educational goals and supplying the encouragement most children need and too often do not receive.

SUMMARY

This paper has been dedicated to the proposition that children who have learned to talk possess the inherent ability — and right — to learn the fundamental skills of reading in such a way that they will be encouraged to read for benefit and enjoyment throughout their lives. A few of the many reasons and circumstances of failure have been mentioned, but the real point is this: *any* problems that are identified as causing or contributing to reading failure or inability should be thought of primarily as starting points for planning strategies or achieving success, rather than as explanations for continued failure.

A newly developed structured beginning reading program, STARTER/ 101, was described as an operational example of the author's philosophy and strategy for helping nonreading children learn to read. Since the general design requirements of this program are independent of the specific content of the program, they are also appropriate for other kinds of teaching situations. Even for reading, all the program design requirements discussed in this chapter (and summarized below) could be met using means other than those used in STARTER/101. The requirements are:

> The materials or activities must be fun and rewarding for the children.

They must be easy for the teacher to implement.

They must take into account specific characteristics of the children for whom the program is intended — characteristics such as mobility, language, etc.

They must include whatever readiness skills are prerequisite to the end (goal) skills.

They must capitalize on the familiar and existing strengths of the target children.

They must present the material to be learned in a systematically and gradually more challenging sequence so that

a) very few specific skills to be learned are introduced at one time;

b) these skills are mastered and then combined with previously learned skills; and

c) the new skills (knowledge) are used immediately, with extensive practice, in a context that is challenging, interesting and exciting to the child.

It *is* possible to help children develop reading skills systematically and successfully in a context that is relevant, familiar, and pleasant for them. This task, this mission, requires our utmost effort in using the most modern techniques at hand for program planning, development, and teacher training. It is to these ends that educators must renew and, where necessary, redirect their effort and dedication.

I wish to thank my colleagues Dr. H. R. Cort, Jr., Miss Margaret Mattis, Mrs. Carol Potter, and Mrs. Naomi Henderson for their helpful comments in preparing this paper.

The program has now been published by Silver Burdett Company, Morristown, N. J.

REFERENCES

Allen, James E., Jr. Statement in "Washington Post," September 23, 1969

Bloomer, R. H. Reading methodology: An experimental test of some alternative organizational principles. **The Reading Teacher,** January 1961.

Chall, Jeanne. **Learning to read: The great debate.** New York: McGraw Hill, 1967.

Davy, Ruth Ann (O'Keefe). An experimental method of teaching reading to severely retarded children. Unpublished M. A. Thesis, College of Education, University of Maryland, 1961.

Davy, Ruth Ann (O'Keefe). Adaption of progressive choice method for teaching reading to retarded children. **Amer. J. of Mental Deficiency,** September 1962, **67,** 274-286.

Davy, Ruth Ann (O'Keefe). Closing the meaning loop through progressive choice structure. **CEC selected convention papers.** Council for Exceptional Children, 1963.

Edward, Thomas J. The progressive choice reading method. In John Money (Ed.), **The disabled reader.** Baltimore: Johns Hopkins Press, 1966.

Engelmann, S. E. **Distar.** Chicago: Science Research Associates, 1969.

Glasser, William. **Schools without failure.** New York: Harper & Row, 1969.

Gibson, Eleanor J. Learning to read. **Science,** May 1965, **148,** 1066-1072.

Gibson, Eleanor J. Experimental psychology of learning to read. In John Money (Ed.), **The disabled reader.** Baltimore: Johns Hopkins Press, 1966.

Lenneberg, Eric H. **Biological foundations of language.** New York: John Wiley & Sons, Inc., 1967.

Leonard, George. **Education and ecstasy.** New York: Delacorte Press, 1968.

McEathron, Margaret. **Your child can learn to read.** New York: Grosset & Dunlap, 1952.

O'Keefe, Ruth Ann. **STARTER/101: A structured beginning reading program for young children.** Morristown, N. J.: Silver Burdett, 1970 (developmental edition; Sept. 1971, commercial edition to be published).

Sherburne, Mary Lela, & Gannon, F. B. Washington, D. C., model school division reading project, 1968-69 academic year. August 1969 (Preliminary draft).

Stevens, George, & Orem, R. C. **The case for early reading.** St. Louis: Warren Green Co., 1968.

Sullivan, M. W. **Reading.** Palo Alto: Behavioral Research Laboratories, 1968. (a)

Sullivan, M. W. **Reading readiness.** Palo Alto: Behavioral Research Laboratories, 1968. (b)

Vail, Edward. **Formula phonics.** Los Angeles: Lawrence Publishing Co., 1969.

Woolman, Myron. **Lift-off to reading.** Chicago: Science Research Associates, 1966.

Perceptual Conditioning for Decoding: Rationale and Method

Gerald G. Glass, Ph.D.
Associate Professor of Education and
Director of Reading and Studies Center
Adelphi University
Garden City, Long Island, New York

RATIONALE

To Teach Reading

Teaching children to read is the responsibility of all who purport to contribute — the reading teachers, linguists, physicians and "researchers" who direct their efforts toward discovering rationale, data and methods. This how-to concern is in contrast to the concerns of teachers of literature and other content areas who make the assumption that the youngster already is able to use the reading medium (their primary responsibility is having the student utilize this ability when studying in the prescribed areas). Instructionally, the former are concerned with the "learning to read" while the latter are concerned with utilizing reading. We here will be primarily concerned with the former, the didactic aspect. Our concerns then are with developing (in children or adults) the ability to use printed language as a stimulus for communicating. (McKee, 1967)

Abilities Already Learned

Previous to reading, children use other communication media which have "naturally" developed without instruction. From birth, children routinely learn to discriminate the world around them by utilizing their inherent senses. Initially what are merely heard as noises soon are clearly discriminated as cues and signals. It is then simple maturation that causes a listening vocabulary to be acquired. In a similar manner, maturation causes (or allows?) *visual ability* to become highly discriminating. In addition, children learn to discriminate and to give meaning to their environments in terms of touch, smell, and taste. Each child, in a uniquely innovative and interdisciplinary way, utilizes the reciprocality of all these senses to direct his overt responses and internal reactions. These are learned. However, very little, if any, of these learnings need to be taught. (Bruner, 1966) Thus, a child coming to the stage of being *ready-to-read* comes with relatively sophisticated visual and auditory abilities which must be utilized in his *learning to read.* (Wardhough, 1969)

76

Reading Is a Different Media

Reading, by design, necessitates that the child learn to use his senses to communicate **without** the dynamic, dimensional media he has used since birth. Meaning must now be drawn from the mute and flat environment of letters clustered together to form words. His seeing and hearing abilities must now utilize cues which are quite different from those utilized in the past. For example, if he looks at markings that we know to be *c, o,* and *w,* he must (minimally) bring to mind the sound *cow* even though what he actually sees is flat and absolutely inert. The word does not look like, feel like, or smell like what he has been seeing in his recent past that brings the sound *cow* successfully to mind. He cannot even have the familiar cue of hearing the sound spoken by someone. The cow he sees in print must bring to mind any thoughts he would have if he actually were to see a cow or the many sound and sight abstractions he has learned for cow. Although he can **see,** vision of the printed word has as much relationship to the cow as vision has in identifying his own mother from a person he has never seen before. He may use his eyes to look at both persons, but the visual ability itself is quite inadequate to interpret the stimuli. He must **learn** something more.

Decoding Comes Before Reading

It is beneficial that persons concerned with the **teaching** of reading see reading didactically; i. e., in a way that allows for the involvement of youngsters in discrete activities which build developmentally upon one another to a level where one can observe that the child "can read." It is also advantageous to see instruction as something that, in its discrete parts, can be offered to children in a relatively parsimonious and simple manner. (It is much less fruitful, for the purpose of teaching, for the teacher to see reading simply as an activity which someone does to gain meaning.)

Most reading authorities would consider that one can **read** only if one

77

is able to decode the written word, obtain meanings of prescribed dimensions from the decoded words, and react to and utilize these meanings for personal growth. (Gray, 1960) It is apparent that if a person is merely able to identify the sound of a word, he is not reading unless he can at the same instant respond with meaning (from noise to signal). However, it must here also be made apparent that, if one is to learn to read, one will never have the opportunity to respond to meanings already known (or develop new meanings via the printed word) if the decoding ability is not *first* there. (Fries, 1962) The person who could not decode would admittedly still have a wide range of avenues open to communicate, but the avenue of "reading" would be blocked.

While decoding is obviously not reading, reading cannot exist without decoding. As a child can learn to listen only after he can hear, a child can learn to read only after he has developed the ability to decode. Hearing is to listening as decoding is to reading. Just hearing a person speak does not assume that the hearer is either listening or understanding (noise vs. signal). However, it would be impossible for listening and understanding to come about were the person not able to hear. Similarly, merely because a person is able to decode does not mean that he is able to read; i.e., to understand and to deal with meanings via the printed word. However, it is crucial to reiterate that it would be impossible to read if decoding ability were not first developed!

Thus, what seems a contradiction may be stated: decoding is at once the least important aspect of reading, and at the same time the most crucial aspect of reading. If a person does not learn to decode efficiently and effectively, he will never be allowed the opportunity to read; i. e., deal with and react to meaning via the printed word. An analogy of relating the steering wheel to the automobile comes to mind. The mere knowledge of the operation of the steering wheel is rather low on the level of importance when one is concerned with the ability to maneuver and make appropriate driving decisions. However, if one does not know this relatively low level skill of steering the car (or if the wheel itself is not there), this could keep one from either developing or utilizing the high level skills needed for driving. The key for the ignition is at once a relatively unimportant factor in the operation of a car but without it the whole process would be at a standstill. The hard fact is that, although decoding is not reading, reading is not without decoding.

Decoding Is Separate From Reading

There are instructional advantages in keeping the teaching of decoding operationally separate from the teaching of reading. Learning to decode is easier than learning to read. Because decoding, unlike reading, is only a limited skill it is much more vulnerable to the effects of simple conditioning or habit formation. Let us attempt to explain why.

In decoding only one sound is wanted — response to the word stimulus. This sound-response is wanted no matter who the responder is. The correct sound of the word is the same no matter who is making the response. The stereotyped bright, creative, culturally advantaged decoder, when he sees *cow*, must come up with the exact same sound-response as a low-achieving relatively phlegmatic, disadvantaged decoder. They both must come up with the sound that is "cow." Thus, in decoding only one correct response is expected — a response that does not allow for any uniqueness and/or creativity. In contrast to decoding, the situation in *reading* is necessarily different. Linguists tell us that no word can ever mean the exact same thing twice. Meaning is dependent upon the word's place in the sentence and that sentence's place in the paragraph. In addition, each child brings to the abstraction "cow" his own individual intelligence, readiness, experiential background, and infinite other factors unique to him. Good reading instruction taps and extends these individual differences and does not aim at making reading something of a homogenous experience. (Betts, 1956)

To reiterate, decoding, in contrast to reading, does not have to allow for individual responses; all are taught to make the *one* correct decoding response. It is from this correct response that each individual can go on his own into reading. Decoding is *merely* identifying a prescribed correct sound; reading has no limits.

Thus one can assume that individual differences in students are less relevant when decoding than when reading, since what is to be learned is simpler. If it is simpler, it should be easier to learn. If the teaching of reading can be separated (and held in abeyance) from the teaching of decoding, more youngsters would probably have an opportunity to learn to decode. This is fortunate for it is an easily observed fact that the overwhelming number of "reading disability" cases are in actuality decoding disability cases. If these youngsters could develop the ability to decode, their reading level would dramatically move toward their expectancy level (generally determined by factors related to intelligence and experiential background.) It is quite common to hear, "He has little difficulty understanding the material if you read to him, but once he has to read it on his own, he is over his head." Substitute decoding for reading and you will see the point we are making. Many youngsters could be helped to improve dramatically (three or four years) in reading level simply by being taught to decode efficiently and effectively.

Hypothesis For Decoding

Because of what is commonly done in the name of decoding (word-analysis) in basal, workbook type and other published programs, it is important to carefully and objectively examine what is involved in the teaching of decoding. It is the purpose of this section to demonstrate that too many of our very widely utilized and accepted methods of teaching decoding are either unreasonable or unwarranted in light of the task involved. It also can be demonstrated that many of the activities which include workbook-type exercises may actually be detrimental to the development of proficiency in decoding.

80

The following points need to be made:

1. From the previous description of a didactic model of reading for the purpose of instruction, it seems wise to consider the teaching of decoding instructionally separate and apart from the teaching of reading. (Chall, 1967) This consideration should not be difficult for teachers of reading. We know that reading, even at its simplest level, must be a response to meaning. Just "calling" a word cannot be considered reading. The reading skill, to be useful in the area of communication, must minimally include the meaning aspect. Thus, in a sense, decoding is an ability that one must have before reading can begin. It may be a pre-reading ability. "Reading" thus comes into play only *after* one knows the sound of a word.

It is important that the reader understand what the writer is attempting to say. If criteria are developed for a program which purports to teach decoding, they may not be the same as (or even similar to) those criteria developed for reading programs. Reading programs must, of necessity, include factors from simple word meanings to high-level critical reading. However, here, the acitivity of decoding is much narrower and shallower in scope and merely includes the identification of the accepted sound of a word in preparation for reading.

Hypothesis: Decoding is not reading. Decoding should be taught separately from reading.

2. Although reading must minimally include the factor of meaning, *decoding* may or may not include the factor of meaning. This can clearly be demonstrated. (The importance of understanding this fact will be seen when recommendations are made for a program to teach decoding.) One can, with ease, decode possible words such as *blant, dexnap, philope, and shantug* without even guessing at their meaning. The decoding is not dependent upon meaning. (In fact, one must be able to decode a word without first discovering meaning because what meaning is applied will depend upon what is decoded.) Those ap-

proaches which ask the pupil to decode on the basis of the possible meaning of the word are dealing with a relatively unstable area. Very few words except for plosives such as *bang, crash,* and *oops* derive their sound from their meaning. One could not even speculate on the meaning of words such as *charm, here, heart,* and *thesaurus* from the sounds represented by the orthography of each word. Thus, for all decoders of the English language, except for possibly the philologists, sound-symbol relationship is a fortuitous thing.

Although the relevance of meaning should be understood in the teaching of decoding, it is actually of little significance and of too much unnecessary concern. All authorities in the teaching of reading agree that students should not be asked to decode words they have not heard before. (Wiley, 1928) Most recommend that the words to be decoded be in the person's listening and speaking vocabulary as well. An examination of the words introduced for decoding in primary basal readers reveals that almost all are already (by design) within the listening vocabulary of youngsters at that grade level. Therefore, the teaching of meanings with the teaching of decoding is not only poor procedure but it is most often irrelevant. If the youngster already knows the meaning of words, then why spend very important time (and dilute the teaching of decoding) by the inappropriate concern for meaning? Meaning has to do with reading and not decoding! Few youngsters at the age of six have less than 4,000 words within their listening vocabulary. (Strickland, 1962) This is more than an ample amount of meaningful words from which to teach decoding. To spend time teaching the meaning of known words is not only wasteful but dull. At the very least it is superfluous.

Hypothesis: Teach youngsters to decode only with words whose meanings they already know. Then meaning is made irrelevant to the instructional session.

3. The use of picture clues may, at times, aid in discovering the sound represented by a word. However, consider how the intrusion of pictures may negatively affect learning to decode. According to the

82

"Gestalt factor," (Hilgard and Marquis, 1940) the child must first utilize those factors in the environment which are instantly recognized. When he sees a picture of a hat with the word "hat" written under the picture, he will have no choice but to respond immediately to the picture of the hat and to think "hat." He will not be allowed the opportunity to deal with (or practice) any activities which would aid in the *decoding* process. The identification of the word through the picture is totally irrelevant to the development of a decoding skill. It is like whispering the sound of the word in his ear and then saying that he is learning to decode.

Likewise, decoding ability may be hampered by teaching decoding through the utilization of words within a phrase or sentence context. To ask a person to determine the sound of a word from its context is an opportunistic approach too dependent upon the lack of ambiguity in the context and the person's sophistication with the language, not upon a decoding ability. The use of both picture and context clues can only divert the learner from developing reliable decoding ability. For example, a reader attempting to discover the sound of "bell" in order to deal with its meaning would only need to use context clues in a sentence such as, "The boy walked to the door and rang the ____." The structure of the sentence is such that without even seeing the word "bell" a child would, with a great deal of confidence, assume it to be "bell." One did not in any way need to use the combined effects of letter-sound elements. All too often it is the consistent use of *context* in word-analysis programs which evolves as a major factor in determining the correct sound of a word. If the formative training in decoding focuses upon the use of context first, it may undermine the use and practice of bona fide decoding skills. Context(and pictures) all too frequently may give both the child and the teacher a spurious idea of decoding ability. They lead to apparent ability not actual ability. One who can decode a word out of context is one who can decode! The child, while working with the teacher, should be free to expose his ignorance and to deal with it in order to develop independent strength in *decoding.* When actually reading (not developing decoding skills), he will have the added clues of context. He will use context if it is there, but he must be able to decode whether or not contextual (or picture) aid is present!

It becomes apparent that only the placement of letters within a word is a reliable determinant of the "sound of a word." Change any letter in a word and it will not represent that same spoken word. Change the sequence of the letters in a word and again it will not represent the spoken word. The particular letters and their placement within the word determine how the word is to be decoded. It may be that many of the word-analysis difficulties which are "discovered" by middle-grade and junior high teachers are the result of the context becoming too difficult to shelter the previously concealed weakness in decoding. This is particularly true for potentially bright youngsters who have been able to take good guesses at the sound of a word because the context in the lower grade was relatively consistent and included little or no meaning problems.

Hypothesis: It would be advantageous to teach decoding in a way that only decoding skills can come into play. This necessitates decoding out of the context of a phrase or sentence and without picture aid.

4. Manuals of basal readers, from second grade on, give teachers information on the teaching of syllabication. Basal and independent workbooks include exercises to give practice in the use of syllabication. We have not been able to find a description of a reading program that does not, at some point, recommend the teaching and use of syllabication as an effective aid to develop independence in decoding (e.g., Heilman, 1964).

It is important to examine such an all-pervasive approach. What does one do when one uses syllabication to discover the sounds in a word? (Glass, 1967) By definition, syllabication is the application of rules or principles which allow the decoder to identify the syllables for the purpose of discovering the sounds made by the letters, particularly the vowels. Thus, according to the most common syllabication rule, when two consonants stand together between two vowels (vccv), the division into syllables occurs between the two consonants as in **pen/cil.** The first consonant (n) ends one syllable and the second (c) starts another. Then we apply the fact that vowels at the end of a syllable (open) are usually "long" and the vowels within the syllables (closed) are usually "short." A reader who wants to determine the sounds in **pencil** can see that the first syllable ends with an **n** and that **e** and **i** are enclosed and therefore short. But he is also taught to watch for consonant digraphs. The two consonants may be digraphs (ch, ph, sh, th), and digraphs are, according to syllabication, treated as single consonants. One cannot split digraphs (machine, mother). The "vccv rule" must be used with discretion.

Another common rule advises that, if a word to be decoded has one consonant (or digraph) standing between two vowels (vcv), the consonant (or digraph) is said to go with the second vowel, with the result that the first vowel is long. Thus, **motor** receives its accepted sound. However, as the child scans a "vcv" word to discover its sound, he again must not be impetuous. The "vcv rule" does not apply if the first syllable is accented. Then the first vowel is short as in **rapid, veteran,** and **cover.**

Syllabication thus asks a child to scan words carefully looking for "vccv" combinations and "vcv" combinations and to know when this does not apply in words where accent determines vowel sound. He would also need to know that a prefix and a suffix usually form their own syllable **regardless** of any rule about consonants between vowels (hunter). However, this does not hold in words such as **mailed,** and **flagged** since the **ed** is not preceded by a **d** or **t**. Also, if a word of more than one syllable ends in **le** (maple, table) one must not apply the "vccv rule" because the **le** plus the preceding consonant form a new syllable. We must also be cognizant of the fact that, when a syllable ends in an **e**, it frequently affects the sound of another vowel in that syllable. Confused?

Obviously, the use of syllabication to aid in decoding is, at its very best, detailed, complex, and often contradictory. The coup-de-grace of the utilization of sequence and frequency of consonants and vowels (the essence of syllabication) is the rule that determines the sounds of the aforementioned *rapid* and *veteran*. This rule advises that in "vcv," the consonant usually goes with the second syllable if the preceding vowel is long and with the first syllable if the vowel is short. The rule actually asks the decoder to know the sound of the unknown word to determine the sound! If the child already knows what the word says, why would he need to apply syllabication to help him discover the sound of the word? In addition, the rate at which a person decodes is such that it would be impossible for one to be applying syllabication rules to determine long and short vowel sounds.

Adults (including teachers) persist in stating that they use "syllabication" to help them identify unknown words. We have checked very carefully with literally hundreds and hundreds of adults and have yet to find one who actually uses syllabication principles or rules when sounding out an unknown word. On close examination, one would observe that syllables are identified *after the sounds* within the word are known. No one in our observation ever used syllabication principles to discover the sounds within a word. The sounds in the word were used to determine the syllable division, and not vice versa. The identification of syllables is apparently a visual process that has no conscious rhyme or reason other than, "the word seemed to sound out that way." In a more esoteric way, certain clusters of letters made sounds which when combined resulted in a word that sounded familiar.or credible. Again, the crucial point to be made is that discovering syllables in a word came after knowledge of the sound of the word and not before. The decoding of a word after one knows the sound of the word is obviously superfluous. Why syllabicate?

This writer is usually wary of extreme positions. However, an examination of "syllabication" forces him to write that he has yet to discover any discernible reason why this activity should be included in a word-analysis program. This statement has been made before countless astute bodies concerned with both language and reading, and the over-whelming majority agree. Yet the teaching of syllabication with the recommended use of syllabication principles is included in every word-analysis (decoding) program that this staff has examined. This includes programs in texts, basals, workbooks, charts, and kits. Why?

An examination of blackboard and workbook syllabication exercises would make apparent the obvious — that they are invalid. In spite of what the directions on a workbook page say, one cannot ever use syllabication in the all-too-common exercises which ask for the identi-fication of syllables within words. The exercises always assume that the reader knows the sound of the whole word and only then asks him to identify the syllables.

Our studies have shown that rarely, if ever, do youngsters syllabicate by the use of rules or principles. (Burton and Glass, 1968) They mere-ly sound out the syllables where the breaks seem appropriate. There is no reasoning or application of principle. The reader might notice how beginners and adults decode an unknown word. It becomes ob-vious that only in a very structured syllabication lesson does one look for "vccv," "vcv," digraphs, and the like.

For further illustration of this demonstration, look at the following word: *prechiming*. Decode it. Did you use syllabication rules? Did you scan and decide, on the basis of principles (or rules), where a syl-lable fell and thus know the sound of the vowel? If you did, you are indeed (according to our information) quite rare. Whatever you did you most surely did not apply syllabication principles.

Hypothesis: Syllabication is not used for decoding. It should not be part of a decoding program.

5. The idea of including syllabication principles in the teaching of de-coding is part of the prevalent thinking that independent word attack

is based upon knowledge which can discriminately and rationally be applied when called for. That if one is to do more than recall whole words at-sight by their configuration, one necessarily has to have a plan of attack. The assumption is that by the intelligent application of so-called phonic and linguistic principles, one can be reasonably certain to become successful in decoding. Fortunately, experience has shown that the ability to decode is based less upon knowledge of rules and principles and more upon an instant response to whole words and/or a conditioned automatic response to the structural parts of whole words (Glass, 1964), not letter by letter. Simply stated, successful decoders simply are able to remember what they have seen and heard before — nothing more! Specifically, successful decoders respond to whole words and clusters of letters within the whole words. They merely remember the sound which common discrete visual elements represent. Because decoders already know the sounds that are common in the English language, they can sequence sounds and produce a whole word sound that makes sense. (Soffietti, 1955)

Hypothesis: Successful decoders do not apply prescribed principles nor do they utilize a conscious reasoning process. Thus, the teaching of decoding does not necessitate the use of rules and principles.

6. There are general factors of learning which need to be taken into consideration when attempting to explore what is involved in learning and utilizing decoding (word-analysis) techniques.

Long ago Gestaltists discovered that the size of a configuration has little or nothing to do with its potential for being learned. The familiarity resulting from meaningfulness and frequency is a major determinant of what one will recall and retain. The eleven-letter word *grandmother* is less difficult to decode and recall than the four-letter word *here*. Since *grandmother* is not seen as eleven separate letters to deal with, it is not more burdensome to identify than *here* which has only four letters.

Size of configuration is also irrelevant in identifying parts *within whole words.* If letter clusters within words can be made residually familiar to a reader, he might find the sound of a four letter cluster such as *ight* in the word *insightful* no more difficult to identify than the sound of *o* in the word *hot.* The point to be made is that a single consonant or a single vowel and the sound it represents are not necessarily easier to identify than clusters of letters which are used to represent a common sound.

Objects composed of discrete elements are initially, because of maturation, seen as wholes and then, if necessary, seen as composed of parts. For example, a very young child first identifies a car, a toy, a house (maybe even a whole word) before he can identify the parts that make up the whole. Only as he matures in his intellectual and perceptual abilities is he able to see parts of the whole. Notice the square with the three numerals $\boxed{\begin{smallmatrix}8 & 4\\ & 3\end{smallmatrix}}$. The three numerals represent "things" that are seen. However, within the next square $\boxed{834}$ one instantly sees only one "thing" on the page. The same three numbers became only one numeral. Depending upon how the stimulus is presented, one can see the numerals as three discrete occurrences and then instantly see the same numerals as one occurrence.

To decode the word *insightful*, no one would deal with each individual letter sound because the letter-by-letter response to English words would not have been reinforced. Instead there was reinforcement when learning to respond to letter clusters which represented sounds that led to the correct whole word. What might be identified is the *in*, the *s*, the *ight*, and the *ful.* This is done because in all of life's experiences of identifying words, this approach has been successful. No successful decoder could possibly deal with the word *insightful* either letter by letter or by clustering the *sig*, the *ht*, the *fu*, and the *l.* Actually there is nothing in the sequencing of the letters that tells what clustering should be made. One just never "sounds out" in a way which would contradict what has been experienced when successful in sounding out previous words.

Hypothesis: Words are initially seen as wholes and then as composed of parts (letter-clusters) which combine to form the correct sound. Size of configuration is not relevant to the ease with which persons learn to decode because decoders do not respond to each letter as separate parts of the word.

7. Anyone who has taught decoding knows how important it is for a person to be able to identify the sounds which are part of a whole word. A decoder is at a disadvantage if he hears a word such as *insightful* as one sound mass similar to the way he hears the sound made by a book that falls onto the floor. The book hitting the floor makes a discernible noise but not noticeably composed of discrete sound elements. However, in contrast, for decoding purposes, he should be able to tell what sounds can be heard within a word — auditory discrimination for decoding. It is also important to decoding that the reader be able to associate the letters that "make" the sound — visual discrimination for decoding. He must correctly see that *ight* makes a discernible familiar sound and that the *ig* or *gh* or the *tfu* in the word *insightful* do not constitute the letter clustering that represents the common sounds heard in the word. (The ability described here is much more discriminating than the global abilities of so-called auditory and visual discrimination.) Any child who can see to live in the every day world and can hear what is being said to him, has all the auditory and visual discrimination ability he will ever need in learning to decode. (In contrast see Money, 1962, 1966) What he may lack is the discriminating ability to identify and respond to the appropriate letters which represent the sounds he hears in words.

Hypothesis: Correct visual and auditory clustering is very important to the decoding process.

8. It is possible to view a broad area and, at the same time, subordinate within that view that to which there is no wish to respond. To explain: Hold a pencil up to anyone and quickly say "What do you see?" Experience has shown that everyone will say, "A pencil." Actually the

observer saw a great deal more. He saw a finger, hand, arm, shoulder, head, torso, the surrounding area, etc. All this was in his view. But he has "learned" to discriminate out of the visual field based upon the question and his learned mental sets. This suggests that in decoding it is possible, and maybe even natural, for a child to find a three- and four-letter combination (such as *ing, ate,* and *ight*) as easy to isolate within the whole word as a single letter sound. As was shown, such clusters of letters may be seen as one whole rather than three or four separate wholes. Thus, one can learn to "see" only a certain part of the complete view (depending upon one's learned mental set), while at the same time observing the whole. If one learns to see the clusters often enough within whole words, then the predictable results of such repetition would cause these clusters to be seen *within the whole word* as routinely as one sees single letters within *the whole word.* In addition, if the clustered letters are also associated with their routine sounds, that is the beginning of a decoding process as a result of a conditioning process which, by definition, is ingrained.

Hypothesis: The correct mental set can cause the decoder to see and respond to the appropriate letter-sound structures within a whole word; i.e., to correctly decode.

A Demonstration

The discussion of the rationale may come to fruition when asked to decode the following possible word: *distenationing.* Say the unknown word aloud. Did you read the word at sight or did you sound out the word? You sounded it out since you have never seen the word before. Did you use syllable or phonic rules such as "vccv," "vcv," open syllable and closed syllable, two vowels together, etc.? Of course not. Not only did you not use syllabication (and the like) but you would have never been able to, in the amount of time you took to decode the word. Did you notice the "little words in the big word" and use the sounds of these words (e.g, *at, on, in*) in the analysis? Hopefully not, for if you did, you decoded the word incorrectly.

What, then, did you do to decode the word? You did something not worthy of being called a process. You decoded the word the way you did because, as a successful decoder, you had no choice. You have been conditioned through your consistent and extensive dealings with words used in English writing to respond to clusters of letters in an un-known word which "naturally" come together. We see (and hear) within the whole word *dis/ ten/ a/ tion/ ing* or possibly *d/ is/ t/ en/-ation/ ing*. But never *di/ ste, ist/ ena, na/ tio* or *io/nin* (all of which are phonically possible). Your correct decoding did not include any of the activities introduced in the word-analysis aspect of reading pro-grams. You did not "cluster" on the basis of a reasoned decision. You did not reason through which were the digraphs, which vowels were long or short, which little words and big words contribute to the cor-rect sound of the whole word. You did not use picture or context clues.

Teach What Is Useful

Actually one is incidentally conditioned to see the appropriate cluster-ing of letters within a whole word. It makes sense, then, that any ac-tivity which fosters seeing the correct clusters would contribute a great deal toward developing a decoding facility. It is this writer's belief that unknown words are correctly identified through a learned response which utilizes a conditioned perceptual *set* which instantly scans a word for its structural sounding elements (letter clusters) as they have been historically consistent in the decoder's experience. You are asked to examine the possible words *blassment, trepulation, trom* and *deplistrationer.* It is most certain that you "read" the words, letter cluster by letter cluster, as you have learned these letters in each word routinely arrange themselves. It is almost as if there were actual spacings between certain letters to form common structures within the words. You used nothing more than your instant (conditioned) knowl-edge of these letter clusters.

Another point. Notice how important *correctness* is. For words that

92

have structures which do not fit a consistent pattern (police, great, mother), one does not respond to the more common sound of "ice," "eat," "her." Familiarity with the language tells you that the whole-word sound produced is not consistent with what you know in the English language. (This was found to be true with first and second graders as well.)

If the method by which successful decoders identify unknown words can be agreed upon, it would be fruitful to backtrack and to develop ways of *learning* decoding which would be consistent with what is desired in the end results. Included will be only that which is (or was) used by successful decoders. An approach utilizing perceptual conditioning methods has been developed to be totally consistent with the factors presented and discussed in this chapter. The approach requires youngsters to examine known words, out of context, both visually and auditorially, in a way that would foster instant visual clustering of letters with their associated sound.

Through the use of *set,* cognitions are developed that involve the organization of the visual and auditory environment into meaningful patterns. The *set* results in the imposition of a meaningful (in terms of decoding) organization upon all incoming sensory data. Each learner is set to respond in one way or another. He is said to be physiologically and psychologically ready to respond to assigned details rather than to others.

Mental sets to "see" correctly are carefully controlled by the teacher's complete direction of how a youngster is to examine a word and identify the sounds within it. The approach evolved from the guidelines set down by the factors discussed in the rationale.

PERCEPTUAL CONDITIONING (GLASS ANALYSIS)

The following approach is deemed to be derived from the rationale presented and the understanding of what method can reasonably be applied in present day classrooms. Perceptual conditioning is thus theoretically based, internally consistent, and applied.[1] It might best be understood if presented in list form that includes steps to follow.

1. Only individual words should be presented to the learner during training sessions. These words may be printed on flash cards, slides, blackboards, or any such material. (The author's group has used 3 x 8 flash cards.) In the training session, the child may never see more or less than the whole word. When the word is first exposed to the child, he is told the sound of the word (e.g., "This word says *catch*.") It is crucial to understand that in this approach, concern is not with the correct identification of the words used in training. The primary objective is to condition the decoders to identify the appropriate sounds and letters (clusters) in a word, as well as to condition him to cluster visually the "correct" letters and simultaneously to make the "correct" oral response when seeing these letters. (Letter clusters are defined as two or more letters that, in a whole word, represent a relatively consistent sound. For example, in *catch* the clusters are *at ch*; in *play* the clusters are *pl ay*; in *standard* the clusters may be *st an and ar ard*.) The child should not use any method which might fortuitously be effective for that particular word but which does not have the potential for generalization as reading letter-cluster by letter-cluster does. Habit formation (for letter clustering) can best come about by the consistent response and appropriate and consistent reinforcement.

The decoder should be looking, at all times, at the word. He is advised not to look away or at the teacher while instructions are given to him. The structuring of the letters and sounds in the word should come

[1]The readers who may be concerned with rationale and consistency might relate each instructional recommendation to its theoretical base as presented in the front section of this chapter.

94

about on the basis of observing the *whole word,* just as it will be seen when read.

2. As stated, the whole word must always be presented. Parts of words may never be covered up to help with identifying letter clusters. The practice of covering part of the word and then exposing that part simply undermines forming the habit of letter clustering within whole words when there are no external clues, as during reading. Similarly, the youngster should not see words which are put together from structural sounding parts. Do not show the *ent* and then add a *t* or an *r* or an *s* to help identify the structure. The correct letter clustering must be seen with the letters before and the letters after, as when seen during actual reading. The *ong* in isolation is not the same perceptual image as the *ong* in the word *stronger.* Again, readers must be conditioned to isolate perceptually the letter clusters as parts of a whole word (such as the reader did with *distenationing*).

3. The teacher always directs how the pupil will examine the word. He is the agent for developing visual and auditory sets. As the youngster is looking at the word, he directs the examination with the following two basic questions to develop the correct mental set:

What letters make (what) sounds?
What sounds do (what) letters make?

For example: In the word *black,* what letters make the *bl* sound? What letters make the *ack* sound? What sound does the *bl* make? What sound does the *ack* make?

In the word *stronger,* what letters make the *st* sound? What letters make the *str* sound? What letters make the *rong* sound? What letters make the *er* sound? What letters make the *ronger* sound? What letters make the *strong* sound? In the word *stronger,* what sound does the *st* make? What sound does the *str* make? What sound does the *ong* make? What sound does the *er* make? What sound does the *strong* make? What sound does the *onger* make?

For students reading at second level or above, it has been found that sounds can be arbitrarily taken off and the students asked to voice the remaining sounds. For example: In the word *stronger,* what sound would be left if the *onger* sound were taken off? *During all this activity the student is looking at the whole word. The configuration of the whole word is never insulted.* He is being conditioned to cluster within whole words.

4. In a similar fashion, the decoder works through the remaining words in a 10- to 15-word list that is controlled for the vowel cluster (e.g., bat, scat, platter, attack, etc.). The vowel cluster (here the *at*) should be seen clustered in the whole word so often that it will be identified (within the whole word) at sight. The question that may immediately come to mind is how many of these letter clusters are there in the English language? Are they so numerous that it would be unreasonable to become conditioned to their existence in words, or, in fact, do they really exist frequently enough for us to depend upon them in sounding out unknown words? This writer and his staff have intensively examined the words used in basals of the first three grades. All new words were examined to determine structural sound makeup. It was discovered that fewer than 100 vowel clusters are included five or more times in the new vocabulary of the first three grades. Forty-two vowel clusters were used 10 times or more. (Chart 1)

If these can be consistently identified in whole words, the youngster will know the vowel sounds introduced in over 90 per cent of the new vocabulary.

Remember that it is just as easy to learn that three or four letters make one sound as it is to learn that one letter makes a sound. Also, it should be noted that if clusters of letters (rather than single letters)

CHART 1

LETTER-CLUSTER FREQUENCY* FOR GLASS ANALYSIS
(RANK ORDER BY VOWEL)

a		e		i		o		u	
ar	47°	er	105	ing	109	or	35	un	20
ai	32	ed (suff)	102	in	28	ow	29	ur	15
an	31	en	58	il(l)	20	oo	27	um	12
ay	19	el(l)	35	id	18	ool	7	ut	10
a	19	ea	33	it	17	oon	8		
ad	17	et	27	ir(r)	15	oom	3	up	9
						oose	2		
at	17	ee	14	ick	15	oop	2	uck	8
						ood	1		
ap	16	ed	13	im	15	oof	2	ure	7
						ooth	2		
as	16	es	12	is	14			us	7
am	12	ess	11	ide	12	oo	26	ush	6
						oot	7	ung	6
ash	11	eat	10	ip	11	ood	8	uf(f)	6
						ool	1		
						ook	10		
ack	11	ex	10	ight	10			ue	6
ake	11	ec	9	ish	10	oa	20	ug	5
and	11	eep	9	ite	9	(n)ow	18		
all	10	est	8	ic	9	on	18		
age	9	ea	8	ink	7	ot	12		
(p)al	9	ev	7	ind	7	op	11		
are	9	eed	7	ire	7	ock	9		
aw	9	ead	6	ice	6	old	9		
air	8	ear	6	ied	6	ou	9		
ame	8	em	6	ies	6	om	8		
ac(c)	7	ean	5	eg	6	oi	7		
ang	7	eas	5	if(f)	5	oke	7		
ant	7	een	5			ol(l)	7		
ave	6	ent	5			one	7		
ace	6					ose	6		
af(f)	6					ove	5		
ank	5					o	5		
ast	5					od	5		
						ong	5		
						ore	5		

* Based upon every new word included in the first three grades of two basal series.
° Numeral after each cluster indicates the number of new words that contained the cluster.

are taught as producing a sound, the problem of teaching vowel sounds and their variations is virtually eliminated. A vowel makes a sound as part of a letter cluster, not because it has a place in a syllable or for any other such "rule."

Careful count was also made of single consonants, blends and consonant digraphs. It was found that, when teaching decoding for perceptual conditioning, these consonant sound elements are learned relatively easily compared to the vowel phonograms. Their random distribution throughout words (in which vowel clusters are controlled) gives enough repetition to bring about the conditioned effect when the consonant elements are seen within a whole word.

Chart 2 includes lists which were developed for thirteen common vowel clusters. Many other words could have been chosen to help bring each of the vowel clusters to perceptual conditioning. These are merely ones the researchers discovered which meet the criteria.

In one perceptual conditioning program which is being conducted in the New York City Public Schools, teachers were asked to identify certain clusters by their relative difficulty. Chart 3 reports on the general consensus. The "mediums" list is a less reliable classification than the "easies" and the "hardzies" lists.

5. What have the foregoing activities attempted to do? The child has been required to examine whole words in a way that will show what will be of benefit to him when he sees other words containing the same letter clusters. It has been required that he *visually* respond to the letters in the word in the appropriate cluster fashion and apply the appropriate sound. It has also been required that he *hear* an appropriate sound and then associate the letters within the whole word that "make" that sound. (What else is decoding?) The child has not been allowed to examine the word in any way other than what is known to be consistent with the way he will eventually examine words when he becomes proficient in decoding. He did not, and never will be

CHART 2

WORDS WHICH MAY BE USED
FOR THIRTEEN VOWEL LETTER-CLUSTERS

Word List 2
Final Positions Only.

and	ot		an		(b)oo(k)	all	
band	cot	rot	ban	tan	book	ball	stall
hand	dot	tot	Dan	van	cook	call	small
land	got	shot	fan	than	hook	fall	
sand	not	trot	can	clan	look	gall	
brand	jot	blot	man	plan	nook	hall	
grand	lot	clot	Nan	span	shook	mall	
stand	hot	plot	pan	scan	brook	tall	
strand	pot	slot	ran		crook	wall	

ay						
bay	jay	pay	clay	pray	slay	
day	lay	ray	play	tray	stray	
gay	may	say	bray	stay	spray	
hay	nay	way	gray	sway		

Varying Positions.

ut	ea	it	et	el
cut	reach	sit	get	bell
butter	teacher	slitting	letter	tell
button	easy	rabbits	upset	held
utmost	peaceful	visitors	lettuce	shelter
flutter	dealer	city	etch	yellow
shutter	reaching	switch	kettle	welcome
mutton	beastly	itch	secretly	melting
crutch	sneakily	kitchen	closetful	skeleton
stutter	steaming	pitcher	forgetful	tunnel
strutted	seated	littlest	settler	televise

(Continued on next page.)

99

(m)oo(n)	id
moon	did
spoon	kid
harpoon	skidding
racoons	middle
saloon	widow
buffoon	idiot
roof	hidden
proof	tidbit
spoof	midnight
goofy	kidnaper
roofing	

CHART 3

PARTIAL LIST OF VOWEL CLUSTERS
AND REPORTED RETENTION DIFFICULTY

Easies	Mediums		Hardzies
(p)an	(m)ap	(m)ight	(h)as
(s)and	(c)ake	(h)is	(h)er
(s)at	(t)all	(p)ick	(p)il(l)
(s)ay	(w)el(l)	(c)ool	(h)ow
(s)ing	(w)et	(b)ook	(kn)ow
(p)in	(s)ent	(f)or	(b)us
(p)it	(b)ed	(h)ut	(f)ur
(h)im	(b)ee	(l)uck	(t)ea
(t)old	(t)en	(d)eck	bai(t)
(s)um	(r)id	(p)on(d)	(p)ie
(s)un			(p)ure
(p)ot			(b)ir(d)
(h)op			

allowed to, insult the integrity of a digraph, vowel cluster, or any of the meaning or pronunciation units which are structurally consistent within the written language. No successful decoder does. It can be stated that if any person (particularly a child), due to the direction of the mental set questions, is consistently required to examine whole words in terms of these internal structures (e.g., team, creamery, steaming, streamline, etc.), he theoretically must condition himself to the appropriate clustering as they are visually isolated within the whole word. This, as has been suggested, is what *all* persons do who are successful in decoding. They use nothing more than a remembrance of how letters cluster in whole words. During training the issue of clustering is literally forced.

6. After a fifteen- or twenty-minute training session in work toward perceptual conditioning of letter clusters within whole words, the child should be required to read orally (at sight) from any basal reader that is at his instructional level. The reading from the basal should include no work in vocabulary or comprehension. If during the at-sight reading from the basal the decoder cannot call a word, the teacher should direct attention (never by pointing to a part of the word) to a major vowel cluster. For example: A child cannot decode *farmer.* One might say, "Notice the *ar,* what sound does the *ar* make?" (If no response.) "It makes the *ar* sound. What sound does *ar* make? Yes, *ar.* Now what sound does *far* make?" Oral reading should rarely go beyond twelve minutes in one session. Its purpose is merely to practice decoding skills and to learn a stock of sight words.

Concerns, Cautions, and Culmination

Although adults do not use rules or principles which allow for a systematic approach to decoding, perhaps this is because they have been successful at the operation for so many years that they have forgotten what these rules were that they used in the past. It might be argued that youngsters in the formative stages of developing a decoding sys-

tem do use rules and principles and thus it would be depriving them of an aid if these were not included in their instruction. A study was conducted (Burton and Glass, 1968) to discover whether or not persons in their formative stages do use rules or principles. Thirty students in grades two and five were tested. All the students were considered excellent readers at their grade level. They were all at least in the top fifth of their classes in decoding ability. The youngsters were asked to "sound out" fifteen words which would be esoteric for them. They also were asked to sound out fifteen possible words. (See Chart 4) Not one child in the group used any method of word attack *before* the word was sounded out. Although some *said* they used "phonics" or "syllabication," it was apparent by their instant recognition of the whole sound of the word that they did not pause to apply any rules or principles. They merely sounded out the words, letter-cluster by letter-cluster, as persons of all ages do.

The list of words used in the Burton and Glass study (Chart 4) has been used as a gross screening of decoding ability. The first 15 words are taken from the list included in the Durrell Analysis of Reading Difficulty test (Harcourt, Brace & World). The remaining are possible words developed by Mrs. Burton. Few if any of the words can be read at sight by persons whose decoding ability is not already excellent. All the Esoteric Words are most probably not within the listening vocabulary and they, at most, may have only incidentally been heard. All the words can be decoded according to commonly accepted sound-symbol responses. Recommended norms are listed below:

Percent Correct	Indications
80-100	No more instruction necessary in decoding.
50-79	Minimum instruction in decoding needed. Do a great deal of oral at-sight reading.
25-49	Routine grade level instruction in decoding.

0-24	Needs careful remedial work if the student is in grade 3 or above. If below grade 3, a score in this range makes the test not applicable.

It should be noted that training for perceptual conditioning is as simple as written. Its very simplicity is causing problems. Many teachers, when they do apply the method, tend to add activities which are acceptable in reading programs but only tend to dilute the effects of working toward perceptual conditioning for decoding. The method does not allow pictures or include the children's writing of any letter

CHART 4

WORDS USED TO DISCOVER HOW EXCELLENT DECODERS DECODE UNKNOWN WORDS (GLASS ANALYSIS TEST)

Esoteric Words	Possible Words
1. intervent	16. fentovite
2. carpolite	17. nugsinbace
3. tonometer	18. bexnayhope
4. introvert	19. hurpolding
5. blastment	20. lishbarness
6. ligulate	21. eckpidseep
7. polarize	22. adzooler
8. stimulus	23. hanfenbine
9. titration	24. mestanglock
10. explicate	25. bishdegnuck
11. isotherm	26. opdangunair
12. astrolabe	27. edstoiyack
13. epithet	28. tuspurstim
14. dissonant	29. torpelnink
15. retrograde	30. hawlatwight

or words. It does not include a discussion of any ideas which might be generated from the sight of a word. (This in teaching decoding, not reading.) Socialization with the child must be kept at a minimum so that as much of the time as possible will be used for learning to decode. Reading activities should not interfere or dilute the fact of meaningful repetition of letters and sounds. This approach represents an abominable way to teach reading, but is effective in teaching decoding.

Reports from teachers state that this method may teach children decoding but it is apt to become boring for the teacher. It is unfortunate that this is so. But experiences have been that, when material is added to make it more interesting both for the teacher and the youngster, there is conditioning leakage and thus, for some children, the acquisition of the decoding skill is slowed down. For some children, particularly the youngsters with learning disabilities, this lessening of the perceptual conditioning effect may be crucial. (Straus, Werner, 1942)

The only materials needed are the carefully selected words (containing common letter clusters), preferably printed on flash cards, and any basal that is at the decoder's decoding level. Again, this is for teaching *decoding* and not the more complex dimensions of reading. The reading program should continue at any time *after* the training session in decoding is completed.

REFERENCES

Almy, Millie C. **Childrens' experiences prior to first grade and success in beginning reading.** New York: Bureau of Publications, 1949.

Betts, E. A. Phonics: Practical considerations based on research. **Elementary English,** 1956, **33,** 357-371.

Beard, Ruth M. **An outline of Piaget's developmental psychology.** New York: Basic Books, Inc., 1969.

Bruner, Jerome S. **Toward a theory of instruction.** New York: W. W. Norton & Co., 1966.

Burton, Elizabeth, & Glass, Gerald G. Students' conception of their decoding skill. Unpublished paper presented at the Education Research Conference, 1968.

Chall, Jeanne. **Learning to read: The great debate.** New York: McGraw-Hill, 1967.

Clymer, Theodore. The utility of phonic generalizations in the primary grades. **The Reading Teacher,** 1963, **16,** 252-258.

Cohen, Alice, & Glass, Gerald G. Lateral dominance and reading ability. **Reading Teacher,** January 1968.

Davidson, Helen P. An experimental study of bright, average, and dull children at the four-year mental level. **Genet. Psychol. Monogr.,** 1931, **9,** 119-225.

Durkin, Dolores. Early readers—reflections after six years of research. **The Reading Teacher,** 1964, **18,** 3-7.

Fernald, Grace. **Remedial techniques in basic school subjects.** New York: McGraw-Hill, 1943.

Flesch, Rudolf. **Why Johnny can't read and what you can do about it.** New York: Harper & Brothers, 1955.

Fries, Charles C. **Linguistics and reading.** New York: Holt, Rinehart and Winston, Inc., 1962.

Gates, Arthur I. The necessary mental age for beginning reading. **Elementary Sch. J.,** 1937, **37,** 497-508.

Gattegno, Caleb. **Words in color.** Chicago: Encyclopaedia Britannica, Inc., 1964.

Gibson, Eleanor J. The role of graphene-phoneme correspondence in word perception. **Amer. J. Psychol.,** 1962, **75,** 554-570.

Glass, Gerald G. The strange world of syllabication. **Elementary Sch. J.,** 1967, **67,** 403-405.

_____. Perceptual conditioning. Proceedings of the International Reading Association, Newark, Delaware, 1964.

Gray, William S. **On their own in reading.** Chicago: Scott, Foresman & Co., 1948, 2nd ed., 1960.

Heilman, Arthur W. **Phonics in proper perspective.** Columbus: Charles E. Merrill Books, 1964.

Hilgard, Ernest R., & Marquis, Donald G. **Conditioning and learning.** New York: D. Appleton-Century Co., 1940.

Holmes, Jack A., & Singer, Harry. The substrata-factor theory; substrata-factor differences underlying reading ability in known groups. Berkeley, California: University of California Press, 1961.

Lorge, Irving, & Chall, Jeanne. Estimating the size of vocabularies of children and adults: An analysis of methodological issues. **J. exp. Educ.,** 1963, **32,** 147-157.

Mazurkiewicz, Albert J., & Tanyzer, Harold J. **Early to read i/t/a program.** New York: Initial Teaching Alphabet Publications, Inc., 1963.

McKee, Paul; et al. **The reading for meaning series.** Boston: Houghton Mifflin Company, 1967.

Money, John (Ed.). **Reading disability: Progress and research needs in dyslexia.** Baltimore: The Johns Hopkins Press, 1962.

_____ (Ed.). **The disabled reader.** Baltimore: The Johns Hopkins Press, 1966.

Morphett, Mabel V., & Washburn, C. When should children begin to read? **Elementary Sch. J.,** 1931, **31,** 496-503.

Orton, Samuel T. **Reading, writing and speech problems in children.** New York: W. W. Norton and Company, Inc., 1937.

Robinson, Helen M. **Why pupils fail in reading.** Chicago: The University of Chicago Press, 1947.

Roswell, Florence, & Natchez, Gladys. **Reading disability: Diagnosis and treatment.** New York: Basic Books, Inc., 1964.

Silver, Archie A., & Hagin, Rosa. Specific reading disability: Delineation of the syndrome and relationship to cerebral dominance. **Comprehensive Psychiat.,** 1960, **1,** 126-134.

Smith, Nila B. **American reading instruction.** Morristown, N.J.: Silver Burdett Co., 1934.

Soffietti, James. Why children fail to read: A linguistic analysis. **Harvard Educ. Rev.,** 1955, **25,** 63-84.

Stern, Catherine. **The structural reading series.** Syracuse, N.Y.: The L. W. Singer Company, Inc., 1963.

Strauss and Werner. Disorders of conceptual thinking in the brain injured child. **J. Nerv. Ment. Dis.,** 1942, **96,** 153-172.

Strickland, Ruth G. The language of elementary school children. **Bull. Sch. Educ.,** Indiana University, 1962, **38** (4).

Traxler, Arthur, with the assistance of the staff of Educational Records Bureau. **Research in reading.** New York: ERB, 1941, 1946, 1955, 1960.

Vernon, M. D. **Backwardness in reading.** London: Cambridge Press, 1958.

Wardbough, Ronald. **Reading, a linguistic perspective.** New York: Harcourt, Brace & World, Inc., 1969.

Wiley, E. G. Difficult words and the beginner. **J. Educ. Res.,** 1928, **17,** 278-289.

Formula Phonics: A Broad Spectrum Reading Method

Edward O. Vail, M.A.
Assistant Superintendent
A B C Unified School District
Los Angeles County Schools
Los Angeles, California

We have come to a point in time when America's poor must have an educational victory. At the same time, America's schools, along with those federal, state, and local agencies which are conducting the war against poverty, must also have a victory. No matter how desperately such a victory may be needed, it cannot be won until a method is devised which will work to teach the nation's poor to read. Teach the poor to read, and the victory may be shared by all.

Since 1965, a major share of the federal, state, and local antipoverty dollar has been spent in attacking the "reading problem". For all that, and despite a thousand promises, the poor are not being taught how to read and there have been no victories. The "hard data," which documents the years of determined effort (and failure) in this area, demands that the poor be freed from the tyranny of conventional reading methods with their "stretched out" or, worse, badly taught "strong phonetic element." This chapter describes the development of a reading method which when used promises an educational victory to those who are involved in the war against poverty. This method is called *Formula Phonics.*

DEVELOPMENT OF FORMULA PHONICS

Capabilities

Formula Phonics has been described as being a broad spectrum reading method. One might inquire, "Before a reading method may be called broad spectrum, what must be its capabilities?" It would seem that such a system would have to teach virtually any non- or near non-reading person to read effectively. Thus, to be truly broad spectrum, a reading system should teach equally well:

Boys (in any population the ratio of boys and girls who learn to read by the method should be the same)

The poor

110

Ethnic minorities

Adults

Adolescents

Beginning readers

Migratory workers and their children

Urban pupils

Rural pupils, and

Most exceptional children

It is suggested here that Formula Phonics has been successful in teaching many members from each of the groups listed above to read.

Formula Phonics is not a cure-all for every type of reading problem, nor is it claimed to be. It has no place in the speed reading class nor in the gifted students' power reading class. The word-attack part of the method would be of little value to the teacher whose pupils know word-attack skills but lack comprehension. Certainly middle and upper income Caucasian first-graders who have good attendance patterns, who are not immature, and who do not present atypical learning patterns, will probably emerge from elementary school reading as well, taught by conventional reading methods, as if taught using Formula Phonics.

Characteristics

The method was originally designed to provide for the poor an alternative to the reading outcome which was afforded in the nation's urban schools. Strategies for developing an alternative system to that which was used with the urban poor made the development of a broad spectrum reading method most complex. Certainly, an acceptable system in addition to teaching reading to nearly any population served by the schools would also demand such characteristics as:

Ease in instruction. The system should be as easily taught to subjects by parent, tutor, or educational aide as by a classroom teacher.

Compatibility with existing reading systems. The system should complement whatever method of reading is being used in a particular school or district.

Lack of expense. The system should not require the use of sophisticated equipment such as reading machines or kits, nor should it require controlled vocabulary materials. The system would have to use those reading materials which are found in the homes of the poor where there are no kits, machines or special books. Further, materials necessary to train one person to teach the method should not exceed a one-time cost of $10.00, while per pupil expense for instructional materials should not exceed a one-time cost of $5.00.

Group or individual use. The system should work as well to teach groups of pupils to read as it does to teach individuals.

Exportability. The system should permit non-school persons to set up successful reading programs.

Speed of instruction. The system should permit both teachers and pupils to understand how the reading process works and to see its application within the shortest possible time. "The shortest possible time" requires that both teacher and pupils should see improvement in most pupils' reading within three or four weeks after the onset of instruction.

History

The search for a broad spectrum reading method started a few years ago. At that time I had already developed a method for teaching reading called Basic Phonics and some years earlier, in the black ghetto of south-central Los Angeles, had demonstrated that Basic Phonics could be used to teach substantial numbers of junior high school youth who had been identified as being educably mentally retarded, to read. Indeed, when exposed to this method, one out of every two of those youngsters who had been classified as mentally retarded learned how to read; and as a result, when retested with a standardized intelligence test for retention in the class, were found to test too high to be eligible for such placement.

Basic Phonics used a *discovery* system to teach word-attack skills. That is, after class members had been told The Story of Language by their teacher, they started to "read" and so discovered, with the teacher's help, word-attack skills. In Basic Phonics the goal of the program was to have the pupils learn enough of those word-attack skills to become independent readers. The method was difficult to teach to many teachers, however, because it demanded that they possess an exceptional memory. (This because the teacher had to remember every word-attack skill and phonetic unit which the class discovered.) For all that, many teachers did learn the method and used it to teach not only black pupils to read but a wide variety of other pupils as well. (These pupils included lower, middle and upper income subjects of all grade levels and ages, large numbers of male problem readers, pupils in institutions, and numbers of Spanish surnamed youth.)

Following the Watts riots, it was seen that no problem in urban education transcended the need to teach the poor how to read. Thus it was with the greatest urgency that the search for a broad spectrum reading system was started. The first research in the area involved teaching parents how to teach their own children to read by way of Basic Phonics. It was discovered during the three years of research which encompassed this project (Los Angeles City Schools, 1965-68) that, while many parents did learn the method and were successful in teaching their own children to read, others were not, for the system demanded certain skills which some of them did not have. Developing a system which would permit parents to teach their own children to read, however, was only a first step in the project. The final design called for the development of a reading system which would permit inner-city high school students to be used as remedial reading teachers. (Crenshaw Community Youth Study Association, 1968)

These limitations led to a decision that an attempt should be made to try to convert the discovery system, Basic Phonics, into a reading system using the learning theory techniques advanced by B. F. Skinner and others. The result was Formula Phonics.

From a discovery system to a learning theory system. The key to converting the Basic Phonics method from a *discovery* system to a *learning theory* system lay in the degree of consistency, or reliability, which could be found in English spelling. Experience with Basic Phonics had shown that rather than being an unphonetic jumble, English spelling is, in truth, highly phonetic. It had been discovered, as well, that only a small percentage of the words which appear in any large dictionary had to be phonetic or even considered, to develop a broad spectrum reading system. This was because only those words which regularly occur in the materials pupils read through grade 6 or 7 had any relevance in constructing such a reading system. It was those words alone whose phonetic construction was of the greatest moment. Finally, earlier work with Basic Phonics had demonstrated that because of Gestalten "closure" in sounding out English words when reading, *close was good enough.* That is, words in English do not have to sound out exactly, if a student is truly reading.

This fact, that "close was good enough," welded the phonetic word-attack system which was developed to the total act of reading. What this discovery meant in fact was that there was no reason at all to attempt to develop a phonetic system which would permit words to be sounded out in isolation. Indeed, a major tenet in Formula Phonics suggests that *one never has his pupils sound out words except when those words come to light in the material being read.* In other words, putting a list of words on the board, one above the other, and asking pupils to sound them out is a totally artificial lesson which bears no relationship to reading and further teaches virtually no essential reading skills. This discovery also ruled out the use of any "artificial" reading systems where words were intentionally misspelled, printed in different colors, or artificial alphabets were used.

Three kinds of phonetic spellings. Research with Basic Phonics also revealed that, so far as phonetic content was concerned, there are three kinds of phonetic spellings of English words. These are:

> *First class phonetic words* sound out exactly. An example of such a word is *cat.* If the standard rules of English spelling and phonetics are applied to this word, it may be only pronounced as *cat.* Hence its pronunciation agrees exactly with its spelling.

> *Second class phonetic words,* when sounded out in isolation, do not say their exact pronunciation and therefore may or may not be guessed by a reader who hears the pronunciation isolated from the context of the material from which the word was extracted. Such words, however, almost always are pronounced correctly by a subject, if they are in his speaking or hearing vocabulary, when placed within the context of material being read. Such a word is *what.* Here, if the rules of English spelling and phonetics are applied, is a word which sounds out to rhyme with the words *that, cat,* or *rat.* Placed in this sentence, *What time is it?* (with *what* rhymed with *that*, a subject who is exposed to the incorrect pronunciation will "close" and call the word *what* correctly. In effect, he will make the word's pronunciation agree with the idealized pronunciation which he knows is necessary to complete the meaning of the material being read.

Third class phonetic words do not sound out at all. Eye is such a word. Fortunately, such words do not occur too frequently in the material emerging readers must attack or else they occur so frequently that they soon become sight words (i.e., *the, one,* or *of.*)

HOW FORMULA PHONICS TEACHES READING

Programming

As has been mentioned, the result of the research carried on to convert Basic Phonics to Formula Phonics was successful. Today nearly any literate person—who has attended either a 12- or 15-hour class such as I have taught, or who has access to a copy of FORMULA PHONICS (Vail, 1969) for himself and copies of THE FORMULA PHONICS READING BOOK (Vail, 1969) for each of his pupils—can teach reading using the method. A person who is going to teach the method is first taught how organisms learn, why the pupils he is going to teach (except in the case of first graders) did not learn how to read, the defensive postures such pupils might be expected to assume in conventional reading situations, and the strategies of the operant conditioner. Some of these data he will pass on to his students, the remainder he will need only for his own use.

Once this is learned, the teacher is ready to *program* or *pattern* his pupils. What he is going to program into his pupils is virtually the entire word-attack system which is used in English spelling.

Except for first (and a few second) graders, any pupils who will *need* instruction in Formula Phonics cannot possibly know phonetics. Such pupils may have been exposed to a part of a phonetic system or they may have been poorly taught, but none of them will have at his disposal a viable phonetic word-attack system. Where there has been poor instruction, the teacher must begin by extinguishing the incorrect sounds or rules which are penalizing his pupils or groups. This

116

he does by showing them that the bad data are hurting them. "Garbage in, garbage out," he will explain. "If you make the sounds incorrectly, they won't blend. Every time you sound out a letter incorrectly, you are adding an extra syllable to the word containing it. Of course, sounding out never worked for you."

Programming also makes every member of a class or of a tutoring group interchangeable. Once a group is programmed, any teacher, parent, aide or tutor who has a knowledge of Formula Phonics or has the books at hand can teach all or any combination of that group to read. Further, once they have been programmed, pupils may be taught to read in science, social studies, or math books, in newspapers or magazines—in any written materials which the teacher holds to be relevant to the particular needs of his class.

Over and above any of the aforementioned reasons, however, is the role programming plays in the strategies of the operant conditioner, the teacher. The teacher who is using Formula Phonics has learned that pupils reinforce best (strengthen a change in behavior until it becomes automatic or *learned*) whatever is being taught them when they conceive that, by their own responses, they are controlling their own destiny. That is to say that each time a teacher calls for a specific behavior or response in a pupil (in this case, an answer to a question about how to sound out a word) and that pupil responds correctly (conceiving that he has not guessed indiscriminately nor answered correctly because of luck or chance) there is positive reinforcement. The less a pupil provides a correct response, the less he will receive reinforcement of what should have been learned by that response. Hence, when pupils are programmed and a teacher calls for a correct response to a question concerning a word-attack skill or phonetic unit, it is more likely that a single pupil, a combination of pupils, or even the entire class will be able to respond correctly rather than offer an incorrect response or no response at all.

The teacher-programmer first programs his group with those data

117

which he knows have the highest reliability or predictability—in English spelling, the sounds of the consonant letters. His group is shown that these consonant letters are binary in nature, being either turned on or turned off. That is, they have a single sound to make and in English spelling either make that sound or make no sound at all. The group is shown that 17 of the consonants have but a single sound and that each of those letters will say that sound or it will say nothing. This being so, the pupils understand that they completely control those 17 letters and that there is nothing that any one of those letters can ever do to "hurt" them. The group is shown that, because of rules they must follow, the reliability of the letters *c* and *w* is nearly 100 percent and that reliability for *g* and *y* is only a tiny bit less. Hence, if they make the sound correctly, pupils may predict with unerring accuracy the action of 21 of the letters in their alphabet.

In Formula Phonics, only two sounds for each vowel are programmed into pupils. These are the vowels' own names and their short sounds. Pupils are given a number of tools which they may use in dealing with vowels. They are shown that two laws and three rules give them nearly as much control over the vowels as they have been given over the consonants. Critical here is the Second Law of Reading. "Always assume a vowel is short" (which renders English spelling phonetic), and the Third Rule of Reading, "A vowel says what it must" (which permits pupils to become self-actuating readers by learning how to attack the only unit in any word which could cause them trouble, the vowels.

Having "programmed" the consonant and vowel data into a group, the teacher is nearly ready to teach the group's members how to read. In a few moments he shows them how to blend letter sounds together, explains "pals," and shows them the difference between *sounding out* a word and *reading* that word. Having accomplished these chores, the teacher is ready to teach his class to read.

Blending causes very little trouble for any pupil who is producing the correct sound for a letter or a combination of letters. Here is certainly a case of "garbage in, garbage out." A pupil who is taught the sounds correctly will be rewarded when they help him sound out words and he accepts phonetics as a tool to help him read. Let the sounds be poorly or incorrectly taught to a pupil, however, and then, when those sounds will not blend and permit him to successfully attack words, he will not only reject those sounds but frequently will reject his teacher-programmer as well.

"Pals" are an important aspect of Formula Phonics and are defined as combinations of two, three, four or five letters whose phonetic reliability is nearly that of consonants. Examples of pals are such combinations of letters as *ing, igh, er, ir, ur,* and *ation.* Pals are treated as though they are long consonants and when a pal contains a vowel or vowels, such letters lose their power to confuse the reader since their sounds may be predicted. Further, the pal in a word such as *sing(ing)* reduces that word to a two-letter word while pals in the word *remembering (em, er, ing)* reduce that eleven-letter word to a six-letter word.

In Formula Phonics the teacher and the students are always aware of the difference between "reading" a word and "saying" that word. This is seen when the teacher asks after any word which has been sounded out, "Did you *say* that word or did you *read* it? If you read it, tell me what it means in that sentence. If you only said it, you have really done nothing more than a parrot can do!" As will be explained, in Formula Phonics one cannot separate word-attack and reading.

It will be noted that in none of the material presented above, which is related to programming, were the words teach, teaching, or taught used. This is because *programming is not teaching.* During this programming phase, there is very little drill, practice, or testing, and the sooner this phase is completed, the better. The maximum time to complete programming for any group would be ten class hours. Pupils *learn* that which is programmed into them during the second, or last phase of the program—reading.

Reinforcement

Once programmed, a group is ready to be taught to read. As a part of this process, pupils read aloud in material which is at their highest level of comprehension. First and second graders usually start reading in anthologies which were compiled for use in fourth grade classrooms; third graders read in fifth grade books; fourth and fifth graders read in sixth grade books, and all others (regardless of their reading level) read in material which is appropriate to their age or grade.

When working in such difficult material, no pupil is expected to read aloud more than three or four words until he is confronted with a word he does not know. In Formula Phonics, when a pupil in a reading group encounters a word he does not know, it is because his teacher has intentionally maneuvered him into a learning situation. The teacher knows that, if a group is reading in "easy" books, he will seldom, if ever, have a chance to teach reading; for his group will be reviewing previous knowledge rather than being confronted with that which must be taught and learned. Because he has forced the pupil who is reading into a learning situation, the teacher must protect that situation at any cost. He must see that no one destroys the learning situation by calling the word aloud. From the very beginning the class has been made to understand that, when a pupil is stuck on a word, learning is going to take place and *no one is to call that word out loud.*

When a pupil is confronted with an unknown word which he has encountered in the normal course of his reading, he is seen to be **thwarted** (he doesn't know the word) and **motivated** (he wants to know the word so that his sentence will be back in balance) and is subject to *tension* (a vague feeling of uneasiness). This is a learning state and that's exactly where his teacher wants him. The teacher, however, cannot be concerned only with the single pupil whom he has forced into the learning situation by having him read aloud in difficult material but must be concerned with the remainder of his group as well. He will wish to involve his entire group in the learning situation. To do

120

this, he will take the unknown word from the exclusive domain of the oral reader by writing it on the blackboard. Placed there, the word becomes a tool which will provide a learning situation for each member of the class.

This phase of the reading process (when the word is on the board) is designed to make the entire group self-actuated readers by teaching them the word-attack skills and phonetic units which earlier have been programmed into them. It is from the strategies used in this process that the name Formula Phonics grew. The formula in Formula Phonics consists of five questions which are asked the class:

1. Does the word have a suffix?

2. Does the word have any silent letters?

3. Does the word have any "pals"?

4. Does the word have any letters which must change their sounds?

5. In this word, how do you mark the remaining vowels?

(At this point the word is ready to be sounded out and its meaning given.)

The teacher asks these five questions of one or another of the members of the class. (Even a pupil who knows at sight the word which is on the board can learn word-attack skills or phonetic units from answering any of the formula questions about the word.) As has been mentioned, because the entire group has been programmed, it is more likely that they will answer correctly any of the questions posed by the teacher than that they will answer those questions incorrectly or have no answer at all. Each time a pupil answers a question correctly or hears another member of the group answer that question when he knows the answer that pupil conceives that he is controlling the sit-

121

uation and that the correct answer given was not just a matter of chance or of luck.

A teacher using classical operant conditioning techniques and desiring to teach a series of word-attack skills into a group might set up a reward system so that for every correct response given, a subject might receive a chocolate candy, a penny, a grade in a roll book, or any tangible reward. With Formula Phonics the teacher is calling for many small bits of information at any given time, and such a reward system was rejected because it was felt that it would be too time consuming or too cumbersome. Further, many of the subjects who are taught to read using Formula Phonics are adolescents or adults who might conceive of such a reward system as being childish.

Equally cumbersome for this purpose are the classical techniques of the contingency manager. Here, if one accepts David Premack's differential probability hypothesis that, "For any pair of responses, the more probable one will reinforce the less probable one," (Premack, 1965) the teacher must accept that each of his pupils will respond for a different reinforcer. This is to say that one pupil might perform a task if allowed to sing and dance, another might perform the same task or another if allowed to sharpen three pencils, while yet another might perform a task if he is allowed to get a drink of water. Unfortunately, the reward a pupil will accept as a reinforcing agent on one occasion may not work at all on the next. This is because the pupil who performed for a drink of water may not wish a drink of water the next time he is asked. However, the person who is teaching reading using Formula Phonics enjoys the very best of operant conditioning and contingency management.

During the time the word is on the board and the teacher is questioning the group, he will acknowledge correct responses with a smile or a word of praise. When an incorrect response is made by a pupil, the teacher neither rewards nor punishes that pupil but instead moves to another pupil whose correct responses will serve as a model for the entire group. If no one in the group knows the correct answer, the

122

teacher simply gives the answer, knowing that the next time the question is asked at least one of his pupils will have the answer and thus be able to serve as the model for the others.

After all questions elicited by the formula have been answered correctly by one or another of the class members, the teacher returns to the student who had been reading aloud. In choosing this pupil, the teacher reestablishes the earlier learning state (thwarting—motivation—tension) but now in a situation where the pupil is ready to successfully attack the word. Before the pupil is encouraged to sound out that word, however, the teacher establishes context by reading a few of the preceding words. At this same time, others in the group are encouraged to sound out the word—but under their breaths. They know, of course, that under no circumstances are they to call that word out loud.

Serving as a model for the group, the original reader sounds the word aloud. Frequently he will not have to sound out the entire word but will "close" and say the idealized (and correct) word after blending only the first few sounds. At the moment of insight, when the word is correctly spoken, it will be seen that the learning state dissolves for every pupil in the group who had not known this word.

Satiated, the pupils are no longer thwarted, their need to know the word is gone, and they experience a resultant reduction in tension. Hence, by requiring pupils to read material which is written at the highest level they can comprehend, the teacher using Formula Phonics forces his class to desire—as reinforcers or rewards—the need to know the very word he wishes to teach. Instead of rewarding with a candy or a penny or by permitting each pupil to engage in whatever type of behavior he is willing to trade for learning, pupils are forced to want (and accept as a reward) the correct pronunciation of the word. In this fashion, the teacher provides them with an external reward, the very word he wanted them to read.

Formula Phonics also offers to each student an internalized reward. That is, the teacher leads his pupils into learning situations and then provides a resolution so that at that moment of resolution (or closure) the pupils experience a reduction in tension. Further, the pupils learn that by applying the formula and knowing all the word-attack strategies, they may have the reward of calling (reading) the word, and they feel good (are subject to reduced tension). (Vail, 1967) This combination of factors, of course, hastens the development of self-actuated word-attack skills in the pupils being taught.

Once the word has been sounded out, the teacher, parent, educational aide, or tutor may start to *teach* reading. This he does by carrying on a dialogue with the group concerning the word which had just been called but always as it relates to what is being read. Now the teacher may say:

Give me a synonym.

Give me an antonym.

Where do you think that word came from?

Why did the author use this word?

Do you think Mary did a good thing?

Can you balance this equation?

How do you read that number?

What do you think a quotation mark means?

What do you think this man means by "Black Pride?"

It is this very type of dialogue which every teacher needs and wants to carry on with his class. This is really what is meant when we read that "Every teacher is a teacher of reading." The word-attack techniques in Formula Phonics permit the fifth grade teacher to teach fifth grade lessons to all of his class; the eighth grade mathematics teacher to teach his entire class arithmetic and reading from the same book; and the high school teacher in the ghetto to teach reading to an entire class in "relevant" material which is presented as it was originally written.

Note that on any given day no teacher using Formula Phonics to teach reading may know where his class is "going" during the reading lesson. He must be ready to teach word-attack skills whenever a pupil encounters a word he does not know. He must also be ready to teach not only vocabulary building and comprehension skills but be able to taken his group wherever the writing or their needs demand.

METHOD OF PRESENTATION

To teach reading using Formula Phonics one needs a single copy of the teacher's programming and reinforcing book, FORMULA PHONICS, and, for each pupil he is to teach, a copy of THE FORMULA PHONICS READING BOOK. The teacher's book is in three sections, two of which are keyed to the pupil's book:

The teacher reads the first section of FORMULA PHONICS to himself. Here he finds out about reading methodology, learning styles, defensive postures, and the strategies he will use in teaching reading.

The teacher reads the second section of FORMULA PHONICS to his pupils. Day by day as he reads his book to them and as they perform certain tasks in their books, the group is being programmed. The same material is used to program any group, whether made up of children or adults, whose members need to learn how to read.

The pupils read to their teacher from *their* books after they have been programmed. As they do, he uses the third part of his book to learn how to teach them Formula Phonics word-attack procedures, along with vocabulary building and comprehension skills. Printed in two kinds of type, and keyed to every word his pupils will read aloud, the third part of the teacher's book shows the teacher how to teach Formula Phonics. He may then transfer his group to whatever reading material he wishes after they have finished the few reading lessons which are found in their FORMULA PHONICS READING BOOKS.

At the same time the two books are teaching the members of his group to read, their content is teaching the instructor how to be a reading teacher.[1] No other materials are necessary to teach either teacher or pupil. This, then, is Formula Phonics—a broad spectrum reading system.

[1]In September of 1970, a series of 12 half hour video tapes were made which may be used to program subjects and, at the same time, teach the method to teachers, parents, tutors, or educational aides. Use of the tapes speeds up the process of programming and provides a uniformity of instruction permitting vastly expanded school-wide and community involvement reading programs, as well as cross-age tutorials and area-wide literacy programs for migrants. Write to: Integrative Learning Systems, Inc., 326 W. Chevy Chase Dr., Number 11, Glendale, California 91204.

REFERENCES

Crenshaw Community Youth Study Association. **Summer crash tutorial project,** 1968. Available (at no cost) through Lawrence Publishing Co., Los Angeles.

Los Angeles City Schools. **Evaluation, adult education project, reading techniques for parents,** 1965-68. Available through Educational Resources Information Center, ED 023 017 AC 002 665.

Premack, D. Reinforcement theory. In D. Levine (Ed.), **Nebraska symposium on motivation.** Lincoln: University of Nebraska Press, 1965.

Vail, E. **Formula phonics.** Los Angeles: Lawrence Publishing Company, 1969.

Vail, E. Formula phonics, an integrative approach to reading. **Psychology,** August 1967, **4** (3).

Vail, E. **The formula phonics reading book.** Los Angeles: Lawrence Publishing Company, 1969.

The Learnable Features of English Orthography

A. Fred Deverell, Ed.D.
Professor of Education
College of Education
University of Saskatchewan
Saskatoon, Saskatchewan, Canada

The title of this chapter implies that some features of English writing and spelling are learnable and others are not. Perhaps more explicitly it should read "The *Most* Learnable Features . . . ." Despite the vagaries of English spelling (American English and Canadian English are included in the term, English), the orthographic system *is* sufficiently predictable from the sounds of spoken English to be, for the most part, both teachable and learnable. This is not to suggest that the orthography is simple; it is not. It is complex, and some features of it are subtle, elusive, or simply archaic. These features—complexity, subtlety, and the quality of being archaic in relation to present-day speech—do not prevent the identification of the principal factors which make it possible for most people who are "schooled" to be quite competent in the encoding (writing and spelling) and decoding (reading) of English.

The position taken by the writer of this chapter is rather effectively illustrated by a statement made by the American physicist, James D. Watson, in writing his account of the discovery of the structure of the D. N. A. molecule. Watson, who worked with the Britisher, Francis Crick, at the famous Cavendish Laboratory in Cambridge, England, began first by describing the *stark simplicity* of the procedures which California's Linus Pauling had previously used in the discovery of the alpha-helix, a group of amino acids important in the life processes. Watson then said of his own work with Crick at Cambridge:

> "We could thus see no reason why we should not solve D. N. A. in the same simple way. All we had to do was to construct a set of models and begin to play—with luck, the structure would be a helix. Any other type of configuration would have been much more complicated. *Worrying about complications before ruling out the possibility that the answer was simple would have been damned foolishness. PAULING NEVER GOT ANYWHERE BY SEEKING OUT MESSES."* (Watson, 1968) [Italics and capital print mine.]

"Pauling never got anywhere by seeking out messes!" The writer wonders whether educators have not gone out of their way to point out and elucidate the irregularities and inconsistencies of English orthography and to develop both reading and spelling instruction schemes around the general concept that "English is not a phonetic language" (whatever that may mean) and that the alphabetic principle—the principle of phoneme-grapheme correspondence—does not really function in the English writing system. Possibly educators have worked so hard on enumerating the messes in English spelling that they have been prevented from seeing the logical patterns of the system. To whatever extent they have done this, they have made more difficult the tasks of learning to read, write, and spell.

Between 1951, when James T. Moore, Jr., completed his Master of Education Thesis at Stanford University (Moore, 1951), and the present year of writing, 1969, a large volume of literature has appeared concerning the English writing system, some of it supporting the concept of generalizations, teachability, and learnability, some of it supporting the idea of modifying the alphabet itself, and still others opposing the "generalizations" concept as being essentially unworkable. The task of reviewing and summarizing this whole body of literature has not been adopted as one of the goals of this chapter. Instead, it will concentrate on significant portions of the literature which stress in general, the teachability and learnability of English orthography. Among the authors who have devoted their energies to understanding and explaining the systematic nature of the English writing system are Paul and Jean Hanna, J. T. Moore, Richard E. Hodges, E. Hugh Rudorf, Charles S. Ross, Gus P. Plessas and Dorothea M. Ladley, Margaret L. Peters, James P. Soffietti, Charles Fries, Rose Sabaroff, Leonard Bloomfield and Clarence Bernhart, Pose Lamb, and Robert A. Hall, Jr. At least one important publication of each is listed in the bibliography. No slight is intended toward those authors who have not been included in this list but who feel that they, too, have made a contribution.

The most notable of those who have proposed modifications in the alphabet is Sir James Pitman of London, England, whose initial teaching alphabet has been the object of well financed and widespread study in England and the United States. Experimentation with it in Canada has not been blessed by commitment of funds to the task and has therefore been meager. Pitman and his advocates have always stressed the use of the initial teaching alphabet of 44 characters, one for each of the 44 phonemes of English, in starting children off. The expectation has been that, having learned to read and write with this relatively dependable or consistent medium for the representation of speech, the children would easily "transfer" to the use of the standard alphabet. Successful as the experimentation has been (Downing, 1969), the community of English speakers as a whole seems to have been slow to pick up the challenge and to adopt the idea on anything approaching a universal basis. Social inertia is difficult to dispell. Interestingly, Pitman supported the need for a revised alphabet (as others before him have done) by gathering together large collections of the inconsistencies in English orthography—here referred to as messes—and, in so doing, contributed unwittingly to the rather popular concept that the English writing system makes no sense at all. However, desirable as the augmented alphabet of Pitman, or some similar type of modification may have been, the present writer is of the opinion that no such change in the writing system for children will ever be adopted throughout the English speaking world unless the governments of at least the major English speaking powers, first by consensus reached through conferences and subsequently by agreed upon legislation, make the new medium obligatory for child and adult alike. This view was expressed by Dr. Hunter Diack of Nottingham University in 1965, when he said to the writer, "I.t.a. is fine, and it makes learning to read and write much less complicated, but it will never succeed with children on anything like a universal scale unless it is adopted by the entire adult community." This, it appears, may have been an accurate prediction.

The number of people who represent or support the third position— the position that "English is not a phonetic language," or that English writing can no longer be classed as an alphabetic system; that it has become an ideographic writing system requiring that each printed word be learned as an independent "meaning" unit—is legion. Most school instruction programs of the past forty or fifty years, in both reading and spelling, have been designed to fit the ideographic principle. For example, Greene and Petty, in a valuable chapter on the teaching of spelling, repeatedly stress the choice of words which are "socially useful" and which are "specifically required for the child's individual needs," but at no point make reference to the importance of providing for transfer of training by teaching the alphabetic principle and by teaching typical spelling patterns. Any spelling program in which children ". . .learn the words specifically required for their individual needs as they arise" is basically a one-word-at-a-time program, each word being treated essentially as an ideograph. Statements made elsewhere in this chapter indicate that these authors are not averse to the alphabetic principle, but nowhere is it clearly enunciated or given prominence in the program (Greene and Petty, 1967).

The authors of the very widely used Curriculum Foundation Series of primary school readers assert that their program aims to have children make an easy, smooth transition from "reading" pictures to "reading" print. This converts the English writing system from an alphabetic kind to primitive picture writing and makes visual word units into "ideational" symbols rather than visual symbols sequences representing the sound sequences of speech. Having said this, the same authors go on to fortify their position by saying that the program does not teach letters, nor does it teach words, but instead it teaches reading with meaning (Murdock MacDonald et al., 1963). Obviously again, the authors are talking about ideographic writing units—units which represent *meanings* rather than the *sounds of speech.*

This kind of attitude toward the English writing system has the effect of making English orthography much more difficult to learn than is the Chinese, which is a true ideographic system. The Chinese system does have common meaning elements which are used in a variety of ideographs. The simplest elements, however, are about 2,000 in number, all of which must be mastered before the system can be said to have been learned.

English orthography employs, basically, twenty-six symbols, not enough to have one symbol for each phoneme in the spoken language. Surely, however, the task of learning twenty-six symbols and their mode of employment is easier than that of learning two thousand or more. Surely also, the common generalizations or concepts which define how the twenty-six symbols are used must bear some relevance to the fact that man possesses, in the cerebral cortex, the powers of differentiation and integration, the powers of "languaging." If the Roman alphabet, as adapted for use in Western languages, were not capable of being subjected to the processes of abstraction and generalization, of differentiation and integration, then I submit that it never would have been adopted for general use throughout the Western world. Why must we persist, mulishly, in denigrating the alphabet? Is it not possibly the most powerful single gift to our culture from the ancient Greeks (who made it a true alphabet of sound) and the Romans (who passed it on to us)?

ENGLISH ORTHOGRAPHY DOES USE IDEOGRAPHIC DEVICES

The first thing to recognize in attempting to describe the "learnability" of English orthography is that it **does** employ many ideographic devices; i.e., devices which signal *meaning* rather than sound. Examples are shown in the word groups which follow.

hear, here   caught, cot

our, hour   plain, plane

Each of the four groups has two visual word forms which, when interpreted, signal different meanings. However, the two items in each case, when spoken, sound (at least in central Canadian English) exactly alike.

134

In speech, only the syntactic relationships of each word in the sentence can serve to identify the specific meaning intended. In writing, however, each *meaning* has a distinctive *form;* the meaning is expressly signalled in the form or spelling of the visual word symbol. To the extent that this phenomenon occurs in English spelling, the writing system can be said to be ideational in character.

The alphabetic principle, however, is not lost in any of the visual word forms in the above pairs. The alphabetic principle simply states that alphabetic symbols (letters) represent phonemes in speech and that the *directional* sequence, from left to right, of letters in printed words and of printed words in sentences represents the *time* sequence of sound in speech. Visual-direction represents sound-time. This principle is readily observable in each of the visual words in each of the above pairs. In every one except *cot,* peculiarities in spelling occur, but, nevertheless, the principal sound elements in each of the spoken words is specifically signalled by a letter or letter combination. That is, *the alphabetic principle functions even in visual word forms which contain ideational elements.* The ideational or ideographic feature does not overrule the alphabetic principle! Once this situation has been established, many of the apparent "messes" in English spelling are not at all as "messy" as the anti-alphabet proponents seem to delight in claiming, and it is possible to proceed to identify those features of English orthography which are most "learnable." They are the alphabet itself, the alphabetic principle of phoneme-grapheme relationship, certain well-defined spelling patterns, and the ability to use all of these in both reading and writing, as well as to overcome without trauma the many minor situations in which what has been learned is contradicted or not usable.

THE ALPHABET IS LEARNABLE

The writer, while working with school beginners who were six years of age (give or take a few months), encountered a little boy who not only was able to name and write both upper and lower case forms of the alphabet symbols but who also was able to read with graceful ease at about a grade three level by standard tests. The conditions under which this child had learned to read were investigated, for the child himself said that he had not learned: he had "always known how." From his father came the statement, "Well, to start with, we learned our alphabet together every evening in the bath when we were two." When questioned further, this parent stated that letter blocks and "alphabet books" had enabled the child to learn to identify both capital and lower-case forms of the letters at age three and that reading had followed very closely after this. The child had been an avid reader for approximately two years before entering grade school.

While working on this particular project, using a sample of over four hundred school beginners randomly selected, the writer found that the average child of six years in a prairie urban setting could name and identify 19 capital letters and 16 lower-case letters and could write 12 letters from dictation. He also found that the only children who could read words were children who knew 20 or more letters and that the ease of learning words was related also to the length of the words in letters, two-letter words being easiest. Moreover, there was no significant difference between the sexes in letter knowledge. Six capital letters and four lower-case letters were known by over 80% of the children, and two letters were written correctly by over 80% of the children. The clear fact seems to be that alphabetic symbols are highly learnable, if opportunity presents itself, for most preschool age children. The "teachers" most frequently mentioned by the children in this study were, in descending order of frequency: 1) mom, or mom and dad, 2) kindergarten teacher, 3) grade one teacher (the testing was done during the third and fourth weeks of September and some "clean-up" testing was done in the first week in October), 4) brother, sister, cousin. Television was mentioned by only one child (Deverell, 1967; 1969).

The extent to which school beginners know the alphabet symbols and the effects of this knowledge on ability to learn to read have been reported by Witty and Kopel (1939), by Wilson (1942), and by Donald Durrell and associates (1958). The latter two of these sources substantiated forcefully the statement made by Witty and Kopel (1939) that no test of reading readiness is so satisfactory as a measure of the ability of the child ". . .to name and sound the letters of the alphabet, singly and in combination."

Two generalizations seem to be justified. First, school-age and pre-school-age children *can* learn the alphabet symbols. Secondly, considerable advantage seems to accrue to those children who do learn the alphabet symbols, relative to learning to read, over children who do not learn them.

THE PHONEME-GRAPHEME CORRESPONDENCE PRINCIPLE IS LEARNABLE

The basic function served by the letters of the alphabet (graphemes) in an alphabetic system of writing is to represent the consonant and vowel sounds of speech (segmental phonemes). As has already been stated, the Roman alphabet used in English writing has only twenty-six letters for the representation of over forty phonemes. This fact, combined with a variety of other concomitant conditions, results in the situation in which:

> Some of the letters are used to represent two, or even three, four or more phonemes. (The letter *a* represents different phonemes in each of *a*t, b*a*ll, c*a*ge, *a*go.)

> A single phoneme may be represented by several letters or letter groups. (The phoneme /f/ has a variety of letter designations, as in *f*ind, sti*ff,* s*ph*ere, cou*gh*.)

The fundamental problems which arise in connection with teaching children to read and write are two:

Are there a significant number of instances in which a regular or constant relationship exists between sound and letter; between phoneme and grapheme?

Where a nonconstant relationship between phoneme and grapheme exists, are there many instances of a single relationship being the most frequently used, the other or errant relationships being relatively few in number and infrequently encountered?

Parenthetically, before proceeding to provide the data which supplies answers to the two questions immediately above, the writer is obliged to assert that the bulk of evidence from research on visual perception in reading favors the viewpoint that not only children but also adults, in reading, tend to see printed words, not as "configurations" or "shapes," but as sequences of letters and that, not merely "cue" letters or "cue groups" of letters, but all of the letters in a word tend to be processed in the reading of print. At the same time, difficulties in letter recognition and in dealing with the sequences of letters are among the principal sources of difficulty in word recognition. The best brief summary of the evidence on this question is to be found in N. L. Gage's HANDBOOK OF RESEARCH ON TEACHING (Gage, 1962). Hunter Diack supplies convincing evidence that children of nursery school age, far from perceiving words as wholes, tend not even to perceive letters as wholes, but to attend to specific small parts of letters (Diack, 1960).

How dependable is the principle of phoneme-grapheme correspondence in the spelling of English? The earliest of recent studies conducted at Stanford University centering on this issue was that of James T. Moore, Jr., in which Moore analyzed the phoneme-grapheme correspondences in the 3,000 words most commonly taught in spelling programs in the United States. The results were subsequently reported by Hanna and Moore (1953). They are summarized in Table 1.

TABLE 1

FREQUENCY AND PERCENT OF REGULAR AND IRREGULAR SPELLINGS OF SPEECH SOUNDS IN 3000 MOST COMMON SPELLING WORDS AS REPORTED BY MOORE

Class of Sounds	Gross Frequency of Occurrence of Sounds	Frequency of Regular Spellings	Percent of Regular Spellings	Percent of Irregular Spellings
Vowel Sounds	4,678	3,059	65.4	34.6
Single Consonant Sounds	5,744	5,242	91.3	8.7
Consonant Blends and Digraphs	1,423	1,312	92.2	7.8
Suffixes and Final Blends	701	427	60.1	39.9
All Speech Sounds	12,546	10,040	80.0	20.0

Thus, 80% or four-fifths of all of the phonemes in these words when they are spoken are predictably represented by graphemic signs (letters) when they are written. Consonant sounds and consonant blends are regularly spelled more than 90% of the time. The investigator stated, regarding the more troublesome vowel spellings, that nearly three-fourths of the vowel sounds present no serious spelling problem, since the vowel speech sounds are spelled regularly from 57% to 99% of the time in the vocabulary analyzed.

The spellings of the vowel sounds which Moore found to be likely to cause the most trouble to learners were:

the spellings of the unstressed or schwa vowel sound /ə/ as in about;

the spellings of the long *e* sound /ē/ as in f**ee**l;

the spellings of the vowel-before-*r* sound, as in v**er**b, b**ir**d, f**ur**;

the spellings of the sound /ŏŏ/, as in b**oo**k, p**u**t, and of the /ōō/ sound as in f**oo**d, s**ui**t;

the spellings of the /ŏ/ or /aw/ vowel sound, as in **a**ll;

the spelling of the /y/ vowel sound as in on**i**on.

The spellings of consonant sounds which were found to be most likely to be troublesome were:

the spelling of the sounds /g/ and /j/, since both may be represented by the letter *g*;

the spelling of the sounds /s/ and /z/, since both are represented by the letter *s*.

Moore found that the single consonant sounds are represented by their regular spellings about 90% of the times they occur. The sounds /b/, /d/, /g/, /h/, /l/, /m/, /n/, /p/, /r/ and /t/ are either spelled by the single letter representing the sound or by the doubled letter.

Thus, Moore's study demonstrated that the sounds of English are regularly represented in English spelling much more often than language experts have supposed and that there is no justification for the claim often made that the alphabetic principle does not function in the English writing system.

Since Moore's study was completed, the precise relationship between

the sound system and the spelling of English has been pursued relent-
lessly by Richard E. Hodges and E. Hugh Rudorf working as part of
the Hanna team and using a total of over 17,000 words (Groff, Glim
and Petty, 1965; Hanna and Hanna, 1965; Hanna, Hanna, Bergquist,
Hodges and Rudorf, 1966; Hanna, Hanna, Hodges and Rudorf, 1966,
1967; Hodges, 1966; Hodges and Rudorf, 1965; Rudorf, 1965). These
studies searched for a rationale for English spelling. They isolated a
variety of factors which, whether the literate individual in the English
language culture is specifically aware of them or not, function in helping him to "learn" how to spell and how to select the correct graphemic option (where two or more options are available) when engaged
in writing. Conversely, the same factors help the individual to interpret writing or print when he is reading. Hanna and associates do not
search out messes. Instead they seek the most simple guidelines to
spelling.

These factors or principles are outlined in the next section.

THE PRINCIPLES OF ENGLISH SPELLING

Principle 1

Letters represent sounds of speech. The consonant sounds are represented more consistently than are the vowel sounds. There is a sufficiently large body of very commonly used words, whose spelling is
completely consistent, to provide the material for initial teaching of
the writing system to school beginners. Detailed discussion and illustration of this principle was made in the previous section of this chapter, as revealed in Moore's study.

Principle 2

*Special spelling variants are frequently signalled by the position of the
sound in the syllable, or the one-syllable word.* An example is the use
of the letter *y* to spell the open long vowel sound /ī/ when it occurs in

the end position, as in b*y*, cr*y*, m*y*. Another is the use of the vowel digraph *ay* to spell the open, long vowel sound /ā/ when it occurs in the end position, as in d*ay* and cl*ay*. The *ck* spelling of the /k/ sound occurs only in the end position after short vowel sounds. In all such cases, it is the equivalent of double *k*. Usually when short vowel syllables or monosyllabic words end in one of the sounds /s/, /f/, /k/, or /l/, the final letter is doubled, as in mi*ss*, blu*ff,* so*ck*, be*ll*, and ba*ll*. These double letters occur in the end position. Another example is the spelling of the sound /v/ in the end position, when it is invariably written *ve*. Examples are li*ve*, sol*ve*, val*ve*, lo*ve* and ha*ve*. (Note that the mute ending *e* in these situations does not necessarily act as a long vowel signaler.)

Thus, *position* in the syllable is frequently a guide to variant spelling options.

Principle 3

Numerous *"internal constraints" or "environmental factors" are guides to particular spelling variants.* An example is seen in the following two groups of words.

　　sta*ck*, sti*ck*, sto*ck*, stu*ck*.

　　sta*k*e, wal*k*, wor*k*, mil*k*.

In the end position, the sound /k/ is spelled *ck after short vowels.* (This is the equivalent of double *k*.) However, when the /k/ sound is preceded by a long vowel sound or by a consonant, the simple *k* spelling is used.

Other examples are numerous. In the initial position, the /k/ sound is spelled *k* when followed by *e* or *i*, as in *kill, kernel, kept, keep*; but it is spelled *c* before *a, o* or *u* and when followed by a consonant, as in *can, cop, cup, clean, crumb*. These patterns are fairly consistent, although significant groups of foreign words adapted into English have retained spellings which violate these models. With respect to the spelling of the /k/ sound, some are:

*k*angaroo, *k*arate, *k*apo*k*, *K*ansas, *k*oda*k*, *k*ula*k*.
words of Greek origin: *ch*emistry, *ch*aracter, *Ch*rist.

Notable also are the number of archaic spellings retained from Old English:

know, knit, knife (the /k/ is no longer pronounced, but the *k* is retained in spelling).

lam*b*, com*b*, de*b*t (the /b/ is no longer pronounced, but the *b* is retained in spelling).

Another familiar environmental constraint is that which states that *c* represents the /s/ sound before *e, i,* or *y*, as in *c*ent, pen*c*il, and *c*yst, but represents the /k/ sound before *a, o,* or *u* or before a consonant as in *c*all, *c*ow, and *c*ulinary and in *c*lose and *c*rown. Familiar is the generalization that *g* usually represents the /g/ sound when followed by *a, o,* or *u*, as in *g*ate, *g*oat and *g*uppy, but represents the /j/ sound when followed by *e, i,* or *y*, as in *g*em, *g*inger and *g*ypsum. Unfortunately, there are many exceptions to this generalization.

The statement that "internal constraints" or "environmental factors" are guides to specific spelling variants is simply a way of saying that, when there is more than one way of using a consonant letter or of spelling a consonant sound, there is often also some other element in the written form which, if known, predicts which variant to use. Knowledge of internal constraints can be a valuable aid to understanding the writing system.

Other Principles

The vocabulary of English is replete with words which use a base word or root word, to which either prefixes and suffixes or special inflectional forms have been added to change or particularize the meaning conveyed by the root. Any word form which can be used independently to convey meaning is known as a **free** morpheme. Prefixes, suffixes, and inflectional changes are known as **bound** morphemes: they convey specific meanings but only as appendages to the base or root word. Many simple but fundamental spelling principles are to be found in the ways in which these "appendages" in the written forms of words are spelled. To understand the spelling, children need also to understand the word structure and the effects which derivational and inflectional changes have on the meanings signaled in the printed forms. A number of examples will illustrate the possibilities.

Word form changes or inflections (of which a few still remain in English) frequently follow easily established patterns of morphemic structure.

The written form of singular nouns which end in the letter *f* frequently change the *f* to *v* before adding the plural indicator, *-es* (leaf—leaves; calf—calves; loaf—loaves). By contrast, nouns in which the spelling ends in double *f* add only *-s*, with no other change (puff—puffs; bluff—bluffs; staff—staffs, but also staff—staves).

Words ending in mute *e* usually drop the *e* before adding an inflectional or derivational ending which begins with a vowel letter (ride—rider—riding; love—lover—loves—loving; love—lovable; prove—provable). However, as Ross (1967) points out, base words which end in the spelling, *-ce*, usually retain the *e* if the form to be added begins with *a, o* or *u* (service—serviceable). This device will be recognized as being useful for protecting the *c* from representing the /k/ sound, which it does if

144

it is followed by *a, o,* or *u* (practice—practicable, when *c* is followed by *a*, or by a consonant, it signals the sound /k/).

Ross (1967) has also pointed to the value of looking at derived forms to help with the spelling of root words, especially in situations in which the position of the main stress changes in the derivatives. In the following words, note how the two-syllable adjectives, with stress on the first syllable, are changed to nouns with the stress shifted to the second syllable:

Adjective		Nominal		Noun
legal	+	ity	=	legality
moral	+	ity	=	morality
senile	+	ity	=	senility

When the stress in the adjective is on the first syllable, the vowel in the second syllable becomes the schwa sound, /ə/, and causes confusion in spelling for those who lack a good visual memory. If, however, the pupil considers the nominal derivative, where the stress is on the second syllable, the vowel value is then readily recognized to be that signaled by a specific vowel letter. From this, the choice of the vowel letter to be used in the adjective can be inferred. Parenthetically, the present writer finds this process tedious. Instead, he helps children to spell multisyllable words by teaching them to exaggerate the vowel sounds in weak-stress syllables (giving each vowel full value) until the spelling of the word has been reasonably well fixed. That is, he teaches pupils to be "spelling pronouncers" for as long as this is necessary. It works.

The nominal endings of "agent" *-er* and its variants, *-ar* and *-or*, cause much trouble. They are attached to verbs to form nouns, and the vowel before *r* is almost invariably pronounced as the schwa sound, giving no clue as to which vowel letter to use in spelling the word:

Verb		Nominal		Noun
run	+	-er	=	runner
bake	+	-er	=	baker
fly	+	-er	=	flier
buy	+	-er	=	buyer
beg	+	-ar	=	beggar
lie	+	-ar	=	liar
gyrate	+	-or	=	gyrator
navigate	+	-or	=	navigator

Note that when the morpheme of agent *-er* is added to the free morpheme, *run*, the *n* is first doubled. This protects the internal vowel in a stressed syllable from being signaled as a long vowel sound, as it would be in *runer*. The doubled letter is an insulator to the short vowel in a stressed syllable. This is a widely used principle (compare măt—mătting—mătted with māte—māting—māted).

Note that in the case of *bake*, the final *e* is first dropped and then the *-er* morpheme of agent is added. Here the vowel in the stressed syllable is already long and no doubling of the consonant letter following it is necessary.

Note that in the case of *fly*, the *y* is changed to *i* before the morpheme of agent is added (cry—crier—cries, but crying; dry—drier—dries—dried, but drying). When the affixed part begins with a vowel letter, the *y* is changed to *i* but the change is not made when the result would be two *i*'s in succession (probably because they would be too easily confused with *u*).

Note that in the case of *buy*, the *y* is retained even when the affixed morpheme begins with a vowel letter. *Buy* is an archaic spelling of uncertain origin. It is probably retained to differentiate it from the preposition *by* (an ideographic differential). Retaining the *u* results in the retention of the entire ideograph when *-er* is added.

146

Of note also are the facts that in *beggar*, the *g* has been doubled just as if the added morpheme had been *-er*; that in *liar* the ending *e* of the free morpheme, *lie*, was dropped before the bound morpheme *-ar* was added.

In the last two examples shown, the variant of the *-er* morpheme of agent is *-or*. Ross (1967) says that about half of the words in which the *-er* morpheme of agent is spelled *-or*, are words in which the root word ends in *-ate*. He suggests this as one of the cues in selecting the *-or* spelling.

A number of other "bound" morphemic structures which are used with great frequency (and which have spelling variants) should be subjected to special study and elucidation. Chief among these are 1) the adjective-forming morpheme, *-able*, and its variant, *-ible*; 2) the nominal, *-ant*, and its variant, *-ent*. The several variants for the prefix, *col-*, which include *cor-, con-* and *com-*, do not seem to present serious problems probably because, since the syllable is in the initial position, the vowel is usually clearly heard.

SUMMARY

This discourse, to this point, has been involved in the presentation of evidence concerning the learnability of various aspects of the alphabetic writing system used in the visual recording system of the English language. It has shown evidence that:

> Children of preschool age and early school age can and do "learn the alphabet." This involves learning the letter forms and their names, both upper-case and lower-case letters, and learning to write or print the letters.

> Children who enter school at about the age of six years and who already "know" twenty or more letters, as defined above, may

have already begun to learn to read, whereas children who know fewer or no letters are unlikely to have made a start in reading.

Measures of letter knowledge are good measures of readiness for learning to read.

Approximately eighty per cent of the phonemes used in the words which comprise the spelling vocabulary of elementary school children adhere to the alphabetic principle in their spelling, i.e., in the letters which are used to represent them. Consonant clusters or blends adhere to the alphabetic principle about ninety-two percent of the time, while single consonant phonemes have consistent letter representation about ninety percent of the time. Vowel phonemes do have most typical letter representation but the level of consistency is much lower than for consonant phonemes. These data suggest that the alphabetic principle is easy to demonstrate and, therefore, learnable.

The English writing system does employ a considerable variety of "ideographic" devices—devices which distinguish meanings of words which, when spoken, have the same sound. However, the alphabetic principle continues to function in these printed forms and is useful in learning to read, write and spell these homonyms.

When two or more graphemic options (i.e., letters or letter groups) are available for spelling a particular phoneme, several factors function to aid the writer or reader in determining which phoneme-grapheme relationship to choose. These are the following:

Position in the syllable.

A variety of "internal constraints" or "environmental factors" which control the choice of grapheme.

The factor of stress position in multisyllable words, In particular, this factor assists in the problems related to the doubling of consonant letters.

The morphemic structure in derivatives and inflected words provides many specific clues in solving spelling problems. The literate user of the English language needs to know the spelling conventions which are associated with making inflectional and derivational changes.

These seven propositions, considered collectively, do not suggest that the English writing system is easy to learn. They establish that it is rather complex. However, they also demonstrate that the whole process begins with the *alphabetic principle* and that most of the special problems involve variants within this principle. Systems of instruction which have been, and in some instances still are, based on the concept of memorizing words by their gross "shape" or "configuration" and which teach children to look at initial and ending consonants as "clues" but which have not taught either the alphabet or the alphabetic principle systematically, have been and still are extremely unfair to children. Taught systematically from the beginning, the basics of English orthography are relatively simple to grasp.

The simplicity of the system, even more dramatically demonstrated, follows in the concluding section on the basic spelling patterns of the writing system.

ENGLISH USES FOUR BASIC SPELLING PATTERNS

English spelling, as has been shown, can be described in terms of the one-to-one relationship between phonemes and graphemes and the variants in these relationships. Another approach to the discussion of English spelling is achieved by considering the patterns or sequences in which series of phonemes are represented by series of consonant and vowel letters. These series are referred to here as spelling patterns.

Spelling patterns have been discussed by Hall (1961), Fries (1963), and by Sabaroff (1966), and the problems of spelling English have been reviewed by Mary R. Key (1969). Hall asserted that there are patterns in English spelling, and he grouped words into three categories, those which are "regular," "semiregular," and "irregular." Fries identified three patterns. They are represented by the three words *man, mane, maid*. The first or short vowel pattern he regarded as the most basic pattern in English. He asserted that children should be taught first the high-frequency, consistently patterned words before being asked to work with varieties of spelling complications.

Sabaroff suggested four main patterns:

The closed, short vowel pattern (can, an)

The open, long vowel pattern (be, go)

The long vowel signaled by mute ending *e* (lane, fine)

The long vowel signaled by two adjacent vowel letters (beat, pain, boat)

In addition, she proposed a fifth pattern, that of the vowel controlled by *r, l*, or *w*.

An independent system of spelling patterns worked out by Deverell over a period of ten to fifteen years in lectures with undergraduate students, and presented in mimeographed materials, has been fully described by Nimfa B. Lorena in her Master of Education thesis at the University of Saskatchewan (Lorena, 1969). Essentially, they are the same as Sabaroff's first four patterns, the *short vowel pattern* and three types of letter grouping which signal or represent *long vowel phonemes*. Deverell, however, provides a category of *x patterns*, namely 1x, 2x, 3x, and 4x, which account for those cases in which the patterns are *visually* those of pattern 1, 2, 3, or 4, but have the

150

vowel heard (or sometimes other differences) and do not actually fit the supposed pattern. These are referred to as *near patterns*. The second special feature of Deverell's system is that he applies the patterns and near patterns to the syllables of polysyllabic words; that is, they account for the spelling of all words, not merely of one syllable words. Finally, Deverell provides a category 5 which he calls *non-patterns*. This is for those cases, few in number, which defy classification.

The Deverell scheme of spelling patterns is laid out in Table 2.

TABLE 2

DEVERELL SCHEME OF SPELLING PATTERNS

Pattern 1. The closed short vowel pattern [(C)VC]

Principle: In a one-syllable word or a syllable, a single vowel letter followed by a terminal consonant is a "closed" vowel and usually signals a short vowel sound. This is identical to Fries' pattern 1.

Examples:

CVC	VC(C)	(C)CVC(C)	CVC.CVC(C)
pat	at	stamp	top.mast (1 + 1)
pet	egg	step	bun.ting (1 + 1)
pit	it	primp	can.cel (1 + 1x)
pot	on	lost	hot.bed (1 + 1)
putt	up	trust	dis.gust (1 + 1)
put (1x)			

Pattern 1 also covers those words in English which double the final consonant after a short vowel, that is, most words ending in /K/, /F/, /S/, /L/.* Double *k* is spelled *ck*.

Examples:

k	f	s	l
back	chaff	lass	ball
deck		less	bell
hick	cliff	miss	kill

151

pock	scoff	boss	dull
luck	puff	fuss	gull

*In this table, a capital letter placed between oblique lines represents the phoneme most commonly associated with that letter. Where a number from 1 to 7 is used following capital vowel letters, the phoneme indicated is that used by Hanna et al. in their monumental study of English spelling (Hanna, Hanna, Hodges, and Rudorf, 1966). The reason for using these symbols rather than those of I.P.A. is that they can be reproduced on the typewriter, a decided advantage.

Pattern 2. The open, long vowel pattern [(C) V]

Principle: When a word or syllable contains a single vowel letter which ends the word or syllable, that vowel letter is open and it usually signals a long vowel sound.
Examples:

be	I	go	gnu
he	by	no	
she	my	so	
we	shy		
me	cry		
thee (2x or 4)	hi(gh) (2x)		

The principle functions also for accented syllables in polysyllabic words.
Examples:

la.dy (2 + 2x)	di.a.lect (2 + 2x + 1)
ta.ble (2 + 5)	i.so.la.tion (2 + 2 + 2 + 5)
ce.dar (2 + 1x)	pho.neme (2 + 3)
tri.al (2 + 1x)	to.tal (2 + 1x)
fi.nal (2 + 1x)	nu.cle.us (2 + 2 + 1x)
my.o.pi.a (2 + 2 + 2x + 2x)	u.ni.verse (2 + 2x + 1x)

Pattern 3. Long medial vowel with terminal mute e [(C) V C e]

Principle: When a one-syllable word or a syllable ends in mute *e*, preceded by a single consonant, the medial vowel letter usually signals a long vowel sound. It

152

is better seen when presented in contrast with pattern 1, as Fries does.
Examples:

Pattern 1	Pattern 3	Pattern 3 in longer words
fad	fade	a.bide (2x + 3)
tap	tape	
rip	ripe	ab.so.lute (1 + 2x + 3)
bit	bite	
at	ate	in.sec.ti.cide (1 + 1 + 2x + 3)
cop	cope	
trip	tripe	hate.ful (3 + 1x)
grip	gripe	
tub	tube	hire.ling (3 + 1)

However, it should be noted that words which end in *-ve, -se* and *-ce* often do not observe this principle.
Examples:

have (1x or 3x)	horse (1x)	lettuce (1 + 1x)
love (1x or 3x)	house (4x)	justice (1 + 1x)
glove (1x or 3x)		preface (2x + 1x or 3x)

Pattern 4. Long vowel signaled by two adjacent vowel letters [(C) V V (C)]

Principle: When a one-syllable word or a syllable contain two adjacent vowel letters, usually the second letter is silent and the first signals a long vowel sound.
Examples:

The vowel digraph *ai* for the sound /A/.

bait	vain
rain	main

The vowel digraph *ea* for the sound /E/.

bead	peat
beast	lead

The vowel digraph *ee* for the sound /E/.

beet	steep
meet	feed

The vowel digraph *oa* for the sound /O/.

boat	coast
coat	Joan
cloak	goat

153

The vowel digraph *ay* for the sound /A/.

hay	gray
lay	slay
may	spray

The vowel digraphs *aw, au* for the sound /O3/.

paw	fault
saw	haul
raw	jaunt

The vowel digraphs *ew, ue,* and *ui* for the sound /U/.

blew	clue	suit
chew	glue	fruit
flew	value	recruit
grew	virtue	conduit

The vowel digraph *oo* for the sound /O6/.

spoon	root	tool
hoop	boot	spool
scoop	shoot	balloon

The vowel digraph *oo* for the sound /O7/.

book (4x)	flood (4x)
look (4x)	blood (4x)
foot (4x)	

The vowel digraph *ow* for the sound /O/.

snow	willow (1 + 4)
sow	yellow (1 + 4)
show	follow (1 + 4)

The diphthongs *oi, oy* /OI/; *ou, ow* /OU/.

Diphthongs are compound vowel sounds which are represented by two adjacent vowel letters. There are only two in English, but each has a spelling variant.

coin	boy	out	owl
coil	toy	house	howl
boil	joy	bout	towel

The "x" variants of the spelling patterns

An "x" variant simply describes any one of the spelling patterns in which the particular example does not run true to form but still displays the visual characteristics of a familiar pattern.

Examples:

Pattern 1x.	*for* (because the vowel sound is modified by *r*)
Pattern 2x.	*be*-longs (because *e* signals a schwa sound not /e/)
Pattern 3x.	*are* (because *a* does not signal a long vowel)
Pattern 4x.	*cook* (because the *oo* symbol does not signal a long vowel)

Pattern 5. The non-pattern

This designation is used to describe a letter arrangement in a syllable which does not resemble any standard pattern. Some examples of these nonpatterns are the *-le* in little and beetle; and the *-ed* graphemic unit when it signals a /T/ sound as in pick*ed* and lock*ed.* In most instances it describes archaic spellings (e.g., bought, night, flight). In others, it designates certain orthographic symbols such as the contraction forms (e.g., won'*t*, don'*t*), possessive forms (e.g., Dan'*s*, Nat'*s*), and abbreviations (e.g., Mr., Mrs.).

ADVANTAGES OF THE DEVERELL SCHEME
OF SPELLING PATTERNS

The major claim made by the writer for his scheme of describing English spelling is that it includes all one-syllable words and all syllables of multisyllabic words in the language. The device of using the *x* patterns provides for a very large number of syllables which are nearly "on pattern" but which do not quite fit. The majority of these are the weak-stress syllables of longer words in which the spelling is on pattern but the vowel sound heard in the normal flow of speech is the schwa rather than the phoneme signaled by the vowel letter or letters which are used.

In her study of the language of the MERRILL LINGUISTIC READERS (Fries, 1966), a set of six books which were judged to be designed for about the first two years of schooling, Lorena found the four spelling patterns to be distributed as shown in Table 3 (Lorena, 1969).

155

TABLE 3

PERCENT OF SPELLING PATTERNS IN ONE-SYLLABLE WORDS AND IN THE SYLLABLES OF POLY-SYLLABIC WORDS IN THE MERRILL LINGUISTIC READERS

Pattern Number	Description	Percent in Total Lexicon	Sub-totals
1	Closed, short vowel	47	
1x	Near pattern	23	70
2	Open, long vowel	4	
2x	Near pattern	1	5
3	Long vowel signaled by ending mute *e*	6	
3x	Near pattern	3	9
4	Long vowel signaled by two adjacent vowel letters (includes diphthongs)	10	
4x	Near pattern	5	15
		Total	99

Predominance (70%) had been given to the closed, short vowel spelling pattern words and syllables, and patterns 2, 3, and 4 occurred in 5%, 9% and 15% of cases, respectively.

In the total lexicon of the program, Lorena found that 62% of short words and syllables were on pattern, 30% were near pattern, and 8% were nonpattern cases (Lorena, 1969). That is, in designing these books, Fries stressed the importance of giving children an opportunity to learn the alphabetic principle by encountering the "regular" spelling patterns of English. When it is recognized that spelling patterns 3 and 4 were not introduced until Book 4 of the series, the significance of the instruction policy becomes very evident. *Learn English orthography by learning how it does work before becoming entangled in its weaknesses and idiosyncrasies. After its system is understood and experience has been gained in dealing with its near misses* (the x patterns or "near" patterns), *the child will zero in on its messes with confidence and glee.* The writer believes that the proportionate distribution of the several spelling patterns in the language sample in the Merrill readers is about the same as for any normal sample of the language.

CONCLUSION

Let us continue a search for the simplicity which exists in the writing system of the English language. Let us start instruction where children start it themselves, that is by learning about the alphabet. Let us teach children the consistent relationships which exist between alphabetic symbols and the phonemes of speech, and between the sequences of letters and the signals which they provide respecting sound. Let us, above all, let children discover the relationship between *visual-direction* in writing or print and *sound-time* in speech. Let us stop confusing children by our methods and allow them to learn the *system* of English writing. Above all, let us start believing in our alphabetic system of writing. It is not perfect, but neither is any other. Even if we were to try to invent a perfect one today, we would be foiled by the variety of dialects of English found in any one country, not to mention the whole wide world. Even if we did invent a perfect one today, it would be outmoded tomorrow by the development of new variants in English speech. We are lucky to have an alphabetic system of writing. Let us make the most of it in teaching our children.

REFERENCES

Bloomfield, Leonard, & Bernhart, Clarence. **Let's read: A linguistic approach.** Detroit: Wayne State University Press, 1946.

Deverell, A. Fred. The alphabet as readiness for beginning reading. Paper read at the annual conference of the Canadian Association of Professors of Education, 1967. Mimeographed.

Deverell, A. Fred. Further studies of symbol knowledge as readiness for beginning reading. Paper read at the annual conference of the Canadian Association of Professors of Education, 1969.

Diack, Hunter. **Reading and the psychology of perception.** Nottingham, England: Peter Skinner Publishing Ltd., 1960.

Downing, John. Initial teaching alphabet: Results after six years. **Elementary Sch. J.,** Feb. 1969, **69,** 242-249.

Durrell, Donald D., & Associates. First grade reading success study. **J. Educ.** (Boston), Feb. 1958, **14.**

Fries, Charles C. **Linguistics and reading.** New York: Holt, Rinehart and Winston, 1963.

Fries, Charles C., & others. **Merrill linguistic readers.** Columbus, Ohio: Charles E. Merrill Co., 1966.

Gage, N. L. (Ed.) **Handbook of research on teaching.** Chicago: Rand McNally, 1962. Pp. 868-873.

Greene, Harry A., & Petty, Walter T. **Developing language skills in the elementary schools.** Boston: Allyn and Bacon, 1967.

Groff, Patrick (Ed.), Glim, Theodore E., & Petty, Walter T. Research critiques (of Hanna and Moore's Spelling—From spoken word to written symbol). **Elementary Sch. J.,** May 1965, **42,** 582-584.

Hall, Robert A., Jr. **Sound and spelling in English.** Philadelphia: Chilton Co., 1961.

Hanna, Paul R., & Hanna, Jean S. Applications of linguistic and psychological cues to the spelling course of study. **Elementary English,** Nov. 1965, **42,** 753-759.

Hanna, Paul R., Hanna, Jean S., Bergquist, Sidney R., Hodges, Richard E., & Rudorf, E. Hugh. Needed research in spelling. **Elementary English,** Jan. 1966, **43,** 60-66.

Hanna, Paul R., Hanna, Jean S., Hodges, Richard E., & Rudorf, E. Hugh, Jr. **Phoneme-grapheme correspondences as cues to spelling improvement.** Washington, D.C.: U.S. Government Printing Office, 1966.

Hanna, Paul, Hanna, Jean S., Hodges, Richard E., & Rudorf, E. Hugh. A summary: Linguistic cues for spelling improvement. **Elementary English,** Dec. 1967, **44,** 862-865.

Hanna, Paul R., & Moore, James T., Jr. Spelling—From spoken word to written symbol. **Elementary Sch. J.,** Feb. 1953, **53,** 329-337.

Hodges, Richard E. The case for teaching sound-to-letter correspondences in spelling. **Elementary Sch. J.,** March 1966, **66,** 327-336.

Hodges, Richard E., & Rudorf, E. Hugh. Searching linguistics for cues for the teaching of spelling. **Elementary English,** May 1965, **42,** 527-533.

Key, Mary Ritchie. The English spelling system and the initial teaching alphabet. **Elementary Sch. J.,** March 1969, **69,** 313-326.

Lamb, Pose. **Linguistics in proper perspective.** Columbus, Ohio: Charles E. Merrill Co., 1967.

Lorena, Nimfa Benito. Language features of the Merrill linguistic readers. Unpublished Masters thesis, University of Saskatchewan, 1969.

Moore, James Thomas, Jr. Phonetic elements appearing in a three thousand word spelling vocabulary. Unpublished Masters thesis, Stanford University, 1951.

Murdock, MacDonald (Consulting Ed.), McCool, Katherine B. (Ed.), & others. **Sally, Dick and Jane: The new basic readers.** Toronto: W. J. Gage and Co., 1963; Chicago: Scott, Foresman & Co.

Peters, Margaret L. The influence of reading methods on spelling. **British J. Educ. Psychol.,** Feb. 1967, **37,** 47-53.

Plessas, Gus P., & Ladley, Dorothea Macie. Some implications of spelling and reading research. **Elementary English,** Feb. 1965, **42,** 142-145.

Ross, Charles S. The writing system. **Elementary English,** Nov. 1967, **44,** 775-778.

Rudorf, E. Hugh. Measurement of spelling ability. **Elementary English,** Dec. 1965, **42,** 889-894.

Sabaroff, Rose. Breaking the code: What method? Introducing an integrated linguistic approach to beginning reading. **Elementary Sch. J.,** Nov. 1966, **66,** 95-103.

Soffietti, James P. Why children fail to read: A linguistic analysis. **Harvard Educ. Rev.,** Spring 1955, **25** (2), 63-84.

Watson, James D. The double helix: The discovery of the structure of D. N. A. **The Atlantic,** Jan. 1968, 77-79.

Wilson, Frank T. Early achievement in reading. **Elementary Sch. J.,** April 1942, **42,** 609-615.

Witty, Paul, & Kopel, Donald. **Reading and the educative process.** Boston: Ginn and Co., 1939.

Comprehension: A Constellation of Many Factors

Gilbert B. Schiffman, Ed.D.
Coordinating Director of Instruction
Prince George's County Board of Education
Upper Marlboro, Maryland

Paul Daniels, Ph.D.
Instructional Consultant
Prince George's County Board of Education
Upper Marlboro, Maryland

For many years we have been interested in developing the concept, "Comprehension—A Constellation of Many Factors." However, the writing had never been completed because it was felt that this aspect of comprehension was so widely accepted by all educators that any writing on the subject would be superfluous.

Recently, we found ourselves resembling the antique dealer who, after collecting certain objects for a long period of time, suddenly finds his market fast disappearing. With alarm, a growing disassociation with the area of comprehension was discovered. Perhaps this is a natural reaction. Years of lip service have been given to the philosophy of reading as a meaningful task; a reconstruction of the meaning behind the symbols. But this has been comprehension of the broadest, most general type, "What did the story say?" In doing this the sequence of mechanical skills of word recognition was relegated to a very automatic role, dictated to day by day by a manual. Consequently, there were in the schools many youngsters with severe word recognition problems. Many of these pupils could not get involved in the comprehension area because they could not unlock that unknown word.

Now the pendulum is swinging the other way. More and more people openly state that they "concentrate on phonics." In a newspaper article it was noted that a new state school superintendent, in instituting new programs, mentioned that his first step would be to develop a phonics program. One rarely hears the other word recognition techniques such as pictures or context clues, structural analysis, configuration, or dictionary usage, mentioned at all.

We have tried to help teachers see the value of having and using word attack skill sequences in their teaching. It is apparent that some children are having reading problems because of difficulties in the word attack area. We have also tried to help teachers see that word attack is a means to an end rather than an end in itself. The ultimate goal of reading is comprehension.

162

However, another type of reading disability could be created if this pendulum continues to swing from the extreme right to the extreme left. (The selection of the directions are purely arbitrary.) With the increased interest in word recognition, there is a growing tendency to omit the basic reason for reading—that of comprehension.

The sudden wide acceptance by classroom teachers of "the swinging pendulum" is a bandwagon effect. It is feared that the pendulum will gain such momentum with this added weight that it will not stop in the middle where it belongs, but continue to the end of its arc. The result will be catastrophic—a generation of verbalizers, students who can pronounce words but do not understand their meanings. Hopefully, educators will use their good common pedagogical know-how and take the valid suggestions of comprehension proponents and weld a topnotch program for their pupils.

CONCEPT OF COMPREHENSION

Of course, one cannot accept the concept of comprehension as an understanding of material in general. As the title "Comprehension— A Constellation of Many Factors" indicates, comprehension is a grouping of many understandings and skills. It is not all of the internal, human factors or the different concepts, ideas or feelings that someone brings to the reading situation. It refers to the different types of comprehension and how the teachers should evaluate comprehension skills and develop comprehension abilities in their students. These skills are varied in type and depth.

These varieties of demands in comprehension are clearly demonstrated in an informal reading inventory used at Temple University. The third reader level selection states that a dog should have one meal in summer and two in winter. To check factual recall, one might ask, "How many meals a day should you give a dog in summer?" Unfortunately, this is a very common type of question. How much more enlightening is the question from the informal reading inventory, "How many meals a day should you give a dog in July?" Too frequently the answer is, "It didn't say" or "July wasn't even in the story." The second question taps a child's ability to do inferential thinking—to manipulate the facts so that a higher level of understanding arises.

Now, any good comprehension check should not only check straight factual recall but deeper critical thinking skills. Many authorities believe it should be roughly fifty percent factual, thirty percent critical, and twenty percent vocabulary, which really cuts across both the factual and the critical areas. However, because of the trend toward verbalism, more weight on critical reading seems appropriate.

Look at a lesson of about 140 words written at the high Fourth or Fifth Grade readability level, and check some of the different types of critical comprehension that might be evaluated:

> On the ridge of a foothill of a small mountain chain, three lone mounted figures could be seen. The feathers of their headdresses hardly moved and their ponies let their heads drop.
>
> In the valley before them, a long black snake-like line moved. Small pads of dust came up from the horses' hooves. This was the First Regiment of the United States Cavalry. These riders were the best troops in the West. These thirteen hundred men carried the flag of the United States always westward.
>
> The three men, Crazy Horse, Sitting Bull, and Bear Claw, looked and saw three thousand of the finest warriors of their nations. Should they attack now or wait? The latter two men wanted to attack immediately; the other said, "This is not the place." Slowly, they turned around and went back to their men. (Reprinted by permission of the author and available from Maddan Publishing, Box 3026, Philadelphia, Pennsylvania 19150)

Below are the types of questions used to tap the various comprehension skills that could be evaluated by this material. It is important to note that the reader should not look back at the material but operate on a recall and recognition basis.

1. Was it a calm or windy day?_____

2. Were these the Rocky Mountains?_____

   How do you know?_____

3. Draw a circle around the word that best fits the three men.
   A. Officers   B. Chiefs   C. Soldiers

4. Draw a line around the answer that best describes the way the troops moved.
   A. In large well spaced groups.
   B. In a file, two or three abreast.
   C. No order.

5. Was this wet or dry country?_____

   How do you know?

6. What was the name of the group of soldiers:
   A. Regiment   B. Battalion   C. Division

7. How many men were in the group?
   A. 13,000   B. 1,300   C. 30,000

8. How many men in a regiment?
   A. 13,000   B. 1,300   C. 30,000

9. Are these troops reinforcements?_____

   How do you know?_____

10. Where were the Indian warriors?_____

11. How many Indians were ready for battle?
    A. 1,300   B. 13,000   C. 3,000

12. Which two men wanted to attack now?
    A. Bear Claw   B. Crazy Horse   C. Sitting Bull

13. Which man was the boss?
    A. Bear Claw   B. Crazy Horse   C. Sitting Bull

14. Were all of these men from the same tribe?_____

    How do you know?_____

COMPREHENSION SKILLS

Basic Elements

Skills tested by these questions include:

1. Inferential thinking—choosing an inference from data provided.
2. Making an inference and then justifying it with recalled data.
3. Making an inference by choosing an appropriate label.
4. Using figurative language to arrive at an inference.
5. Selecting an inference and then justifying it with specific factual data.
6. Factual recognition—all that is required is that the reader recognize which of the three responses appeared in the material.
7. Factual recall is required in this question as the factual data were written in English but the responses were in Arabic.
8. This requires a student to draw a conclusion from the data presented in #6 and #7.
9. This question taps vocabulary, reinforcements; the making of an inference about this word; and the use of figurative language, the flag of the United States always westward, to make the inference.
10. In this question the reader must use the factual information involved with *ridge* and the data given in the material, "went *back* to their men."
11. Factual recall is required as in question #7.
12. This question is based on the manipulation of the word *latter.* First as a vocabulary understanding and then as source of direction.
13. Inferential thinking is required in that the usually democratic process was not adhered to.
14. This inference is based on a precise piece of factual data, notions.

From the material above it is obvious that certain elements of comprehension are basic and that our differentiated skill sequences in most respects are variations on these themes. The acquisition of factual data would appear to be a first step; its manipulation in various ways would follow.

Factual Recognition and Recall

It is obvious that, if comprehension is to be developed, the facts must be obtained from the printed matter and then recalled at the appropriate time. This requires the reader to set purposes for reading and then to recognize the factual data that are encountered in the material that are appropriate to the purposes. Once the factual material has been obtained its manipulation in many ways can begin.

However, factual recognition in itself would not be very valuable if there was no ability to recall the material once it had been obtained. Many teachers complain that the students "can't remember from one day to the next." Children feel upset also about their inability to recall information. In many cases, this is the direct result of the failure to organize material in some fashion once it has been obtained.

Read the following line of words once, cover them and then try to recall what you read. Tabulate it by writing the line on a sheet of paper.

house west gun by drop girl dry lonely one game

Now do the same thing with the following line of words and follow the same procedure.

Yesterday for breakfast I had coffee with cream and sugar.

Which line did you recall with the most accuracy? Nearly everyone does far better with the second line of ten words. These words have been organized. The most important factor here is that tomorrow you will be able to recall the second line in more detail than the first.

Manipulation of the Data

Once data have been obtained, they can be handled in many ways. They might be brought together to arrive at a higher level idea or more abstract idea usually called an inference. They might be put into organizational schemes based on systems such as alphabetical order, chronological sequence, cause and effect relationships, and so forth.

It appears then that the ability to comprehend depends in a large measure on the degree to which material can be organized for retention, for recall, and most importantly, for inferential thinking of whatever type.

Fundamental abilities. Certain fundamental abilities must be brought to bear on materials when we talk about manipulating data. First of all, the reader must be able to appreciate the data of the same level of abstraction that is available. He must then choose those that go together based on his purposes, and finally he must be able to label those choosing data in some fashion if he is to communicate the ideas. This appears to be the system in its developmental sequence. To facilitate retention of material, the reader must be helped to integrate the new material with previously learned material whenever possible.

Organizational skills. A basic element in comprehension which requires the abilities noted above is paragraph analysis. If the ability to analyze is to be acquired, an overall ability to organize material must be developed. These skills are usually labeled the organizational skills.

The term *organization* has long been used by teachers in their discussions of factors involved in reading. However, few authors or textbooks appear to clearly define the term or place it in any developmental sequence in their Language Arts Program. Sometimes the term is referred to as an independent factor appearing in certain particular types of reading. At other times it is recognized as an integral part of all comprehension to be developed at every level. It is hoped that the previous material will state our point of view about organization and what it entails.

Webster defines organization as the process of arranging or forming into a complete and functioning whole. Dr. Nila B. Smith probably gives the most functional definition when she says "To organize is to put together ideas that belong together." No matter which definition we accept, it appears obvious that organization is an important factor in reading, particularly in study or work type reading, and it consists of a constellation of many complex skills as noted above.

This complexity may be one of the major factors causing the obvious frustrations of many students when faced with a content teacher's assignment calling for the organization of a long selection or passage. Without question, all authorities agree that organizational skills are extremely important in preparing all pupils to read efficiently. To classify material into several categories, to distinguish relevant from irrelevant ideas, to perceive a sequence of events, to summarize or telescope material, and to understand the mechanics of outlining are some of these important skills.

Paragraph organization. One of the most important of the organizational skills is the ability to distinguish between the main idea and the subordinate details. This basic skill is taught by giving specific attention to the organization and meaning of paragraphs. (Robinson says first at the sentence level, but it might need to start at the word level.)

One can demonstrate the importance of understanding paragraph organization by the following example:

> If I put the letters *c-a-t* on the blackboard and ask you to pronounce the word they form, you would have no difficulty saying the word *cat*. But, if I asked you what the word *cat* meant or what was my meaning of the word *cat,* as the author, you might have some difficulty. It could mean a type of woman, it would mean a four-legged animal, or it might mean some slang expression. If I put it in a phrase, "A cat with a blade," you would then probably think of a "cool cat" or a human being or a type of tractor. If I put it in a complete sentence "I saw a cat with a blade come down the road," you possibly still would not be sure of my meaning. Only when I put the word in a meaningful paragraph do you really understand the situation. Therefore, it is important that the reader recognizes the basic value of reading the paragraph.

Comprehending a paragraph depends upon an understanding of the interrelationship of its parts. The most important part of a paragraph is the main idea but this is an *outcome* of personal understanding of the parts, rather than the cause of understanding. Too frequently we begin helping children understand paragraphs by using the topic sentence which is merely the vehicle that carries the main idea. Both of these, the main idea and topic sentence, should be arrived at by appreciating the coordinated details that lead to the main idea. In reality, the reader must be able to recognize the factual details, put those that go together (for a reason) together, and then draw a conclusion or make an inference about them. This inference or conclusion is the main idea. (Note the same idea presented earlier with terms to fit paragraph analysis.)

Once a reader is well versed in this procedure, he is then able to begin to use topic sentences to manipulate paragraphs. There is no doubt that recognition of main ideas and topic sentences is a key to paragraph analysis.

Types of paragraphs. From the point of view of topic sentence placement (in relation to supporting details), there are five basic types of paragraphs. Children should learn these types as early as possible. Both authors of this material and others in the field have demonstrated this concept through the use of geometric forms.

A paragraph might be built in triangular form with the apex up. This form represents the topic sentence occurring initially. This is seen very frequently in newspaper writing and in textbooks; it represents learning through a deductive process.

A paragraph represented by a triangle with the apex down would indicate that the topic sentence is last. Learning through this paragraph depends on induction.

A third paragraph can be represented by two triangles with their apexes joined. In this paragraph ideas are presented, a conclusion drawn and elaboration provided.

A diamond is representative of a paragraph in which the main idea is stated initially and finally. It is often found in advertising copy and classically in debates. Its function is to highlight an important idea.

The fifth type of paragraph resembles a rectangle. It has no topic sentence. In this type of paragraph, the reader must infer the main idea with no aid from the author. These paragraphs are often the source of difficulty when reading learned journals. This type of paragraph is also known as the so-called "transitional paragraph." In reality, it is really a series of sequential statements that are organized in paragraph form for typographical reason. (We write in paragraphs.)

The following paragraphs developed by Dr. Daniels might be helpful in demonstrating these organization patterns.

We read the plans and bought the wood, nails, and cement we needed. Then we carried these down the hill to the site. It is not easy to build a summer cottage in the mountains. Next we dug the foundation and poured the cement. By then the summer was gone and we hadn't gotten far.

This paragraph represents the two joined triangles.

Here is the next paragraph. What form fits this paragraph?

Dark clouds rolled in from the west and lightning flashed through the trees and great drops of rain exploded on the dust. The thunderstorm had finally reached us.

This is the inverted triangle.

Here is the next paragraph.

My Uncle Harry was a swell guy. In the spring he would take me to a ball game. Sometimes we would visit the waterfront and talk about ships. He could throw and catch a ball better than anyone I knew. When he left I always had some change to buy what I wanted. My Uncle Harry was a great guy.

This represents the diamond shaped paragraph.

Look at the next paragraph.

We have many things to get ready for a picnic. We have to plan the food to be taken, and we have to prepare it. We must decide on the place for the picnic. We must ask the people to go to the outing, and we must find a way to get there.

This represents a triangle with apex up.

Try the last paragraph.

> Billy White's father held him in the chair and Billy screamed.
> When I came close to him with my scissors he tried to bite me.
> His head was never still long enough to use clippers and he
> ripped the pocket of my barber's jacket. When he left, I was
> still shaking.

This paragraph has no topic sentence; the reader must infer the key
idea.

Of course, it must be understood that this is just one technique to
develop adequacy in paragraph comprehension. Many texts describe
additional pedagogical procedures and activities to reinforce this skill.
An interesting follow-up project, for the reader, might be to investi-
gate and record some other approaches to developing this competency.

Organizational activities of this type enhance comprehension, facilitate recall, and further the development of good study procedures.
They are often called the "tools of study"—the skills that are needed
every day and that must be developed into habits.

CONCLUSIONS

In the authors' opinions, it seems evident that a major factor in reading disability is an unorganized approach to learning on the part of
the learner. Secondly, many teachers do not structure their instruction on organized patterns because they do not know the value of
organization in facilitating retention and recall. It might well be said
that some, possibly many, children have trouble with word recognition because they have not been helped to comprehend.

This problem stems from a pedagogical view of schools that has divorced this social institution (school) from the rest of the learner's sociology. Comprehension problems occur too frequently because the school does not provide the setting for comprehension to develop. It is beyond the role of this chapter to discuss the problem in all of its ramifications. However, if the school does not provide problem-solving situations in which material can be manipulated, then the real purpose for comprehension never develops. We comprehend to solve problems—lessen anxiety. It is difficult to imagine this happening in a school where learning to decode is an end in itself. If children are to learn to comprehend, they must use reading to help solve problems and the procedures should be used to solve the problem called decoding.

Development of various aspects of comprehension, of course, is not only in the hands of the reading teacher or of the elementary classroom teacher. All teachers have a responsibility to check comprehension and to develop comprehension skills using the critical reading area. There is no question that this type of comprehension lends itself very easily to social studies and science material. There is no question, also, that these materials were just a small sampling of the different kinds of comprehension that could be developed. When one looks at all of this, one realizes the tremendous responsibility that is placed upon the educator. Not only must he develop good word recognition skills and good comprehension skills in the proper proportion, not only must he look warily at all of the biased groups, not only must he question all of the magic panaceas and cure-alls, but he must also keep in mind the different types of comprehension, and before him he must see the ultimate goal—that the pupil should read for meaning, for enjoyment, and for learning.

Editor's Introduction

Some hold that educational diagnosis ought to be the process of finding out what to teach a child. Others add that it should also assist in deciding how to teach him. Some also want diagnosis to clarify reasons for past failure to learn in the expected fashion. As in other facets of the prevention and correction of reading failure we have less than perfect agreement among professionals. In the last paper of this section, Cohen takes a strong stand for what he calls the "so what" diagnosis, in which only those diagnostic findings or observations which have treatment implications are of concern. The treatment is recorded immediately following each observation. Clearly much of what is called educational diagnosis today has no such treatment implications. Cohen believes that etiology is usually irrelevant to treatment of behavioral disorders such as reading failure. One purpose of his paper is to demonstrate that most reading retardation results from the dreaded psychoeducational disease called dyspedagogia (poor teaching). Interestingly, if dyspedagogia is the major etiological factor in poor reading then this is an instance where etiology is relevant to treatment! The treatment is to improve the instruction offered to teachers of reading. Since colleges of education have by and large failed to do an adequate job of preparing teachers to teach reading, we must develop a dual approach — improved in-service training for those teachers who were not given adequate preparation in college and revolutionized methods courses for teachers still in college. There are the same urgent needs in teaching teachers as there are in teaching children — just as we need new decoding emphases for children "the first time around" and improved remediation for those already in trouble, so we need better college preparation for teachers the first time around and greatly improved in-service for those already in the field. And as is readily recognized, this is easier said than done.

The other papers in this section—by Ray, Wallen, Sipay, and Powell—vary on a continuum that might be described as one of specificity of focus. Powell deals with the nature of diagnosis itself and with the characteristics of relevant diagnosis and of the effective diagnostician. Ray provides a specific model for a comprehensive and educationally relevant diagnosis which incorporates learning preference, performance level, specific skill instruction, nature of deficiencies, reinforcement and the teaching-learning environment. Wallen discusses the failure of standardized reading achievement tests and of standardized and informal diagnostic tests to identify and assist in arranging specific instructional procedures for children who need help. He advocates and describes the design and use of informal education tests which assess mastery of specific tasks essential to reading. If a child's performance is inadequate on a test item, the appropriate instruction then closely resembles the test item. Implications and directions are also implied for the assessment of effectiveness of reading instruction. Wallen's approach is consistent with much currently being advocated in regard to criterion-referenced testing and teaching. The reader may note similarities between Wallen's Informal Testing and Cohen's "so what" diagnosis. Sipay provides a highly detailed procedure for the precise and specific diagnosis or examination of word identification difficulties.

The authors represented in this section differ in their emphases. They largely agree, however, that educational diagnosis must yield specific teaching strategies. An interesting question which is not treated extensively by any of the papers is that of whether diagnosis can yield information about both what to teach and how to teach it. Determining exactly what reading skills are deficient in a given child is not as difficult as a common failure to do it would suggest. However, once it has been determined that a child does not, e.g., blend sounds adequately, can we diagnostically pursue the question of how to best teach that particular skill to that particular child? Most assume so.

One of the important questions which advocates of thorough, individual diagnosis must be prepared to deal with is whether remediation should be directed to the child's strengths or weaknesses. So far, there is little agreement and less evidence on this apparently critical issue. The assumption underlying some diagnostic efforts is that there is an interaction between the child's learning styles or modalities and the method by which he is taught. The evidence is elusive, even on this fundamental problem.

Diagnosis conducted to assess relevant entering behavior, i.e., to determine which reading skills a child possesses and which he does not, is an important part of teaching any child who needs special help in reading. However, there is some question about the necessity and/or value of diagnosis directed toward determining how to teach a given skill to a given child.

One detailed and comprehensive system for "diagnosing" reading behavior is presented in the paper by Starlin, "Evaluating Progress Toward Reading Proficiency," which appears in the final section of this book. Some readers may wish to read it in connection with individual diagnosis; others may be more interested in Starlin's proposals as they relate to upgrading all reading teaching, developmental and remedial. He describes and advocates Precision Teaching which derives from a purely behavioral approach and the reader who finds this emphasis somewhat neglected in the present section might also wish to refer to Starlin's paper.

Specificity in Remediation

Darrel D. Ray, Ed.D.
Assistant Professor Education
Oklahoma State University
Stillwater, Oklahoma

The act of reading is one of the few human behaviors that cannot be learned through imitation of others performing the act. The receptive nature of the process precludes learning through imitative behavior and the unique nature of the learning process for a reader suggests that even a successful method of instruction cannot be imitated and thus be generalized from one remedial situation to another. Historically, however, remedial techniques for disabled readers have been selected primarily on the basis of a professional bias for a method, a preference for a type of material, or an assumption that readers progress through material in identical fashion. The resulting remedial program frequently relegates the learner to a secondary role in either the determination of direction for the program or the procedures utilized in the program.

The point of view expressed here is that no remedial program should be initiated unless that program is based upon the careful consideration of the learner and the behavior of the learner in the reading situation. This chapter outlines a structured approach to remediation involving specific identification of:

The learning preference of the disabled reader.

The level of performance of the reader and the range of acceptable performance around that level.

The specific skill deficiencies of the reader functioning below the range of acceptability.

The nature of the deficiencies as related to the reading act.

A planned reinforcement of skills developed.

An understanding of the teaching-learning environment specific to the learner.

LEARNING PREFERENCE

The reader response to the process of learning to read must be considered to allow the selection of a suitable method of instruction. In analyzing the act of reading it is apparent that the mature reader uses a rapid visual recognition approach to trigger meaningful responses from material. However, in learning to read the learner will demonstrate a preference in the selection of recognition cues based upon visual or auditory learning modality strengths.

The disabled reader frequently has not been offered the opportunity to utilize preferred strengths in the teaching-learning situation in the classroom and therefore fails to make adequate progress. Behaviors exhibited during the diagnosis of the reading problem will identify the strengths of the learner and will direct the clinician to the appropriate method of instruction.

In evaluating methods currently available to the clinician, there appear to be four methods of reading instruction in use. Table 1 outlines these methods of instruction including primary modality emphasis, units of instruction, skill development procedures, skill transfer projection, pace of skill development and the learner strength requirements. A study of Table 1 will allow the clinician to select the most appropriate method for the learner.

Clinical evidence supports the hypothesis that the majority of disabled readers will respond in an instructional situation where some combination of vision and audition abilities are emphasized. It is not infrequent, however, to find disabled readers who exhibit depressed areas of skill development which require modification of the selected method to include additional sensory involvement in the teaching-learning situation. For example, a learner with strengths in audition development (acuity, identification, discrimination, perception, memory), but who reflects the lack of ability to integrate auditory and visual stimuli should respond to an auditory-visual method of instruction within an educa-

TABLE 1

METHODS OF READING INSTRUCTION

Primary Emphasis	Visual-Auditory Method	Auditory Visual Method	Linguistic Word Structure Method	Language Experience Method
Unit of instruction	Word	Letter	Word Pattern	Meaningful Structure
Skill Development	Accumulation of sight word vocabulary. Analytical approach to decoding.	Accumulation of sound-symbol relationships. Synthetic approach to decoding.	Accumulation of spelling pattern associations. Minimum contrast approach to decoding.	Transfer of learner oral communications to visual recognition. Language anticipation approach to decoding.
Skill Transfer	Immediate in controlled vocabulary reading material. Delayed in general application.	Immediate in consistent sound-symbol patterns. Early in general application.	Immediate in consistent spelling patterns. Delayed in general application.	Immediate in learner written material. Early in general application.
Pace of Skill Development	Slow	Accelerated	Slow	Accelerated
Learner Strength Requirements	Vision: —Acuity —Identification —Discrimination —Perception —Memory Visual-Auditory Integration.	Audition —Acuity —Identification —Discrimination —Perception —Memory Auditory-Visual Integration.	Vision: —Acuity —Identification —Discrimination —Perception —Memory Visual-Auditory Integration.	Language Skills Auditory Memory Auditory-Visual Integration

tional framework of additional sensory involvement, that is AVK or AVKT. Additional sensory involvement maintains its utility only in skill introductory activities and therefore should not be included as a part of the skill reinforcement program.

PERFORMANCE LEVEL INSTRUCTION

When the learning task is considered, there are three developmental bands of reading performance. The first of these, the Foundation Band, is included in reading performance between the levels 1.0 - 2.4 grade equivalencies and includes the growth of perceptual and language skills facilitating the development of an adequate sight vocabulary and basic decoding skills. The second band, extending from 2.5 to 3.9 is the Skill Acquisition Band which includes accelerated development of refined decoding skills and an expansion and maintenance of a rapidly recognized core of words. The last band, the Skill Application Band, is represented by reading performance of 4.0 grade e-quivalency or above, where previously developed skills are utilized in self-directed reading activities. Once the instructional level of performance for a reader has been established, and an evaluation of subskill abilities has been made, certain educational objectives become apparent with expectations based upon specific teaching-learning task requirements found within each band.

Performance variability around the instructional level in subskill growth can be expected from disabled readers and the range of acceptable variation will be dependent upon the band of performance in which the reader operates. Reader performance within the Foundation Band will accept only a range of .5 year from the instructional level, with performance within the Skill Acquisition Band allowing a .75 year range and Skill Application Band allowing a 1.0 year range. For example, if a diagnosis has established an instructional level of 2.75 for a disabled reader, then a range of performance in reading subskills between 2.0 and 3.5 can be accepted as maintaining a developmental balance for this reader and an adjusted developmental program can be pursued utilizing the preferred method of instruction. Performance level instruction reflects the strengths of the disabled reader and the range of that strength in the reading act including development of all reading skills found at that level.

SPECIFIC SKILL INSTRUCTION

Specific skill instruction for the disabled reader is determined through identification of weaknesses in subskill performance that reflect an unacceptable balance in total reading growth. Unlike skill development at the performance, or instructional level, where needs are developmental in nature, subskill growth is depressed in relation to the reader's own level of performance and therefore becomes a disability within a disability. For example, severely disabled readers operating developmentally within the Skill Acquisition Band will frequently exhibit behaviors reflecting a failure to visually track from left to right, a skill not associated developmentally with the Skill Acquisition Band.

The profile of behaviors of a disabled reader will illustrate specific subskill deficiencies operating in the reading act below the acceptable range of variability and will reflect the need for specific remediation, *in addition to* the adjusted developmental program for the reader. The instruction is provided at a level of performance that will allow an exclusion of interfering reading behaviors. That is, the skill is isolated and taught at an independent level. For example, if a specific comprehension difficulty has been identified for skill instruction, the exercises will be designed at a level where word recognition difficulty does not exist. A reader profile will not identify all of the specific skill needs of a reader; therefore, error behavior must be analyzed to permit specific skill development exercises to be used. Errors to be classified include visual perception errors, visual-auditory perception errors, sight word errors, behavioral errors, and language errors.

Visual perception errors consist of immediate incorrect responses to stimulus words using only a part of the visual pattern as a cue. These errors—Locational (initial, medial, and final), Syllabic Division, and Directional Confusion (rotations and reversals)—reflect the failure on the part of the reader to use total configuration, or pattern, in recognition of words. This failure will be manifested in dependency on a single portion of a word as a recognition trigger, failure to perceive total word pattern, and failure to track from left to right. Clinic subjects who are operating developmentally within either the Foundation Band or the Skill Acquisition Band frequently exhibit visual perception errors. In classifying visual perception errors, the clinician is interested in:

Dependency on a single portion of the word as revealed by the location of the error.

Directional confusion as revealed in reversals of letters, word parts, words, and word sequence.

At reading levels above 3.5, the failure to see visual patterns of multi-syllabic words.

Visual-auditory errors—consonant (single, blend, digraph) and vowel (single, digraph, diphthong)—are those errors reflecting faulty perception of sound-symbol relationships, application of phonic principles, or lack of application of alternative word recognition techniques to sound-symbol associations. Behaviorally, these errors are evidenced by difficulty with recognition of unknown words. Unlike visual perception errors, where immediate response to a stimulus is given, the visual-auditory errors include an obvious attempt on the part of the reader to associate sound and symbol or sound units and symbols. The term visual is retained in this classification because of the relationship between the visual pattern of a word and the sound associated with that pattern, e.g., the final *e* must be perceived (visually) before the "long" sound of *a* can be associated with the letter *a* in a word like *came.* In classifying visual-auditory errors, the clinician is concerned with:

Consonant errors (single, blends, digraphs, clusters) where the error is one of faulty sound-symbol association.

Vowel errors (single, digraph, diphthong) where the error is one of faulty sound-symbol association within the framework of visual patterns.

Sight word errors are those errors occurring where no situational clue is used by the reader; that is, the absence of use of sound-symbol, visual pattern, or anticipation from context.

Behavioral characteristics of the reader reveal task security or the lack of security in the oral reading act. Behavioral errors include omissions, additions, repetitions, and self-corrections.

Omissions and additions, as observed clinically, indicate unsatisfactory eye-voice span, unsatisfactory rate of reading, or refusal of stimulus. Repetition of words indicate insecurity with the reading task, insufficient word recognition skills, speech deficiencies, and to a limited degree, unsatisfactory eye-voice span. Self-corrections reveal the failure of the reader to utilize context, visual clues, and phonic generalizations selectively and accurately.

Language errors are those errors associated with the use of language, vocabulary development, anticipation of meaning, and involvement with the reading material. Comprehension errors include both type of comprehension (main idea, supporting details, sequence) and quality of comprehension (imagery, delayed recall, percentage of accuracy).

Vocabulary errors are those reflecting failure to recognize structural changes of words (affixes, derivatives, etc.), dialect errors (frequently identified incorrectly as decoding errors), anticipation of meaning, and expressive and receptive understanding of words.

Because of the unique nature of the reading behavior of the disabled reader no expected frequency of error type can be established. For the purposes of preparing remedial exercises, an examination of patterns, or clusters, of errors is made and corrective exercises are developed.

NATURE OF DEFICIENCIES

In attempting to determine what is the cumulative effect of the reading disability, and adjusting the remediation accordingly it is necessary to identify types of behavior within the reading act itself which may be causal of the current status and lack of progress in reading. Several conditions within the reading act can be identified as restrictive including:

The capacity to learn to read is impaired due to a failure to master a skill prerequisite to more advanced skills.

The capacity to learn to read is impaired due to compensatory activity detrimental to additional skill development.

The capacity to learn to read is impaired due to the interference of a skill in the performance of the reading act.

The capacity to learn to read is impaired due to a language deficiency.

Impairment due to a failure to master a skill prerequisite to more advanced skills occurs with a high frequency among reading disability samples. The reader behavior typifying this kind of deficiency can best be illustrated using the sentence "He hit the nail with the hammer," with "hammer" as the unknown word and the generalization VCCV as the skill to be applied where the reader who has failed to master position as a clue to vowel sounds (as in the first syllable of hammer) or the function of the vowel controller (as in the last syllable of hammer) cannot utilize the VCCV syllabic division generaliza-

187

tion even though he appears to have mastered the mechanical application of the generalization. Errors will reflect lack of basic learning as in calling "hammer," "hamer."

The second type of disability within the reading situation, compensatory activity detrimental to additional skill development, occurs when a reader compensates for a skill deficiency by accelerated development in another skill. For example, if we assume that hammer is the unknown word in this sentence, "He hit the nail with the hammer," and the reader has compensated for lack of phonic skills with the use of context clues, little difficulty will be expected in reading the word hammer even though the reader could not recall the word in isolation and could not recognize it in this context, "If I had a hammer." Frequently the reader has an unsatisfactory relationship between word recognition in context (usually high) and recognition in isolation (usually low) with comprehension of material inexact.

The stage at which compensatory activity fails to allow progress in reading will occur when, and in those situations where, the particular skill is removed from the reading situation through level or type of performance, when the compensatory activity modifies the meaning of what is read, and when reading becomes a self-oriented experience.

The third type concerns the interference of a skill in the performance of the reading act. Again using the sentence "He hit the nail with the hammer," with the unknown word "hammer," this point can be illustrated. The mechanics of determining the pronunciation of "hammer" require literally a shift from silent to oral reading and a shift from reading for meaning to reading to recognize words. If the task is difficult for the reader; that is, if context cannot be used as an aid or if the recognition skill is laborious, then the meaning is lost. Frequently the reader has an unsatisfactory relationship between word recognition in isolation (usually high), comprehension (usually low), and speed of reading (usually low). This type of reader occurs most frequently as the result of a failure to adjust the instructional method to the needs of the reader. The fourth type of disability within the reading act, language deficiency, occurs in those cases where the reader masters the mechanical skills of reading but fails to understand the material read without direct and constant guidance from some outside agent. Typically these readers come from a restricted environment where language exchange, if present at all, is primarily directive. These readers frequently are not identified as disabled until the level of operation requires self-directed activities. Behaviors in the reading situation include vocabulary weakness, failure to read orally with rhythm, responses in monosyllables, no memory for sequence of ideas or events, and an obvious lack of involvement with the material read (poor imagery).

The identification of the disability by the clinician will allow for more specific direction in the remedial program as performance will determine if remediation is primarily a matter of establishing a developmental level for a skill or re-education and retraining of a skill.

PLANNED REINFORCEMENT

Frequently the clinician is so intent on continuation of the developmental program that structured reinforcement of skills already developed is not considered. Skill introduction for the reader is an other-directed activity where the reader's participation is primarily responsive. Before mastery of a skill is accomplished, the application of that skill must be self-directed.

In the structured remedial program, the self-actualization, or the process of transference from clinician directed activities to learner directed activities becomes a matter of providing independent level reading to reinforce the level of developmental growth and self-directed skill activities at an independent level to provide reinforcement of specific skills.

TEACHING-LEARNING ENVIRONMENT

No remediation technique can be successful without careful consideration given to two major aspects of the teaching-learning environment: the span of concentration and the task-response time. The span of concentration of the disabled reader can be identified through the use of observation of behavior in tasks requiring sequencing of objects, ideas, or events, tolerance level for new word introduction, response to self-directed manipulative activities, and ability to reconstruct or record an experience. Initial remediation should be directed, within the frameworks of the appropriate method, to increasing the space of concentration.

The task-response time, while primarily acquired, can be an innate part of the learning style of the disabled reader. The resultant lack of speed in completing a task will result in an unsatisfactory relationship existing between the ability to decode and comprehend and the speed of perception or task-response time. The tasks in the remedial teaching-learning situation, with the exception of developmental level instruction, should be organized with the task-response factor in mind.

SUMMARY

The specific nature of remediation, as outlined in this chapter, becomes in essence, an extension of the diagnosis with educational objectives evolving from a careful study of learner behavior as examined from the reading task requirements, the approach to the reading task and the nature of the reading disability. The learner's approach to the teaching-learning situation will identify the method of instruction (visual-auditory, auditory-visual, linguistic word structure, language experience), the need for additional sensory involvement, the concentration span, and the task-response time. From the reading task requirements will come specific direction for a developmental program (determined by strengths) and a supportive skill program (determined by weaknesses) along with a reinforcement program (determined by the self-directed activity level of the reader). Examining the nature of the disability within the reading act will identify those behaviors of the reader in the remedial program that are developmental in nature as well as those behaviors that are remedial in nature.

Informal Testing

Carl J. Wallen, Ed.D.
Associate Professor of Education
Department of Curriculum and Instruction
University of Oregon
Eugene, Oregon

Reading tests can serve four functions in classrooms. First, they can be used as a basis for assigning grades. The highest scorer on a given test is assigned an A and the lowest scorer is assigned an F. The remainder of the class is distributed between the poles. Second, they can be used to identify children who particularly need additional instruction. Third, they can be used as a means of identifying the specific instruction appropriate for each child in a classroom. The test would enable the teacher to "start where the child is." Fourth, they can be used as a guide in selecting and organizing instruction. The test provides guidance in how to teach for a specific objective.

This chapter will deal with the second, third, and fourth uses of class-room tests.

Four types of reading tests will be discussed: standardized achievement, standardized diagnostic, informal diagnosis, and informal testing. Three criteria will be utilized in evaluating the four types of tests.

How well does the test identify children who particularly need additional instruction?

How well does the test identify the specific instruction appropriate for a given child?

How well does the test provide guidance in selecting and organizing the appropriate instruction?

The three criteria are based upon three of the four functions of class-room tests. The best classroom tests will be those which meet all three criteria. The three criteria are not met by three of the four types of classroom tests: standardized achievement, standardized diagnostic, and informal diagnosis. The informal testing procedures described in this chapter do meet the three criteria, primarily because the procedures were designed to meet the criteria.

194

STANDARDIZED ACHIEVEMENT TESTS

Overview

Standardized achievement tests are designed to rank individuals. Test items are selected which differentiate among children. Test items which all or nearly all children can do, as well as test items which only a few can do, are eliminated because they do not give much discrimination.

The only legitimate conclusion which can be made from an achievement test score is the relative placement of the score. If Johnny received the same score as the reported score for beginning third grade children, Johnny would receive a reading grade placement score of 3.1. Johnny's performance is the equivalent of the score reported for children in the third grade, first month. Mary's reading grade placement score of 3.5 signifies the equivalent of third grade, fifth month. Johnny scored lower than Mary. Mary scored higher than Johnny.

An achievement test score could be reported as a percentile. Johnny's reading grade placement score of 3.1 could have a percentile score of 45, indicating that forty-five percent of the people with whom Johnny is being compared performed more poorly than Johnny. Mary's reading grade placement score could have a percential score of 64, indicating that sixty-four percent of the people in the comparison group performed more poorly than Mary. Mary performed better than Johnny and sixty-four percent of the people in the comparison group. Eighteen percent of the people in the comparison group received scores which were higher than Johnny's and lower than Mary's.

The difference between the child's actual achievement and potential achievement can be determined by comparing his achievement test score with his aptitude test score. The California Short-Form Test of Mental Maturity (Sullivan, Clark, Tiegs, 1963) shows Anticipated Achievement Grade Placements for the ten areas of the California Achievement Tests (Tiegs and Clark, 1957). An Anticipated Achievement Grade Placement score for Reading Vocabulary of 5.2 indicates that Harry has the potential of attaining a grade placement score of 5.2 on the Reading Vocabulary subtest of the California Achievement Tests. If Johnny actually received a grade placement score of 4.2 on the Reading Vocabulary subtest, he is an underachiever. If he actually received a grade placement score of 5.8 on the Reading Vocabulary subtest, he is an overachiever, theoretically an impossibility.

Attainment of Criteria

Criterion one. Achievement tests meet the first criterion. When achievement tests are used alone, they identify the best and the poorest readers in any group, a school district, a school, or a classroom. When coordinated with certain aptitude tests, the two tests identify the difference between a child's actual and potential reading achievement. Achievement tests, especially when used in conjunction with aptitude tests, do enable the teacher to identify children who particularly need additional instruction. If Roger has an Anticipated Grade Placement score of 5.1 and an actual achievement grade placement score of 4.2, he needs additional instruction more than Susan who has an Anticipated Grade Placement score of 5.2 and an actual achievement grade placement score of 5.0.

Criterion two. Achievement tests do not meet the second criterion. An achievement test score does not indicate the specific instruction appropriate for a given child. A reading grade placement score of 3.2 on Word Meaning does not indicate whether Karen needs a specific lesson on *phonics-initial consonant blend br* or a specific lesson on *phonics-initial consonant digraph th* or both.

Criterion three. Achievement tests only partially meet the third criterion. A Reading Vocabulary grade placement score of 2.6 does in-

196

dicate a suitable initial placement for a child. The test does not indicate future placement. Mary might receive a grade placement score of 2.6 in October and a grade placement score of 3.5 in January. But achievement tests are seldom administered more than once a year or once every two years. The teacher is left to operate on the erroneous assumption that a child will make one month of progress for each month of school: 2.6 in October, 2.7 in November, 2.8 in December, and 2.9 in January. Mary's reading instruction will grow progressively more inappropriate until the next standardized reading achievement test is administered, twelve or twenty-four months hence.

A Reading Vocabulary grade placement score of 2.6 does not indicate how a vocabulary lesson should be organized and taught so that the child will score higher on the achievement test the next time. Achievement tests have no value in selecting and organizing specific instructional procedures.

STANDARDIZED DIAGNOSTIC TESTS

Overview

Standardized diagnostic tests are designed just like standardized achievement tests. Test items are selected because they differentiate between children. Test items are not selected because they indicate attainment of some particular reading skill objective.

The primary difference between diagnostic and achievement tests is in the number of reported subtest scores. The California Achievement Test reports three reading scores: Reading Vocabulary, Reading Achievement, and Total Reading. The Stanford Diagnostic Reading Test (Karlsen, Madden, Gardner, 1966) reports seven scores: Reading Comprehension, Vocabulary, Auditory Discrimination, Syllabication, Beginning and Ending Sounds, Blending, and Sound Discrimination. The actual differences between the two types of tests are often misunderstood. Subtests of diagnostic tests are identical with subtests of achievement tests. The Stanford Achievement Test: Reading (Kelly, Ruch, Terman, 1943) contains the same two subtests as the Stanford Diagnostic Reading test. What the Stanford Achievement Test: Reading calls Word Meaning and Paragraph Meaning is called Vocabulary and Reading Comprehension on the Stanford Diagnostic Test.

Tyler (1967) has criticized diagnostic tests because the test designers are so obsessed by the ranking of individuals that they have ignored what is the most important consideration in diagnostic tests, mastery. Mastery tests are not intended to provide scores that will rank individuals; rather, they are intended to separate students into two groups, those who can do a certain item and those who cannot do the item. When mastery scores are computed for groups, Tyler (1967) maintained that the scores should be reported in a binary fashion:

> *For the sample of seventeen-year old boys of higher socioeconomic status from rural and small town areas of the Midwest, it was found that: 93% could read a typical newspaper paragraph like the following. . . (p. 14)*

Attainment of Criteria

Criterion one. Diagnostic tests are not as useful as achievement tests for identifying children who particularly need instruction. Diagnostic tests do not allow for the determination of the actual and potential reading achievements because they are not coordinated with aptitude tests.

Criterion two. Diagnostic tests do not perform the one function for which they are supposedly designed. They do not indicate the specific instruction appropriate for a given child. The test does not specify tomorrow's reading lesson for the child scoring in the sixty-fourth percentile in Blending on the Stanford Diagnostic Reading Test. What is the teacher supposed to do tomorrow or the next day? The manual

198

for the Stanford Diagnostic Reading Test defines blending as "the ability to blend the sounds of a word after the word has been divided into meaningful elements and the sound of each element has been determined." Where does one begin teaching blending to a child scoring in the sixty-fourth percentile? Presumably, one begins at a different place from the one when teaching blending to a child scoring in the forty-third percentile. The only children the teacher can feel secure about are those scoring in the zero percentile—they need everything— and the children scoring in the ninety-ninth percentile—they need nothing.

Criterion three. Diagnostic tests meet the third criterion about as well as achievement tests. The grade placement scores can be used to indicate initial placement for a reader. Both types of tests lose their value if not administered three or more times a year.

INFORMAL DIAGNOSIS

Overview

Most reading methods texts describe procedures for informal diagnosis with the apparent assumption that, as Mazurkiewicz (1960) said, "No test score is diagnostic, nor are so-called diagnostic tests usually diagnostic. Diagnosis is the job of the teacher." Informal diagnosis generally accompanies formal standardized testing because, as Bond and Tinker (1957) noted, "The diagnosis of reading ability and deficiencies is best achieved through using standardized tests and procedures. It is possible, however, and sometimes desirable to make a preliminary diagnosis by less formal procedures." (p. 169) Bond and Tinker did not go on to justify even the *sometimes* use of informal diagnosis.

Informal diagnosis is conducted by obtaining samples of a child's language behavior. A child reads aloud, reads silently, listens, or writes. The teacher records the child's responses and performs one of two tasks. 1) The teacher compares the child's errors to established criteria and identifies appropriate level reading materials for the child. 2) The teacher interprets the child's errors as indicating the need for instruction in specific reading skills.

Reading levels. The identification of appropriate level reading materials for children has been clearly defined by Betts (1946). Betts called the procedure the Informal Reading Inventory. With the Informal Reading Inventory the teacher compares a child's oral and silent reading behavior with established criteria of reading levels for the purpose of identifying the child's independent, instructional and independent reading levels.

The three reading levels are defined in two ways: in terms of children's reading behavior and in terms of implications for instruction. The reading behavior of the instructional level is defined as that reading selection where the child correctly pronounces at least 95% of the words and correctly answers at least 75% of the comprehension questions asked by the teacher. If in reading a fifth level reader a child correctly pronounces 96% of the words and correctly answers 80% of the questions asked by the teacher, the child can be said to be reading instructionally at the fifth reader level. The instructional implication of the instructional level is defined as that reading level which is appropriate for organized reading instruction. The teacher should conduct reading instruction at the fifth reader level with a child whose instructional reading level is five.

Specific reading instruction. The identification of instruction for specific reading skills has never been clearly defined in reading methods texts. For example, in a text designed for remedial reading teachers, Bond and Tinker (1957) provide a sample Informal Diagnosis Blank which the teacher could use in recording and analyzing children's reading errors. The child reads aloud from word lists in selected readers. The teacher interprets the child's responses by completing the blanks shown in Figure 1.

200

FIGURE 1

Word Pronunciation from Word Lists in Basic Books (Bond and Tinker, 1957, p. 173)

1. Name and grade level of book_____
2. Nature of phonetic attack_____
3. Blending skill_____
4. Resorts to spelling attack_____
5. No method of word analysis_____
6. Skill in syllabication_____
7. Recognition of familiar parts_____
8. Recognition of parts of compound words_____
9. Recognition of word roots_____
10. Handling of suffixes_____
11. Handling of prefixes_____
12. Trouble with consonants_____
13. Trouble with vowels_____
14. Sounds omitted_____
15. Sounds added_____

Bond and Tinker do not provide any criteria which can be used in assigning children's responses to any of the categories, nor do they provide definitions of the categories which have instructional implications. The criteria for some categories can be presumed from the category names. An example of "Sounds Omitted" might be *sees/ see.* An example of "Sounds Added" might be *had/haved.* The names of most of the other categories give little direction for assignment of response to categories. In a later chapter on correcting word recognition difficulties, Bond and Tinker provide examples of appropriate instructional exercises, but the instructional exercises are not given the same names as the categories on the Informal Diagnosis Blank. Bond and Tinker do not provide instructional exercises which are appropriate for children identified as having "trouble with consonants" or "resorts to spelling attack." No wonder Bond and Tinker consider informal diagnosis of little value.

The same lack of direction appears in a text designed for classroom teachers (Veatch, 1966). The text describes the individualized reading method. In a chapter on teaching reading skills, Veatch describes a testing procedure where children's independent writing is interpreted. Figure 2 shows a sample of the spelling errors of two children and the categories to which Veatch assigned the errors.

FIGURE 2

INTERPRETING SPELLING ERRORS
(Veatch, 1966, pp. 360-361)

Spelling Errors		Instructional Interpretation	
Mary B.	Girl/gril	**Reversals**	
	are/out	Mary B.	girl/gril
George C.	quart/kwort	**Vowels Affected by r**	
	sing/sint	Mary B.	girl/gril
		George C.	quart/kwort
		Word Drill on Hard-To-Remember Words	
		George C.	quart/kwort
		Endings	
		George C.	sing/sint

Veatch gives no guidance in assigning spelling errors to instructional interpretation categories or in how to overcome any of the reading difficulties identified. The diagnosis appears to have little to do with instruction.

The inadequacies of the procedures for identifying specific reading instruction become clearer when compared with the procedures for identifying appropriate level reading materials. The steps involved in the two procedures are shown in Figure 3.

FIGURE 3

STEPS IN INFORMAL DIAGNOSIS

	Identifying Reading Levels	Identifying Specific Reading Instruction
STEP 1	Child reads aloud or silently from graded reading selections.	Child reads aloud from word lists or graded reading selections. Child spells words during independent writing.
STEP 2	The percentage of pronunciation and comprehension errors are computed. The data are then compared with the criteria for the three reading levels: independent, instructional, and frustrational.	(missing)
STEP 3	The child's reading level is identified for each graded reading selection. Level 2 may be independent and Level 4 may be instructional.	The child's reading errors are identified. A reading error may be identified as Reversals or Trouble with Vowels.
STEP 4	The categories are defined in terms of the appropriate instructional response. Reading instruction should be conducted at the instructional level. Independent reading should be conducted at the independent level.	(missing)

When informal diagnosis is used for identifying the appropriate levels of reading materials for a child, the procedures for conducting the diagnosis and the implications for instruction are clear. When informal diagnosis is used for identifying needed specific instruction, the procedures for conducting the diagnosis and the implications for instruction are so unclear that the whole procedure appears to be nothing more than unexamined intuition.

Attainment of Criteria

Criterion one. Informal diagnosis is not as useful as achievement tests for identifying children who particularly need instruction. Informal diagnosis could be used if achievement tests were not available, especially for identifying a child whose actual reading achievement (instructional reading level) was below his possible achievement level, as determined by a test of mental maturity. A fifth grade child with an IQ of 100 is an underachiever if his instructional reading level is third.

Criterion two. Informal diagnosis gives no help in identifying the specific instruction appropriate for a child. The reading methods texts which describe informal diagnosis do not suggest what lesson the teacher might have tomorrow for Mary B., who was diagnosed as needing instruction in reversals and vowels affected by *r* because she spelled girl as gril.

Criterion three. Informal diagnosis is only useful in selecting the appropriate level reading materials for a child. Informal diagnosis has an advantage over achievement tests and diagnostic tests because informal diagnosis can be conducted as often as necessary while the standardized tests are seldom conducted more than once a year. On the negative side, informal diagnosis provides the teacher no guidance in selecting and organizing instruction for specific reading skills.

INFORMAL TESTING

Informal testing was designed to remedy the inadequacies of standardized achievement tests, standardized diagnostic tests, and informal diagnosis. The three types of tests do not attain Criteria two and three: they do not enable the teacher to identify the specific reading skill instruction appropriate for each child, and they do not provide the teacher guidance in selecting and organizing the appropriate reading skill instruction.

The attractive notion of individualizing reading instruction can be realized only when teachers utilize classroom tests which meet Criteria two and three. When suitable tests are not available, teachers, whether in special remedial reading classrooms or in regular classrooms, have no recourse but to stick religiously to the manual or to abdicate responsibility for reading skill instruction. Those who follow the manual carry out the lesson prescribed on pages 15 and 16 of the manual, regardless of the children's actual reading skill attainments. The teacher may abdicate responsibility by depending exclusively upon the so-called programmed skill builders or by taking the position that children will learn reading skill on their own if only interesting books are provided.

Tests to Meet Criteria Two and Three

In order to meet Criteria two and three, a classroom test must provide procedures for relating observed pupil behavior to the appropriate reading skill instruction. The Informal Reading Inventory, described earlier, provides guidance in how children's behavior and reading skill instruction might be related. The Informal Reading Inventory relates pupil behavior to the appropriate level of reading materials through a four -step procedure for 1) observing the child reading graded reading selections; 2) analyzing the child's observed reading behavior by relating performance to criteria; 3) assigning a category name to the child's reading performance; and 4) selecting the appropriate level reading materials for the child.

Informal testing is the name given by the author to classroom testing procedures designed to accomplish with specific reading skills what the Informal Reading Inventory accomplished with reading levels. Informal testing provides procedures for relating a child's performance on specific skill tests to the selection and organization of instruction appropriate for those specific reading skills.

Informal testing provides the same four-step procedure as the Informal Reading Inventory. 1) The teacher observes a child doing a test designed for a specific reading skill. 2) The teacher analyzes the child's performance on the test. 3) The teacher categorizes the child's performance. 4) The teacher selects or organizes the appropriate reading skill instruction.

Informal testing, like the Informal Reading Inventory, is based upon a test designed for the purpose of the procedure. The Informal Reading Inventory consists of reading selections graded for difficulty level, because the inventory is used to determine the appropriate level of reading material for a child. The informal test consists of exercises for specific reading skills, because the informal test is used to determine the child's attainment of specific reading skills.

The designing and conducting of informal tests will be discussed in the remainder of this chapter.

Designing Informal Tests

Informal tests are designed according to Tyler's (1958) definition of an education test.

> *We now think of an education test as a series of situations which call forth from the student the kind of behavior defined in the*

objective and permit a record to be made of the student's actual behavior. . . . this means that the testing device would obtain a sample of the kind of behavior stated in the objective. (p.6)

Tests for specific reading skills are constructed by operationalizing reading skill objectives. The reading skill objectives are those identified in most reading methods tests, children's reading texts, and reading curriculum guides. A test for a specific reading skill objective is constructed by answering the question: How does a child behave who has attained the specific skill objective?

In order to relate a reading skill objective with instruction, the test must define a relationship between a category of reading skill objectives and a type of learning. Each type of learning would have a distinctive set of instructional conditions. By relating a category of reading skill to a learning type, the teacher is provided guidance in selecting and organizing instruction for a specific reading skill objective. If a child inadequately performs the test for a specific reading skill objective, which is related by definition to a type of learning, the teacher can select or organize instruction according to the instructional conditions specified by the type of learning. For further clarification of learning types and instructional conditions, see CONDITIONS OF LEARNING (Gagne, 1966).

The categories of reading skill objectives and the corresponding types of learning defined by the author are shown in Figure 4.

Informal tests for specific objectives belonging to the same category of reading skill will have the same test format. The test format is logically derived from both a definition of reading and a definition of learning types. The format of tests for sight word skill objectives will be consistent with a definition of reading and with the type of learning Gagne called verbal association. The format of tests for vocabulary will be consistent with a definition of reading and with the type of learning Ausubel called representational learning.

FIGURE 4

CATEGORIES OF READING SKILL OBJECTIVES
AND TYPES OF LEARNING

Category of Reading Skill	Type of Learning
Sight word skill	Verbal association (Gagne, 1966)
Visual discrimination skill	Multiple discrimination (Gagne)
Auditory discrimination skill	Multiple discrimination
Phonic word attack skill	Word attack (Wallen, 1969)
Structural word attack skill	Word attack
Syllabic word attack skill	Word attack
Vocabulary skill	Representational learning (Ausubel, 1968)
Recall skill	Propositional learning (Ausubel)
Interpretation skill*	Propositional learning
Extrapolation skill*	Propositional learning
Analysis skill*	Propositional learning
Rate skill	Propositional learning

*Adapted from Bloom (1956).

Informal tests designed for three specific reading skill objectives are shown in Figure 5. The three specific reading skill objectives all refer to the same category of reading skill, visual discrimination, so the three informal tests follow the same format.

The teacher need not accept the definition of visual discrimination given in Figure 5. What is important, however, is the identification of some test format which the teacher considers to be logically related to learning conditions. If the teacher fails to identify test formats which are related to instructional conditions, he will find that he will be able to identify children's specific reading skill deficiencies (Criteria two) but be unable to provide the appropriate instruction for the skill deficiency (Criteria three).

FIGURE 5

EXAMPLES OF INFORMAL TESTS FOR THREE READING SKILL OBJECTIVES BELONGING TO THE CATEGORY: VISUAL DISCRIMINATION

TEST 1

Reading Skill Objective
Visual discrimination of the initial consonant *b*
Exercise
Give each child the worksheet shown below. Ask the children to circle the word in each row which starts with the same letter as that italicized in the first word. A child should do the worksheet without help.

*b*oy/ toy dig but	*b*ang/ dunk bill pang
*b*ust/ big dust past	*b*an/ tan ball doll

Adequate Answer
In order to be considered adequate, a child must make no mistakes.

TEST 2

Reading Skill Objective
Visual discrimination of the initial consonant *m*
Exercise
Give each child the worksheet shown below. Ask the children to circle the word in each row which starts with the same letter as that italicized in the first word. A child should do the worksheet without help.

*m*an/ mope nill wan	*m*ill/ not me will
*m*ust/ but noon mean	*m*ole/ mine nail not

Adequate Answer
In order to be considered adequate, a child must make no mistakes.

TEST 3

Reading Skill Objective
Visual discrimination of the initial consonant blend *tr*
Exercise
Give each child the worksheet shown below. Ask the children to circle the word in each row which starts with the same two letters as those italicized in the first word. A child should do the worksheet without help.

*tr*ap/ tree twine tap	*tr*ip/ tip print tram
*tr*eat/ tweet trave dream	*tr*olly/ trump dolly twist

Adequate Answer
In order to be considered adequate, a child must make no mistakes.

Conducting Informal Tests

Once the informal test for a specific reading skill objective has been constructed, the conduct of the first three steps of informal testing is clear. 1) The teacher administers the informal test. With one of the informal tests shown in Figure 5, the children would be asked to do a worksheet. When the children finish the worksheet, the teacher would collect and correct them. 2) The teacher determines whether each child attained the criteria specified in the adequate answer. With any of the informal tests shown in Figure 5, a child must make no mistakes in order to have an adequate performance. 3) The teacher interprets each child's paper by making one of two possible conclusions: either the child passed the informal test and thus has attained the specific reading skill objective or the child failed the informal test and thus has not attained the specific reading skill objective. In informal testing a child's performance can be interpreted in only two ways: either the child needs instruction for the specific reading skill objective or he does not need instruction for the specific reading skill objective.

The fourth step for conducting informal tests is implied in the design of the informal test. The most appropriate instruction for a specific reading skill objective will be those instructional exercises which cause a child to pass an informal test he could not previously pass. The child would be given instruction for the specific reading skill objective, visual discrimination of the initial consonant *b,* if he failed an informal test designed for that objective. If instruction for the specific reading skill objective is successful, the child will be able to perform adequately on the next informal test designed for the objective. The second informal test would follow the same format as the first informal test, but different words would be used.

The most logically appropriate instruction for a specific reading skill objective will be instructional exercises which look like the test exercise. If a test exercise asks the child to point to words which look like the first word in a row—*b*oy/ toy dig but—then the instructional exercise should require the same response—*b*oat/ coat big dole. The primary difference between testing and instruction would be the guidance the teacher provides the child. The child starts the lesson unable to make the required visual discrimination. During the lesson the teacher provides the guidance which will enable the child to respond correctly to the instructional exercise. The distinction between testing and instruction is shown in Figure 6.

FIGURE 6

DIFFERENCE BETWEEN TESTING AND INSTRUCTION FOR ONE SPECIFIC READING SKILL OBJECTIVE

Reading Skill Objective
Visual discrimination of the initial consonant *b*

Test Exercise	**Instructional Exercise**
Ask the child to circle the word which begins with the same letter as that italicized in the first word. Give the child no assistance.	Provide the child guidance so that he will be able to circle the word which begins with the same letter as that italicized in the first word. The guidance might consist of tracing the first letter of all four words, or of comments about the look of the first letter—the *b* has a belly on the line and the belly faces the word, the *d* has a belly on the line and the belly faces away from the word. Continue giving guidance and new groups of words until the child can respond adequately.
*b*ust/ dill by past	*b*ean/ big dean pig

The less an instructional exercise resembles a test exercise, the more questionable the instruction. Instructional exercises containing pictures to be matched according to the way they look or the direction they face would be a very questionable instructional exercise for the reading skill objective, visual discrimination of the initial consonant *b.* The informal test for the visual discrimination objective, shown in Figure 5, did not contain pictures, it contained words. An instructional exercise having different drawings of houses which the child is supposed to match might be an appropriate instructional exercise for the objective, match drawings of houses. But house matching is a questionable procedure when the objective is to teach the child to match words beginning with the initial consonant *b.* If the teacher wishes to teach a child to match words beginning with the initial consonant *b,* then the teacher should provide instructional exercises where the child will have guided practice in matching words beginning with the initial consonant *b.*

SUMMARY

Three commonly used classroom tests—standardized achievement, standardized diagnostic, and informal diagnosis—do not provide the teacher with procedures for determining the specific reading skill instruction needed by a child and do not provide the teacher guidance in selecting and organizing instruction appropriate for specific reading skills.

Informal testing is designed to enable the teacher to determine specific skill needs and to provide the appropriate skill instruction. Informal testing is equally useful in regular classroom and in remedial classrooms.

REFERENCES

Ausubel, D. P. **Educational psychology: A cognitive view.** New York: Holt, Rinehart and Winston, Inc., 1968.

Betts, E. A. **Foundations of reading instruction.** New York: American Book Company, 1946.

Bloom, B. S. (Ed.) **Taxonomy of educational objectives.** New York: David McKay Company, Inc., 1956.

Bond, G. L., & Tinker, M. A. **Reading difficulties: Their diagnosis and correction.** New York: Appleton-Century-Crofts, Inc., 1957.

Gagne, R. M. **The conditions of learning.** New York: Holt, Rinehart and Winston, Inc., 1966.

Karlsen, B., Madden, R., & Gardner, E. **Stanford diagnostic reading test: Level I.** New York: Harcourt, Brace & World, Inc., 1966.

Kelly, T. L., Ruch, G. M., & Terman, L. M. **Stanford achievement test: Reading.** New York: World Book Company, 1943.

Mazurkiewicz, A. J. What does a test battery tell a teacher? **Proceedings** of the 41st and 42nd Annual Education Conferences held at the University of Delaware, 1959-60, **IX**, 91-94.

Sullivan, E. T., Clark, W. W., & Tiegs, E. W. **California test of mental maturity.** Monterey, California: California Test Bureau, 1957, 1963.

Tiegs, E. W., & Clark, W. W. **California achievement tests.** Monterey, California: California Test Bureau, 1957.

Tyler, R. W. What is evaluation? In H. M. Robinson (Ed.), **Evaluation of reading.** Supplementary Educational Monographs, The University of Chicago Press, Number 88, December 1958. Pp. 4-9.

Tyler, R. W. Changing concepts of educational evaluation. **Perspectives of curriculum evaluation.** American Educational Research Association Monograph Series. Chicago: Rand McNally & Company, 1967. Pp. 13-18.

Veatch, J. **Reading in the elementary school.** New York: The Ronald Press Company, 1966.

Wallen, C. J. **Word attack skills in reading.** Columbus, Ohio: Charles E. Merrill Publishing Co., 1969.

Determining Word Identification Difficulties

E. R. Sipay, Ph.D.
Reading Department
State University of New York
Albany, New York

The main purposes of this chapter are to discuss the skills and tacks involved in word identification; and to present a procedure for determining possible word identification difficulties.

It is probably easier for a reader to identify words whose meanings are known to him because he will need to apply fewer word identification skills; he will have a model with which he can compare his partial response and thereby receive some feedback about its correctness. However, word meaning (reading vocabulary) is not considered in great detail in this chapter because the ability to attach meaning to graphic symbols is not a prerequisite for pronouncing a word. That is, a reader need not know a meaning of a word in order to be able to pronounce the word(s). Of course, if the child does not have a usable understanding vocabulary, his comprehension of printed material will be limited and word analysis may become a meaningless activity.

The term *determining* rather than *diagnosing* is used because diagnosis denotes the ability to determine the exact causes of the disability. In the author's opinion, at the present time we very often are unable to pinpoint the contributing factors. Therefore, the following limitations of our knowledge concerning the reading act and our ability to diagnose a given child's word identification problems are readily admitted:

> We cannot state with certitude that we know exactly what sensory, perceptual, and cognitive processes occur when a given child is confronted by a word which he does not recognize immediately. It is quite possible that different children use different processes and/or information for arriving at the same response.

> Although there have been correlational and predictive studies and although logically there appears to be such a relationship, there is no clearly established cause-effect relationship between the skills at the various levels of difficulty outlined in the diagnostic procedure.

We do not know what level of competency in a subskill or what combination level of subskills is necessary for success in what is considered to be a higher level skill. For example, there is evidence that auditory and visual discrimination skills are related to success in reading; however, we do not know if there is a cutoff point below which a child will have extreme difficulty in learning to read. Then too, children vary in their ability to compensate for weaknesses. Furthermore, it is quite possible that the level of competency necessary for success depends, at least in part, on the approach used to teach reading.

We do not know exactly what effect certain factors (e.g., cognitive style, personality, receptive or expressive language handicaps) have upon the acquisition and use of the various word identification skills.

There is little evidence as to when a majority of children have acquired or should acquire a certain skill or what relative levels of skills exist at various levels of general reading ability.

The evidence is unequivocal as to the sequence in which all skills are acquired or should be taught. Some children seem to abstract and internalize generalizations before such skills are formally taught.

Although skills are discussed separately, they do not function in isolation. Many skills are combined in the complex act called reading. Furthermore, it is difficult, if not impossible, to obtain a pure measure of many skills. That is, other skills may enter into the task required of the subject. For example, when testing for visual discrimination, most likely the directions are given orally so that weak receptive language skills and poor short-term auditory memory are possible factors contaminating the obtained results.

Word identification is a complex process; therefore, it is not possible to be extremely accurate in isolating which skills or contributing factors are operating against the acquisition of the body of skills commonly known as word analysis or word identification.

The above limitations, however, do not preclude making an evaluation of a child's ability to perform certain tasks which presently are considered important in word identification. It is the author's belief that certain skills influence ability to perform what are defined as higher level word identification skills. Furthermore, it is believed that the subject can be presented with a task which can be defined in behavioral terms. Then, based upon the subject's performance, one can infer the presence or absence of the skills and perhaps gain some idea of the degree to which the skill is intact. Therefore, diagnosis involves determining as accurately as possible which word identification skills and subskills a subject does or does not display and how effectively he uses those he does employ.

The plan for determining word identification difficulties assumes there is a hierarchy of skills. Furthermore, it holds that acquisition of skills at one level influences success at the higher level. (Wiener and Cromer, 1967) And finally, the plan rests on the assumption that, within the limitation imposed by the tests available, the skills can be measured accurately. Verification of these assumptions needs to be obtained. For example, does specific instruction in a weak "lower level" skill result in or facilitate improved ability in a high level skill? (Silver, Hagin, and Hirsch, 1967)

WORD IDENTIFICATION SKILLS AND POSSIBLE TACKS

Reading is an associational process whereby the reader makes some mental response, perhaps accompanied by an emotional or physical response, to printed or written material. The printed words have no meaning in themselves; their meaning lies within the mind of the reader. In order for the reader to make the necessary associations (bring meaning to the words or comprehend them), he must recognize or identify these words as being in his understanding vocabulary or, perhaps make use of context clues to gain meaning.

It is very unlikely that anyone is ever taught directly every word that he needs to recognize at sight in order to become an independent efficient reader. Therefore, the individual must assimilate some procedure for identifying words which are not in his sight vocabulary. This chapter deals with determining the child's ability to identify words which are not recognized immediately. It treats the child's ability to decode — to pronounce correctly — rather than with the process of associating meaning with the printed words (reading vocabulary).[1] Hopefully the pronunciation leads to a correct association with meaning.

Word identification is a complex process which is not yet fully understood (Bryant, 1962). What follows undoubtedly is an over-simplification of the steps involved in word identification. In order to translate the graphic representations into their spoken counterpart, the individual probably goes through basically three steps; 1) he visually analyzes the word into elements; 2) he applies phonics to the separate elements which he does not recognize; and 3) he mentally blends (auditorily blends - visually synthesizes) the elements into a whole word which he can pronounce orally, subvocally, or mentally. The manner in which individuals go through these steps probably differs from child to child and may even differ from word to word when applied by the same child.

[1]There is some difference of opinion as to whether a word is or must be pronounced, either orally or subvocally or mentally, before meaning is or can be associated with it. In other words, does the reader go directly from the graphic representation to its meaning; or, is there an intermediate step involving the pronunciation of the word? Perhaps the first time, or after a varying number of exposures (depending upon the individual), a child encounters a printed word and pronounces or needs to pronounce the word. Perhaps such a step is necessary to obtain a model against which to monitor his response (giving correct meaning) because of the reinforcement with meaning supplied by the pronunciation. However, the use of, or need for, pronunciation may be reduced as the individual encounters the word more frequently.

Context

The context in which a word is set and the reader's oral language pattern (the probability that certain types of words or even the exact words are likely to occur) may assist the reader in determining the pronunciation or meaning of an unknown word (a word not recognized at sight).[2] It is possible for an individual to infer the meaning of a word without knowing the pronunciation of or even attempting to pronounce the word because the contextual setting makes it obvious. It should be pointed out, however, that, although words derive their exact meaning from context, the context does not necessarily reveal the word's meaning or pronunciation. Furthermore, such factors as intelligence, reading ability, experiential background, and language facility influence the ability to use context clues. Probably more often than not, the reader combines some other skill(s) with context clues as an aid to word identification. (Carter and McGinnis, 1962)

Configuration

Some use may be made of the word's configuration (i.e., its general outline). However, it is likely that "the pattern functions as a cue only when the words are familiar." (Anderson and Dearborn, 1952) Furthermore, a child who relies too heavily on configuration cues will never become an efficient independent reader. Therefore, it is likely that the good reader combines the use of configuration and context clues and even more likely that such cues are used in conjunction with the initial letters.

Substitution

At times, the child may use substitution principles; that is, he recog-

[2]As Wiener and Cromer (1967) pointed out, ". . . comprehension can facilitate identification if the reader has highly advanced language skills available, e.g., vocabulary, sequences, appropriate generating grammar, (in Chomsky's sense). To the extent that each of these skills facilitates identification by decreasing the range of possibilities of what is likely to occur in the written material, less information is necessary from the visual input to elicit the whole sequence."

nizes through visual analysis that the unknown word is similar to a known word except for one or a few letters. He then mentally substitutes known symbol-sound associations for the letter that is different in the unknown word. For example, if the unknown word is *bake*, the child may recognize that it is similar to the known word *take* except for the initial consonant. Provided that he can make the symbol-sound association for *b,* he can arrive at the correct pronunciation.[3]

Spelling

Some children, usually because they have been instructed to do so, spell out the word, that is, name each letter in a left to right sequence. This technique appears to work fairly efficiently for some children when dealing with short monosyllabic words; however, difficulty often arises when they are confronted by longer words, particularly those which are polysyllabic.

Little Words

Other children, perhaps because they were taught to do so, look for the *little* word in the *big* word. *Although this method may work with some words, it does not have a high utility ratio.*

Visual Analysis—Phonics-Blending

Although aspects of this procedure occur in the previously mentioned tacks (e.g., in substitution, visual analysis is used when the similarity and differences are recognized within the graphic representation of the unknown word, phonics are utilized when the known sounds are substituted for the different elements, and blending takes place in order to pronounce the word), this procedure is categorized separately because of the variety of tacks a child may take. Some possible tacks are:

[3]After applying word identification skills, the child should be encouraged to ask himself two guiding questions: 1) "Does it sound like a word I know?" and 2)"Does it make sense in this sentence?"

Visual analysis of the whole word (e.g., unscramble = un scram ble)

Application of phonics to all elements necessary[4] (e.g., un = ŭn; scram = skrăm; ble = b'l)

Visual analysis of an element (e.g., un)

Application of phonics to that element (e.g., un = ŭn)

Repetitions of steps 1 and 2 (e.g., scram, scram = skrăm; ble, ble = b'l)

Blend the elements into a whole word (e.g., ŭn + skrăm = ŭnskrăm; ŭnskrăm + b'l = ŭnskrămb'l)

Visual Analysis. Visual analysis is the term used by Bond and Tinker (1967) to indicate the ability to see the structural elements in words. Some authors refer to this ability as structural analysis; others consider it as a part of phonics. Perhaps the term *visual-mental* would be more appropriate because, although there is a visual component to the act, the process takes place mentally (as do other processes in word identification). Furthermore, the component parts must be kept in mind (therefore attention and short-term memory may become factors) because, in the reading act, there are no extraneous visual cues telling where the word should be divided or was divided by the individual (except for words hyphenated at the end of a line of print). Be that as it may, the term *visual analysis* will be used in this chapter.

As the child views the word, he employs his ability at visual analysis to "break down" the word into some component parts which are

[4]The sequence in which this and other steps are done may vary. For example, the child may focus first on the root words and their component parts and then proceed to the affixes. Probably, however, the most efficient and least confusing procedure would involve a left to right sequence. Application of phonics may be the first step for a child who employs single letter phonics (e.g., pronounces the sound of each letter).

known units to which he can also apply his skills at phonic analysis. Basically, he may (not *should*) divide the word into the following:

Root (base) word(s) and affixes, including derived or inflected forms [5]

Syllables (which may be roots or affixes)

Common elements (which may be affixes or phonograms)

Letter combinations
    Consonant blends
    Consonant digraphs
    Vowel digraphs
    Vowel diphthongs
    Vowels modified by *r*
    Silent letter combinations

Single letter
    Consonants
    Vowels

Although there is no infallible method of determining in what ways a child attempts to visually analyze an unknown word, it is likely that he divides it into the largest units of pronunciation or meaning he can handle. Possibly some children attempt to analyze words into syllables most of the time and only on occasion find it necessary to break down the syllable into component parts in order to arrive at a pronunciation. Even for such children, differences in mode of operation probably exist. Some may attempt to apply only a few syllabication generalizations; others may attempt to apply many such generalizations but apply only one or two efficiently. On the other hand, some may only attempt to analyze words into units smaller than syllables. There

[5]There are generalizations concerning inflected endings.

223

also are those who have not assimilated any consistent or efficient method of visual analysis as well as those who never attempt any type of visual analysis. And there are children who analyze almost every word they encounter. Over-analysis also can be a problem.

Although we are never certain as to how a child visually analyzes an unknown word, there are syllabication generalizations which are fairly commonly taught in the schools. The wording of the generalizations varies from program to program as does the sequence in which, and rapidity with which they are introduced. Though most children have been exposed, they may not have assimilated many of the major syllabic generalizations by the fourth grade.

Blending. Blending, sometimes referred to as synthesis or fusion, is the ability to blend the separate sounds together to form a word. After the child has visually analyzed the word and applied phonics to those elements not immediately recognized, he must hold in mind his responses to the separate elements and, proceeding from left to right, visually synthesize or mentally blend the elements into a word which he can pronounce orally, subvocally, or mentally.

It would seem that visual skills such as perception, discrimination, and memory and the ability to make the necessary left to right eye movements are factors which may influence the ability to blend. Beyond that, it is difficult to state exactly what factors are involved. Perhaps similar factors are involved in visual synthesis (the ability to blend parts into a whole when looking at a whole word) as are in auditory blending (the ability to blend the parts of spoken words into a whole). Certainly there are differences in the tasks, but since auditory blending appears to be related to neuro-physiological development, perhaps visual blending is also a function of maturation. The age at which auditory blending ability occurs varies and the extent to which competency in blending is influenced by instruction is not known. (Roswell and Chall, 1956)

Systematic Coordination

A child must not only be able to perform the separate tasks involved in word identification, but also must possess the ability to systematically coordinate the skills. It is feasible that a child may display adequate ability when tested on the separate skills but yet be unable to "put them all together" to a degree that will allow him to identify unknown words.

Associated Factors

Undoubtedly there are factors associated with success and style in word identification which have not been discussed in this chapter. Such factors as intelligence, language facility, motivation, cognitive style, attention to the task, and psychological make-up[6] may influence the ability to identify words. At the present time, however, it is not known to what extent these factors are operative.

PROCEDURE FOR DETERMINING POSSIBLE DIFFICULTIES

Outline and Rationale

It would be desirable to arrange the tasks involved in word identification in a hierarchical system because failure to reach a certain level on a lower level skill implies that the higher level skills will not be well learned. Unfortunately, however, it presently is not known what level of competency in a lower level skill is necessary for success at what might be considered the next higher level, nor is it known if strength in one factor compensates for weakness in another. In fact, there is little research evidence that good and poor readers differ greatly in the skill areas. Except for the classification of errors, what follows is an attempt to order the tasks involved in word identification from what appears to be the highest to lowest level. Theoretically, the skills

[6]Refer to Kagan (1965) for a discussion of the possibility that one factor, reflection-impulsivity, may influence a child's behavior on word pronunciation or recognition tests.

measured in steps 3 to 5 influence the ability measured in the first step. Likewise, the skills measured in steps 6 to 8 are felt to influence those measured in the preceding steps. The order of the tasks also was influenced to some extent by the frequency with which certain types of weaknesses are encountered.

It is recommended that except when it is anticipated that failure will adversely influence test performance, testing begin at the highest level — correct word pronunciation — and proceed toward the lowest level until the child's difficulties have been determined, that is, until an estimate has been made that skills at a lower level(s) are adequate. The procedure is outlined as follows:

1. Word pronunciation

2. Classification of errors

3. Visual analysis and Phonics

4. Blending

5. Discrimination
     visual
     auditory

6. Visual acuity

7. Visual perception

8. Visual memory

The rationale for so ordering the tasks includes these considerations:

The highest level of word identification is displayed by the ability to pronounce correctly words which are not recognized at sight.

If the child cannot pronounce unknown words correctly, he may be unable to:

make the necessary symbol-sound associations (phonics)

visually analyze the words

blend the parts into a whole

The child may not be able to use phonics because he cannot apply or perhaps even does not know the generalizations and principles involved in making the symbol-sound association.

The child may not be able to associate sounds with symbols because of weak auditory or visual discrimination; that is, if the child has difficulty distinguishing visually between and among visual stimuli (in this case, letters and words), it will be very difficult to learn which grapheme signals certain sounds. Likewise, if the child has difficulty distinguishing between and among auditory stimuli, it will be difficult to learn what sounds should be assigned to a certain grapheme. Visual discrimination may also influence visual analysis.

The child may be weak in visual or auditory discrimination because of poor acuity. A child whose keenness of hearing or seeing is impaired may have difficulty discriminating because he is not seeing or hearing the stimuli properly. For example, a child with a hearing loss in a certain range may not be able to discriminate among the speech sounds in that range. Visual acuity also may influence visual analysis.

A child who is weak in the other visual skills may be weak in visual perception. If the visual images are distorted or inconsistent, acuity and more likely discrimination may be affected.

A child who is extremely weak in the above tasks may be having difficulty storing and retrieving stimuli which were visually or auditorily received. A child who has a poor or no memory of previously seen or heard stimuli would find it almost impossible to perform most of the higher level tasks.

It is realized that some of the factors listed as being lower in order can be influenced by higher level abilities. For example, visual memory may be influenced by visual perception; for, if the percepts are distorted or constantly changing, the memory of the percepts very probably will be affected.

The following are the suggested steps in determining possible word analysis problems. If the examiner has valid evidence that the child is weak or strong in any of the tasks, further testing is not necessary.

Step 1: Word Pronunciation.

Task. To pronounce correctly words presented in an untimed situation.

In order to perform this task, the child must possess a majority of the skills discussed (depending on the words presented and the tack taken by the child). An untimed situation is employed because timed presentation involves speed of recognition; and, except for the child who is over-analytical,[7] the individual who has difficulty with words is further handicapped by presenting the stimuli for only short durations.

Test. The ability to pronounce unknown words may be checked by having the child read words in isolation or in context. Except when

---

[7]The child who attempts to analyze almost every word he encounters may do better when the words are flashed because he is forced to respond quickly to the stimuli.

nonsense syllables are used, there is no way to predetermine[8] exactly which words a given child will or will not be able to recognize at sight.

Words in isolation. Presenting words in isolation rules out the subject's use of context as an aid to word identification. In this sense, it is a purer measure of his ability to pronounce unknown words, albeit one which is less similar to the actual reading situation. Use of words in isolation may uncover a child who is heavily reliant on context clues. Also, it rules out the possibility that the testee is distracted by the other words which occur in context. If words in isolation are used, the child's ability to use context and language cues also should be checked.

Either real words or nonsense syllables can be used as stimuli. If real words are employed, it is difficult to ascertain whether delayed (a rough cut-off point is three seconds) correct responses are a result of slow recognition or an application of word identification skills.

If nonsense syllables are used they should be readily pronounce-able and in general follow the orthography found in real words (e.g., "cxa" would be difficult to pronounce and the "cx" pattern is un-usual).

Whether real or nonsense words are used, the task should progress from easy to the more difficult. In the case of real words, perhaps the majority of the initial words should be commonly used words or words which are monosyllabic "phonetically correct" words involving single consonants and vowels, progressing to consonant and vowel com-binations and then to polysyllabic words.

It is advisable to engage the subject in conversation prior to testing

---

[8]The words introduced in the materials used in school might be used as a guide. However, it should be understood that the term "new word" simply means that is has not been used in that text before. In some cases new words are better known by the child than are certain "old words."

not only to establish rapport but also to estimate his verbal facility and his pronunciation of words. The obtained information better enables the examiner to evaluate the child's performance. Because the subject's pronunciation differs from that of the examiner does not necessarily mean that the child has decoding problems. The examiner must consider the subject's regional or cultural dialect because people from different parts of the country and from different sub-cultures pronounce sounds differently, particularly vowel sounds. In such cases, the "mispronunciation" of the printed symbol probably does not indicate an inability to make the "proper" symbol-sound association, but rather that the subject has correctly translated the printed symbol into its spoken counterpart in accordance with his own dialect. A somewhat similar situation occurs with certain sub-cultural speech patterns in which word endings often are omitted and in which there frequently is lack of noun-verb agreement. When reading, the individual may perceive the letters and words correctly but pronounce them in accordance with his oral speech pattern.

Word pronunciation tests may be found in the following tests: Botel, 1961; Durrell, 1955; Gates and McKillop, 1962; Monroe, 1932; Roswell and Chall, 1963; Spache, 1963.[9]

Words in context. When words are presented in context, the child may use context and language cues to infer the pronunciation of words not recognized at sight and thus have to rely less on other word identification skills. A comparison of the child's performance on isolated words with words in context may reveal the extent to which a child makes use of or relies on context as an aid.

[9]All these tests do not measure exactly the same skills, because they require differing tasks. The same is true for the tests listed in the other areas. There are other test which also measure the skills listed in the procedure. Listing a test in this chapter does not indicate endorsement.

The ability to pronounce words in context may be evaluated by having the child read from a book of appropriate difficulty or by administering an informal reading inventory or a standardized oral reading test. (Durrell, 1955; Roswell and Chall, 1963; Gilmore, 1952; Gray, 1963; Spache, 1965)

An analysis of the child's performance on tests which require him to attempt pronunciation of words which are not recognized at sight may reveal a weakness in this area. If so, the testing should continue to determine the child's strengths and weaknesses in the subskills.

Step 2: Classification of Errors

One factor which may influence the child's performance is the level of difficulty of the material. A child may make errors in reading material at his frustration level that he would not make in reading material at his instructional or independent levels. (Betts, 1946) It is therefore suggested that the word recognition errors be classified as to the reader level or level of the selection at which they were made. It also should be recognized in analyzing the child's performance, either with isolated words or words in context, that: 1) a child cannot display his ability (or lack of ability) if words that call for that skill are not presented (e.g., a child may be weak in consonant digraphs; but, unless words containing digraphs appear in the stimuli, he cannot display this weakness); and 2) if the words used contain a large number of one or a few types of elements with which the child has difficulty, he may appear to be poorer in word pronunciation than he really is. In short, the stimuli words may influence the obtained results. It should be further realized that one cannot expect most children to be able to perform tasks which involve skills they have not been taught.

When the word pronunciation testing has been completed, the errors made can be classified into four major categories:[10] 1) mispronuncia-

[10]Refer to Kerfoot (1965) for a more detailed plan for oral reading analysis.

231

tion - substitutions, 2) words pronounced for the child, 3) omissions and 4) additions.

Mispronunciations - substitutions. Some writers distinguish between mispronunciations, words that are not pronounced correctly and do not fit the meaning of the sentence (e.g., *horse* for *house*), and substitutions or words that are incorrectly pronounced but whose meaning fits the context (e.g., *home* for *house*). There could be two categories instead of one, or all words which are pronounced incorrectly can be placed into one category and then the errors can be checked to compare the number of relevant (errors allowed the child while retaining the meaning of the sentence) with the number of irrelevant mispronunciations-substitutions. Of course, judgments as to this type of difficulty only can be made if words are presented in context. Frequent substitution of words having irrelevant meaning may be due to not being aware that context can be used as a clue to word pronunciation.

The errors also may be classified as to the position in which they occur: initial, medial, final, and mixed or complete.[11] Errors are more likely to occur in the final position than in the medial, and more likely in the medial than in the intial position. [Ed. note: Many believe medial errors are most frequent.] Pronunciations which reflect regional or cultural dialects should not be counted as word recognition errors because the child probably is only responding to his own language cues.

According to Bond and Tinker (1967), initial errors indicate that the child as he inspects words is neglecting to notice the beginnings of words closely enough, while medial errors may be brought about by hurried inspection of unfamiliar words to a point where he neglects the middle of words; or they may be the result of limited knowledge

[11]Since the same incorrect response may appear in more than one category, (e.g., nonphonic, irrelevant, medial position; *don* for done) care should be exercised in tallying the total number of errors lest an error be counted more than once. Errors of omissions and additions also may be classified into these categories.

of vowel sounds. Errors in the final position may be due to a lack of attention to word endings or difficulty with inflected endings or errors in suffixes. Errors of the mixed type may indicate that the child is relying on one element, usually the initial letter (which indicates that he at least has those phonics skills), and guessing at the rest of the word, frequently without regard to meaning. Complete substitutions often are of two types: substitution of similar parts of speech (e.g., *a* for *the* or vice versa) and completely irrelevant words.

A judgment also should be made as to the frequency and type of reversal errors. Young children frequently make reversals, but it is not until they persist into the second grade that there is much need for concern. Reversals may involve single letters (e.g., rotations such as *b-d-p-q* and inversions such as *u-n*), transposition of letters (e.g., *girl* for *grill*), or complete word reversals (e.g., *saw* for *was*).

Words pronounced for child. Children for whom a number of words have been pronounced may be weak in word identification skills or may be unwilling to attempt unknown words (they may possess few or many word identification skills). Some children have learned either to overrely on the teacher when confronted by an unknown word or have learned that if they make no attempt, they cannot fail. In any case, if the analysis of errors indicates words frequently were pronounced for the subject, word identification skills should be checked in detail.

Omissions. When reading words either in isolation or in context, the child may omit parts of words or whole words (the latter is more likely to occur when words are presented in context). Parts of words may be omitted because of carelessness or the inability to pronounce an element, or the pronunciation may reflect a speech pattern (e.g., the frequent omission of final *s*). Complete words may be omitted because of carelessness or the inability to pronounce the word or an element, or because the child did not anticipate the word occurring in a particular sequence of words. The latter type of error is not a common one. Therefore, omissions usually reflect a lack of ability or carelessness. When groups of words are frequently omitted, it may indicate an inability to keep place along a line of print or a faulty return sweep.

Additions. Occasionally children add parts of words or complete words. The latter is found only when reading words in context. For the most part, additions are caused by carelessness and unless they occur frequently or distort meaning, there is little need for concern. Additions may be the result of inattention to the details within words, most frequently in the final position.

Step 3: Visual Analysis and Phonics

If the child is unable to pronounce a word, a comparison should be made between the manner in which the word should be divided and the apparent division indicated by his pronunciation of the word, especially when polysyllabic words are employed. In such cases the child may:

Syllabicate the word correctly (in accord with the commonly taught generalizations) and pronounce the word in accord with they syllabication, an indication that he can apply a syllabication generalization, phonics, and has the ability to blend.

Syllabicate the word correctly and mispronounce the word, an indication that he has good visual analysis skill but is weak in phonic or blending skills.

Syllabicate the word incorrectly but pronounce the word correctly, an indication that the child really is not aware of where or why he syllabicated the word as he did.

Syllabicate and pronounce the word incorrectly but pronounce it in accord with the manner in which he syllabicated the word, an indication of weak visual analysis but adequate phonic skills and blending ability.

Syllabicate and pronounce certain elements within the word incorrectly, an indication of weak visual and phonic analysis but with adequate blending ability.

Syllabications tests may be found in Bond, Clymer, and Hoyt (1955), Botel (1961), Gates and McKillop (1962), Karlsen, Madden, and Gardner (1966), and McCullough (1963). Whatever test is employed, an analysis should be made to determine which generalizations the child can and cannot apply consistently. Tests of visual analysis with root words and affixes are contained in Bond, Clymer, and Hoyt (1955) and McCullough (1963).

There are some children who may have difficulty pronouncing words correctly, not because of any basic weakness in visual analysis, phonic analysis, or blending, but rather because they seem to forget where they divided the word. If such a situation is suspected, the child can be presented with words which have been marked off or separated into syllables (e.g., *be/gan* or *be gan*) and asked to pronounce them. The same test may be employed to check the phonic and blending skills of children who are weak in visual analysis. If a child can pronounce correctly only words that have been marked off or separated, he probably has difficulty in visual analysis or in remembering where he divided the word. The child with the latter type of problem is able to relate correctly where he would divide the word.

Step 4: Blending

Task. To blend or fuse word parts into wholes.

Test. The ability to blend word parts into whole words may be checked in various ways depending to some extent on the other skills which the

235

child possesses. In some cases, blending testing can be combined with tests of visual analysis and phonics.

If the child has phonic skills, he can be asked to pronounce each element after the word has been divided into components in the visual analysis test and then asked to blend the elements into a whole word. If the child is weak in making symbol-sound associations or if the examiner does not wish to introduce this aspect of testing, the following procedure may be employed:

Pronounce the first element for the child.

Ask the child to repeat what he heard in order to determine if he heard the element properly (speech reproduction also may be a factor).

Steps one and two are repeated.

Ask the child to blend the two elements (auditory memory and attention become factors).

Steps one and two are repeated.

Ask the child to blend his response from step four with the response from step five (the response may be repeated for child).

Steps are repeated as often as necessary.

Some examiners may prefer to repeat steps one and two until all elements have been pronounced and then ask the child to blend them into a whole word. The differences in procedures may produce different results depending upon such factors as the child's attention to the task and his auditory memory because in one instance he must remember only the pronunciation of the last element and the present one and in the other all of the elements must be recalled at once.

The cause(s) of the inability to blend elements into wholes is unknown. Durrell (1955) speculated that the child may enunciate the phonic units so slowly, focusing attention upon them as completely isolated units, that they defy integration into a total word sound. Another possibility was offered by Vernon (1957) who wrote, "The inability to blend speech sounds correctly to form words may be due in part to poor perception of temporal order (succession of letter sounds) and rhythm."

If the child has difficulty blending elements which are presented visually, his auditory blending ability can be tested. On such tests, the examiner pronounces word parts with intervening pauses and then asks the child to pronounce the word he has heard. No visual stimuli are involved. Auditory blending may be a subskill involved in visual blending. The child probably must hear the sounds and blend them together mentally before he gives a response to an unknown printed word. It should be remembered that 1) auditory blending apparently is a function of maturation (Roswell and Chall, 1963) and 2) the obtained results may be influenced by the words used in the test (the parts of some words are not easily pronounceable or require the inclusion of additional speech sounds such as the schwa) and the enunciation and pronunciation of the tester.

The following tests are or contain tests of visual synthesis: Bond, Clymer, and Hoyt (1955), Gates and McKillop (1962), and Karlsen, Madden, and Gardner (1966). Auditory blending tests are found in McCullough (1963), Gates and McKillop (1962), and Roswell and Chall (1963).

Step 5a: Visual Discrimination

Task. To distinguish visually (to see likenesses and differences) between and among visual stimuli which are in view.

Test. Barrett's (1965) review of the research led him to formulate three generalizations: 1) visual discrimination of letters and words has a somewhat higher predictive relationship with first grade reading achievement than does visual discrimination of geometric designs and pictures; 2) several tasks requiring discrimination of geometric designs and pictures have predictive possibilities and warrant additional study; and 3) there is no clear-cut information as to whether discrimination of letters or discrimination of words has a superior relationship with early reading achievement. As is the case with auditory discrimination, there is no evidence of cause and effect relationship nor is it known what level of visual discrimination is required for success in word identification. Still, it seems logical to assume that poor visual discrimination may impair the ability to make symbol-sound associations because the child needs to be able to distinguish among and between letters in order to associate the sounds with those letters. Because of the possibility that it may be a contributing factor to poor phonics skills, the child's visual discrimination should be checked.

Step 5b: Auditory Discrimination

Task. To distinguish auditorily (to hear likenesses and differences) among and between phonemes.

Test. The author uses the Wepman Auditory Discrimination Test (1958) which has norms for five- to eight-year-olds and supplements it with the subtest involving vowel sounds from the informal test suggested by Schack (1962) because the Wepman contains only a few items on vowel sounds. Other tests of auditory discrimination may be found in Gates and McKillop (1962) and Roswell and Chall (1956).

238

Step 6. Visual Acuity

Task. To see visual stimuli clearly.

Test. The research (Malmquist, 1968; Flom, 1963) has not established visual defects as a major causal factor. In fact, Arner (1966) stated that the only consistent correlation with reading disability from an optometric viewpoint is binocular instability. However, this does not rule out the possible need for a visual examination. As Gates (1947) pointed out,

> In general, the safe point of view to take is this: printed words are small objects and some of them. . .are very much alike. Defects in vision even if they do not cause conspicuous errors in word recognition may make the activity more difficult and in any event are likely to make continuous reading more fatiguing and less satisfying. The child who can maintain clear vision only by means of effort may be subject to eyestrain, irritation, general fatigue, and restlessness. Not only in reading but in other phases of school work it is important to detect all defects and deficiencies in vision and to correct them whenever possible.

The reading specialist or school psychologist should not attempt to diagnose visual defects. They can, however, give some visual screening tests. Peters (1963) has written a comprehensive chapter on vision screening, and Harris (1961) and Bond and Tinker (1967) discuss procedures for visual screening.

If a child fails a visual screening test, a problem arises as to whom he should be referred. The dilemma was best summarized by Peters (1963):

> There are other conflicts, too, such as: who should be responsible for vision screening, public health or education; who should do the screening, laymen, teachers, nurses, optometrists, or oph-

thalmologists; how should referrals be made, by whom and to whom? Even the need for any vision screening is questioned by some.

There is a particularly debilitating conflict between optometry and ophthalmology, a conflict that more often than not leads to confusion and frustration in developing a vision-screening program. Ophthalmologists reflect their interest and training in eye pathology, squint (an amblyopia), and the more gross refractive errors by insisting (Vaughan, 1960) that "visual acuity testing with the Snellen chart is the only important test which need be performed in the schools." Or, as stated by Foote (1954), "The Snellen test, combined with careful teacher observation, is recommended." Optometrists reflect their interest and training in functional vision performance and particularly their interest in near point performance by insisting that vision screening include not only visual acuity but also tests of coordination between the two eyes, ability to maintain adequate focus at the near point, identification of refractive errors that produce stress in the visual system, as well as organic integrity. These two points of view are not easily reconciled, and great tact, patience, and understanding are required of all parties to arrive at a mutually satisfactory program. [12]

Each examiner will have to reconcile the problem of visual screening and referrals based upon the best available information.

Step 7: Visual Perception

It is impossible to define the task or tasks involved in visual perception. In the literature, it seems to be defined on the basis of the task(s) re-

[12]Refer to Campion (1965) for an ophthalmologist's viewpoint on visual problems and reading disorders.

quired on the test used to measure visual perception. When measured, the tasks often require motor skills. Moreover, the relationship between visual-perceptual or visual-motor skills to reading ability has not been clearly established. (Cohen, 1966; Olsen, 1966a, b) This is another area requiring more intense research, especially with the increasing number of visual perception tests on the market.

Step 8: Visual Memory

Task. To recall and identify visual stimuli which are no longer in view.

Test. As best as can be determined by the author, the available tests of visual memory (without calling for an association) involve short term or immediate memory.

REFERENCES

Anderson, Irving H., & Dearborn, Walter F. **The psychology of teaching reading.** New York: Ronald Press Co., 1952.

Arner, Robert S. **A rationale for developmental testing and training.** Duncan, Oklahoma: Optometric Extension Program, Inc., 1966.

Bailey, Mildred H. The utility of phonic generalizations in grades one through six. **Reading Teacher,** Feb. 1967, **20,** 413-418.

Barrett, Thomas C. The relationship between measures of pre-reading visual discrimination and first grade reading achievement: A review of the literature. **Reading Res. quart.,** Fall 1965, **1,** 51-76.

Betts, Emmett Albert. **Foundations of reading instruction.** New York: American Book Company, 1946.

Birch, H. G., & Belmont, L. Auditory-visual integration in normal and retarded readers. **Amer. J. Orthopsychiat.,** Oct. 1964, **34,** 852-861.

Birch, H. G., & Belmont, L. Auditory-visual integration, intelligence, and reading ability in school children. **Percept. mot. Skills,** Feb. 1965, **20,** 295-305.

Bond, Guy L., Clymer, Theodore, & Hoyt, Cyril J. **Silent reading diagnostic tests.** Chicago: Lyons and Carnahan, 1955.

Bond, Guy L., & Tinker, Miles A. **Reading difficulties: Their diagnosis and correction.** New York: Appleton-Century-Crofts, 1967.

Botel, Morton. **Botel reading inventory.** Chicago: Follett Publishing Co., 1961.

Bryant, N. Dale. Reading disability: Part of a syndrome of neurological dysfunctioning. **Challenge and experiment in reading,** International Reading Association Conference Proceedings, 1962, **7,** 139-143.

Campion, George S. Visual problems and reading disorders. In R. Flowers, et al. (Eds.), **Reading disorders: A multidisciplinary symposium.** Philadelphia: F. A. Davis Co., 1965. Pp. 41-44.

Carter, Homer L. J., & McGinnis, Dorothy J. **Teaching individuals to read.** Boston: D. C. Heath and Co., 1962.

Clymer, Theodore. The utility of phonic generalizations in the primary grades. **Reading Teacher,** Jan. 1963, **16,** 252-258.

Clymer, Theodore, & Barrett, Thomas C. **Clymer-Barrett prereading battery.** Princeton, N. J.: Personnel Press, 1967.

Cohen, Ruth I. Remedial training of first grade children with visual perceptual retardation. **Educ. Horizons,** Winter 1966, **45,** 60-63.

Cordts, Anna D. **Phonics for the reading teacher.** New York: Holt, Rinehart and Winston, Inc., 1965.

Durrell, Donald. **Durrell analysis of reading difficulty.** Yonkers-on-Hudson, New York: World Book Co., 1955.

Durrell, Donald D. **Improving reading instruction.** Yonkers-on-Hudson, New York: World Book Co., 1956.

Dykstra, Robert. Auditory discrimination abilities and beginning reading achievement. **Reading Res. quart.,** Spring 1966, **1,** 5-34.

Emans, Robert. The usefulness of phonic generalizations above the primary grades. **Reading Teacher,** Feb. 1967, **20,** 419-425. (a)

Emans, Robert. When two vowels go to walking and other such things. **Reading Teacher,** Dec. 1967, **21,** 262-269. (b)

Flom, Bernice C. The optometrist's role in the reading field. In Monroe Hirsch and Ralph Wick (Eds.), **Vision of children: An optometric symposium.** Philadelphia: Chilton Books, 1963. Pp. 371-398.

Flowers, Arthur, & Crandell, Edwin W. Relations among central auditory abilities, socio-economic factors, speech delay, phonic abilities and reading achievement. Cooperative Research Project No. 6-8313. May be obtained from ERIC.

Flower, Richard M. Auditory disorders and reading disorders. In Richard Flower, et al. (Eds.), **Reading disorders: A multidisciplinary symposium.** Philadelphia: F. A. Davis Co., 1965. Pp. 81-102.

Flower, Richard M. The evaluation of auditory abilities in the appraisal of children with reading problems. Mimeographed.

Gates, Arthur I., & McKillop, Ann S. **Gates-McKillop reading diagnostic tests.** New York: Bureau of Publications, Teachers College, Columbia University, 1962.

Gates, Arthur I. **Gates reading readiness tests.** New York: Bureau of Publications, Teachers College, Columbia University, 1939.

Gates, Arthur I. **The improvement of reading.** New York: Macmillan Co., 1947.

Gilmore, John V. **Gilmore oral reading test.** New York: Harcourt, Brace and World, 1952.

Gray, William S. **Gray oral reading tests.** Indianapolis, Indiana: Bobbs-Merrill Co., Inc., 1963.

Harris, Albert J. **Effective teaching of reading.** New York: David McKay, 1962.

Harris, Albert J. **How to increase reading ability.** New York: David McKay, 1961.

Kagan, Jerome. Reflection-impulsivity and reading ability in primary grade children. **Child Develpm.,** Sept. 1965, **36,** 609-628.

Karlsen, Bjorn, Madden, Richard, & Gardner, Eric. **Stanford diagnostic reading test: Forms I and II.** New York: Harcourt, Brace and World, Inc., 1966.

Kerfoot, James E. An instructional view of reading diagnosis. **Reading and inquiry,** International Reading Association Conference Proceedings, 1965, **10,** 215-219.

Krese, E. Morley. Reversals in reading: A problem in space perception? **Elementary Sch. J.,** Jan. 1949, **49,** 278-284.

Leavell, Ullin W. The problem of symbol reversals and confusions. **Peabody J. Educ.,** Nov. 1954, **32,** 130-141.

Malmquist, Eve. **Factors related to reading disabilities in the first grade of the elementary school.** Stockholm, Sweden: Almquist and Wiksel, 1968.

McCullough, Constance. **McCullough word-analysis tests.** Princeton, New Jersey: Personnel Press, Inc., 1963.

Monroe, Marion. **Reading aptitude tests.** Boston: Houghton-Mifflin Co., 1935.

Monroe, Marion. **Diagnostic reading examination for diagnosis of special difficulty in reading.** Chicago: C. H. Stoelting Co., 1932.

Muehl, Siegmar, & Kremenak, S. Ability to match information within and between auditory and visual sense modalities and subsequent reading achievement. **J. Educ. Psychol.,** Aug. 1966, **57,** 230-238.

Olsen, Arthur V. Relation of achievement test scores and specific reading abilities to the Frostig developmental test of visual perception. **Percept. mot. Skills,** Feb. 1966, **22,** 179-184. (a)

Olsen, Arthur V. Frostig developmental test of visual perception as a predictor of specific reading abilities with second grade children. **Elementary English,** Dec. 1966, **43.** 869-872. (b)

Peters, Henry B. Vision screening. In Monroe Hirsch and Ralph Wick (Eds.), **Vision of children: An optometric symposium.** Philadelphia: Chilton Books, 1963. Pp. 333-359.

Roswell, Florence G., & Chall, Jeanne S. **Roswell-Chall auditory blending test.** New York: Essay Press, 1963.

Roswell, Florence G., & Chall, Jeanne S. **Manual for the Roswell-Chall auditory blending test.** New York: Essay Press, 1963.

Roswell, Florence G., & Chall, Jeanne S. **Roswell-Chall diagnostic reading test of word analysis skills.** New York: Essay Press, 1956.

Schack, Vita G. A quick phonics readiness check for retarded readers. **Elementary English,** Oct. 1962, **39,** 584-586.

Silver, Archie A., Hagin, Rosa A., & Hirsch, Marilyn F. Reading disability: Teaching through stimulation of deficit perceptual areas. **Amer. J. Orthopsychiat.,** July 1967, **37,** 744-752.

Smith, Henry P., & Dechant, Emerald V. **Psychology in teaching reading.** Englewood Cliffs, New Jersey: Prentice-Hall, Inc., 1961.

Spache, George D. **Diagnostic reading scales.** Monterey, California: California Test Bureau, 1963.

Sterritt, G., & Rudnick, M. Auditory and visual rhythm perception in relation to reading ability in fourth grade boys. **Percept. mot. Skills,** June 1966, **22,** 859-864.

Vernon, M. D. **Backwardness in reading.** Cambridge, England: Cambridge University Press, 1957.

Wechsler, David, & Pignatelli, Myrtle L. Reversal errors in reading: Phenomena of axial rotation. **J. Educ. Psychol.,** March 1937, **28,** 215-221.

Wechsler, David. **Wechsler intelligence scale for children.** New York: Psychological Corp., 1949.

Wepman, Joseph M. Auditory discrimination, speech, and reading. **Elementary Sch. J.,** March 1960, **60,** 325-333.

Wepman, Joseph. **Wepman auditory discrimination test.** Language Research Associates, 1958.

Wiener, Morton, & Cromer, Ward. Reading and reading difficulty: A conceptual analysis. **Harvard Educ. Rev.,** Fall 1967, **37,** 620-643.

The Nature of Diagnosis

William R. Powell, Ed.D.
Professor of Education and
Director, Center for Reading Research and Instruction
University of Illinois
Urbana, Illinois

The purpose of this chapter[1] is to examine the nature of the diagnostic process and to identify its common elements, regardless of how or where that process may be used. While medicine and psychology have been the main sources of ideas concerning diagnosis, the following discussion will attempt to employ these concepts within the framework of learning disorders, with special reference to reading.

DISTINCTIONS IN USING "DIAGNOSIS"

Communication too frequently breaks down between members of different professions. One reason is that each profession has its own terminology, jargon, and special meanings for words. Each may be using the same word, but with different connotations and nuances. These hazards of communication are as common within a profession as they are between several of them.

In education, for example, many individuals use terms such as "clinical teaching" and "diagnostic teaching," yet meaning may not be effectively transmitted. Careful analysis reveals that people are not talking about the same thing, only using the same terminology. Certain word usage can become abstruse, profuse, and jargon-laden—employed only because it fits the popular conception of the day. Unfortunately, as some professional terms become popular and move from the specific to the general, they lose their special reference in the process. The term diagnosis is now in such a transitional state.

Many fields now claim use of the diagnostic process. For example, advertisements such as the following are common. "Stop by A & B Garage to have a diagnostic motor checkup." "Call XYZ Electrical Service and one of our expert technicians will make a complete diagnosis of the wiring in your home." A football fan might hear the sports announcer exclaim, "The linebackers certainly diagnosed that

[1] Acknowledgment is given to Robert E. Smith, University of Illinois, for assistance in the final preparation of this manuscript.

play well." The trend today is to extend the use of the term diagnosis, giving it greater and greater application in all fields of endeavor.

This transitional state and trend suggest several questions. What is diagnosis? What are its basic elements? Does the diagnostic process contain factors that are common to several fields? What are these common factors? What implications would such a set of characteristics have for the diagnostician? These questions and others like them provide the motivation for this chapter.

WHAT IS DIAGNOSIS?

The term itself is a compound of two Greek elements, *dia* and *gnosis.* *Dia* means thorough, apart, completely; *gnosis* means knowing, understanding, knowledge. Diagnosis, then, means simply to know something thoroughly. The derivation of the term implies that to know something completely, the diagnostician must know its components— the subparts.

The inference might be made that one cannot know the whole without a knowledge of the parts. One then examines the parts in relation to the whole. To diagnose, an individual has to recognize, distinguish, differentiate, have knowledge of, and designate.

Diagnosis is not the mere application of a label. It must evolve from the classification and name stage to the stage of attempting to provide a clinical picture where understanding is discovered in how this disability affects this subject. Diagnosis in this sense answers a series of questions: How is the subject disabled? How disabled is the subject? How does the disablement affect the subject? How did the subject become disabled? Diagnosis results in some decision for action based on the data under examination.

BASIC CONCEPTS IN DIAGNOSIS

Five concepts used mostly in the medical field apply directly to the understanding of the nature of diagnosis. These concepts are: symptom, sign, syndrome, type, and class.

Symptom

A symptom is any functional evidence of an anomaly. The term is derived from the area of symptomology, a branch of science dealing with symptoms. They are not always what they seem to be; they are subjectively determined, that is, they are not completely quantifiable. That does not mean, however, that they do not exist and that they do not have direct bearing on any disorder. Symptoms are apt to appear some time before striking objective data become evident and before many tests are useful in detecting the anomaly.

Symptoms must be interpreted. Indeed, they almost always are, and it is here that many an untrained clinician goes astray. Interpretation may be faulty if it is based on inaccurate or incomplete information. Therefore, analysis of the symptoms must precede interpretation. One must not only determine the nature of the symptoms but decide whether a reticular formation of symptoms is involved. Not all symptoms are of equal diagnostic importance, and it is the clinician's role to decide clearly which ones are important. The considerations must be: What does this symptom mean to this subject? What part does it play in his life? How does it affect him?

The purpose of the interpretation of the symptoms is to lead to an understanding of the related aspects of the basic difficulty. The gradation between the simplest and most confounding cases is not so much in the intensity of the symptoms present as in the degree of their reversibility. Those behaviors that offer maximum potential for reversibility are of prime consideration to the clinician.

By interpreting the symptoms, the clinician selects the most valuable tests but avoids collecting useless data. The wise clinician will protect his subject from even the slightest danger, smallest anxiety, or expense of his time unless warranted by possible gains. Testing will not be pursued for sake of testing.

Sign

Semiology, a branch of science dealing with the systematic study of the signs of an anomaly, provides the framework for the more objective, quantifiable evidence for analysis. A sign is objective evidence relating to the disorder. It is sometimes referred to as the "raw" or "hard" data pertaining to the case. Quite often, clinicians tend to regard this data component as the main, if not the sole characteristic of diagnosis—forgetting the other concepts of the diagnostic process.

Psychologists and educators tend to use various standardized tests to collect the "sign" language of a case, while the medical profession relies heavily on laboratory analysis of the data. Assuming an accurate approach to the collection of the objective data is done, the clinician needs to be aware that the increase in the number of tests may increase the reliability of the signs; but more tests will not likely change the scope of the appraisal.

Syndromes

A useful aid in the interpretation of symptoms and signs consists of grouping them together to form recognizable complexes or syndromes. A syndrome is a group of signs and symptoms that cluster together and characterize an anomaly. The parts are coordinated and partially dependent on one another. Indeed, it is this very interdependence that makes them a syndrome.

Disorders are not necessarily mutually exclusive. The features of two or three reaction types often coexist in the same subject. For example,

253

it is not uncommon for a subject to have a speech and reading disorder simultaneously. However, the medical model indicates that syndromes are mutually exclusive. The designation of a specific syndrome automatically excludes all others for that subject, excepting the syndrome of stress.

For learning disorders, specific syndromes have not been clearly identified. Hence, it is impossible to tell whether the mutually exclusive syndrome model would be appropriate.

In all situations, it is important for a clinician not to rely solely on commonly accepted syndromes but to examine each case thoroughly in order to understand how these signs and symptoms are related and why the anomaly process results in these particular manifestations.

Type

Type refers to a given set of subjects possessing a common set of characteristics that clearly distinguish them from all other sets. Different groups of subjects are collected into a subclass on the basis of their common manifestations, because they are more alike than any other set of subjects. Case typing normally implies that a name is attached to the identifiable group possessing this common set of characteristics.

Case typing, or attaching a name to a disorder, generates controversy and presents an obstacle to the system, especially in certain fields— psychiatry, for example. It is true that mere labeling does not, in itself, add much to a diagnosis. Typing can be a technique of hiding behind labels because there is too little knowledge. It can also be a technique for adding order, stability, and structure to a diverse and diffuse area.

If typing leads to name-calling, with emphasis on the product and not on an effort to understand and describe the process, then it becomes a disservice to the endeavor.

Class

A class is a set of types discretely ordered in a given system. Classes are useful when they facilitate communication among professions. They reflect not only our needs but our current knowledge about a field as well. The less effective the classification system, the greater the need.

A basic requirement for an effective classification system is that the subclasses be mutually exclusive. This requirement may explain why there still is no such system for learning disorders. Whether or when a classification system with mutually exclusive subclasses can be constructed remains to be seen. However, if a classification system is developed on the principle of gradation as well as of exclusion, it might be more applicable to the problems of learning disorders.

THREE PERSPECTIVES OF DIAGNOSIS

A Medical Perspective

The goal of the medical practitioner is clear; his concern is with the health of his patient. With that in mind, he can then proceed to carry out his examination. He has been trained to view the patient as a whole entity. He looks for symptoms of ill health; he assesses the weak and the strong points of the case and attempts to relate them to the pathological processes underlying the classified disease entities.

When it comes to the method to be perused by the physician in taking a case, there is much divergence of opinion among practitioners. Almost every one devises his own style, and these differ widely. There is, however, one essential quality in their approach to taking a case. It must be both comprehensive and concise.

In taking a case, the general plan used by most physicians consists of two parts: 1) interrogating the patient and 2) giving him a physical examination. The pattern is illustrated as follows:

History + Examination → Diagnosis → Treatment

The first portion of the diagnosis involves the collection of data in order to obtain an objective history of the complaint so the doctor can attempt to etiologically reconstruct the nature of the disturbance and its significance within the individual's life.

The second phase is the physical examination, during which the physician views the patient's general state, i.e., his whole being and actions. The examination continues in the sequential order of inspecting (viewing closely the body or any of its parts by the eye), palpation (touching or feeling by the hand parts of the body), percussion (tapping the surface of the body with the hand or a small hammer for information about the underlying structure through emitted sounds or vibratory sensations), and auscultation (listening for sound, often through a stethoscope, arising from within the various organs, namely, the heart and lungs). The clinical physician's procedure involves the general state, inspection, palpation, percussion, and auscultation—in that order.

It is important to note that the process described for the medical practitioner leads to a clinical judgment based on his perception of things through the primary senses and supported only by simple instruments. Laboratory tests or objective signs may not be available at this time. The way the physician utilizes his knowledge and skills depends on his conception of physiological function as well as anatomic structure and localization, plus his inference of the pathological process.

Unless the physician chooses to rely on signs obtained from various laboratory tests, the likelihood of accuracy in his diagnoses is not particularly high. Even with laboratory tests, the level of accuracy is not necessarily as high as it could or should be. Assuming an accurate diagnosis, the practitioner still may not be certain of the treatment because of the many alternatives open to him. Frequently, he relies on trial and error. However, he constantly reevaluates the situation and adjusts for the best possible cure.

The important characteristic of the medical approach to diagnosis is that in the absence of better technique, the physician has been trained to think *clinically.* He has learned to assimilate his knowledge of anatomy, physiology, pathology, pharmacology, and other disciplines, into a preconscious level with which to make quick and efficient responses during the physical examination. He has developed a conceptual understanding of what is typical or normal (within individual variance) and has learned to look for atypical variance. If the scanning mechanism for his models makes an error or lacks the essential residue to draw from, then the diagnosis and probable treatment will be mismatched and readjustment will have to follow.

Medical science has been and continues to be a pragmatic rather than theoretical science. The physician has a vast literature from various intellectual disciplines to draw on. He also has voluminous case history and other medical data at his disposal. On the basis of his diagnostic evaluation, he prescribes treatment in order to bring about a cure. Implicit in his understanding of diagnosis is that it must lead to a reversal of the abortive condition and back to normal health, or at least must arrest the condition and prevent it from progressing further. Without much theory, the medical profession has been productive in medical science.

A Psychological Perspective

Through the systematic study of psychology, human behavior has been evaluated with a greater degree of accuracy and sophistication. The psychological approach to diagnosis is to observe the subject's behavior and relate it to the theoretical model the psychologist believes best explains human behavior in general. Because of the number of disparate theories used to explain behavior, different interpretations of the same behavior are frequent. It is also possible that within the operating framework used for interpretation, all are correct. The basic orientation to the study of behavior can conflict sharply, and this conflict can cause approaches to diagnosis and treatment that differ as markedly.

To help systematize and stabilize his observations, the psychologist has developed instruments that supposedly measure selected skills, knowledge, attitudes, aptitudes, personality, and other characteristics representative of the sampled behavior. Using these instruments the psychologist has attempted with some degree of success to infer and predict an individual's behavior. These inferences and predictions are made on the basis of standards, norms, or guidelines that are often geared to statistical specifications accompanying the test. However, the standards are relative and depend on the population from which they were derived as well as a host of other technical factors.

In interpreting his data, the psychologist tends to group both signs and symptoms under the single rubric of symptoms. Therefore, when the psychologist refers to the symptoms of his case, he is including both objective and subjective data. He does not always separate the two concepts, as the medical practitioner does.

In an educational situation, the psychologist has been concerned typically with placement (both grade placement and assignment to special classes), promotion and retention decisions, and the manageability of selected children. Operationally, more time is spent by the psychologist on the first two of these functions—placement and promotion-retention. Interest is extended, however, into the causative factors operating in learning problems and conflict situations operating within the learning environment.

Diagnostically, the school psychologist is concerned with the area of measuring intelligence and identifying potential as accurately as possible. He often uses just mental age as a measure of expectancy, and achievement areas are usually measured by survey instruments. He is less sensitive to the differential aspects of diagnosis as these relate to learning. For example, he may not be concerned with identifying the instructional reading level but may be content with the results of a power test (which often produce frustrational level scores). He is probably concerned with the global reading abilities of a subject and may not differentiate significantly between word recognition and comprehension.

If the psychologist is sensitive to these two aspects, he probably will not proceed to identify the specific strengths and weaknesses within each of these areas. Thus, he leaves many of the specifics of a diagnosis to the teacher or to other specialized personnel such as a reading teacher. Unfortunately, many schools have no reading specialist and the teachers are often unaware of how to assess such a specific area themselves. Yet these specific areas are the very ones the teachers so badly want and need the most for instructional objectives.

The school psychologist generally works with the teacher, helping alleviate factors that may be having an adverse effect on the child's performance. His approach is through the teacher rather than working directly with the child, although he may spend some time with the child. He is concerned with the differential reinforcement used to shape the child's behavior, also with helping to change the teacher's perception of the child, if this is necessary. He would also be very concerned about the teacher's level of expectation for a child, encouraging her to modify her instruction. However, the psychologist's unfamiliarity with actual teaching techniques and classroom procedures causes many of his recommendations to become abstractions for the teacher. Since the teacher is the instrument for treatment, a good continuity of communication about recommendations between the teacher and school psychologist is important. If this breaks down, the diagnosis will be rendered ineffective, no matter how accurate it may be.

An Educational Perspective

Certain aspects of an educational diagnosis may be traced back to the Greek and Roman civilizations. In THE REPUBLIC, Plato describes the stages necessary for the proper education of the guardian. To select those of the warrior class most qualified by temperament and training for higher education, Plato had to make an assessment of each individual. Through a series of tests, he was able to chose those individuals best qualified for this rigorous training.

A careful examination of Plato's procedures reveals a positive perspective for an educational diagnosis. He had a goal (the educational development of the guardian class), he could observe signs and symptoms (physical and affective qualities), and he could identify the ones relevant to the achievement of his goal (the selective process). Unfortunately, Plato was not interested in treatment. His concern was with the creation of an elite, not with helping individuals who could not achieve selected standards. From a modern viewpoint, the judgment could be made that the process was correct but incomplete.

Even though the past methods and procedures used by teachers to appraise children's performance may have been crude, the process was there just waiting for refinement. Today, much of that refinement has been accomplished. But now there is a longing for an even greater revision of technique.

Most people are usually impressed with scientific methods and statistical inferences. Teachers are no exception. Therefore, the educational approach to diagnosis is similar to the psychological one. The chief difference is in the type and quality of instruments used.

Psychologists and educational personnel both give a battery of tests, in the hope of discovering an individual's abilities and conversely, by default, his disabilities. The objective for the administration of some of these tests may not always be clear, but both educators and psychologists label the process of testing, finding symptoms, and classification as diagnosis. Although the psychologist tends to work closely with individual measuring devices, the educator has had to rely on group-type instruments for part of his assessment. Hence, the validity and reliability of measuring devices becomes even more suspect because of this approach.

The classroom teacher has little support for the evaluation of skill differences at present, except through informal means. The tools generally available lack the specificity necessary for clearly identifying assets or deficits. Thus, some children's skills may be skipped or overlooked, while others are given inappropriate instruction.

Even if suitable tests were available, there is some evidence that teachers will tend to ignore the findings anyway, preferring to operate toward the treatment process with the inclinations, predispositions, and biases they had prior to testing. Instruments are needed that will pinpoint strengths and weaknesses more effectively, along with an emphasis on the proper interpretation of the tools used in making a diagnosis.

CHARACTERISTICS OF AN EFFECTIVE DIAGNOSTICIAN

A careful analysis of the three perspectives reveals four characteristics of an effective diagnostician. These are: 1) insight, 2) conceptual framework, 3) objective data, and 4) experience. If the diagnosis is to be a concise, comprehensive, and well-directed one, these qualities are essential in the individual conducting the diagnosis.

Insight

Insight is the quality that permits the diagnostician to have command and control over the total diagnostic process. His ability to know which tests to select, when to use them, and how to interpret the findings will depend largely on his skill in analyzing and interpreting symptoms. As objective data are collected, the clinician's skill in observing and detecting the nonquantitative aspects of the subject's behavior provides the cues to subsequent steps for evaluation. While objective instruments are essential for an effective diagnosis of learning disorders, no test or device can ever substitute for the informed mind of the clinician. Tests and other assessment techniques are only as valuable as the insight and wisdom of the individual directing the process. However, insight is not achieved without effort and experience. Many an effective technician fails to be an effective diagnostician simply because he has failed to develop the kind of disciplined mind that needs to be added to his effective technique.

Conceptual Framework

Insight and intuition operate within the conceptual background and belief system of the diagnostician, and are usually limited by them. The conceptual framework of the clinician provides the basis for his style and approach to diagnosis, and certainly tints his interpretations. The type of training he has received, the philosophy of his mentors, his own background of experience, his adopted value system, and the depth of his knowledge in his field and related areas all contribute to this conceptual framework from which a diagnostician operates.

One point should be clear. By definition, diagnosis means to know something *thoroughly.* One cannot make an effective diagnosis otherwise. This means the diagnostician has to know his area totally and specifically—the whole and all of its parts. Specificity is a matter of degree, and so is an effective diagnosis.

Objective Data

No diagnostician working with reading problems or any other learning disorder can operate effectively without objective data derived from valid and reliable instruments. Tests are part of his stock-in-trade, but they are not his master. Rather, they are his able servants, helping him gather the most essential information.

Not all tests have to be of the standardized variety to be useful. Indeed, some of the best and most useful diagnostic data can be obtained through criterion tests developed by the clinician for a specific purpose. However, the desire to have discriminating objective data should not become an end in itself and lead to excessive testing. More tests will not replace a lack of insight or background on the part of the diagnostician.

Experience

All of the previous characteristics—insight, conceptual background, and objective data—are a function of the quantity and quality of the diagnostician's experience. Knowing how to determine the substantive features in the diagnostic process can only come from a background of clinical experience. The quality of this experience provides the ingredients for a solid yet flexible conceptual model for effective diagnostic strategies. Unlike various devices and tests, experience cannot be met with a substitute. An effective diagnostician must get his "feet wet in the field of experience and at least keep them damp."

STRATEGIES FOR AN EFFECTIVE DIAGNOSIS

Diagnosis can be a meaningful term, have relevance for any profession, and serve as a frame of reference if it contains the following components:

An objective or goal, either stated or implied.

A description of the physiological and/or behavioral signs and symptoms.

An exact pinpointing of the problem area(s).

Cues for remediation.

Each component of diagnostic strategy can be identified in part from the three perspectives presented earlier. A lack of clarity in any of these four components will reduce the total effectiveness of the diagnosis.

The Goals or Objectives

The goals of the educational process are not easily defined. In fact, questions such as these readily suggest themselves: Whom to teach? What to teach? When to teach it? How to teach it? Why? These have been and still are controversial issues. One of the goals of education is to perpetuate the democratic way of life. Inherent in the democratic ideal is the sanctity of the individual: each individual should be educated to reach his full potential (ideally), not only for the good of society but for his own personal fulfillment.

This educational objective (the maximum fulfillment of the potential of each child) is a long-range one. The teacher must be alert to the individual learning and behavior patterns of each child, in order to determine suitable short-range objectives.

Description of Signs and Symptoms

As part of the daily contact with students, the teacher needs to observe closely and note patterns of responses and the behavioral characteristics of the child. This collection of quantitative as well as qualitative data is a process as well as a product. A teacher must constantly be assessing as well as testing her pupils. She must build on their knowledge and skill and help them with their difficulties.

As the teacher works with the child over a period of time, she can observe his response in a specific learning situation. If she observes success in mastering a specific task, she may reassess the child's ability to undertake tasks that are more complex. If a child fails to master a task, then the teacher must make a judgment about why this happened and must make the appropriate adjustment.

Specifying the Problem Areas

A battery of tests is only as good as the help it provides in illuminating the strengths and weaknesses of the subject's skills. In many instances, tests delimit the area of exploration. Yet, unfortunately, they do not have the capacity to specify particular problem areas.

To say this is not necessarily to criticize the current test market, because many of the tests now available were not designed for great specificity. Therefore, criticizing an instrument for not accomplishing a task it was not designed to do would not be justified.

With a reading problem case, the diagnostician attempts to locate the essential skills that need modification because they deviate too far from the expected patterns of reading behavior. By observing two or more conditions with similar signs and symptoms and distinguishing a real difference where normally no difference would be expected, a teacher or diagnostician can differentiate appropriately between skills.

Using a diagnostic procedure with youngsters who are experiencing great difficulty often shows that the subject is deficient in many skills and needs help of a broad nature. The diagnostician's task is then to identify the most relevant items, that is, those of major or first-order concern for instruction.

For a diagnosis to be specific, the following factors must be clearly identified in terms of the basic minimum needed:

The exact nature of the skill instruction required and the order in which the skills should be presented.

The level of difficulty involved in materials to be used for instructional and independent activities.

The types of material suitable for use in developing this specific skill.

Cues for Treatment

Direction for correction is an important aspect of any diagnostic strategy and it is contingent upon a clearly stated goal or objective. Too frequently a diagnosis ends with a label being attached to the outcome which may result from the lack of specificity in the process.

After a diagnosis, it is not at all uncommon to find terms and phrases indicating that the child needs help in auditory discrimination, blends, suffixes, comprehension, phonics, and so forth. Or one may find that the subject has a language deficiency, is emotionally disturbed, or that he has a problem of lateral dominance. The classroom teacher or the reading clinician has the right to ask and expect answers to questions such as: Which blends? What particular comprehension skill(s)?

The diagnosis that results in nothing more than a labeling process is a waste of time, energy, and materials. Broad labels do not help the subject and offer little help for the teacher attempting to direct the treatment procedures. What is needed from the diagnosis is the specific identification of the skills or rules of behavior that the child must learn in order to overcome unwanted characteristics. The specific elements within categories appropriate for instructional purposes should also be pointed out.

The remedial teacher functions in terms of identifiable teaching units that can be presented to the subject in a sequential manner. In short, to be complete, the diagnostic strategy must be precise, specific, prescriptive, directional, and translatable into the language of the individual applying the treatment. Remedial efforts are enhanced or diminished by the number of cues obtained for remediation.

SUMMARY

An examination of the nature of diagnosis reveals that the term can have relevance for any vocational field which has accepted standards that form the base line from which judgments may be made. To diagnose in any given area, the diagnostician must have a complete understanding of the inputs normally expected so any significant deviations from the standard may be observed. The inputs may be subjective (symptoms) and/or objective (signs) and these data may form mutually exclusive clusters (syndromes) that can be labelled (typing) and arranged into a system (classification). In the ideal diagnostic situation, the diagnostician uses his insight and draws from his conceptual background and experience to evaluate the objective data so he can determine for his subject 1) an objective or goal, 2) note and record significant behavior patterns, 3) pinpoint areas of difficulty and of progress, and 4) a plan for future direction (remediation, if necessary).

Dyspedagogia as a Cause of Reading Retardation: Definition and Treatment

S. Alan Cohen, Ed.D.
Associate Professor and
Director, Reading and Language Arts Center
Graduate School
Yeshiva University
New York, New York

DEFINITION

What Causes Reading Retardation?

If the retarded reader is black, urban and poor, his retardation is considered a concomitant of being disadvantaged. Being *disadvantaged* means to lack a father in the home, to speak with a dialect, to have deficient conceptual vocabulary (liberals prefer the word *different* to *deficient*), to have a "nonverbal" communications style, and to suffer the insults inflicted by a racist, segregated environment. (Cohen, 1969a)

If the retarded reader is white, suburban and middle class, his retardation is often labeled dyslexia or is explained as the result of perceptual dysfunction.

Black or white, the retarded reader is analyzed, prodded, observed, tested, exposed to instruction, re-exposed to remedial instruction, diagnosed, written up, and—if he is one in 100,000—referred to a university clinic.

What Do We Find in the Referral Records to Explain the Child's Reading Problem?

Psychiatrists, psychologists, learning disability experts, pediatricians, neurologists, guidance counselors, reading specialists, and principals supply us with the following diagnostic labels to explain the retarded reader:

Dyslexia	Perceptually handicapped or impaired
Emotionally disturbed	Learning disability
Mixed dominant	Cross dominant
Lazy	Hyperactive
Hyperkinetic	Hypoactive
Lack of impulse control	Passive aggressive

Distractibility   He's not ready
Minimal brain dysfunction   Delayed maturation
Minimally neurologically impaired

The list goes on and on—the etiologies conforming to the latest vogue
as determined by TIME, NEWSWEEK, READER'S DIGEST or the
state legislature's most recent definition of "learning disorder."

What Do These Labels or Etiologies Tell Us About Treatment?

Nothing. The list of etiologies and labels may in fact describe conditions that exist in individuals or groups who are retarded readers, but
the accuracy of the labels and etiological conditions is irrelevant to
the treatment of most cases of reading retardation. One purpose of
this chapter is to demonstrate that:

> Research indicates that most reading retardation stems from the
> dreaded psychoeducational disease we have labeled *dyspedagogia*
> —poor teaching.

> Even in cases of neurological impairment or perceptual dysfunc-
> tion, the etiology of a behavioral condition that is not within the
> realm of medical pathology (endocrine imbalance, neurological
> deterioration) is usually irrelevant to its treatment.

In addition to establishing this point of view and supplying the data
to verify it, this chapter presents specific suggestions on how to treat
victims of dyspedagogia by using the "so what" diagnosis and high intensity instruction.

Clarifications and Limitations to the Argument

The point of view expressed in this chapter is that etiology is usually
irrelevant to treatment of behavioral disorders. We call this the "Etiology Be Damned" or EBD point of view. The EBD argument is often

271

distorted by overextending it to realms of medicine and prevention. Medicine deals with physiological pathology in which etiology is a key to treatment. Overt seizures, for example, take on special significance according to etiology. In such cases, etiology influences whether or not surgery, psychotherapy or chemotherapy is prescribed. EBD is limited, therefore, to behavioral disorders and does not apply to medical pathology.

EBD does not apply to prevention. Etiology is crucial to behavioral research that is meant to pay off some day in preventive programs. To prevent future reading retardation, we must isolate the etiological variables that cause that condition. EBD does not apply. But to solve the reading problems that exist currently in children, etiology is irrelevant. EBD does apply.

Two other points must be clarified before considering the data in support of EBD. First, the specific conditions described by diagnostic labels and etiologies are often accurate. EBD does not deny the existence of psychosocial, psychophysical, psychodynamic, psycholinguistic, economic and ecological variables implied in diagnostic labels and etiological descriptions. Second, many of these variables are important to consider and to treat for reasons other than literacy. The point is, that in most treatments of reading retardation, these variables are irrelevant.

The Case for Dyspedagogia

According to Mary Austin's study, American reading instruction in general is weak. (Austin, et al., 1963) More dramatic, perhaps, than Austin's observations were the classroom achievement level patterns that emerged from the Cooperative Reading Research projects conducted in the mid 1960's by the U.S. Office of Education. (THE READING TEACHER, 1966a, b, 1967a, b) One of the best of these studies, Albert Harris's CRAFT project, demonstrates the existence of dyspedagogia. (Harris, et al., 1968)

272

Harris found what most other Cooperative Reading Research studies found and what most researchers predicted he would find: When we compare various published beginning reading programs (e.g., ITA with sight basal with language experience with "linguistic" with phonics) matching the classrooms both within each program and across each program, the difference between one classroom's achievement and another's *using the same program* is greater than classroom achievement levels across programs. Most researchers interpreted this as: "The teacher variable is more potent than the 'method' variable." This, of course, is an oversimplification. The published material is a program, not a method. What each teacher does with a published program is *the method.* In other words, the research does indicate that *methodology* makes a difference in achievement. The question that needed to be asked was not: Which beginning reading program gets better results? Instead, the question should have been: What is it that more successful teachers do that less successful teachers do not do? The researchable problem should have been: What is the *pedagogy* in the more successful classrooms? (Cohen, 1968)

As an experienced researcher, Harris anticipated the teacher variable or what this chapter defines as pedagogy. He built into the CRAFT project attempts to isolate variables that could identify more successful teachers. Earlier studies have attempted to isolate these same variables. (Chall and Feldmann, 1966) One of the most promising studies indicated two variables which appear to be most significant: (Tannenbaum and Cohen, 1967)

> More successful teachers (as defined by higher reading achievement levels of pupils) tended to differentiate (individualize) reading instruction more than less successful teachers.

> Classes with higher reading achievement tended to spend more time in reading instruction than classes with lower reading achievement.

Call these variables *differentiated instruction* and *time.* The problem with most classroom observation schemes is that they concentrate on the wrong phenomenon—the teacher. When they look at the pupil, they do so either in interaction with the teacher or in an unsystematic, clinical observation. Tannenbaum and Cohen, on the other hand, developed a different classroom analysis scheme. Instead of observing the teacher, they analyzed pupil behaviors in reading classes. (Tannenbaum and Cohen, 1967) They analyzed systematically what reading skills and subskills each child was learning, at what level he was operating, what channel of communications input he was using, through what communications channel he was responding, the types of media delivering the stimuli, the learning strategy utilized by the learner and the pupil grouping employed. This technique allowed the observer to analyze a class and to define not only what the class was doing, but what individuals were doing on all eight dimensions listed in the Taxonomy of Instructional Treatments (Figure 1). This observation scheme revealed that more successful classes had a higher "participation-in-learning ratio" (*P* ratio) than less successful classes. This study is important for two reasons: First, it focused on the learner rather than on the teacher, demonstrating that learner performance, not teacher performance, is the more accurate measure of classroom efficiency. Second, it defined what *differentiation* and more *time* meant in other studies that had similar findings.

The Tannenbaum-Cohen technique indicated *why* individualizing instruction and increasing time caused reading achievement to increase. The factors appear to be *efficiency* and *intensity.* Given a period of time in which pupils are programmed to read, the more successful classes are ones in which 85 to 95% of the clock time is spent by the pupils working in prescribed learning-to-read activities. The best way to achieve this intensity is to adjust *what* a child learns to each individual's needs and to allow each child to learn that skill or content at his *level* and at his own *rate.* This is called "individualizing" or "differentiating" instruction. The degree to which the teacher does *not* differentiate can be partially compensated for by increasing the amount of

FIGURE 1

TAXONOMY OF INSTRUCTIONAL TREATMENTS
(Developed for Project #OEG-1-6-062528-2092)
by Abraham J. Tannenbaum and S. Alan Cohen

CONTENT

BASIC SKILL	BASIC SUBSKILL	SEQUENTIAL LEVEL
1. Word attack	1. Consonants	1. Easy/Initial
	2. Vowels	2. Average/Intermediate
	3. Word structure	3. Difficult/Sophisticated
	4. Sight vocabulary	4. Ungradable
	5. Word meaning	
	6. Context inference	
	7. Symbolic discrimination	
2. Comprehension	1. Details-Main ideas	
	2. Sequence-Relations	
	3. Follow directions	
	4. Sentence structure	
	5. Paragraph structure	
	6. Recreational reading	
3. Study skills	1. Dictionary	
	2. Maps and graphs	
	3. References and texts	

CHANNEL OF COMMUNICATION

COMMUNICATION INPUT	COMMUNICATION OUTPUT
1. Auditory	0. Nonobservable
2. Visual	1. Oral
3. Kinesthetic	2. Motoric
4. Auditory/Visual	3. Oral-Motoric
5. Visual/Kinesthetic	
6. Auditory/Kinesthetic	
7. Visual/Auditory/Kinesthetic	

STRATEGY

INSTRUCTIONAL MEDIA	INSTRUCTIONAL STRATEGY	INSTRUCTIONAL GROUPING
1. Visual-Projector	1. Play-Chance	1. Teacher/Large group
2. Auditory-Recorder	2. Play-Competition	2. Teacher/Small group
3. Skill drill text	3. Play-Puzzle	3. Teacher/Individual/Student/Tutor
4. Games-Role playing	4. Test-Response	4. Student/Small group
5. Books	5. Exploration	5. Student/Large group
	6. Programmed response	6. Student/Student team
	7. Creative problem solving	7. Individual self instruction

275

clock hours devoted to reading instruction. In other words, three hours daily of inefficient reading instruction may yield a little better results than one hour of daily inefficient reading instruction. Most traditional teacher-directed classrooms operate, according to this research, at 30 to 45% *P* ratios. By increasing time in these inefficient classrooms, achievement increases slightly. But if we increase both efficiency and time, achievement jumps.

Use of the Tannenbaum-Cohen observation scheme results in the conclusion that most classrooms operate at shockingly low efficiency. Using the eight taxonomy dimensions (Figure 1), this observation scheme shows little *real* instruction occurring in most classrooms. "Real instruction" is systematic, sequential management of prescribed stimuli and contingencies. But most classroom instruction is simply exposure. The assumption, for example, that all children are certainly taught letters and words (Frostig, et al., 1969) does not stand up under careful behavioral analysis. The fact is that most children certainly do *not* receive intensive instruction in letters and words. They are merely exposed to letters and words, and a pedagogical universe exists between simple exposure and systematic contingency management which is the key to learning.

Dyspedagogia is, therefore, what most children get in school. And for most children, dyspedagogia is good enough, for they read in spite of it. Some children, however, do have unique combinations of negative psychosocial, psychodynamic, psychophysical, psycholinguistic variables that require something more than dyspedagogia. Their problems are not in these unique combinations, but in the dyspedagogia. For the Harris CRAFT study, among others, shows us that in the presence of intensive negative etiological factors, a *slight* increase in the intensity of instruction eliminates a measurable amount of the effect of these etiological variables at the beginning reading stage. To assume that, just because a child has been exposed to a course called "remedial reading" or "special help," he has received intensive instruction is an error.

276

Harris's populations were disadvantaged urban children who manifest what we call in middle class children the learning disorder syndrome. The disadvantaged syndrome is the learning disability syndrome at its most intensive. (Cohen, 1969a, 1966) In poor black children, we often call it deprivation. In the CRAFT research, teachers were closely trained and supervised, resulting not in optimal pedagogy, but in slightly better-than-average pedagogy. In third grade, these disadvantaged children in the CRAFT study were reading on grade level — a rare phenomenon in these particular ghetto schools. The crucial factor was pedagogy. Stated in reverse, dyspedagogia ("low intensity" pedagogy) causes most reading retardation. Stated positively, in spite of intensive negative psychosocial, psychodynamic, psychophysical, psycholinguistic factors, a little better pedagogy makes a big difference in achievement.

The Case for EBD

Etiology of a behavioral disorder is irrelevant to treatment. A child's present behaviors define his problems; correct identification of etiology should have little influence upon treatment. For example, a child with no male identity model in his home may range from neurotic attraction to neurotic repulsion in the presence of adult males. What matters is his neurotic behavior *now*. The etiology is an after-the-fact reflection — a psychoanalytic relic that has not survived careful research — a hold over from medical diagnosis where it is valid. If a therapist needs to know that a child's neurotic attraction to males is the result of a fatherless home before that therapist can understand and change that behavior, then that therapist is both insensitive and incompetent. In the first instance, sensitivity is a quality of human interaction with behavior, not with etiology. In the second instance, few therapists know how to supply fatherless homes with fathers; and, even if they could do so, there is no evidence to show that a new father, as such, would change the child's behavior. Knowledge of the history of a behavior's development adds not an iota to the management of that behavior. To know that reading retardation, or any aspect of it, can be traced to prenatal, paranatal or postnatal psycho-

277

dynamic, psychosocial, psychophysical or psycholinguistic factors does not, nor should it, influence what a teacher or therapist does to a child. The presenting behavioral patterns and the stimuli that trigger these behaviors *now* are the essentials of the issue. The argument that knowledge of etiology adds a perspective to the problem is evading it.

Even the psychoanalytic method of behavior modification is subject to the EBD principle. Prodding one's past is a treatment method one may use to attack present neurotic behaviors. The therapist does not need to know the etiology in order to use that treatment.

Another example of the EBD principle is in the treatment of those learning disorders which have been conveniently labeled as the "disadvantaged condition." To eradicate that condition by preventing future generations from suffering the effects of racism and poverty, the etiological factors that cause it need to be identified and eliminated. But this is not the same thing as saying that ghetto children presently afflicted with reading retardation cannot be taught until racism and poverty are rooted out. Consider just one etiological factor that seems to contribute to reading retardation in this population-poor visual perception development. (Cohen, 1969a) A series of studies indicates that perceptual motor behaviors, as defined by the Frostig and other similar tests, or programs derived from such tests, may be valuable in themselves, but are practically unrelated and functionally independent of reading behaviors. (Cohen, 1969b) Here is a case of etiological factors translated into behavior modification strategies that have little effect on reading. Harris's populations were these same ghetto children. Improved pedagogy taught them to read. They were not subject to special programs geared to specific etiological factors such as poor visual perception as defined by a Frostig test. (Cohen, 1961)

In extreme cases of perceptual dysfunction, a child may need perceptual training before he can orient himself to a near point task. He may need hand-eye-motor coordination training at such a gross level, that instruction in reading and writing is impossible. But even in these cases, the etiology of the dysfunction — be it a developmental problem, a paranatal or prenatal trauma — is irrelevant to the treatment. What matters to the trainer, or therapist, or remedial clinician is the presenting behaviors. These behaviors determine the problem and, in the final analysis, determine the treatments.

TREATMENT OF DYSPEDAGOGIA

The SO WHAT Diagnosis

The treatment for dyspedagogia is intensive instruction. The first step in intensive instruction is prescriptive diagnosis distinguishable from classical diagnosis by the former's utility. Classical diagnosis assigns numbers (third grade level) or etiological labels (developmental dyslexia, or primary reading disorder with passive aggressive tendencies) to a child's behavior. Obviously, the classical diagnosis is useless to the child and to the clinician who must find a way to teach the child to read.

The prescriptive diagnosis may also record a child's specific deficiencies by using numbers, by standard scores, or by percent correct. But the prescriptive diagnosis has five characteristics that differentiate it from the classical diagnosis:

It defines the specific reading behavior measured, usually by the nature of the test used.

It describes the behaviors operationally, usually by the nature of the test item. ("Select one of four alternative titles that expressed the paragraph's main idea.")

It defines the conditions of behavior on such dimensions as: a timed test, in a classroom, etc.

279

It defines the criterion of success in such terms as "grade level achievement" or "percent correct." This is called *expectancy level* and is determined by the teacher, who considers the entering level of the child; his general ability level, his degree of retardation and the level of the materials available. The expectancy level is set at a level higher than the child is presently operating, but low enough for him to reach in a relatively short time.

It answers the question *"so what?"* of its findings. The teacher or clinician is not allowed to record a qualitative or quantitative designation to any test behavior unless he also records a "best guess" *"so what"* to indicate what strategy, grouping, medium or level (see Figure 1) will remediate the deficiency. The teacher usually records in the *"so what"* column the name of a piece of published material to help remediate the deficiency.

Figure 2 is an example of a *"so what"* diagnosis for a retarded reading seventh grader. It covers lower level reading skills. Another form is used for higher level or comprehension skills. That form is shown as Figure 3. The behaviors listed on a diagnosis form are determined by the nature of the pupil populations, available teaching resources, and biases and talents of the teacher or clinician. The first four characteristics of the diagnosis are defined by the diagnostic tests used, which may be parts of published standardized batteries, teacher-made checklists, or reading samples. Using the test as the instructional objective forces the teacher to define the behavioral outcomes and admit to himself what he conceives the reading act to be, preventing the stereotyped excuse, "I don't believe in standardized reading tests. Reading is much more than what the Metropolitan Achievement Test taps. I teach for those other things that tests don't measure."

The *"so what"* diagnosis does not advocate teaching *to* the test. It demands teaching for the types of behaviors defined by a criterion test. Reading is always "more than the test measure." But whatever more one cares to teach must be defined in a criterion test. Teachers who

280

FIGURE 2

EXAMPLE OF SO WHAT DIAGNOSIS FOR BASIC READING SKILLS

Name   Tommy   Age   13   Grade   7

Date of Tests   10 - 1   Expectancy   6

Behaviors	Score	"So What"
1. Visual discrimination of letters	OK	Have him work in spare time on letter form board for b,p,d,q,u,v,w,x,y,z.
2. Alphabet knowledge	OK	
3. Visual memory for words	poor	Tachistoscope Training-EDL spelling, Spelling 2,3,4 Psychotechnics 1 and 2.
4. Word-Recognition (Sight)	poor	Same as 3; also **Word Bank** system, Dolch list and Chandler Basals.
5. Word analysis	poor	Visual tracking/Michigan books 3-5.
6. Conceptual vocabulary	OK	No work needed now.
7. Auditory discrimination sounds in words	weak	Medial and ends weak. Michigan Auditory Discrimination.
8. Phonic spelling	poor	Do 3-5 and 10-14 first. Then use 10-dictations daily.
9. Initial consonants	good	No work needed.
10. Final consonants	weak ⎫	Work on 3-5, 7 first. Then program
11. Initial blends	weak ⎬	to Michigan. Back up with BRL and worksheets.
12. Final blends	poor ⎫	Intersperse with word and card
13. Short vowel sounds	poor ⎬	games. If this doesn't work, use
14. Visual discrimination of vowels	poor ⎭	Speech To Print one-to-one.
15. Auditory syllabication	good	No work needed.
16. Visual syllabication	poor	Ignore for now.
17. Structural analysis	poor	After 3-5, 7 use Macmillan.
18. Common confusions	weak	Scott Foresman, programmed spelling and other work books.
19. Oral reading comprehension	good	No work needed.
20. Silent reading comprehension	good	(No code busting skills.)
21. Listening comprehension	weak	EDL listening.
22. Following written directions	poor	Barnell Loft **Follow Directions** A and B.
23. Following oral directions	weak	Listening skills cassettes.

FIGURE 3

EXAMPLE OF SO WHAT DIAGNOSTIC REPORT
FOR HIGHER LEVEL SKILLS

Name   Age   Grade

                                               Date of Test   Expectancy

Behaviors	Score	"So What?"
VOCABULARY		
General		
Science		
Math		
Social studies		
FOLLOW DIRECTIONS		
Definitions		
Simple choice		
Mathematics		
Map		
REFERENCE SKILLS		
Parts of a book		
Newspaper		
Dictionary		
Index		
Contents		
Graphs		
Classifying		
Reference books		
Maps		
Organizing		
Recall of sequence		
COMPREHENSION		
Recall of details		
Recall of main ideas		
Inference		
Self initiated reading		

claim to teach children "a love of books" have been forced to define what they mean operationally. How does one know that Johnnie loves to read books? Figure 3 defines this objective as **self-initiated reading,** an operational definition measured by a teacher checklist.

A more detailed description of specific tests appears in other sources. (Cohen, 1969a) Different clinicians prefer different tests. Whatever tests one uses, they should help the clinician pinpoint the specific behaviors that must be learned and how the learner is most likely to learn those behaviors. Many tests, including informal teacher-made instruments, can isolate the behavioral deficits. But practically no test reports **how** a pupil learns. The Harris Learning Test (Harris, 1961) or the Illinois Test of Psycholinguistic Abilities (Kirk, et al., 1968) are two examples of tests that attempt to provide information on **how** children learn. But information from these tests is of questionable validity, because a specific stimulus in a specific environment is different from the **same** stimulus in another environment. For example, visual decoding of geometric shapes in an artificial test environment may not be the same problem as visual decoding of letters on a page, and to generalize from the former that a child has a visual decoding problem may be invalid. So the best analysis of **how** the child may learn is a calculated guess based on **how** the child tends to perform on a test. That guess is recorded under **"so what"** (Figure 2). When treatment begins, the clinician may need to correct his guess. To do so, the clinician varies any combination of the eight variables listed in the Taxonomy (Figure 1) to engineer the types of responses defined by the criterion tests.

High Intensity Instruction

Intensified instruction is a system by which a learner responds to prescribed stimuli 85 to 95% of the lesson time. The prescription insures that the individual works on the specific skill or information he needs according to the **"so what"** diagnosis. The individual's schedule is simply parts of the **"so what"** column (Figure 2) fitted into a time schedule with one time slot devoted to straight reading comprehension, regardless of how deficient the reader is in basic decoding. Thus, the three-hour schedule for the seventh grader whose *"so what"* diagnosis is shown as Figure 2 appears as Figure 4. In most cases, a child's schedule is conveniently split into three areas: word study, comprehension, work study skills.[1] When dealing with large numbers of retarded readers, we find it efficient to train teachers as specialists in one of those three areas. This delimits each teacher's responsibility, allowing him to become expert in materials and strategies in one of the reading areas. The disadvantage of splitting reading into three areas is to fragmentize a naturally integrated process. To compensate for this disadvantage, the three specialists form a teaching team—working together to re-integrate what was artificially split.

The materials and physical setting for this type of prescriptive, high intensity reading clinic or center have been described elsewhere. (Cohen, 1969a, 1967)

A simple model is used to determine which materials to use, how to structure the physical environment and which strategies to employ. To intensify instruction, the *content, level* and *rate* of learning must be adjusted to each individual. The materials, strategy and resources must:

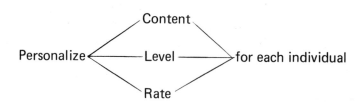

Applied to this model are a number of classical learning principles, four of which are especially important:

[1]In Figure 4, Tommy is so deficient in basic decoding skills that most of his activities are concentrated in word study.

FIGURE 4

CLASS SCHEDULE FOR RETARDED READER SHOWN IN FIGURE 2

Word Study

9:00 to 9:15	Visual tracking
9:15 to 9:35	Tach training, EDL and Psychotechnics
9:35 to 10:00	Michigan Words Bks. 3-4

Comprehension

10:00 to 10:30	Read for comprehension in Reading Attainment (Red) and in *Step Up Books.* *
10:30 to 11:00	EDL Listening Skills tapes

Word Study

11:00 to 11:20	Auditory discrimination, Michigan listening
11:20 to 12:00	Word bank, word games to preteach vocabulary in Chandler readers

*Note: Regardless of how deficient a child is in basic word analysis, some kind of high interest and low vocabulary book or kit is programmed into his schedule to give him a feeling of what reading really is.

---

1) *The individual's presenting behaviors determine what and when to teach him.* Presently, most schools and clinics predetermine what a child will learn. For example, most first grades have a set of basal readers that largely determine the content, rate and level of instruction. The child either fits the program at a prescribed rate and level or he flunks. Some teachers manage to divide the learners into three subgroups and write this off as "adjusting instruction to individual needs." This, of course, is an absurdity, for it implies only three possible combinations of rates, levels and content needs. Such absurdities contribute to dyspedagogia.

2) *Motivation management is the major determinant of learning.* Ironic as it may seem, one of the most insidious forces to undermine learning in the classroom is the teacher training institution and the school administration that require the traditional lesson plan. The lesson plan is the "fifth column" of the school. It misrepresents motivation. As a result, many practicing clinicians and teachers do not understand, nor do they appreciate the significance of motivation.

What the lesson plan calls *motivation* is really attention-getting. Attention-getting is a useful external device such as yelling, "Shut up!" or telling a humorous story or "introducing" a subject. Motivation, on the other hand, is what a learner feels when he responds to a stimulus and knows *immediately* whether or not his response is adequate. If he discovers the response is adequate, he feels good. We call it *positive reward.* If he discovers the response is inadequate, he receives (or feels) *negative* reinforcement. That reinforcement system in a high intensity learning clinic or classroom is translated into material rewards or points or simple charts, graphs or records of some kind. The formal or informal reinforcement system sets an affective tone which is *motivation.* In other words, *motivation is the result of a learner experiencing the contingencies or payoffs or results of his behaviors.* This is a fact of life intrinsic to all behavior, but it is rarely used in the classroom or clinic as a management technique in learning to read.

If the schoolmen understood the nature and significance of motivation, the entire instructional system would be modified to present each stimulus or set of stimuli to each learner immediately following each learner's active, overt response to a previous stimulus. This is intensive learning and is different from what is allowed to occur in the traditional, teacher-directed large or small group lesson.

3) *Immediate feedback is provided for each response.* Motivation management depends upon the learner knowing immediately the appropriateness of his response. How else can the learner

experience positive or negative reinforcement which becomes the impetus to attend to the next stimulus?

4) *Whatever is to be learned should be a reinforced (rewarded) response to an appropriate stimulus or set of stimuli.* Teaching is behavior management. The teacher structures an environment in which prescribed stimuli are presented to the learner, and the learner's responses are appropriately reinforced. Too often, teachers expose children to information and assume that information is learned. But intensified learning is more than mere exposure. Learning occurs when the learner overtly responds, and that response is immediately reinforced positively and negatively. Mere knowledge of the response's adequacy or inadequacy is usually sufficient reinforcement for most normal children. The important point is that unless an overt response to programmed stimuli is reinforced, the teacher cannot assume learning to have taken place.

Applying these principles to learning requires a very different teacher or clinician than traditionally sought in remedial work. The teacher must be a manager, not a dispenser of wisdom. The manager determines the target behaviors to be achieved. The manager diagnoses. He programs the learner according to the *"so what"* diagnosis and then matches sets of hardware and software to the content needs and levels of each learner. The instruction becomes largely self instruction or small pupil-team learning. The manager or teacher adjusts resources using Taxonomy (Figure 1) as a guide. Taxonomy offers eight variables the teacher can manipulate until he gets the desired response from the learner. The learner controls his own rate of learning and almost all the record keeping.

The list of materials to teach reading used in this type of learning center appears elsewhere. (Cohen, 1969a) The teacher's job is to manipulate these materials in relation to pupil needs, to modify materials so that they can be used as self directing and self correcting learning experiences, and to give on-the-spot first aid to the learner when the materials to teach a specific behavior are unavailable or non-existent.

CONCLUSION

Can high intensity instruction work in regular classrooms with 30-to-one one pupil-teacher ratios? The system described in this chapter was designed for inner city ghetto classroom serving severely retarded readers. Variations of the system have been used in such classrooms all over the country with excellent results. To satisfy skeptical conservatives, the system was demonstrated successfully with delinquent boys who were severely retarded in reading. (Tannenbaum and Cohen, 1967) The system was also demonstrated for beginning reading in grades one and two where, until recently, self directing materials were unavailable.

By definition, intensifying instruction prevents dyspedagogia. The data available from the above projects indicate this. For children already victims of dyspedagogia, intensified instruction compensates markedly for poor teaching. Intensive instruction is, therefore, a prevention as well as a treatment.

Perhaps the most important point to consider is the possibility that from a treatment point of view, etiologies of learning disorders may be irrelevant in the light of applied principles of learning. The vast amounts of energy, time and money expended on researching and treating reading disabilities from the perspectives of visual perception and visual motor development, psycholinguistics and chemotherapy may be largely a waste. Instead, applying simple principles of learning may be the key to most of these learning disorders. One thing is certain—we can no longer assume that retarded readers who have not responded to remedial or "special" help need an etiological approach that restructures perceptual, linguistic, cognitive or metabolic processes underlying reading. Behavioral analyses of these remedial or special programs indicate that they are hardly more intensive than the run-of-the-mill dyspedagogia perpetrated upon children in regular classrooms. Usually, the only variables that change in special programs compared to regular classrooms are time and class size. More dyspedagogia will yield, at best, only meager results.

How many retarded readers would be left after trying high intensity instruction? Until we find out, we ought not hide behind systems of cross patterning, dexedrine, angels in the snow, and so on. And after we find out and cross pattern the "N.I.'s" and drug the "hyper-kinetics," and perceptually train the "dyslexics," we will still need to teach them all to read. In which case, intensive instruction will be the prescription.

REFERENCES

Austin, Mary; et al. **The first R.** New York: Macmillan, 1963.

Chall, Jeanne, & Feldman, Shirley. First grade reading: An analysis of the interactions of professed methods, teacher implementation and child background. **The Reading Teacher,** 1966, **19,** 569-575.

Cohen, S. Alan. **Teach them all to read: Theory, methods and materials for teaching the disadvantaged.** New York: Random House, 1969. (a)

Cohen, S. Alan. Studies in visual perception and reading in disadvantaged children. **Journal of Learning Disabilities,** Oct. 1969, **2,** 8-13. (b)

Cohen, S. Alan. **Research and teaching reading to disadvantaged learners: Implications for further research and practice.** Paper delivered at the Convention of the International Reading Association, Boston, Mass., 1968. (Available in mimeo from the Reading and Language Arts Center, Graduate School, Yeshiva University.)

Cohen, S. Alan. Reading and language arts skills. **Imperatives for change.** New York: Ferkauff Graduate School. Yeshiva University and New York State Department of Education, 1967.

Cohen, S. Alan. Some learning disabilities of socially disadvantaged Puerto Rican and Negro children. **Academic Therapy Quarterly,** Fall 1966, **II,** 37-41.

Frostig, Marianne; et al. Reading, developmental abilities, and the problem of the match. **Journal of Learning Disabilities,** Nov. 1969, **2,** 22.

Frostig, Marianne; et al. **Developmental test of visual-perception.** Palo Alto, California: Consulting Psychologists Press, 1961.

Harris, Albert; et al. **A continuation of the craft project: Comparing approaches with disadvantaged urban Negro children in primary grades.** U. S. O. E. No. 6-10-063, Division of Teacher Education, City University of New York, 1968.

Harris, Albert. **How to increase reading ability.** New York: Longmans, Green and Co., 1961.

Kirk, Samuel; et al. **Illinois test of psycholinguistic abilities.** University of Illinois, 1968.

The Reading Teacher. May 1966, **19.** (a)

The Reading Teacher. October 1966, **20.** (b)

The Reading Teacher, May 1967, **20.** (a)

The Reading Teacher. October 1967, **21.** (b)

Tannenbaum, Abraham, & Cohen, S. Alan. Taxonomy of instructional treatments. Final Report, U.S.O.E. No. G-1-6-062528-2092: **Development and demonstration of a self instruction reading and mathematics program for emotionally disturbed boys** by A. H. Tannenbaum (U.S. Office of Education, 1967).

PART III. DIAGNOSIS AND REMEDIATION:
MEDICAL-EDUCATIONAL VIEWS

Editor's Introduction

Discussion about the value of the term *dyslexia* certainly will not cease with the opinion of the HEW Committee that it serves no useful purpose. In fact it seems reasonable to expect even more discussion. After all, even if the term were abandoned, it would not have any effect on the children whose reading behaviors or lack of them prompted someone to call them dyslexic. The idea is now being expressed by some that rather than give up the term dyslexia, efforts might be directed toward clarifying its use. The HEW Committee's view was that agreement on its meaning was impossible. At this point, then, the burden is clearly on authors who use the term to make their own meaning crystal clear. We believe this is done well in the chapters of this section.

Boder proposes three subtypes of specific developmental dyslexia—dysphonetic, dyseidetic, and combined. The differential diagnosis is made by a careful evaluation of patterns of reading and spelling errors. Boder has developed practical, direct diagnostic screening procedures which can be used by a variety of multidisciplinary personnel. She advocates management of the dyslexic child by a neuropsychoeducational team approach. Her paper describes the diagnostic screening procedure and the three distinctive patterns of reading and spelling which have been found. The diagnostic screening procedure is based on how the child attempts to spell words which are in his reading sight vocabulary and words which are unknown to him. The idea is an intriguing one and we hope it will stimulate new and useful research. Many educators who have objected to the diagnosis of dyslexia based on factors far removed from actual reading performance may find Boder's approach exciting and relevant—perhaps enough so to overcome some of the objections to the word dyslexia! A large portion of some educators' discomfort with the concept of dyslexia is that it seems to place the cause for reading failure solely within the child. These same educators believe that a more profitable approach is to behave as if the difficulty were in the reading instruction being offered the child, since that is within the educator's realm of possible change. Boder's approach offers the possibility of examining in a new way the extent to which types of reading-spelling error patterns vary with the instruction received. For example, those who hold that dyspedagogia is a more valid concept than dyslexia would predict a high incidence of dysphonetic types among children who have received whole-word, traditional meaning-emphasis basal approaches and a low incidence of dysphonetic types among children who have had intensive decoding emphases in their early reading instruction. The possibility exists that excellent instruction can compensate for dyslexia-proneness to the point that the child would not be educationally dyslexic, but he would nonetheless reveal dyslexic error patterns when confronted with reading material substantially above his reading level. (Boder, private communication, 1970)

Blau, Blau and Schwalb also acknowledge that little agreement exists about the meaning of dyslexia and believe this is at least partially due to inadequate promulgation of a uniform classification system. They emphasize that a diagnosis of dyslexia is not an end product in itself, but rather is a means toward planning educational treatment. Remedial techniques are discussed in the final section of their chapter. These techniques include a bookless curriculum, modality adapted learning, non-visual AKT, modality overloading, taped dictation, and phonics. Illustrative cases are also included. The concept of non-visual AKT, in which the visual modality is blocked out during the early stages of learning to read, is an extremely important technique as it demonstrates that the role of vision in reading is not an essential one. Evidence continues to mount from a variety of sources indicating that the auditory component is the critical one in reading, due to the very nature of the reading response which is converting a stimulus (usually, but not necessarily visual) into its *sound* equivalent.

294

Blau, Blau and Schwalb have performed a particularly important task in drawing attention to the general educational deprivation experienced by the child who has been in school for several years and been unable to use reading for information input. Too often, as they point out, dyslexia is treated as if reading were the sole area of deficiency. Their general remedial strategy is to utilize the modalities most likely to be effective, i.e., teach to the areas of strength. This approach is generally accepted by medical and para-medical practitioners.

Together, these chapters by Boder and by Blau, Blau and Schwalb confirm the fact that the term dyslexia is not used identically by all, but more importantly they suggest that the term may still have usefulness if it is clearly defined by all who do use it and if it serves as the first step in educational planning.

Developmental Dyslexia:
A Diagnostic Screening Procedure
Based on Three Characteristic Patterns
of Reading and Spelling

Elena Boder, M.D.
Associate Clinical Professor of Pediatrics
School of Medicine
University of Southern California
Los Angeles, California

INTRODUCTION

There is growing awareness that specific learning disabilities, notably developmental dyslexia,[1] underlie academic underachievement and school behavioral problems far more frequently than has been heretofore recognized. (Boder, 1966; Boder and Foncerrada, 1967; Critchley, 1964; Thompson, 1966) It is now widely accepted that early diagnosis of developmental dyslexia, whatever the coexisting contributory factors may be, is of central importance both for successful remediation and to prevent school failure with its concomitant emotional overlay and loss of self-esteem.

There is therefore a widely felt need for practical, direct diagnostic screening procedures that can be used by a variety of multidisciplinary personnel—by teachers, who are usually the first to observe a child's learning difficulties, as well as by psychologists and physicians. Developmental dyslexia is clearly a multidisciplinary problem, and a team approach, which may be termed neuropsychoeducational, is essential to its diagnosis and management.

The purpose of this chapter is 1) to describe a *diagnostic screening procedure* for developmental dyslexia and 2) to describe *three distinctive patterns* of reading and spelling revealed by the diagnostic screening procedure which appear to provide a basis for classifying dyslexic children into three main subtypes.

[1]Terminology: Developmental dyslexia is viewed here as a *neurodevelopmental,* and frequently *neurogenetic,* disorder. (Critchley, 1964, 1968) The terms dyslexia, specific dyslexia, and specific developmental dyslexia are used here interchangeably with developmental dyslexia. None is used as a broad term encompassing nonspecific reading disorders. Other synonyms are specific reading disability (Bakwin and Bakwin, 1966; Eustin, 1947), strephosymbolia (Orton, 1937), developmental alexia (Jackson in Heller, 1963), primary reading retardation (Rabinovitch, 1968), Gestalt-blindness (Bender, 1959; deHirsch, 1952), and specific language disability (Gallagher, 1960). The older term congenital word blindness is still widely used.

Preliminary papers were published earlier. (Boder, 1968a, b, 1969) The current chapter presents a more fully developed description of the diagnostic screening procedure, a survey of a larger sample of dyslexic children, and an illustrative case report.

The diagnostic screening procedure described in this chapter represents an effort to approach the diagnosis of developmental dyslexia *directly* through objective patterns of reading and spelling. It is based on familiar school tasks which are readily adaptable to use by a variety of professional personnel—in schools, clinics, or private pediatric practice. This approach can be expected to facilitate diagnosis and suggest means for dealing with developmental dyslexia on a broader scale within the realistic limitations of current shortages in skilled personnel and special facilities.

As an empirically evolved procedure, it calls for further study and refinement. As a screening procedure, it has recognized limitations and does not supplant the standard diagnostic tests of psychological and psycholinguistic functions when more precise evaluation of reading ability and achievement is indicated.

DIAGNOSTIC SCREENING PROCEDURE
FOR DEVELOPMENTAL DYSLEXIA

The screening procedure for developmental dyslexia is used as an integral part of the complete neuropediatric evaluation that is done on every child referred for school behavioral or learning problems to the School Neurology Clinics in the Health Centers of the Los Angeles City Schools and at Cedars-Sinai Medical Center. The overall approach to the diagnosis and management of such children has been described in a previous report. (Boder, 1966)

The purpose of the screening procedure is to do not merely a quantitative evaluation of the child's ability to read and spell but a qualitative one. It is the qualitative analysis of *how* he reads and spells, rather than *at what grade level,* that enables the examiner to identify deficits in the functions prerequisite to reading, and thus to make a diagnosis of specific dyslexia and give guidelines for remedial teaching. The sequence of tasks is designed not merely to disclose the number and kinds of dyslexic errors the child makes in reading and spelling but to enable the examiner to ascertain his reading-spelling pattern and the subtype into which he falls (Table 1).

Reading Test

Screening for dyslexia in the school Neurology Clinics begins by utilizing the word recognition inventory that is used widely in the Los Angeles City Schools as an informal test of reading achievement (see Appendix 1). It consists of 8 lists of 20 words each, graded from the pre-primer level through the sixth grade.[2] Adapting a technique that is standard among reading specialists, the presentation of the word list at each level has two sections, for each of which a column is provided: the "flash" section, which determines the child's *sight vocabulary* (i.e., the words he reads as whole-word configurations or gestalts), and the "untimed" section, which calls upon the child's ability to employ phonetic word-analysis in reading words *not* in his sight vocabulary.

Two copies of the word list are used, one for the child to read and the other for the examiner's record of the child's performance so that the child is not distracted by the notations or discouraged by

[2]The Informal Word Recognition Inventory, based on word-frequency counts of basal readers (Ginn and Allyn; Bacon) commonly used in grades 1 through 6, was developed by Millard H. Black when he was Elementary Reading Supervisor in the Los Angeles City Schools. (Black, ND) The additional two word lists, used at the Junior High School and Senior High School levels respectively, were originally developed by Gilbert B. Schiffman of the Baltimore County Schools, Maryland. (Schiffman in Boder, 1966)

his mistakes. In presenting the word list to the child, the examiner says, "Here's a list of words for you to read. Do the best you can. It's all right to make mistakes, and it's all right to guess. This isn't a test; you won't be graded. We just want to see how you read so we'll know better how to help you." The child is then asked to go down the list, looking at each word in turn and reading it aloud. He is permitted to move the edge of a card down the list, if he likes, uncovering one by one the words to be read. Some children need to be assured that the test results are for use only at the clinic and will not be sent to the school.

If the child identifies a word correctly within two seconds, this is recorded with a checkmark in the flash column. If he misreads the word on sight or does not read it at all, he is asked to "take another look and try again." If he now identifies the word correctly, a checkmark is entered in the untimed column. If, given about ten seconds, he offers no meaningful approximation or misreads the word on one or more trials, the examiner records this with a dash in the untimed column. These words that the child cannot read correctly on either flash or untimed presentation are termed his *unknown vocabulary.* Actual misreadings and wrong guesses are also recorded—the immediate misreadings in the flash column and the delayed ones in the untimed column—for later evaluation of the child's characteristic errors and the deficit functions they may reflect. Words that are correctly read untimed, but with unusual difficulty, are circled for possible later use in the spelling test.

If the child is disturbed by his inability to decipher a word, the examiner may say, "If you don't know the word, you can read the letters," or "It's all right, we can come back to this word later," and the child is asked to go on to the next word. When it becomes obvious that the child has reached the reading level at which it is difficult for him to proceed, he is asked to look down the list quickly and pick out the words he recognizes. The test is continued until he reaches the grade level at which none of the words can be identified correctly.

The highest grade level at which the child's sight vocabulary includes at least 50% of the word list is considered his reading level.

The number of correctly read words in the flash and untimed columns is recorded at each grade level presented. The ratio between the two totals is helpful in analyzing whether the child is reading through both whole-word configurations and phonetic analysis or predominantly through one or the other. Finally, the examiner notes whether the child's sight vocabulary includes both phonetic and nonphonetic words.

Spelling Test

Following the administration of the word recognition inventory, the child is screened for atypical spelling patterns. The spelling test, like the reading test, has two sections and is presented in two columns—"known words" and "unknown words." The list of known words is intended to tap the child's ability to revisualize words in his sight vocabulary, and the list of unknown words to tap his phonetic concepts, specifically his ability to write good phonetic equivalents of words not in his sight vocabulary. Thus, the two columns are designed to tap the central auditory and visual processes prerequisite to spelling, in the same way that the flash and untimed columns of the reading test tap the central visual and auditory processes prerequisite to reading.

The child is first asked to write eight or more known words selected from the flash column of his reading test, and then to write the same number of unknown words selected from the untimed column. If too few unknown words are available for a given child, his second list is supplemented with words from the untimed column that the child read correctly but with unusual difficulty, and cannot therefore be considered to be in his sight vocabulary. The known words should be selected from the flash column at the child's actual reading level and down to two grades below, whereas the unknown words should be selected from the untimed column at his reading level and up to two grades above. An effort is made to present an equal number of phonetic and nonphonetic words in both the known and the unknown spelling lists. An additional effort is made to include some relatively long phonetic words (three or four syllables) in one or both columns as a means of eliciting omitted-syllable errors.

In introducing the spelling test, the examiner gives the child a lined page divided into two columns by a center line and says, "I'm going to give you two short lists of words to write. All of the words in the first list are words you know. Write them as well as you can." The child is given a pencil to use rather than a pen. No erasures are allowed, but the child may cross out and rewrite a word as many times as he wishes. If the child is having some difficulty in spelling a word, the examiner can say, "If you don't remember what this word looks like, it is all right to guess."[3]

Before dictating the unknown list the examiner explains, "This is the second list. These are words you don't know. We don't expect you to spell them correctly. They are guess words. Listen to the word carefully; then write all the letter-sounds you hear, so we can see how close you get to writing the word just as it sounds." The examiner says the word and may use it in a simple sentence. If the child hesitates, the examiner encourages him to say the word out loud once or twice before starting to write, to be sure he can repeat it correctly and to give him the kinesthetic reinforcement of articulating the word. If the child still makes no progress in writing the first word, an example of phonetic analysis of a spoken word is given, utilizing a simple word in his sight vocabulary. For example: *"No is nnn-oh and the letters are N-O."*

The percent of correctly spelled words is indicated at the bottom of each column. In the list of known words the examiner notes in addition whether the correctly spelled words include both phonetic and

[3]The procedures used in giving the Spelling Test may have to be modified for individual children. A severely dyslexic child should not be asked, for example, to spell full lists of 8 or 10 words, and the examiner's explanations of the tests should be adapted to the age and intelligence of each child.

nonphonetic words. In the list of unknown words the examiner notes whether the misspelled words are good phonetic equivalents of the dictated words and how many misspellings are so dysphonetic that the original word is not recognizable—not even to the child himself.

One can be quite certain that analysis of a child's spelling list of unknown words reveals his phonetic concepts and his ability to write phonetically; it is less certain that his spelling list of known words can reveal his ability to revisualize sight vocabulary independently of phonetic concepts—except when the task word is strikingly nonphonetic (e.g., talk, flight), so that the child must rely very specifically on visual memory.

Supplementary Tasks

If a child gives evidence of being unable to decipher words phonetically, the examiner goes back to the word recognition inventory at the conclusion of the reading and spelling tests. Several phonetic words in the unknown vocabulary are selected to explore whether the child can read them if given help in dividing the words into syllables. The child's performance enables the examiner to determine whether the marked deficit in phonetic abilities is at the analytic level of letter-sound association or at the synthetic level, i.e., the blending of component letter sounds into syllables and the syllables into words.

In addition, reciting and writing the alphabet may be presented as preliminary tasks to the diagnostic screening procedure in order to test the child's auditory and visual sequential memory as well as his ability to recognize and reproduce the individual letters. Finally, the reading of a paragraph from a textbook at the child's grade level or below may be included among the tasks to determine if his ability to read is improved in context. Illustrations are covered to avoid giving clues.

Comment

It should be noted that the exploration of the child's differential ability to spell known and unknown words to dictation is the unique feature of our diagnostic screening procedure, not previously described to the writer's knowledge. It was the designing of the spelling tasks to parallel the reading tasks and to utilize information revealed by the reading tasks that ultimately disclosed a consistent relationship between how a dyslexic child reads and how he spells, and led to the delineation of the three distinctive reading-spelling patterns described in this chapter (Table 1).

The diagnostic screening procedure permits an empirical clinical analysis of a child's reading and spelling performance, qualitative as well as quantitative. The possibility that a standard scoring method can be devised to make the qualitative analysis more objective is recognized, and is being explored. Certain quantitative criteria have already proved to be useful in further differentiating the three subtypes of dyslexic children from each other and from the poor readers whose reading-spelling pattern is normal and whose reading retardation is assumed therefore to be nonspecific. These criteria will be discussed elsewhere. (Boder, to be published)

READING-SPELLING PATTERNS
AMONG CHILDREN WITH DEVELOPMENTAL DYSLEXIA

We recognize that a variety of complex psychoneurologic functions, perceptual and integrative, are being tapped by the reading and spelling tasks in our diagnostic screening procedure. *Reading* requires visual perception and discrimination, visual sequential memory and recall, and directional orientation. (Benton, 1962) It also requires *visual-auditory integration*—that is, the translation of visual letter symbols into meaningful auditory equivalents, which includes the synthesis of letter-sounds into syllables and syllables into words. (Bauza, et al., 1962; Ingram, 1963; Myklebust, 1965; Rabinovitch, 1968) (The still higher level of integration required for reading comprehension is not tapped by our screening procedure.) *Spelling,* in contrast, requires the translation of speech sounds into their visual letter symbol equivalents. In addition to the visual functions prerequisite to reading, this *auditory-visual integration* requires auditory perception and discrimination, and auditory sequential memory. (Bannatyne, 1966; Bateman, 1968; Ingram, 1963; Isom, 1968; Wepman, 1962) *Writing* calls, further, upon fine motor and visuomotor coordination and tactile-kinesthetic memory. (Bannatyne, 1966; Johnson and Myklebust, 1967; Myklebust, 1965)

In the final analysis reading may be said to be essentially a *two channel function,* requiring the integration of intact visual and auditory processes, peripheral and central. It is essential for normal reading that these component processes go forward automatically. (de Hirsch, 1963; Rabinovitch, 1968; Wiener and Cromer, 1967)

A normal reader recognizes the familiar words constituting his sight vocabulary through the "visual channel," so to speak, as whole word configurations or instantaneous *visual gestalts* without having to discriminate individual letters or component syllables. In brief, he reads the words in his sight vocabulary *globally* rather than analytically. On the other hand, unfamiliar words, like words in a foreign language, are read by the normal reader through the "auditory channel," by a process of *phonetic analysis and synthesis.* In brief, he sounds out, or reads "by ear," the words that are not in his sight vocabulary.

In the dyslexic child, the normal reading process is fragmented or *dissociated.* (Heller, 1963) The normal automatic interplay of integrative and analytic processes is disrupted. The dyslexic child reads and spells differently from the normal reader *qualitatively as well as quantitatively.* (Boder, 1966; Eisenberg, 1966; Ingram, 1963; Orton, 1937; Rabinovitch, 1968) The writer's observations, consistent with those of other investigators (Ingram, 1963; Johnson and Myklebust, 1967; Myklebust, 1965; de Quiros, 1964; Rabinovitch, 1968), suggest that

306

dyslexic children have basic functional deficits in either the visual or the auditory channel, or in both, which are reflected in abnormal patterns in their reading and spelling performance.

Our diagnostic screening procedure has gradually revealed *three distinctive patterns of reading and spelling* among dyslexic children. One or another of these three reading-spelling patterns is found consistently, in the writer's experience, in all severely retarded readers who fulfill standard criteria for the diagnosis of developmental dyslexia by exclusion. None of the patterns is found among normal readers and spellers. The correlation between a child's pattern of reading and his pattern of spelling has been found to be so consistent that one is predictive of the other. From the way the child reads, it becomes possible to predict how he spells, and vice versa. It would appear that the same functional assets and deficits underlie both the reading and the spelling of dyslexic children. Thus, the three reading-spelling patterns appear to have diagnostic, prognostic, and remedial implications.

On the basis of the three correlated patterns, three subtypes, or groups, of dyslexic children have been delineated (Table 1). The description of the reading-spelling patterns is purely clinical. No attempt is being made to relate the patterns and the deficit functions they reflect to neurophysiological mechanisms.

Group I. Dysphonetic Dyslexia

Reading pattern. The child in Group I typically has a limited "sight vocabulary" of whole words that he recognizes on presentation and reads fluently. He reads words through *whole-word visual gestalts,* the component letters of which he may not be able to identify in the early grades. When he confronts a word, however simple, common, or phonetic, that is not in his sight vocabulary he is typically unable to decipher it. Lacking phonetic concepts, he has no word analysis skills and is unable to sound out or blend the component letters and syllables of a word.

307

TABLE 1

CLASSIFICATION OF CHILDREN
WITH DEVELOPMENTAL DYSLEXIA
BASED ON DIAGNOSTIC READING-SPELLING PATTERNS

Group I: Dysphonetic Dyslexia	Children whose reading-spelling pattern reflects primary deficit in symbol-sound (grapheme-phoneme) integration and in the ability to develop phonetic skills.
Group II: Dyseidetic Dyslexia (Gestalt-blind)*	Children whose reading-spelling pattern reflects primary deficit in the ability to perceive letters and whole words as configurations, or visual gestalts.
Group III: Combined Dysphonetic and Dyseidetic Dyslexia—Alexia	Children whose reading-spelling pattern reflects primary deficit in both ability to develop phonetic skills and ability to perceive letters and whole words as visual gestalts.

---

*Both "dyseidetic" and "dysphonetic" are coined descriptive terms. Dyseidetic is used to denote the subtype of dyslexia characterized by impairment in perception or recognition of the visual gestalts of whole words (from *eidos* meaning form or shape in Greek, as *Gestalt* does in German). It is synonymous with "gestalt-blind," the term applied by Bender (1959) and de Hirsch (1963) to all dyslexic children.

He tends to read words better in context than separately, since he may guess a word from minimal clues; for example, from the first and last letters. However, he may substitute a word similar in meaning though quite different phonetically.

In severe cases, he may not achieve a sight vocabulary beyond the fourth or fifth grade level even in high school, unless he has had reme-

308

dial reading therapy. However, even after he has gained phonetic concepts through remedial teaching his word analysis seldom becomes as
effortless and automatic as that of normal readers.

Spelling pattern. The dysphonetic child may be said to read and spell
by sight and not by ear, since he has difficulty learning what the letters sound like. He is a poor speller, his spelling level being typically
below the level of his sight vocabulary. Unable to read phonetically,
he cannot spell phonetically. His correctly written words are islands
in a hodgepodge of misspellings, typically *nonphonetic,* in which the
original words can seldom be identified even by himself. He spells
correctly to dictation only those words he can revisualize in his sight
vocabulary, regardless of whether they are phonetic or nonphonetic.
(Myklebust, 1965) In his spelling list of words selected from his
sight vocabulary a nonphonetic word may be written correctly, whereas in his spelling list of words *not* in his sight vocabulary a phonetic
word as simple as *go* or *did* may be bizarrely misspelled (Figure 1).

The most striking dyslexic errors of this group of children, observed
primarily in their reading but also in their spelling, are substitutions
of words that are closely related conceptually but not phonetically,
which may be termed *semantic-substitution errors.* Some examples
are funny for laugh, human for person, yesterday for tomorrow,
quack or chicken for duck, animals for cattle, airplane for train, Los
Angeles for city.

Group II. Dyseidetic Dyslexia

Reading pattern. The child in Group II reads laboriously, as if he is
seeing each word for the first time. Just as the dysphonetic child
has difficulty learning what the letters sound like, the dyseidetic
child has difficulty learning what they look like. The term "letter-
blind" can often be aptly applied to the Group II child. Although
he can usually recite the letters of the alphabet fluently and without
error, he may not be able to recognize or write the letters until the

FIGURE 1

ILLUSTRATING NONPHONETIC SPELLING
OF A DYSLEXIC CHILD IN DYSPHONETIC GROUP I

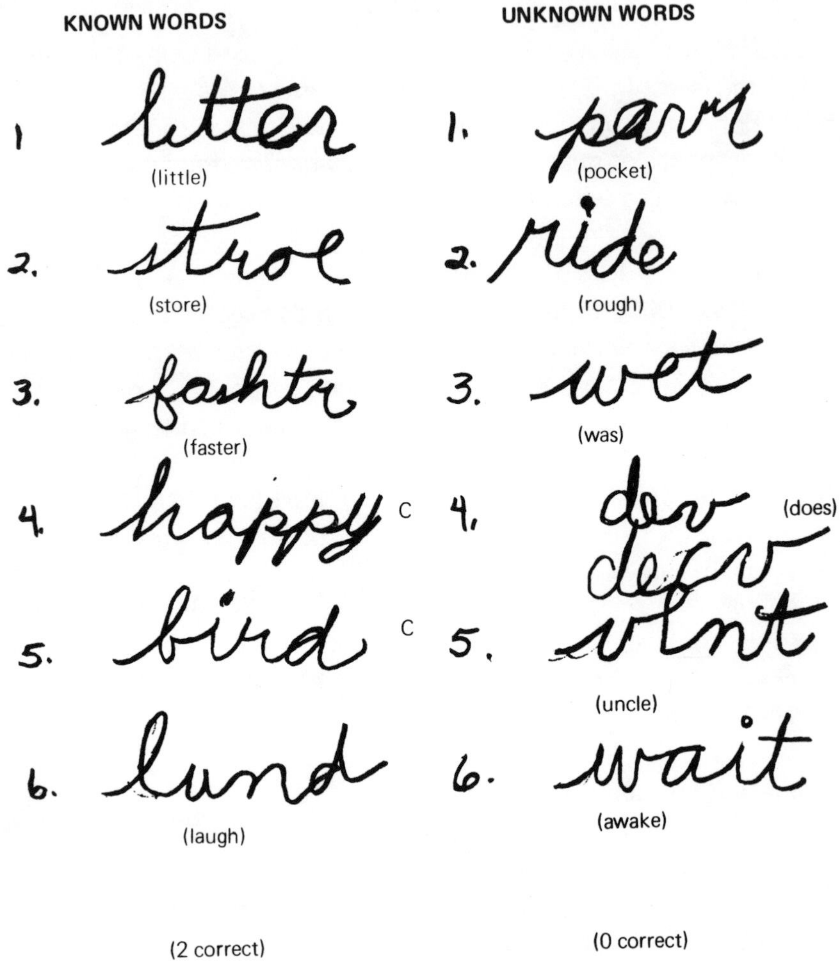

KNOWN WORDS

1. *litter* (little)
2. *stroe* (store)
3. *fashtr* (faster)
4. *happy* C (happy)
5. *bird* C (bird)
6. *lund* (laugh)

(2 correct)

UNKNOWN WORDS

1. *parm* (pocket)
2. *ride* (rough)
3. *wet* (was)
4. *dev* / *defv* (does)
5. *vlnt* (uncle)
6. *wait* (awake)

(0 correct)

10½-year-old boy, grade 4, average intelligence (Binet, Form LM). Reading level: Between grades 1 and 2 (sight vocabulary); word-analysis skills minimal. (See Case Report, Appendix I.)

FIGURE 2

ILLUSTRATING PHONETIC SPELLING OF A DYSLEXIC CHILD IN DYSEIDETIC GROUP II

Danny   9 YeRSe   GRaD – HiY 3

KNOWN WORDS		UNKNOWN WORDS	
1. Hoss	(house)	1. Bisshis	(business)
2. Blowe	(blue)	2. PRomiS	(promise)
3. afteR	c	3. Stor	(store)
4. then	c	4. WuDeRFuL	(wonderful)
5. Uncil	(uncle)	5. Lisin	(listen)
6. motheR	c	6. into	c
7. Litil	(little)	7. faster	c
8. GRen	(green)	8. Wet	c
9. funey	(funny)	9. awaK	(awake)
(3 correct)		(3 correct)	

9½-year-old boy, grade 3, IQ 92 (Binet, Form LM). Reading level: Primer to grade 1 (sight vocabulary); grade 3 (word-analysis skills). Note that in the lists of "known" and "unknown" words the only correctly spelled words are the phonetic ones.

311

fourth or fifth grade, unless he has had the benefit of remedial teaching. Even when no longer letter-blind he may still be said to be "word-blind" or "gestalt-blind," for he has little or no visual memory for whole words. He is an *analytic* reader and reads by ear, by a laborious process of phonetic analysis, sounding out familiar as well as unfamiliar combinations of letters, rather than by whole-word visual gestalts.

In contrast to Group I, the Group II child can often read the word list by phonetic analysis at or near his grade level, missing only words that cannot be decoded phonetically. For example, the word laugh may not be read at all or read as log or loge; the word bird may be misread as beard or by-erd; the word talk as talc.

Spelling pattern. The Group II child, like the Group I child, spells poorly, though not bizarrely as a rule. He spells as he reads—phonetically, by ear. In contrast to Group I, his *misspellings are phonetic,* and the original word can usually be readily identified in his spelling list by himself and others. Some examples are letl for little, lisn for listen, sos for sauce, rit for right, bisnis for business, onkl for uncle, tok for talk, laf for laugh.

His occasional nonphonetic bizarre misspellings seem to manifest an effort to spell a word in his sight vocabulary list by revisualizing it, and failing to make use of his more efficient auditory channel. Some examples are glaf for laugh, hwisper for whisper.

A striking finding is that simple *nonphonetic* words in this child's limited sight vocabulary are usually written incorrectly, whereas a long and unfamiliar *phonetic* word *not* in his sight vocabulary may be written correctly. It is also striking that he can write good phonetic equivalents of nonphonetic words that he cannot read at all (Figure 2).

312

FIGURE 3

ILLUSTRATING NONPHONETIC SPELLING
OF A DYSLEXIC CHILD
IN COMBINED DYSPHONETIC-DYSEIDETIC GROUP III

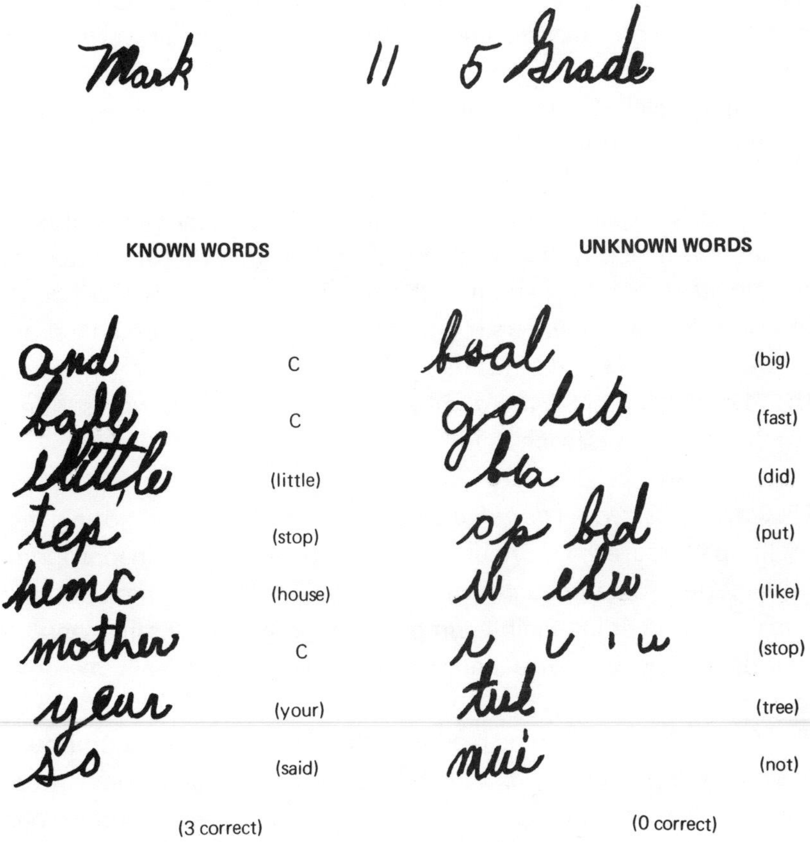

KNOWN WORDS		UNKNOWN WORDS	
and	C	*boal*	(big)
ball	C	*go lib*	(fast)
little	(little)	*ba*	(did)
tep	(stop)	*op byd*	(put)
hemc	(house)	*ib ebw*	(like)
mother	C	*u v i w*	(stop)
your	(your)	*tul*	(tree)
so	(said)	*mui*	(not)
(3 correct)		(0 correct)	

11-year-old boy, grade 5, IQ 97 (WISC: Verbal IQ 84, Performance IQ 113). Reading level: Pre-primer (sight vocabulary); no word-analysis skills. Note that the only correctly spelled words, as in Group I, are in the list of "known" words, phonetic or not, selected from the child's very limited sight vocabulary.

Group III. Combined Dysphonetic and Dyseidetic—Alexia

Group III comprises the "hard core" dyslexic children who tend to be the most severely handicapped educationally and may be properly termed *alexic.* The child in Group III, combining the deficits of both Group I and Group II, cannot read either by sight or by ear. Even in high school he may remain a virtual nonreader or alexic, unless he has had intensive remedial reading therapy. The occasional word that he recognizes on sight or can write correctly is typically on the primer or pre-primer level. Characteristically, his response to usual remedial teaching is painfully slow.

As would be expected, since he cannot read, he cannot spell. Like children in Group II, he has difficulty in learning what the letters of the alphabet look like, and like children in Group I he has difficulty in learning what the letters sound like. He often has marked visuo-spatial difficulties and tends more than children in Group I to confuse the reversible letters, *b-d-p-q, m-w,* and *n-u,* and letters with subtle graphic differences, such as *h-n, g-q, v-y.*

His *spelling pattern* is *nonphonetic,* like that of Group I, but his mis-spellings appear even more bizarre: sometimes a single inappropriate initial letter; sometimes a formless scribble, as if imitating rapid writing; usually an unintelligible jumble (Figure 3). In the same sense that he may be said to be a nonreader, he is a nonspeller.

The Group III child can be readily differentiated from Group I by the much lower grade level of his sight vocabulary, and from Group II by his lack of word analysis skills. His sense of defeat and his phobic withdrawal from reading and writing tasks are often striking.

Additional Comments on the Three Groups

It should be noted, in summary, that although there is a fundamental *qualitative association* between how a given dyslexic child reads and how he spells, there is a *quantitative dissociation* between his achievement levels in reading and spelling. In all three groups, spelling achievement is consistently at a lower grade level than reading achievement. Dyslexic children can seldom spell correctly more than 50% of the words in their sight vocabulary at their reading level and below, and usually much less (Figures 1, 2, 3). By contrast, normal readers in the writer's experience can usually spell correctly 80% to 100% of their sight vocabulary at their grade level or below and, commensurate with their grade level, write good phonetic equivalents of words not yet in their sight vocabulary.

The classic dyslexic errors—confusion of reversible letters, the so-called *static reversals,* and mirror-reading and -writing, the so-called *kinetic reversals* (Clements and Peters, 1962; Orton, 1937; Orton in Thompson, 1966, pp. 26-60)—have been observed in all three of our groups, particularly among the younger children, and are viewed as valuable diagnostic signs. Although such visuospatial reversals are ubiquitous among normal young beginning readers, it is generally agreed that they are diagnostically significant when they are very frequent or persist beyond the age of eight. (Money, 1962; Schiffman, 1962) *Letter-order errors,* found by Kinsbourne and Warrington (1966) to be characteristic of dyslexic children with the developmental Gerstmann syndrome, have also been observed in all three of our groups and are viewed as diagnostically significant.

As noted earlier, visuospatial reversals appear to occur more frequently in Group III and to persist for a longer time. However, the distribution of reversals and letter-order errors in Groups I, II, and III has not yet been statistically evaluated, and no conclusions can be drawn that any of these errors or the functional deficits they reflect are definitely more characteristic of one of the three groups than another.

IMPLICATIONS FOR REMEDIATION

The three delineated reading-spelling patterns reflect the child's functional assets as well as his functional deficits, and suggest the sensory modality, or channel, upon which the initial remedial techniques should be based. This permits the reading therapist to teach to the child's assets, not to his deficits, i.e., to his abilities rather than to his disabilities, and thus insure the initial successes that will help to motivate the dyslexic child and encourage a positive attitude toward learning.

Ultimately, of course, a multisensory approach to reading remediation will be used for all three groups of dyslexic children, but the techniques used initially will vary with each group.

The dysphonetic child (Group I) can be called "visile" rather than "audile." (Wepman, 1962) (Table 1) Since his primary deficit is in the auditory channel and he is unable to *auditorize*[4] letters and words, his dyslexia would be called "auditory dyslexia" by Myklebust (1965). The initial remedial approach for these children—contrary to general practice and belief—might well be through whole-word techniques. Only after he has developed sufficient sight vocabulary (reinforced by tactile-kinesthetic clues) to provide an adequate foundation should the teaching of remedial phonetics be initiated. It is important, of course, for the teacher to be aware from the outset that phonetic concepts will not come easily to such a child, because this is precisely the area of his primary deficit.

This child, like the Group III child, is typically a nonphonetic speller, whose spelling tends to be unintelligible except for those words in his sight vocabulary that he is able to revisualize. The initial remedial efforts to improve his spelling, therefore, should realistically be directed

---

[4]Myklebust's terms "to auditorize" and "to visualize" refer, respectively, to the central auditory and visual processes prerequisite to reading.

toward converting him from a nonphonetic speller to a phonetic speller so that everyone, including himself, can correctly interpret what he has written.

The dyseidetic child (Group II) can be called "audile" rather than "visile" (Table 1), and since his primary deficit is in the visual channel and he is unable to visualize letters and words, his dyslexia would be called "visual dyslexia" by Myklebust (1965). The implications for remedial teaching would be to start with tactile-kinesthetic techniques (Fernald in Schiffman, 1962), if the child has not yet learned to recognize the letters of the alphabet. Remedial phonetics, e.g., the Orton-Gillingham technique (Schiffman, 1962), would be the indicated initial method if he can recognize the visual forms of the letters.

In contrast to Group I, the child in Group II will learn through phonics readily. To develop a sight vocabulary, i.e., visual gestalts of whole words, the use of tactile-kinesthetic techniques would also be required.

The dysphonetic-dyseidetic child of Group III is neither visile nor audile, but has the combined deficits of both Group I and Group II children. The initial remedial approach of choice for this child would have to be the tactile-kinesthetic method for learning letters and whole words, until there is some sight vocabulary as a basis for subsequent remedial phonetics and multisensory techniques. The remedial approach to this child's spelling disability would be the same as for the child in Group I, that is, to convert him from a nonphonetic to a phonetic speller. At the same time, the development of nonlanguage skills at which the child can succeed should be encouraged.

Reading-Spelling Patterns in Grouping for Remedial Teaching

The three reading-spelling patterns delineated here offer a rational basis for grouping dyslexic children into homogeneous groups for prescriptive remedial teaching, the groups being set up according to

317

shared functional assets and deficits in their visual and auditory processes, or channels, i.e., their abilities and disabilities. This may make it possible to meet individual remedial needs on a group basis and prove more effective than the teaching of undifferentiated groups of dyslexic children in the usual remedial classes. In view of current shortages of skilled remedial reading teachers and special classes, this approach offers immediate practical advantages.

DISTRIBUTION OF THE THREE READING-SPELLING PATTERNS AMONG DYSLEXIC CHILDREN

The distribution of the three reading-spelling patterns among dyslexic children seen at the Clinics during the first six months of 1968 was determined in a preliminary survey. Of the total group of children who fulfilled the standard criteria for the diagnosis of developmental dyslexia *by exclusion,*[5] 107 were selected according to the following criteria: 1) All of the children were in the third grade or beyond. 2) All were two or more years retarded in reading according to the Jastak Wide Range Achievement Test and the Informal Word Recognition Inventory. 3) All of the children were of normal intelligence. They generally attained IQ scores of 90 or more on the Stanford-Binet Form L, or on either the Verbal Scale or the Performance Scale of the Wechsler Intelligence Scale for Children. A few had IQ scores between 80 and 90, but showed wide scatter in their test results, reaching well into the normal range. 4) All had essentially normal hearing and vision. 5) All were in good general health and free from gross neurologic defect and overt primary psychiatric disorder.

In the total sample of 107 children, 92 were boys and 15 were girls. These children represent essentially a random sample of dyslexic chil-

[5]Diagnosis of developmental dyslexia by exclusion is well illustrated by Eisenberg's (1966) widely quoted definition: "Operationally, specific reading disability may be defined as the failure to learn to read with normal proficiency despite conventional instruction, a culturally adequate home, proper motivation, intact senses, normal intelligence, and freedom from gross neurological defects."

dren in the regular clinic population, although a special effort was made to include the dyslexic siblings of the patients. Of the 107 in the sample, 67 (63%) fell into Group I, 10 (9%) into Group II, 23 (22%) into Group III. Of the total sample, only 7 patients (6%) had to be placed in an undetermined group, to be studied further.

Most of the children were readily classified into the three groups. Some of the children in the sample have been followed for as long as seven years, and their reading-spelling patterns on the whole have remained consistent even when their levels of reading achievement have risen significantly.

It has become apparent, however, from a comparative study of long-term records that differentiating certain Group II children from Group III children may present difficulties. Their reading-spelling patterns may be indistinguishable, in fact, if Group II children are seen before they have had the benefit of remedial phonetics. Thus, some of the children in the sample now classified in Group II showed reading-spelling patterns at an earlier age that would have placed them in Group III.

Long-term observation and trial of remedial phonetic instruction may be required to distinguish such Group II children from Group III children. Group III in our sample may therefore contain some Group II children who have not yet been taught phonetics.

It should also be noted that although the spelling patterns of children in Groups I and III may be very similar, the children can usually be clearly differentiated by the disparity they exhibit in sight vocabulary, that of Group III being at a much lower grade level. Young Group III children may have no sight vocabulary or letter recognition, while the sight vocabulary of older Group III children is typically at the primer or pre-primer level, unless they have had the benefit of intensive remedial reading therapy.

It is of interest that Group I is the largest of the three groups, and it

319

is the one to which the terms word-blind or gestalt-blind—widely used as synonyms for developmental dyslexia—are not really applicable, although these terms can be aptly applied to Groups II and III. The higher incidence of the dysphonetic reading-spelling pattern of Group I corroborates the observations of Ingram (1963) and others (Warrington, 1967; Wepman, 1962) that deficits in auditory discrimination in letter-sound integration or in word analysis and synthesis are more important as causes of developmental dyslexia than visuospatial perceptual deficits.

DISCUSSION

The prevailing diagnostic criteria for developmental dyslexia have evolved in the fields of medicine, psychology, and education, independently or through interdisciplinary collaboration. The criteria invoked tend to vary with the professional disciplines of those involved in making a diagnosis. It tends to be diagnosed either indirectly on the basis of neurological and psychometric concomitants, directly by the frequency and persistence of certain types of errors in reading and writing, or by a process of exclusion. (Critchley, 1964; Eisenberg, 1966; Rabinovitch, 1968)

A critical review of the prevailing diagnostic criteria is not within the scope of this chapter. Such a review, indicating how the writer's concept of direct diagnosis of developmental dyslexia through objective patterns of reading and spelling fits into the context of prevailing diagnostic criteria, will appear in a subsequent paper. (Boder, to be published)

The delineation of three main clinical subtypes of dyslexic children on the basis of their reading-spelling patterns is consistent with a growing number of observations by other investigators, notably those of Bateman (1968), Ingram (1963), Kinsbourne and Warrington (1966), Myklebust (1965, 1968), de Quiros (1964), and Wolf (1968), indicating

320

that children with developmental dyslexia are a heterogeneous group both etiologically and clinically.

The validity of the three reading-spelling patterns as direct evidence of specific deficits in psychoneurologic functions essential to reading is well supported. In addition to the consistency with which the patterns occur in retarded readers who fulfill standard diagnostic criteria for developmental dyslexia, particularly diagnosis by exclusion, none of the patterns has been found in normal readers, i.e., children who are up to grade level, or above, in both reading and spelling, or whose achievement in reading and spelling is commensurate with their mental age.

Long-term observation of some of the children in the sample indicates that their reading-spelling patterns, though they may be compensated to a large extent through remedial teaching, have remained consistent, even when the level of their reading and spelling has risen significantly. The single exception has already been noted: the dyseidetic Group II child whose early reading-spelling pattern, before he has been taught phonetics, is indistinguishable from the pattern of a Group III child. Clearly, neither variations in teaching methods nor in levels of maturity can account for the observed reading-spelling patterns.

Further evidence for the validity of the reading-spelling patterns as diagnostic indicators of three distinct subtypes of developmental dyslexia is provided by their frequent familial incidence within the sample, and their association with the classic dyslexic errors and "soft" neurologic signs. The familial incidence of developmental dyslexia is impressive and is widely viewed as corroborative evidence for the diagnosis. (Childs, 1970; Critchley, 1964; Crosby and Liston, 1968; Hallgren, 1950; Herman and Norrie, 1958) Within this sample, a positive family history of reading disability has been elicited for most of the children in all three groups. In fact, there is suggestive evidence that a genetic factor may exist in each of the three reading-spelling patterns in that the dyslexic siblings tend to exhibit the same reading-spelling pattern.

Additional suggestive evidence that the reading-spelling patterns are neurogenic is found in the frequency with which they are associated with a variety of minimal, or soft, neurologic signs, pointing to a parieto-occipital dysfunction (Cohn, 1964; Critchley, 1964; Whitsell, 1965) and neurophysiological immaturity. (Bender, 1959; de Hirsch, 1963) Among these neurologic concomitants are crossed-dominance, right-left confusion, cerebellar signs, nonspecific fine and gross motor clumsiness (Bakwin, 1968), developmental dysgraphia, finger agnosia (Kinsbourne and Wellington, 1966), developmental speech and language disorders (Ingram, 1963), and the hyperkinetic syndrome. (Boder, 1966; Ingram, 1963) Associated mild electroencephalographic abnormalities are also frequent.

Cumulatively, the evidence is strong that the three reading-spelling patterns can be viewed as specific and diagnostic in themselves of developmental dyslexia, each of the subtypes delineated by the patterns having a different prognosis and calling for different remedial reading techniques.

The direct diagnostic approach to developmental dyslexia through dyslexic reading-spelling patterns—reflecting both the child's functional assets and his deficits—offers a fuller range of prognostic and therapeutic implications than the traditional direct diagnostic approach through dyslexic errors, which reflect the child's functional deficits alone.

The identification of the three reading-spelling patterns reveals that most of the errors made by dyslexic children do not occur at random among them but in patterns of errors, thus highlighting the heterogeneity of dyslexic children and the fact that they misspell in different ways for different reasons. It has been standard practice to refer to the so-called dyslexic errors as bizarre, and even to say that the very bizarreness of the errors is diagnostic of developmental dyslexia. Understood as patterns of errors in reading and spelling, the errors cease to be bizarre; they become direct reflections of specific functional deficits in the dyslexic child. It becomes evident that most of the spelling errors that have been described as typical of dyslexic children fall into two main groups—the intelligible phonetic errors and the unintelligible nonphonetic, or dysphonetic, errors. The often bizarre errors of Groups I and III are seen to be consistently nonphonetic (Figures 1, 3), with semantic-substitution errors in both reading and spelling being unique to Group I and virtually diagnostic, whereas the errors of Group II are seen to be consistently phonetic (Figure 2).

Reading-Spelling Patterns in Differential Diagnosis

Along with other clinicians in the field, the writer views specific developmental dyslexia as essentially a *neurodevelopmental reading disorder* that is frequently neurogenetic and only infrequently due to brain damage. (Bannatyne, 1963; Critchley, 1964; Hallgren, 1950; Hermann and Norrie, 1958) In its milder and transient forms developmental dyslexia may represent a normal variation in psychoneurological maturation, i.e., a maturational lag in reading-readiness. (Bender, 1959; de Hirsch, 1952) On the other hand, nonspecific reading disorders, or "secondary reading retardation" (Rabinovitch, 1968), may have a variety of nonspecific causes: physical, mental, emotional, cultural and educational.

The concept that specific developmental dyslexia is by definition of neurologic origin greatly simplifies differential diagnosis. The diagnostic objective becomes, in essence, to differentiate between specific dyslexia and nonspecific reading retardation. The differentiation has a direct practical bearing, since specific dyslexia calls for certain remedial reading techniques that are not essential in the management of nonspecific reading disorders. (Boder, 1966; Money, 1966)

A child with a *nonspecific reading disorder* reads poorly but has a normal reading potential. In the writer's experience and that of other investigators (Bauza, et al., 1962; Ingram, 1963; Myklebust, 1965,

323

1968; Rabinovitch, 1968), the reading and spelling performance of such a child is quantitatively different from that of a normal reader, but not qualitatively, whereas a dyslexic child reads differently both quantitatively and qualitatively.

The child of normal intelligence whose reading retardation is nonspecific reads and spells normally at whatever grade level he has achieved, his performance in terms of sight vocabulary and word-analysis skills being indistinguishable from that of an average younger reader at the same grade level. In writing to dictation he is able to spell correctly most of the words in his sight vocabulary and to spell unfamiliar words phonetically. There are none of the dissociative reading and spelling patterns characteristic of dyslexic children and no persisting dyslexic errors, such as static and kinetic reversals, beyond the age of eight.

Unlike the reading disability of dyslexic children, which is often selective and in sharp contrast with their other abilities and achievement, nonspecific reading retardation is usually part of a global underachievement, particularly in the emotionally disturbed or poorly motivated child. Nor, in the writer's experience and that of Rabinovitch (1968), is reading retardation secondary to emotional factors ever as severe in relation to grade level and mental age as the reading retardation of dyslexic children—one to two years at most.

The reading retardation secondary to mental retardation is also part of a global underachievement, but one that is commensurate with the child's mental age. It should be noted, however, that developmental dyslexia and mental retardation may coexist. In the writer's judgment a diagnosis of developmental dyslexia can be made in a mentally retarded child, and it is important to do so, since a retarded dyslexic child also needs remedial reading therapy if he is to learn to read. The diagnosis should be considered if the retarded child's reading level is two or more years below his mental age and grade level, particularly if he presents one of the delineated reading-spelling patterns or meets other criteria standard in the diagnosis of developmental dyslexia in children of normal intelligence. The screening of mentally retarded children for developmental dyslexia is particularly important, since a dyslexic child characteristically shows a wide scatter in his psychological test results which may bring his overall IQ score into the mentally retarded range. Unless the diagnosis of developmental dyslexia is made in such a child, he may be erroneously labeled and assigned to a class for the mentally retarded, rather than to a special class for children with specific learning disabilities where he properly belongs.

The utilization of atypical patterns of reading and spelling as diagnostic criteria also permits diagnosis of developmental dyslexia in a child of superior intelligence. Although his reading and even his spelling may be at grade level or only slightly below, a diagnosis of developmental dyslexia should be considered if his performance in reading and spelling is two or more years below his mental age and he exhibits one of the three delineated reading-spelling patterns.

Reading-Spelling Patterns in Prognosis

Long-term observations have shown that the reading-spelling patterns have prognostic implications differing for each group. The prognosis for Group I and II, in which the primary deficit is in only one sensory channel, has been found to be more favorable than that for Group III, in which both the auditory and visual channels are deficient. The prognosis for children in the combined dysphonetic-dyseidetic Group III must be guarded. Without intensive remedial reading therapy, they are not likely to achieve any degree of proficiency in either reading or spelling.

Reading-Spelling Patterns in Counseling

Parent and child counseling is of paramount importance in dealing with the dyslexic child and has been discussed in some detail in a previous publication. (Boder, 1966) The reading-spelling patterns, readily de-

monstrable, can be effectively used to help parents gain better understanding of the child's dyslexic problem and the specific goals toward
which remedial reading instruction will have to be directed. Interpreting deficit functions in visual and auditory processes for learning to
read in terms of channels that are open or closed is readily grasped
and accepted by the parents and the child, who have been equally be-
wildered by his inability to read. The concept of three subtypes of
dyslexic children based on reading-spelling patterns is also effective
in interpreting the dyslexic problems of individual children to school
personnel.

SUMMARY

A diagnostic screening procedure for developmental dyslexia is described, revealing three distinctive, atypical patterns of reading and
spelling among dyslexic children. It is based on familiar reading and
spelling tasks which are readily adaptable to use by a variety of multidisciplinary personnel—in schools, clinics, and private pediatric practice.

The diagnostic screening procedure permits an empirical clinical analysis of a child's reading and spelling performance, qualitative as well as
quantitative, emphasizing how he reads and spells rather than at what
level. It was the designing of the spelling tasks to parallel the reading
tasks that ultimately disclosed the consistent relationship between the
reading and spelling performance of dyslexic children, and led to the
delineation of the three atypical reading-spelling patterns. A unique
feature of the screening procedure is its exploration of the child's differential ability to spell to dictation words that are and are not in his
sight vocabulary.

One or another of the three reading-spelling patterns has been found
in all severely retarded readers who fulfill standard diagnostic criteria
for developmental dyslexia. None of the patterns has been found
among normal readers and spellers. The three dyslexic reading-spell-

ing patterns appear to be specific, therefore, and diagnostic in themselves. As such, they provide a basis for classifying dyslexic children into three main subtypes, and suggest a useful direct diagnostic approach. In addition, these three patterns—since they reflect the dyslexic child's functional assets as well as deficits in the visual and auditory processes prerequisite to reading—appear to have prognostic and therapeutic implications, differing for each of the three subtypes.

The diagnostic screening procedure is systematically used by the writer as an integral part of the neurological examination of every child referred for behavioral or learning problems. However, developmental dyslexia is viewed as a multidisciplinary problem, and a team approach that may be termed neuropsychoeducational is viewed as essential to its diagnosis and management.

The identification of three clinical subtypes of developmental dyslexia on the basis of three atypical reading-spelling patterns has not been previously reported to the writer's knowledge. Although the usefulness of the patterns as diagnostic indicators awaits assessment by other investigators, their identification already offers a fresh point of departure for further studies of developmental dyslexia.

The writer wishes to express her appreciation to Dr. Harriett B. Randall who, as Administrator of the Health Services Branch, Los Angeles City Schools, initiated the Neurology Clinics in the School Health Centers and has given consistent support to the writer in developing the program out of which evolved the diagnostic approach to dyslexia described in this chapter.

Acknowledgment is also due to the invaluable contribution of Anne Ross Silver, M.A., in preparing statistical surveys of the 107 dyslexic children and to the skillful volunteer participation of Mrs. Esther P. Gunther, Mrs. Frances D. Nordhoff, Mrs. Reba Phillips, and Mrs. Suzanne Stein in the administration of the diagnostic screening procedure. The writer is indebted to Dr. C. Edward Meyers for his practical statistical consultation, to Sylvia Jarrico, M.A., for her thoughtful editorial assistance and suggestions in the preparation of the manuscript, and to Drs. Joseph E. Bogen, Marcel Kinsbourne, and Anita Whiting for their helpful criticism.

APPENDIX I.

INFORMAL WORD RECOGNITION INVENTORY

(Vocabulary Common to Ginn and Allyn and Bacon Readers,
Pre-Primer Through Grade 6)

NAME _____ AGE _____ GRADE _____

EXAMINER _____ DATE _____

| | Pre-Primer | | | Primer | |
Stimulus	Flash	Untimed	Stimulus	Flash	Untimed
1. and	_____	_____	are	_____	_____
2. big	_____	_____	black	_____	_____
3. ball	_____	_____	came	_____	_____
4. fast	_____	_____	did	_____	_____
5. go	_____	_____	eat	_____	_____
6. green	_____	_____	farm	_____	_____
7. help	_____	_____	house	_____	_____
8. I	_____	_____	like	_____	_____
9. little	_____	_____	now	_____	_____
10. mother	_____	_____	on	_____	_____
11. not	_____	_____	paint	_____	_____
12. play	_____	_____	put	_____	_____
13. red	_____	_____	ready	_____	_____
14. ride	_____	_____	saw	_____	_____
15. said	_____	_____	store	_____	_____
16. stop	_____	_____	tree	_____	_____
17. the	_____	_____	your	_____	_____
18. to	_____	_____	too	_____	_____
19. we	_____	_____	white	_____	_____
20. work	_____	_____	yes	_____	_____

INFORMAL WORD RECOGNITION INVENTORY

	First Reader			Second Reader		
	Stimulus	**Response**		**Stimulus**		**Response**
		Flash	**Untimed**		**Flash**	**Untimed**
1.	after	_____	_____	across	_____	_____
2.	away	_____	_____	ask	_____	_____
3.	blue	_____	_____	bird	_____	_____
4.	call	_____	_____	city	_____	_____
5.	dinner	_____	_____	does	_____	_____
6.	faster	_____	_____	ever	_____	_____
7.	funny	_____	_____	five	_____	_____
8.	guess	_____	_____	girl	_____	_____
9.	here	_____	_____	happy	_____	_____
10.	into	_____	_____	just	_____	_____
11.	like	_____	_____	listen	_____	_____
12.	money	_____	_____	miss	_____	_____
13.	now	_____	_____	next	_____	_____
14.	pocket	_____	_____	over	_____	_____
15.	sat	_____	_____	pull	_____	_____
16.	stay	_____	_____	rolled	_____	_____
17.	then	_____	_____	step	_____	_____
18.	toy	_____	_____	talk	_____	_____
19.	was	_____	_____	uncle	_____	_____
20.	with	_____	_____	wet	_____	_____

INFORMAL WORD RECOGNITION INVENTORY

(From Ginn Basal Reader Series, Grades 4 through 6)

	Third Reader			Fourth Reader		
	Stimulus	Response		Stimulus	Response	
		Flash	Untimed		Flash	Untimed
1.	almost			automobile		
2.	awake			blindfolded		
3.	believe			characters		
4.	business			cottage		
5.	chance			delight		
6.	deep			environment		
7.	earth			flight		
8.	farther			goggles		
9.	front			human		
10.	great			lame		
11.	heavy			marry		
12.	important			natural		
13.	laugh			pain		
14.	minute			prisoners		
15.	other			rough		
16.	promise			shallow		
17.	remember			soared		
18.	should			study		
19.	traffic			tourists		
20.	wonderful			whisper		

INFORMAL WORD RECOGNITION INVENTORY

	Fifth Reader			Sixth Reader	
	Stimulus	Response		Stimulus	Response
		Flash	Untimed		Flash	Untimed

	Fifth Reader Stimulus	Flash	Untimed	Sixth Reader Stimulus	Flash	Untimed
1.	astronomy	_____	_____	apparatus	_____	_____
2.	astonished	_____	_____	badge	_____	_____
3.	curious	_____	_____	burlap	_____	_____
4.	crocodiles	_____	_____	conceited	_____	_____
5.	doubt	_____	_____	decisions	_____	_____
6.	equator	_____	_____	earthquake	_____	_____
7.	forge	_____	_____	foreign	_____	_____
8.	genius	_____	_____	hibernation	_____	_____
9.	height	_____	_____	immense	_____	_____
10.	inventor	_____	_____	knapsack	_____	_____
11.	lizard	_____	_____	legendary	_____	_____
12.	marmalade	_____	_____	marvelous	_____	_____
13.	opposite	_____	_____	necessary	_____	_____
14.	position	_____	_____	persuade	_____	_____
15.	recognized	_____	_____	quest	_____	_____
16.	scrambled	_____	_____	substituted	_____	_____
17.	scholar	_____	_____	treacherous	_____	_____
18.	tomato	_____	_____	utter	_____	_____
19.	vowed	_____	_____	varnish	_____	_____
20.	witness	_____	_____	wisdom	_____	_____

WORD RECOGNITION INVENTORY

	Jr. High (Grades 7-8)				Sr. High (Grades 9-12)	
Stimulus	Response		Stimulus	Response	
	Flash	Untimed		Flash	Untimed
1. abate			abandoned		
2. armament			armada		
3. blunt			blurt		
4. charitable			Charlemagne		
5. coolie			cookery		
6. devoted			detestable		
7. Elsie			elude		
8. fireman			Finland		
9. graciously			graduation		
10. Hungarian			hundredth		
11. jeer			islet		
12. loveliness			lovable		
13. morrow			morose		
14. stretched			outsider		
15. poorly			pollute		
16. recline			recital		
17. saucepan			Saul		
18. snuff			snuggle		
19. Susan			surveying		
20. trudge			truant		

Note: From Gilbert B. Schiffman. Cited in Boder, E., **Learning Disorders,** Vol. 2, 1966.

APPENDIX II.

Case Report

The following letter from the mother of a dyslexic child is presented to illustrate the importance of correctly diagnosing developmental dyslexia and of making the diagnosis as early as possible. Apart from the use of a fictitious name to avoid identifying the child, the letter is presented virtually verbatim. It reflects the reluctance of many professionals in the field to make a specific diagnosis. Every possible alternative to developmental dyslexia is considered as the family makes its rounds of the specialists. With the accumulation of negative findings, often at substantial cost, there is a tendency to diagnose a primary emotional problem as the cause of the child's inability to read, although the presence of an emotional disorder, primary or secondary, should not exclude the possibility that the child may also be dyslexic.

The letter is striking as a description of the confusion, anxiety, and bewilderment that may be experienced by the dyslexic child and his parents in the absence of a coordinated and specific diagnosis. Here, ironically, it remained for the mother herself to first suspect the diagnosis, on the basis of a newspaper account of an interview with the author.

Sept. 24, 1968

Dear Dr. Boder,

I am writing in regard to an article we read in the TIMES giving your explanation of a condition called "dyslexia."

This is the first time we have ever read anything that explains our youngest son's problem. The fact that he had a problem became apparent in the 1st grade. It was recognized as something unusual by his teacher who consulted the school psychologist. Our boy not only transposed letters and wrote backwards; he could not follow the written line, he would drop to the line below midway. He also drew squares around the words as if he was trying to pin them down. The school psychologist suggested a neurologist. We took him and he was tested, including a brain wave test. He was found to be perfectly normal. So he was returned to the regular class work. At this point he was found to be very quick at figures; had a good memory of things that were read to him, also could express himself well but made no progress at all in reading. They passed him to second grade and his problems worsened. He did not want to go to school as the children were making fun of him. He cried and was almost hysterical every morning. When I did get him to go, he would actually become ill and be sent home. I then took him to our family doctor. He found nothing physically wrong, except he was overactive and had a very short attention span. He put him on tranquilizers. This did not improve his reading, but it did help him to get through the school day.

Since there was no improvement we decided to take him to an ophthalmologist to see if it was his eyesight. This proved his eyesight was fine but it was noted he had a lazy muscle in one eye and when he did not get enough rest it "floated" for just a few seconds in the morning. We finished the cycle by having a thorough hearing test made. This also showed nothing wrong. His perception was normal also.

(Before I go any further here is one thing I left out that might be important. He had trouble learning to talk correctly. When in kindergarten and 1st grade he was sent to the speech therapist and the condition was completely corrected. His problem was not being able to say certain letters such as "l", "s", etc.)

When they passed him to 3rd grade I again had a conference with the principal. He felt it would only add an emotional problem if they held him back. So when the 3rd grade teacher called us in, she felt he had a mental block against reading and suggested a psychiatrist. The psychiatrist was completely baffled. She could not find anything to go on. The only sugtestion she had was a remedial reading class. By the end of the 3rd grade I felt he was showing some improvement and my hopes rose. This brings us up to the present.

He is now in 4th grade and although school has just started the problem has already loomed up as strong as ever. In 3rd grade I had been able to help him study the spelling words the night before the test and he would manage to pass it. But this year they are given sentences to write with the spelling words in. He is lost as he cannot come up with the other words.

Yesterday I called the school to ask about remedial reading classes. I was told they aren't having any this year. I was told about a new program but understand this is for children mainly in the 1st and 2nd grade. My son now almost 10 years old (Dec. 25) is showing his concern by asking such questions as "What will they do with you if you keep getting older and older and never learn to read." I do not know how to answer him.

I feel I must add Timothy has never been a problem in school behavior-wise. He is well liked by his teachers and has many friends. He has a pleasant disposition. He is the youngest of 4 children. The other three have had no learning problems and have even been outstanding in school. Timothy has natural building ability and even shows some inventiveness. He can recall things that happened long ago but cannot recall simple words.

By this time I'm sure you can understand why we are desperate parents. We do not know where to turn for help. Everything we have tried has been useless. We are not wealthy people but have not turned down any suggestion the school has made to help him. At times it proved very expensive and still useless.

I am writing to you now to ask what if anything can be done for this child. Your explanation seems to fit so exactly that I had to write to you. Is there any way I can help him myself? (I have tried phonetic books but had a very difficult time keeping his attention.) I thought of a private tutor but the psychiatrist advised against it.

Can you help us? Whatever you could tell us or suggest would be so greatly appreciated.

I know you must be a very busy Dr. but if you could answer this letter we would be so thankful.

Yours truly,

Mrs. _____

335

P. S. At age 18 months Timothy had a severe convulsion and was uncon-
scious for 8 hours.

SUBSEQUENT HISTORY

In the author's followup a few months later, the child, then 10½ years old, was
found to have a sight vocabulary two and a half years below grade level and to
exhibit the reading-spelling patterns of dysphonetic dyslexia (Group I) in classic
form. (See Figure 1.) The neurological examination was found to be entirely
negative except for the following "soft" signs: 1) mixed dominance (right handed and left footed, with a left eye preference); 2) right-left confusion in relation
both to his own right and left and to the examiner's; 3) mild deficit in fine motor coordination, with digital awkwardness on the fingers-thumb test; and 4) minimal ataxia on tandem walking. His drawing of his family consisted of stick figures, like the product of a much younger child, suggesting some deficit in visuomotor coordination as well as in body-image concept.

The school psychologist's reports confirmed the mother's impression that Tim's
overall school adjustment was good. He related well to other children, accepted
school routine and other responsibilities, and was not a discipline problem. It
was noted that his occasional complaints of feeling sick in the classroom were related to his realization that many school tasks were too hard for him. His personality development, apart from such feelings of inadequacy, was considered good.
At chronological age 7-7 he was found to be in the average range of intelligence.
The Wide-Range Achievement Test indicated that he was at grade level in arithmetic but was selectively retarded in reading, which was at the kindergarten level.
His performance on the Bender Visual-Motor Gestalt Test was poor and was interpreted as indicative of a visual-perceptual problem that was the sole factor underlying his inability to read.

It became clear that he had indeed been seen by a variety of qualified specialists.
Without a coordinated team approach, however, the numerous referrals to specialists led to some misconceptions and further confusion on the part of the parents,
and no action was taken on several recommendations for a remedial reading program.

A year later he is in the fifth grade, still in a regular classroom because of the limited facilities for children with specific learning disabilities in his school district. His parents have had to rely on private tutoring to supplement the limited amount of remedial reading he gets at school. In both, the teaching of phonetics is emphasized. His sight vocabulary, now between the second and third grade level, has risen one year but is still two and a half years below his grade level. His reading-spelling pattern has not changed, although he shows some evidence of improvement in phonetic concepts. He is under increased pressure in the classroom — as might be expected, since a reading problem tends typically to become a learning problem in the upper grades. He continues to get passing marks in spite of his severe handicap, apparently because of his good motivation and generally good school adjustment. Nevertheless, his anxiety about his reading problem has increased.

REFERENCES

Bachmann, F. Cited in Heller (1963).

Bakwin, H. Develpmental disorders of motility and language. **Pediat. Clin. N. Amer.,** 1968, **15,** 565.

Bakwin, H., and Bakwin, R. M. Difficulties in reading. In **Clinical management of behavior disorders in children.** Philadelphia: W. B. Saunders Co., 1966. Pp. 347-357.

Bannatyne, A. The etiology of dyslexia and the color phonics system. In J. Money (Ed.), **The disabled reader: Education of the dyslexic child.** Baltimore: The Johns Hopkins Press, 1966. Pp. 193-215.

Bateman, B. D. **Interpretation of the 1961 Illinois test of psycholinguistic abilities.** Seattle, Wa.: Special Child Publications, 1968.

Bauza, C. A., de Grompone, M. A. C., Ecuder, E., and Drets, M. E. **La Dislexia de evolucion.** Montevideo: Garcia Morales-Mercant, Graficos Unidos, S. A., 1962.

Bender, L. **Psychopathology of children with organic brain disorders.**

Springfield, Ill.: Chas. C. Thomas, 1959.

Benton, A. L. Dyslexia in relation to form perception and directional sense. In J. Money (Ed.), **Reading disability: Progress and research needs in dyslexia.** Baltimore: The Johns Hopkins Press, 1962. Pp. 81-102.

Black, M. H. Personal communication.

Boder, E. A Neuropediatric approach to school behavioral and learning disorders: Diagnosis and management. In J. Hellmuth (Ed.), **Learning disorders,** Vol. II. Seattle, Wa.: Special Child Publications, 1966. Pp. 15-44.

Boder, E., and Foncerrada, M. Disfuncion cerebral minima. In R. H. Valenzuela (Ed.), **Manual de Pediatria, 7th Edicion.** Mexico City: Interamericana, 1967. Pp. 589-597.

Boder, E. Developmental dyslexia: A diagnostic screening procedure based on three characteristic patterns of reading and spelling. A Preliminary Report. In M. P. Douglass (Ed.), **Claremont Reading Conference 32nd Yearbook.** Claremont, Calif.: Claremont University Center, 1968. Pp. 173-187.

Boder, E. Developmental dyslexia: A diagnostic approach based on patterns of reading and spelling. In **Proc. XII international congress of pediatrics,** Mexico City, December 1968.

Boder, E. Developmental dyslexia: A diagnostic screening procedure based on three characteristic patterns of reading and spelling. (A summary). **Academic Therapy,** Summer 1969, **4,** 285-287.

Boder, E. Developmental dyslexia. In H. R. Myklebust (Ed.), **Progress in learning disabilities,** Vol. II. New York and London: Grune and Stratton, in press.

338

Boder, E. Developmental dyslexia: A new diagnostic approach based on the identification of three subtypes (A summary). **J. Sch. Hlth,** June 1970, **40,** 289.

Childs, B. The genetics of reading disability: Present and future. Paper read at the Conference on Biological bases of Human Behavior, California Institute of Technology, Pasadena, Calif., March 18, 1970.

Clements, S. D., and Peters, J. E. Minimal brain dysfunctions in the school-age child. **Arch. Gen. Psychiat.,** 1962, **6,** 187.

Cohn, R. The neurological study of children with learning disabilities. **Except. Child.,** 1964, **31,** 179.

Critchley, M. **Developmental dyslexia.** Springfield, Ill.: Chas. C. Thomas, 1964.

Crosby, R. M. N., and Liston, R. A. **The waysiders. A new approach to reading and the dyslexic reader.** New York: Delacorte Press, 1968.

Eisenberg, L. Reading retardation: 1. Psychiatric and sociologic aspects. **Pediatrics.** 1966, **37,** 352.

Eustis, R. R. Specific reading disability: A familial syndrome, associated with ambidexterity and speech defects and a frequent cause of problem behavior. **New Engl. J. Med.,** 1947, **237,** 243.

Fernald, G. Cited in Schiffman (1962).

Gallagher, J. Specific language disability: Dyslexia. **Bulletin Orton Society,** 1960, **10,** 5.

Hallgren, B. Specific dyslexia — A clinical and genetic study. **Acta Psychiat. Scand.,** Suppl. 65, 1950.

Heller, T. M. Word-Blindness — A survey of the literature and a report of twenty-eight cases. **Pediatrics,** 1963, **31,** 669.

Hermann, K., and Norrie, E. Is congenital word-blindness a hereditary type of Gerstmann's syndrome? **Psychiat. Neurol.** (Basel), 1958, **136,** 59.

de Hirsch, K. Specific dyslexia or strephosymbolia. **Folia Phoniatrica,** 1952, **5,** 231.

de Hirsch, K. Concepts related to normal reading processes and their application to reading pathology. **J. Genetic Psychol.,** 1963, **102,** 277.

Ingram, T. T. S. Delayed development of speech with special reference to dyslexia. **Proc. Roy. Soc. Med.,** 1963, **56,** 199.

Isom, J. B. Some neuropsychological findings in children with reading problems. In M. P. Douglass (Ed.), **Claremont Reading Conference 32nd Yearbook.** Claremont, Calif.: Claremont University Center, 1968. Pp. 188-198.

Jackson, E. Cited in Heller (1963).

Johnson, D. J., and Myklebust, H. R. Learning disabilities: Educational principles and practices. New York: Grune and Stratton, 1967.

Kinsbourne, M., and Warrington, E. K. Developmental factors in reading and writing backwardness. In J. Money (Ed.), **The disabled reader: Education of the dyslexic child.** Baltimore: The Johns Hopkins Press, 1966. Pp. 59-71.

Money, J. Reading disability: Progress and research needs in dyslexia. Baltimore: The Johns Hopkins Press, 1962. Pp. 9-33, Post Conference Review.

Money, J. Reading disorder. In S. S. Gellis and B. M. Kagan (Eds.), **Current pediatric therapy,** 2nd Ed., Philadelphia: W. B. Saunders Co., 1966. Pp. 46, 47.

340

Myklebust, H. R. **Development and disorders of written language.** New York: Grune and Stratton, Inc., 1965.

Myklebust, H. R. Learning disabilities, definition and overview. In H. R. Myklebust (Ed.), **Progress in learning disabilities,** Vol. I. New York and London: Grune and Stratton, 1968. Pp. 1-16.

Orton, S. **Reading, writing, and speech problems in children.** New York: W. W. Norton and Co., 1937.

Orton, S. Cited in Thompson (1966). Pp. 26-60.

de Quiros, J. B. Dysphasia and dyslexia in school children. **Folia Phoniatrica,** 1964, **16,** 201.

Rabinovitch, R. D. Reading problems in children: Definitions and classifications. In A. H. Keeney and V. T. Keeney (Eds.), **Dyslexia: Diagnosis and treatment of reading disorders.** St. Louis: C. V. Mosby Co., 1968. Pp. 1-10.

Schiffman, G. B. Cited in Boder (1966).

Schiffman, G. B. Dyslexia as an educational phenomenon: Its recognition and treatment. In J. Money (Ed.), **Reading disability: Progress and research needs in dyslexia.** Baltimore: The Johns Hopkins Press, 1962. Pp. 45-60.

Thompson, L. J. **Reading disability: Developmental dyslexia.** Springfield, Ill.: Chas. C. Thomas, 1966.

Warrington, E. K. The incidence of verbal disability associated with retardation reading. **Neuropsychologia,** 1967, **5,** 175.

Wepman, J. M. Dyslexia: Its relationship to language acquisition and concept formation. In J. Money (Ed.), **Reading disability: Pro-**

gress and research needs in dyslexia. Baltimore: The Johns Hopkins Press, 1962. Pp. 179-186.

Whitsell, L. J. Neurologic aspects of reading disorders. In R. M. Flower, H. F. Gofman and L. I. Lawson (Eds.), **Reading disorders, A multidisciplinary symposium.** Philadelphia: F. A. Davis Co., 1965.

Wiener, M., and Cromer, W. Reading and reading difficulty: A Conceptual analysis. In **Harvard University Educ. Rev.,** Fall 1967, 620-643.

Wolf, C. W. A Statistical study of specific dyslexia — Characteristics and syndrome patterns. Unpublished doctoral dissertation, University of Houston, Texas, June, 1968.

Developmental and Symptomatic Dyslexia: Differential Diagnosis and Remediation

Eugene Schwalb, M.D.
Medical Coordinator, Learning Disabilities Center
Long Island Jewish Medical Center, Department of Pediatrics
New Hyde Park, New York
        and
Department of Pediatrics
East Nassau Medical Group
Hicksville, New York

Harold Blau, M.A.
Educational Coordinator, Learning Disabilities Center
Long Island Jewish Medical Center, Department of Pediatrics
New Hyde Park, New York
        and
Director, Learning Disabilities Study Center
Long Island Reading Institute
Hollis, New York

Harriet Blau, M.A.
Director, The Learning Institute
Flushing, New York

PART I

Dyslexia, both as a semantic unit and as a physiological dysfunction, is marked by an inordinate degree of domain indeterminacy. (Wallace and Atkins, 1960) Educators, physicians, and psychologists use the word differently and often there is little agreement even among members of the same discipline as to what the word means. A uniform classification system has been inadequately promulgated and the criteria used for identifying the problem vary from author to author. While many definitions and explanations of this multifaceted syndrome exist, all are agreed that dyslexic children find it very difficult to learn to read.

It is the purpose of this report to define, to identify, to differentiate, to give clues and to illustrate the many faces of dyslexia. It should be noted that the diagnosis is not a sufficient end product but has been helpful in establishing treatment goals and clarifying prognosis. This examination is designed to assess the child's abilities and handicaps in order to provide the educator with information regarding the child's strengths and weaknesses and to identify children who are functioning below their age capacity level. Accordingly, he may then design an appropriate, modified curriculum and hope to prevent further emotional sequelae.

DEFINITION

There is a tendency to define dyslexic children as those with normal eyesight (or corrected visual capacity) and with normal intelligence who show difficulty in learning how to read with ordinary teaching methods — the majority of poor readers are included, regardless of whatever their neurological symptoms might be. This term is meant to include developmental dyslexia (primary or specific) and the various forms of symptomatic (secondary) dyslexia (Table 1). Although we believe this differentiation is of practical significance in remedia-

344

TABLE I

READING RETARDATION

Primary dyslexic (Developmental Dyslexic of Critchley 1964, Congenital Word Blind of Morgan 1896, Primary Reading Retardation of Rabinovitch 1954)

Secondary dyslexic

Brain Dysfunction

Delayed motor development
Behavioral aberrations — hyperkinesis
Delayed language development — developmental aphasia
Delayed cerebral dominance
Visual perceptual problem
Auditory indiscrimination

Environment deprivation with

deficiencies in the "sensory cognitive stimulation" resulting from

poverty and disadvantage or
institutional care

poor instruction

poorly prepared teachers of reading
English as a second language, i.e., Puerto Rican

deficiencies in motivation

social — "ghetto life"
emotional problem secondary to family, etc., problems
illness

emotional problems — primary or secondary

tion and prognosis, one diagnosis does not exclude the presence of the other.

It has been helpful to define developmental dyslexics as a mixed group of individuals who have a common defect in learning to read related to an inability to recognize and interpret verbal symbols by visual channels depsite normal IQ, normal vision, normal motivation, normal auditory discrimination, and normal two-dimensional visual perception. In its pure form, a normal neurodevelopmental and psychiatric examination is found. The ability to recognize words by tactile or kinesthetic means may be present. We agree with Critchley (1964) who is reluctant to "visualize in developmental dyslexia any focal lesion" despite its similarity to dyslexia seen following acute neurological insult. Interestingly, only one of more than 50 cases diagnosed as developmental dyslexia here in the past six years had any "hard" neurological findings. Critchley also believes that reading retardation as a result of brain trauma at birth is different from developmental dyslexia. He believes that developmental dyslexia represents more of a "developmental inefficiency" in functioning that handicaps learning rather than a traumatic disruption of existing skills. Our classification is, however, not based on etiological factors but on the actual pathophysiology found.

Symptomatic dyslexia may be divided into brain dysfunction and environmental deprivation. It may be associated with developmental dyslexia and may be the result of a variety of factors interacting either singly or in combination.

Brain Dysfunction

Children classified in this group appear to have various neurodevelopmental problems which can manifest themselves in varying degrees of severity and can involve any or all of the more specific areas, e.g., motor, sensory, or intellectual. The term refers to children with average general intelligence with certain learning or behavioral disabilities, ranging from mild to severe, which are associated with deviations of

346

the central nervous system. These deviations may manifest themselves by various combinations of impairment in perception, conceptualization, language, memory, and control of attention and impulsivity. (Clements, 1966) Impaired motor function, particularly fine and rapid coordination and delayed cerebral dominance and auditory verbal indiscrimination, is also prominent. In these patients, the neurological examination must recognize the possibility of borderline or forme fruste lesions of the central nervous system. Table 2 compares some of the overt gross "hard" signs of cerebral palsy with subtle "soft" lesions found in brain dysfunction. These symptoms are physiologically analogous to similar reactions that appear in normal infants and children during different stages of development but acquire their symptomatic significance by virtue of their persistence into ages where these manifestations have long disappeared in the normal child. Recent reports on the diagnosis and remediation of brain dysfunction have been published. (Schwalb, 1967; Schwalb, Blau and Blau, 1969)

Environmental Deprivation

Dyslexia associated with environmental deprivation is a result of the various factors listed in Table 1. Undoubtedly, the cultural and linguistic environment of the reader is a factor in this subdivision of symptomatic dyslexia in view of the fact that peoples of different cultures organize their perceptual apparatus in different ways. (McDermott) Biology and culture work in a feedback system, and the development of perceptual equipment prerequisite to reading may be peculiar to a certain cultural milieu. Working from a phonological and semantic system different from that used in print, it is understandable then why blacks may be shown as demonstrating a high rate of reading disability with a predominance of dyslexic symptoms. When a careful consideration of social psychological factors is also brought into focus, such as the visual and auditory sensory deprivation common to an overcrowded and noisy ghetto life, an explicative pattern emerges. (McDermott) Jensenism then cannot explain the differential in reading retardation between blacks and whites.

TABLE 2

BRAIN DYSFUNCTION

	Cerebral Palsy Gross Lesion	Borderline Lesion
Motor	Palsy	Inability to perform certain tongue and facial movements. Fine and rapid motor incoordination Equilibrium disturbances—inability to adjust to changes in posture and to orientation in space Minor choreoathetosis or tremor Increased reflexes Delay in acquisition of new functions and abilities Retention of primitive motor patterns Motor disinhibition
Mental	Mental deficiency	Minimal retardation Impulsiveness Distractibility Short attention span Low frustration tolerance Perseveration Dyscalculia Abstract and conceptual problems Reading problems
Sensory	Cortical blindness	Visual perception and integration problems
	Cortical deafness	Auditory verbal indiscrimination and imperception
	Visual field defect	Impaired spatial concept
	Astereognosis	Visual or tactile inattention
	Sensory defect	Positive face—hand test Finger agnosia
Language	Aphasia	Delayed speech Persistence of infantile speech pattern Language problems
Convulsions	Epilepsy	Abnormal EEG

DIFFERENTIAL DIAGNOSIS

The above classification (Table 1) has been found useful in evaluating the dyslexic, although most younger children may appear with mixed components and a clear-cut diagnosis is often only made with time. In our experience, we have found this classification to form a useful base for different approaches to therapy (subsequently described). This classification considers that in a particular child many factors come into play, such as linguistic factors, poor motivation, gross physical disabilities, emotional problems, and poor instruction.

DEVELOPMENTAL DYSLEXIA — DIAGNOSTIC CLUES

Dyslexia typically occurs in boys of normal intelligence. Reading is significantly below grade level. Material is read haltingly and simple errors are made. A word may be recognized in one sentence but remains unrecognized in the next. Guessing at words on the basis of the initial letters, sound, or length and story context is rampant. Usually, the dyslexic has little trouble with consonants but he becomes confused in reading vowel sounds, particularly when present in a word. There is usually no difficulty in pronouncing vowel sounds after hearing them, and he can usually blend two or three sounds when the sounds are heard separately.

In contrast, he has difficulty in blending letter sounds when he has to produce the sounds from visual presentation of the letters, even though he might be able to produce the specific letter sounds if each letter is presented independently. His is a problem in retaining a visual image of a word. He has poor memory for words and for letter sequences but excellent audio-verbal language ability. His reading skills and errors are like those of young readers, but he has learned to recognize a number of words so that he can read some at higher grade levels. He still, however, makes errors like beginning readers. Usually, maturity only slowly improves the problem, so that the axiom that the older child with normal intelligence referred to as a nonreader or extremely poor reader is invariably a developmental dyslexic, is valid.

Strong auditory verbal abilities are characteristic of the developmental dyslexic even if there are auditory memory problems for spelling present. Difficulty in picture interpretation is absent. Auditory verbal scores as measured by a variety of picture word vocabulary tests, such as the Ammons Quick Test or the Peabody Picture Word Vocabulary Test which are exceptionally good.

Usually, the developmental dyslexic has right-left disorientation plus some confusion about months, seasons, and judgment of time, direction, and size. He is also more likely than a normal child to have male relatives with similar difficulty in learning to read. As in all cases of children with learning difficulties, he feels inadequate, stupid, and guilty.

Characteristically, developmental dyslexia persists into adult life. Occasionally, with great effort, a modicum of literacy may be achieved. Spelling, however, generally remains erratic. Critchley (1964) suspects that Hans Christian Anderson's spelling, which reveals many such errors as noted later, was that of a dyslexic. Critchley (1964) and Hermann (1959) relate stories of several dyslexics who achieved modest social and professional positions despite their developmental dyslexia. Unfortunately, few accounts of long-term follow-up are available, and it seems unlikely that the majority of developmental dyslexics have been so fortunate.

Major areas in which developmental and symptomatic dyslexia are involved are as follows:

Reading

For the purpose of this paper, reading is assumed to be made up of the following characteristics:

350

perception or awareness of visual symbols,

association of these symbols with auditory, tactile, and other perceptions,

translation of the symbols into words,

translation of words into meaning,

relating words in a meaningful way to each other, and

memorizing the word by stowing it in a memory bank.

The developmental dyslexic has problems in all areas except awareness of visual symbols and thus his reading is characterized by problems that may be grouped under the heading of word attack and recognition and comprehension.

Word attack and recognition.
Inability to recognize printed words and written characters by sight.

Inability to acquire visual memory of words and rarely letters, despite the same kind of education and training that other children receive who acquire them in a normal way.

Guessing at words on the basis of initial letters, length of the word, and other insufficient clues.

Confusing vowel sounds in a word.

Inability to blend sounds when presented visually, i.e., *com mune cat tion,* but they have no problems in pronouncing and understanding the word *communication* after hearing it.

Inability to organize letters and words in relation to each other. Critchley (1964) lists 17 diagnostic errors common to dyslexics, including:

inability to keep place on a page,

reversal of letters showing, for example, *b, p, q, d,* as interchangeable or *h, n, m, v, w,*

reversal of letters within words, as *was* for *saw* (transposition),

confusion of letters phonetically similar — *v, f,*

word substitution — usually words with similar meanings, *cat* for *kitten, mom* for *mother,*

addition and omissions of letters or sounds,

inability to handle many phonic units, especially in blends, and

mirror reading.

Luchsinger calls this disability a synthetic-analytic incapacity. (Luchsinger and Arnold, 1959) Myklebust equates the developmental dyslexic's problems with an inability to "reauditorize" and "revisualize." (Myklebust and Johnson, 1962)

Many of these errors are normal in children learning to read, but in the developmental dyslexic their frequency and persistence (past age eight) make them abnormal.

Essentially, then, one tests *how* the child reads and not at what level he reads. The Clements Word Recognition Test (Glaser and Clement, 1965) the Houston Independent School District Paragraph Reading

Tests (1961-62) are used. The latter test has been preferred over the Gray and Gilmore by the physician because of its high interest stories which are relatively free from stereotypes. Most students queried have found the contents of the Gray and Gilmore limited in interest.

Comprehension—using any reading tests. All developmental dyslexics appear to have a large gap between "auding" capacity, which is often superior, and visual comprehension capacity, which is handicapped by the lack of good word recognition and word attack abilities. "Auding" capacity, or the capacity to comprehend when material is read orally, is found to indicate a high expected reading potential, a potential the developmental dyslexic cannot attain visually.

It should be added that it is the configuration of the total pattern that adds up to the diagnosis of developmental dyslexia, since educators already have categorized the various reading and spelling errors made by the nonreader.

Spelling Problems

Spelling includes the oral as well as the written arrangement of letters in print or script. Errors are closely related to those listed under word attack and recognition.

The developmental dyslexic:

fails to recall letters of words in the correct order, for example (Figure 1), *instead* is spelled *insahtam,* etc.;

often has the ability to write the initial consonants, especially when it is also phonic (although some have no ability to provide the appropriate letter symbol). For example, *saw* is written as *see* (at least the patient knows the word has something to do with "seeing"), or *mountain* is spelled as *mong, president* as *prought* (Figure 1);

353

makes errors in letter order with reversal of letter pairs (Figure 2), such as *pale* as *pla,* or *secret* as *serci;*

makes substitutions (Figure 3), *want* as *wiht;*

concocts word jumbles resulting in an anagram of words (Figure 3), *quarterback* as *codrb* (or Figure 4);

omits letters (Figures 1, 2, 3, 4);

spells, orally and written, with letter reversal and omission—of course, these errors are also quite common in the normal younger child (Figures 1, 2, 3, 4);

spells on a phonetic basis (Figures 1, 2, 3, 4);

does mirror image spelling (Figure 5) or reverse mirror image (Figure 6).

FIGURE 1

Spelling test of 9½ year old dyslexic after first use of AKT to teach words:

A. Following is characteristic bizarre spelling (of words taught by conventional methods)

1. mong - mountain
2. prought - president
3. insahtam - instead
4. sonsw - straight

B. Following were first words taught via AKT - all were spelled correctly on test:

1. anyone
2. excuse
3. ink   D.D. 54 B.C. 42
4. bottom
5. horn

FIGURE 2

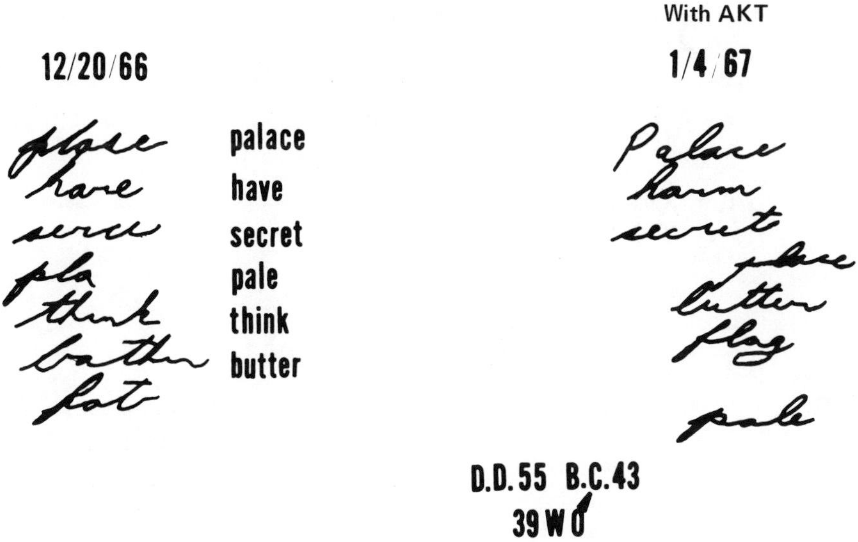

12/20/66

palace
have
secret
pale
think
butter
fat

With AKT

1/4/67

Palace
harm
secret
place
butter
flag
pale

D.D. 55   B.C. 43
39 W ♂

FIGURE 3

I want to go to the movies on Saturday and yesterday.

They voted in America.

Joe Namath is a great quarterback.

Writing to dictation   9½ yr. W ♂   95246
                                    O.C. 92
                                    D.D. 42

355

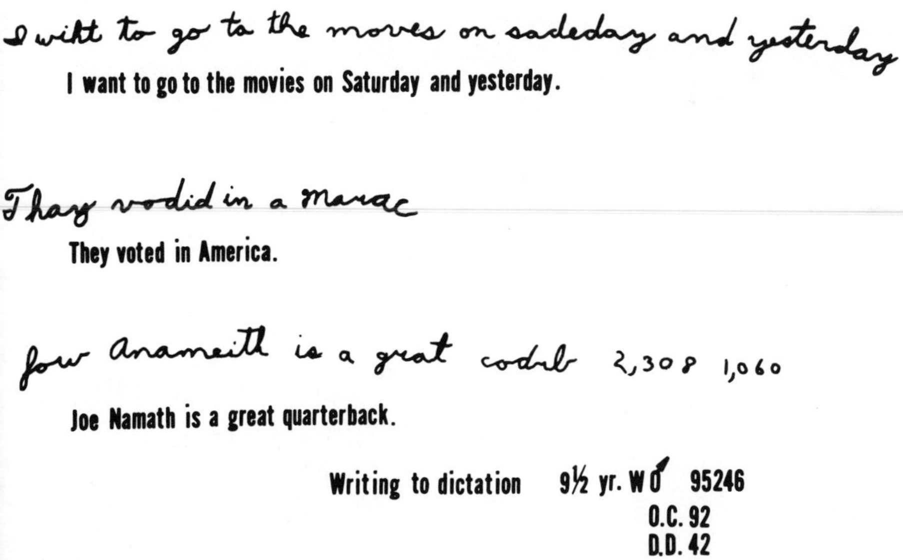

FIGURE 4

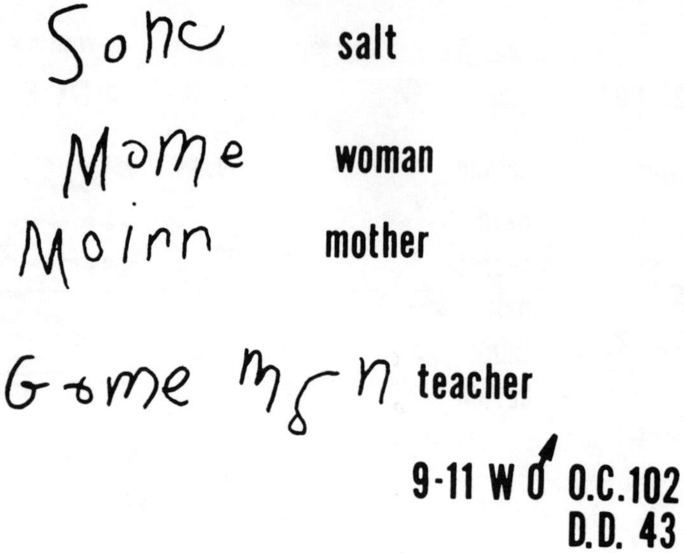

Sohc   salt

Mome   woman

Moirn   mother

Gome mɛn teacher

9-11 W ♂ O.C.102
D.D. 43

FIGURE 6

FIGURE 7

Reverse
mirror image

Hσ /ᴑ ι

10, 37
4 6ſ
13, 40
17,50

11·3 W ♂ premir reader
O.C. 211
DD 51

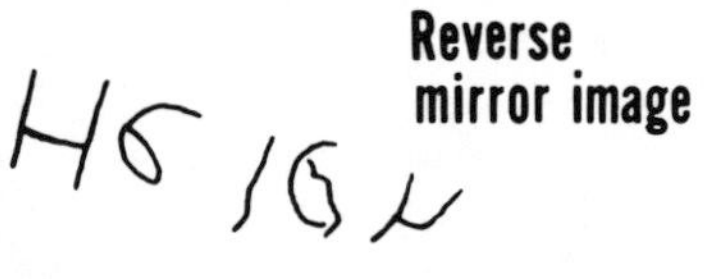

FIGURE 5

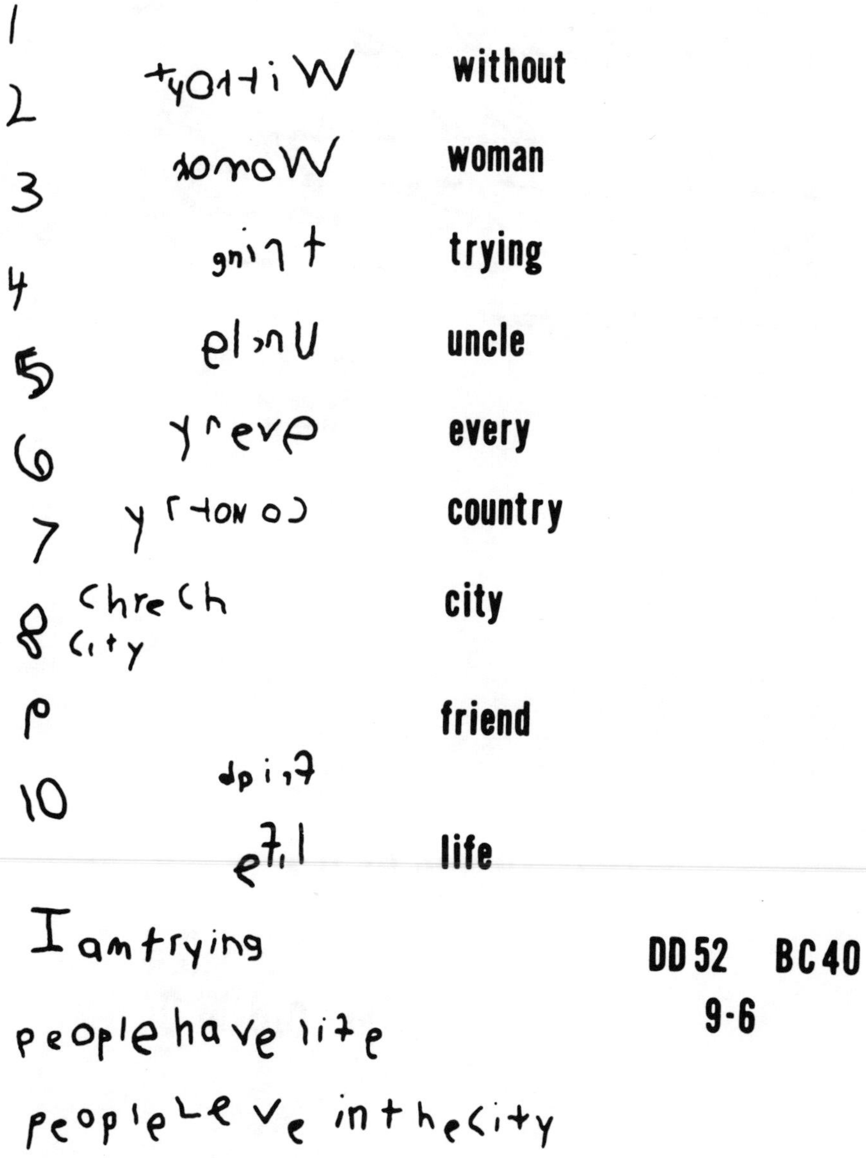

	(handwritten)	
1		
2	†yO1†iW	without
3	ʌonoW	woman
4	gni⅂t	trying
5	elↄnU	uncle
6	yⁿeve	every
7	yⁿↄonoↄ	country
8	chrech / city	city
9	ꝑ	friend
10	ꝺpiⁿꟼ	
	eⁿil	life

I am trying

people have life

people Le ve in the city

DD 52   BC 40
9-6

FIGURE 8

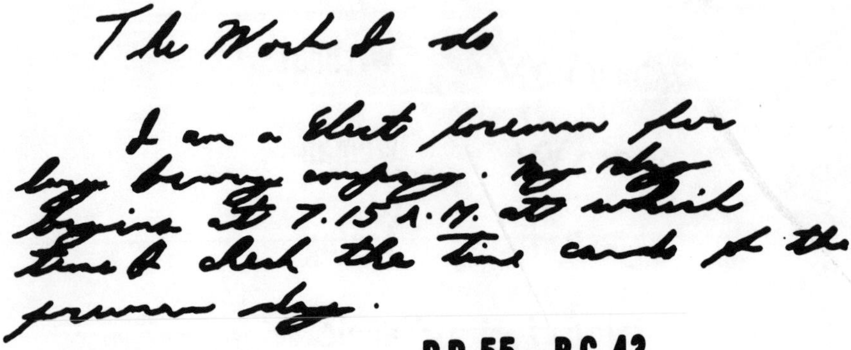

The Work I do

I am a Elect foreman for
large timbering company. By day
begins at 7.15 A.M. at which
time I check the time cards of the
previous day.

D.D. 55   B.C. 43
39 W ♂

FIGURE 9

t͟he

the: fusion of h & e

D.D. 2 O.C. 4
13 yr. old W ♀

All patients were able to spell words out loud letter by letter when given the letters orally; but, when asked to recognize them by sense of sight alone, they could not. All test words used were well within the patient's vocabulary as tested by the Ammons Quick Test (Ammons and Ammons, 1962) and the Clement Word Recognition Test. (Glaser and Clement, 1965)

In our experience, as the spelling demands increase (longer and more complex words), the problem accentuates. The spelling difficulty improves little and often appears to be aggravated with maturity.

Arithmetic

The power of retaining, storing, and reproducing visual memories of numbers is often also disturbed, although some developmental dyslexics are extremely proficient in both concrete (arithmetic) and higher conceptual mathematics. Most developmental dyslexics, however, do poorly in the latter—despite good arithmetic grades in primary school. Cohen (1961), in his article on dyscalculia, lists mathematical errors as the following:

> Disturbed horizontal positioning of number sequences. Critchley calls this number dyslexia. (Critchley, 1964) Essentially, there is difficulty in writing to dictation of long numbers with many digits. There are often too many or too few zeros and the commas are incorrectly placed. This sign appears to be extremely significant in children nine years of age or over with normal intelligence and increases in validity with increasing IQ's (Figure 7).

> Failure to use a separating line to differentiate the factors from the product.

> Disarray of the vertical alignment of numbers.

Transposition of numbers; for instance, writing *13* for *31.*

Faulty memory for arithmetic tables.

Failure to carry over correctly.

Handwriting

Brain (1965) states that writing is more complex than reading. Cursive handwriting in both developmental and symptomatic dyslexia is usually, but not always, abnormal. Printing, however, is usually normal when one considers the pure developmental dyslexic.

Examples of the abnormalities noted include:

Distortion which may be so gross that none of the letters are recognizable (Figure 8).

Letters may be badly formed and improperly joined (Figures 2, 9), or there may be an unusual manner of joining adjacent letters or poor alignment of letters.

Letter reversals and small word reversals are common; i.e., *was* for *saw.*

In addition, Critchley describes "an untidiness of the penmanship." (Figure 8) Some developmental dyslexics, however, do write neatly and clearly, possibly due to persistent efforts by the school.

Other common errors are malalignment, rotation of letters, and odd punctuation marks.

Critchley also feels that the linkage between letters is either too long or too short (Figures 8, 9).

Mirror image writing is often found in the developmental dyslexic (Figure 5). Orton in 1937 demonstrated that, in developmental dyslexia, mirror writing, however, was secondary to mirror reading. He felt that this tendency was related to incomplete left hemispheric dominance. Mirror writing is also performed by normal right handers who write with the left hand and is found in the right handed who develop right hemiplegia and who then have to write with their left hand. (Brain, 1965)

In left-handed children, mirror writing is also found even if they use their right hand (consistent sinistral orientation of letters and the sinistral progression of words). In fact, this is thought to be the left-handed normal pattern of writing, and it is felt that the changeover to normal writing is culturally inspired. Some observers feel that one of the reasons for this is that the left-handed individual can write easily from right to left but cannot from left to right. A Semitic language might be more appropriate for such individuals. In the normal right handed, most observers opine that mirror writing coexists with confusion of language.

Certainly, mirror image writing was not unusual in developmental dyslexics, but the incidence of mirror image writing in the nondyslexic population is not available, making conclusions of substance unwise.

Vertical inversion, that is writing letters upside down, is not the reserved domain of the developmental dyslexic either. Normal children to age six commonly substitute *b* for *p,* but apparently it is only occasionally found normally thereafter. It is common in both primary and secondary dyslexics of all age groups, and its persistence after six years of age is abnormal.

Right-Left Orientation

It should be noted that when children learn to write, letter reversal is common. It may in part be related to right-left orientation. This ability to discriminate between right and left begins at two and reaches adult levels at ten. Usually, the average seven-year-old knows his right hand from his left with early discrimination related to a high functional IQ. Deficient right-left orientation is found in most dyslexics, including those with brain dysfunction, and in normal pre-seven-year-old children.

One point of differential diagnostic importance is that normal children have systematic reversals similar to pre-five-year-old children. Patients with brain dysfunction tend to randomize their responses during right-left testing.

Right-left orientation tends to be divided into four groups (Table 3). For developmental dyslexics, sections C and D have been found useful. Most of these patients have built-in clues in differentiating right from left. Tests listed in sections A and B have been more significant in pre-nine-year-old patients with brain dysfunction. Tests for dominance have often documented mixed patterns, i.e., left eyed in right handed, right legged. The significance of these findings has not been ascertained. However, evidence has mounted that crossed or mixed dominance has nothing to do with either symptomatic or developmental dyslexia. The distribution of so-called mixed dominance appears to be the same in developmental dyslexics as in the superior readers. (Bettman and others, 1967)

Brain Dysfunction Symptoms Mixed with Developmental Dyslexia

Developmental dyslexia is often associated with symptomatic dyslexia, particularly brain dysfunction in the younger pre-teen-age child. These symptoms appear to improve with maturity and/or medication and are uncommon in the older developmental dyslexics. Table 4 compares the pertinent findings in brain dysfunction and developmental dyslexia. Symptoms of brain dysfunction include:

Behavioral aberrations consisting of hyperactivity, short attention

TABLE 3

RIGHT-LEFT ORIENTATION SCALE

		Correct	**Incorrect**

A. Body Concept

    Primitive orientation

        Show me your left hand _____

        Show me your right leg _____

        Show me your left eye _____

        Show me your right ear _____

B. Crossing the Midline

    Cross your left leg over your right knee _____

    Touch your left elbow with your right hand_____

    Touch your right ear with your left hand _____

C. Objective Tests

    Folding arm _____

    Clasping hand _____

    Schilder's Extension Test _____

    Preferred lateralization on color plate _____

D. Shifting Concept into Space

    Point to my left ear with your right hand _____

    Point to my right eye with your left thumb _____

E. Test for Dominance (circle correct response)

    Right eyed   Left eyed

    Right handed   Left handed

    Right legged   Left legged

TABLE 4

SYMPTOMATIC DYSLEXIA

	Brain Dysfunction	Developmental Dyslexia	Mixed
Likely age for diagnosis	5-9	9-16	
Ratio of male to female	3:1	10:1	
Race	Unknown	94% white	
Familial history	No	Yes	
Behavior			
Hyperkinesis	Yes	No	Yes
Short attention span	Yes	No	Yes
Poor concentration	Yes	No	Yes
Emotional overlay	Yes	Yes	Yes
Mental block*	No	Yes	Yes
Visual perceptual problems	Yes	No	Yes
Visual memory problems	Yes	Yes	Yes
Auditory indiscrimination	Yes	No	Yes
Auditory memory problems	Yes	No**	Yes
Right-left disorientation***	Yes	Yes	Yes
Primitive orientation	Yes	No	Yes
Crossing midline	Yes	No	Yes
Objective tests	Yes	Yes	Yes
Shifting concept into space	Yes	Yes	Yes
Mixed dominance	Yes	Yes	Yes
School problems			
Reading			
Word attack and recognition	Yes	Yes	Yes
Word memory	No	Yes	Yes
Visual comprehension	Yes	Yes	Yes
Auditory comprehension	Yes	No	Yes
Spelling (rote memory)	No	Yes	Yes
Arithmetic			
Concrete	Yes	No	Yes
Conceptual	Yes	Sometimes	Yes

Handwriting	Yes	Yes	Yes
Mirror writing	No	Often	Yes
Neurological problems			
Coordination problems	Yes	No	Yes
Positive soft motor signs	Yes	No	Yes
Finger agnosia	Sometimes	Often	Yes
Language problem	Yes	No	Yes
History of			
Prematurity	Yes	No	Yes
Brain injury	Yes	No	Yes
Neonatal abnormalities	Yes	No	Yes
Soft EEG abnormalities	Yes	Yes	Yes
Prognosis			
Maturational improvement	Yes	Unlikely	Yes

*See definition p. 367.
**Yes for auditory dyslexics.
***See Table 3.

---

span, poor concentration, easy frustration, and emotional lability. These symptoms are usually improved with the use of dextroamphetamine, a drug well tolerated in such children in large doses.

Auditory indiscrimination.

Abnormal visual perception as measured by the Bender-Gestalt or Frostig.

Poor fine and rapid motor coordination.

Abnormal "soft" motor[1] neurological examinations.

[1]Divided into four sections: a) Measuring the ability to perform certain tongue and facial movements. b) Evaluating equilibrium disturbances, i.e., the ability to adjust to changes in

Abnormal "soft" sensory[2] examinations except for the fact that finger agnosia, which represents a difficulty in selecting, naming, and distinguishing the fingers which are touched, often persists to be found in the older individuals with developmental dyslexia.

Differential Normal Findings

Normal findings in the developmental dyslexics which differentiate them from some other dyslexics:

Most developmental dyslexics have normal, and usually above average, IQ's.

They have normal power of reasoning.

They have normal vision.

They are usually not color blind.

They have normal binocular vision.

They have normal memory for forms, colors, persons, objects, and places. It should be noted, however, that the presence of an ocular defect due to a disease or refractive error may be considered "normal" and is not related to developmental dyslexia.

They have normal memory of all sorts except visual.

---

posture and orientation in space. c) Ability to duplicate directed acts. d) Tests measuring interrupted normal maturation, including test evaluating the retention of primitive reflex patterns and tests evaluating delays in acquisition of new functions and abilities. Twenty separate tests are performed and a score is obtained. (Schwalb and Blau, 1968)

[2]Tests include: test for finger agnosia, test for tactile agnosia, tactile figure writing, position sense testing, two-point discrimination test, test for optokinetic nystagmus, auditory tune out test (ringing a bell and simultaneously touching the child's hands or legs), and the face-hand test.

They usually have no neurological nor primary emotional problems.

Psychiatric Considerations

Most psychiatric examinations reveal frustration, anxiety, resignation, poor motivation, uncooperativeness, and adjustment reactions of childhood.

"Mental blocks"[3] were reported in 17 of the first 35 developmental dyslexic cases examined by psychiatrists. Although the reading disability is often not considered the primary problem, it is our belief that the emotional and behavioral disabilities are secondary reactions to reading disability. Proper diagnosis and remediation often dramatically improve the child's emotional outlook in school and at home. We therefore feel that the concept of mental block is inappropriate.

Body Image and Body Concept

Developmental dyslexics have considerable difficulty in drawing human figures (Figure 10). Nevertheless, they are usually able to point to body parts. We have not found the Goodenough Draw-A-Man test particularly useful in differentiating developmental from other forms of dyslexia.

Electroencephalographic Findings

The significance of the electroencephalograph soft signs found (excessive random slowing, prolonged response to hyperventilation, occipital spiking, and 6-14 positive spiking) is not known. They may represent subliminal discharges and often clear with motor maturation. A bet-

---

[3]Simple blocking (mental block) is the inability to recall something very familiar and is apparently not caused by emotions but may lead to an emotional block which inhibits thinking or other forms of adjustive response due to excessive emotions, usually of the fear group (English and English, 1958).

ter way to discern a subliminal spike is being sought. Electroencephalographic computer averaging of an auditory click helped Barnett, et al. (1966) uncover deafness in congenital rubella within the first week of life. This may prove to be the best diagnostic test, since the developmental dyslexic's discharge may require the additive effect of a computer to become visible.

FIGURE 10

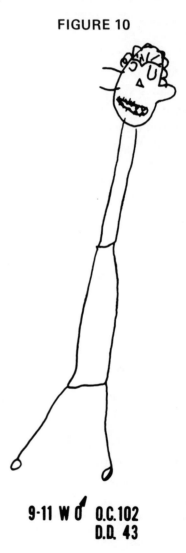

9-11 W ♂ O.C. 102
D.Q. 43

Kellaway (1965) believes that some occipital spiking reported in the developmental dyslexic or in brain dysfunction are not from intracerebral abnormalities but are conditioned by peripheral events similar to occipital discharges in amblyopia ex anopsia or blindness from birth from, i.e., congenital glaucoma. He thus postulates a "peripheral sensory deprivation phenomena" without direct cerebral insult. In all events, it seems that only with improved sorting out of the heterogeneous clinical material will the EEG provide differential validity.

A summary of EEG findings is found in Table 5. Interestingly, these findings are most common in the younger child with associated brain dysfunction and appears to normalize with age. Further long term follow-up of the developmental dyslexic

TABLE 5

EEG NONSPECIFIC ABNORMALITIES
IN DEVELOPMENTAL DYSLEXIA

		Ages				
		7-8	9-10	11-13	14-16	Over 16
Total tested	35	4	14	7	7	3
Abnormalities*	15	4	7	3	1	

* 1. Polymorphous slowing, similar to dysrhythmia, similar to excessive random slowing.

2. Prolonged response to hyperventilation (normal 90-100 seconds).

3. Occipital spike.

4. 6 and 14.

---

and his EEG are needed to substantiate these postulates. It should be added that the EEG can never help establish the diagnosis of developmental dyslexia nor should a normal EEG detract from such a diagnosis. At present, the EEG has no pragmatic value in this disorder but is only of use from a research point of view.

CONCLUSION

This section has been presented in the hope that some standardization can be achieved in the evaluation and diagnosis of dyslexia. Once this has been accomplished, it appears to us incumbent on the educator to conceptualize and implement a technique for teaching each child based on the characteristics of the abnormal condition found. The next section is then devoted to these latter thoughts.

PART II

REMEDIATION

The approach to the remediation of dyslexia, in this section, may be described as a functional one. By this, we mean an approach which is specific for the symptoms presented. Four such possibilities will be offered here. The first has to do with the education of the dyslexic in general. Although the interrelationship between remediation and education could hardly seem less than intimate, there is, oddly, very little about education in the material dealing with dyslexics. Most of it is concerned with remediation as if this were the only learning the dyslexic could be expected to absorb; or as if data absorption, education, the learning of facts and ideas were some kind of automatic process on the one hand or, on the other, so far from solution as to be beyond discussion. Those who have worked with dyslexics can appreciate the promptness with which the last alternative presents itself as the most likely one. Educational deprivation, therefore, tends to be a problem with dyslexics and is therefore properly the concern of a paper on remediation.

Bookless Curriculum

From that standpoint, the dyslexic is probably the most important candidate for what is now boldly being called "The Bookless Curriculum." (Silberberg and Silberberg, 1969) When we first took this approach some years back, it was with the thought that the dyslexic should be taught as if he were blind. Instead of a "bookless curriculum," though, we spoke and still speak of a curriculum that would make use chiefly of the auditory modality, much as work with the blind does, and in which books would be used as supplementary material, quite reversing the usual order of things. If a dyslexic child at age 12 could not *read* The Moffats, he should have an opportunity to hear it, we thought. An so it was provided on tape. The exact function of books will be indicated shortly.

Modality-Adapted Learning

In general, no procedure normally associated with the blind should be overlooked in the education of the dyslexic or, more aptly in this context, the "word-blind." In either case, what is being used may be called modality-adapted learning or using the modality most likely to be effective. Extending this concept a little further, one may anticipate that some day the dyslexic would be routinely admitted to college, his materials read to him or taped for him, his oral responses accepted and his written communication aided as in the case of, again, the legally blind.

One would imagine that this principle of reading material to those who cannot read, especially the dyslexic, or of having it read to them would be pretty much self-evident by this time, especially in our technologically oriented society, with a tape player almost as universally available as the transistor radio. Nothing of the kind has taken place. Commercially produced material is only just becoming available in quantity (and not merely for the dyslexic, of course) in the form of prerecorded tapes. Library of Congress recordings and tapes, hitherto available without charge only to the legally blind, may only now be secured by all those so handicapped as to be unable to read, including dyslexics. (TALKING BOOKS, Wash., D.C.)

A serious obstacle seems to have been the somewhat widespread conviction that dyslexia, in the absence of an obvious etiology, represented a desire to perpetuate a childish dependency and that to read aloud to the dyslexic would strengthen the evasive behavior. Considering the complexity of the problem, this may indeed have been true in some cases, but it would seem more likely that constant failure and humiliation would be even more destructive. There is no avoiding the constant need for careful case differentiation. Almost uniformly, parents of dyslexic children report having been discouraged from reading school material aloud or report having done so with varying degrees of guilt feeling.

371

To discuss the parallel with the blind a little further before proceeding with other remedial processes brings us to a consideration of the Braille book, the book for the blind. The dyslexic has no equivalent resource except the not so insignificant one of being able to see, of course. To use this properly, we insist on his following in a text everything, or almost everything, that he is hearing, whether from an individual or a tape or a recording. To repeat, *he must follow in a text!*

This is clearly not a bookless curriculum. The rationale is obvious, though; he might improve his word recognition and thus his reading, if only through repetition—and he does. Actually, if there were any real danger of reinforcing dependency trends, it would be precisely in letting the dyslexic simply listen, which is the way he functions anyhow, instead of insisting on simultaneous use of an accompanying text. Also, what might be described as an automatic integrating process is thus instituted in which there may become apparent the results, if any, of the remedial procedures being used, especially those which are to be described at this point.

Nonvisual AKT

The first of these is a modification of the multisensory approach more widely known as the Fernald method (Fernald, 1943), or as VAKT, meaning visual, auditory, kinesthetic, tactile, in which words are literally structured of clay or sand, or simply traced, and then incorporated into some kind of connected written discourse. The proposed variation is called nonvisual AKT and is the most important of the methods to be discussed. Some preliminary comments are required, however. In no case of dyslexia is there any significant difficulty in associating reality items with their oral or verbal descriptors. That is, a dog is clearly known and named as such; similarly with *auto, ball, mother,* and so forth. Most, if not all, of the other details of the environment are usually correctly tagged, verbally at least, by age five, if not sooner. The auditory encoding-decoding process seems to offer no problems to these children. Where the problem does arise is, to continue the use of currently popular terminology, in the area of abstract representation or in visual encoding-decoding or, to put it simply, in reading. In other words, the dyslexic child who says, "dog," and knows what it means cannot be brought to spell it or to read it, nor can he decode *brother, fire, baseball,* or *airplane,* to cite just a few of the more conspicuous gaps.

It is possible that this happens because, as current hypotheses will have it, the "memory bank" for symbols is defective in a fashion similar to the defect in the processing system which is supposed to cause color blindness or there is some other neurological anomaly or, at bottom, for the dyslexic there is no reality corresponding to the symbols or letters that we want him to learn. He cannot, apparently, look at D-O-G and really see the thing that walks on four feet and makes certain characteristic noises. As John Money once put it, it is as if we demanded that he hear the color green. (Money, 1966)

For most parents and teachers, this is totally bewildering. "How," they seem to ask, "can this child learn to say the word and not be able to learn to read it?" Our basic rejoinder is that while the auditory modality seems to function properly (otherwise there would be no speech), something in the visual modality seems to cut off or to interfere with word recognition, and therefore with reading, instead of facilitating it.

Blocking Visual Modality

This is a deduction based primarily on functional considerations; if simply looking were an answer, there would be no adult dyslexics. They would long since have *looked* enough to learn to read reasonably well. From this we deduce further, therefore, that *not looking,* or blocking the visual modality, that is blindfolding or at least closing a dyslexic's eyes at the start, in the process of teaching him to recognize words may help him to remember them better. This seems to be true of from 65-95% of the words presented in this way and

373

with about 75% of the individuals concerned. While his eyes are shut or covered, he receives the usual multisensory experiences, auditory, kinesthetic and tactile, or AKT, but all directed toward substituting other input for the blocked visual modality.

The student, as described in one of the earliest papers describing the initial use of and rationale for this technique:

> *. . . is blindfolded or closes his eyes, and the word to be learned is traced on his back. As the teacher traces the word, she spells it aloud, letter by letter. Often, the second or third time around, the student can identify the letters being traced and he, too, spells out the word. Usually (until the student becomes too advanced for this), three-dimensional letters, arranged to spell out the word, are placed before the student and still blindfolded (he) . . . arranges the letters in the proper sequence. The blindfold is then removed, the student sees what he has done (often his first experience with coherent sequencing) and writes the word on paper, or at the board, and then on a file card for future review. . . . In general, once a word has been mastered by the "Non-V" method, it seems to be handled by the student with complete normalcy.* (Blau and Blau, 1968) (Figure 1)

Some variations have been introduced since then, such as having the student trace the three-dimensional letters at the same time as they are being traced on his back or picking the letter out of a group and then placing it in correct sequence to form the word.

In this way not only does the dyslexic begin to learn but he is more willing to try. This seems to be especially true with respect to adolescents and adults to whom it comes as a welcome relief not to have to try to fix these evasive symbols in the mind visually with the sure knowledge that they will undoubtedly fail, as before.

Tansley (1967), working in the St. Francis Residential School in

Birmingham, utilized for more limited goals a similar process called "haptic training," in which the child is not allowed to see various forms and shapes but has to identify or classify them by touch or movement. (Blau and Blau, 1968)

Parenthetically, it might be noted that the printing or tracing on the back

. . . was first adopted to reinforce a sense of left to right directionality (Orton, 1966) *and to establish some limited kind of physical contact analogous to guiding the hands of the blind. It was then observed that printing a word on the child's back . . . seemed to touch off a "closed eye reflex" and to compel exactly the kind of "introjection" or focusing of the mental image needed by the nonreader.* (Schwalb, Blau, and Zanger, 1968)

For the dyslexic, the basic problem is word recognition through the visual channel. He generally is intelligent enough to read quite well once this hurdle is overcome so that the foregoing word recognition technique is particularly applicable.

Modality Overloading

Different from the simplicity of the functional approach, a more developed theoretical base may be found in the concept of a failure in "modality integration." An article on psychoneurological disturbances by Myklebust (1964) makes the point that input systems can and sometimes do function "semi-independently." Children "with minimal brain damage" are reported to have:

. . . serious difficulty when the learning task entails interrelated functions, such as both auditory and visual learning. . . . These children may learn what the letters look like but find it exceedingly difficult to learn what they sound like or the opposite.

375

> When presented with one aspect of the word, the visual, they
> cannot normally convert it to the auditory. . . . Apparently,
> when two or more types of information are delivered to the
> brain simultaneously, a breakdown in neurological processes
> occurs. The clinical manifestations are confusion, poor recall,
> random movements, disturbed attention. . . .

It did not seem far-fetched to apply this description to the dyslexic
and to the nonvisual AKT technique which obviously was a way of
avoiding delivering "two or more types of information. . .to the brain
simultaneously," especially since further elaboration was provided
only a short time later with the concept of "modality overloading."

> The multi-sensory approach, if used promiscuously, can be
> damaging. . .even normal systems within the brain can be over-
> loaded. . . . The information being received through a given
> sensory modality (may) impede integration of that being re-
> ceived through another. (Johnson and Myklebust, 1967)

This concept of overloading was of special significance because regardless of the name given to the "exceptional child: specific language disability, brain injured, perceptually handicapped, dyslexic, . . . aphasic,
dysgraphic, interjacent, and so forth," (Bateman, 1965) the multisensory approach turned out finally to be the only treatment. Hopefully,
greater differentiation in treatment may now be anticipated and not a
moment too soon since:

> . . . there may be a number of children, especially in the early
> grades, classified as. . .non-learners (young dyslexics perhaps),
> who really suffer from a kind of modality conflict (or "over-
> loading") and for whom instruction centering around modality
> blocking may be required prior to, or at least simultaneously
> with, any other program for the amelioration of their difficul-
> ties. (Blau and Blau, 1968)

Taped Dictation

Another remedial technique, again functionally derived, is "taped dictation." It is likewise based on the apparent visual-auditory input conflict of the dyslexic. "They," he will often complain about words, "don't look the way they sound."

To change this, he is helped to improvise or to read any simple material on to a tape and encouraged to play it back phrase by phrase as a dictation exercise. Experience suggests that, whereas previously it was his teacher's voice and words that failed, the use, instead, of his own voice and his own words heard and written, is often successful in persuading him of the fact and nature of the connection between speech sounds and the printed symbols for them.

In using this technique for spelling, which often requires special attention, the student creates his own version of what may be called a simple "responsive environment":

> *The student gets ready to record his voice. He pronounces his first word into the microphone. With the tape recorder still running, he writes or copies the word twice, marks off the syllables, if any, says the word again, and spells it aloud. He does the same with the next word and the next for a total of five or ten words.* (Blau, 1969)

The general procedure should be clear. The student does as many words as he likes, studies them, and plays the whole thing back as a self-checking test. The use of an earphone makes the entire process private.

Phonics

The final remedial technique to be considered is phonics. Oldest of all and still a vital factor in the remediation of dyslexia, it is detailed, intense, and usually individual. It claims many successes and a whole organization is devoted to proselytizing on behalf of a specific phonic system. (Orton, 1966) Its function is also to establish sound-symbol linkage. Unfortunately, by the time most dyslexics are recognized for what they are, their intolerance of and resistance to phonics are monumental. Purely from a functional point of view, one can again resort to the tape recorder. The phonics used is programmed and recorded. (Carroll, 1967) The dyslexic listens only as long as he desires, with earphones, and repeats the material as often as he must. Failures are few, successes many, as would be expected from programmed material. Mastery is carefully checked. Most cases are promptly aware of an improvement in spelling, at least, and subsequently in reading.

Cases

Cases illustrative only of nonvisual AKT will be cited. One is that of a bright, male, fourth grade child, a secondary dyslexic with diagnosed minimal brain damage. Reading was on a third grade level; spelling and auditory sequencing were both poor. There was no medication. After intense use of the nonvisual method over a six-week period, reading rose to a fifth grade level and spelling became superior.

The second case is that of a medicated, because of hyperactivity, minimally brain-damaged child whose reading grade rose from 2.1 to 2.8 also over a seven-week period after intensive use of the nonvisual method. There had been no change in a seven-month period before that.

The third and fourth cases are more involved. Ilse is that rarity, a female developmental dyslexic. Age fourteen and presenting the customary symptoms, bizarre spelling, inability to read what she wrote, poor comprehension, she was also reported to be bright and creative. Five weeks after beginning intensive work with the new method, her oral reading improved from 4.9 to 7.0 in word recognition and her "visual-auditory" comprehension (on the Gilmore Oral Reading Test) from 4.5 to better than 9.8. It was as if suddenly a window had been opened

378

and her improvement was prompt and satisfying but apparently not permanent or at least not consistent. Later testing within a two-month period produced a word recognition score of only 4.0. At this writing, the contradiction has not been resolved.

The last is that of a developmental dyslexic. He was first seen when he was 17, a school drop-out and a total nonreader. Every technique was tried at that time, including mirror-board work and the Fernald method, as well as drill on vocabulary drawn from work experience. There was some improvement from a negative score to 2.9 over a period of two years. Work was then terminated. After a lapse of two more years and with the development of the new technique, he was recalled. He had regressed somewhat, his best score being only 2.4. He found the new method interesting and worked well. Approximately a year later, his best score was 4.1; this was approximately twice the rate of his previous growth. He contended that his actual functioning was even better. This seemed to be confirmed by his performance with a controlled reader which permitted no regressions, his usual mode of functioning. On this, his comprehension ranged up to 80%. It was concluded that his functioning was indeed, and not surprisingly, better than his test scores would indicate.

CONCLUSION

In conclusion, although research data are far from complete, there is some indication that both symptomatic and developmental dyslexics may benefit from a partial suppression of visual input at strategic stages in the learning process. Experience suggests that secondary, or symptomatic dyslexics, may progress toward normal competence with only tutorial aid. Primary, or developmental dyslexics, show only limited gains and provision for them must include the modified "bookless" curriculum previously described, with the addition of one other factor, a special school environment.

There are several reasons for this. First is the obvious one that the auditory input technique is simply more time consuming than the traditional pattern. Another is the damage caused by the hopeless competition with more fortunately endowed peers. In other words, the dyslexic would feel inferior in the ordinary school environment even if it were more accepting and understanding than it usually is. The special class is only too quickly and derisively characterized. Finally, his sense of his own status, his self-image, is enhanced if he can refer to himself as attending a special school rather than as a member of a special class.

The authors would like to thank Frank Desposito, M.D., for his assistance in reviewing this manuscript; Joel Herring, Medical Artist, Queens Medical Center, Jamaica, N.Y.; Floyd Jackson, B.P.A., Medical Photographer, Queens Medical Center, Jamaica, N.Y.; and Alfred Sepe, Assistant Medical Photographer, Queens Medical Center, Jamaica, N.Y.

REFERENCES

Ammons, R. B., & Ammons, C. H. **Quick test (QT) provisional manual psychological reports** (Monograph Supplement), 1962, **1,** 111-161.

Barnett, A. B., & Lodge, A. Diagnosis of deafness in infants with the use of computer averaged electro-encephalographic responses to sound. **J. Peds.,** 1966, **69,** 753.

Bateman, B. An educator's view of a diagnostic approach to learning. In J. Hellmuth (Ed.), **Learning disorders I.** Seattle: Special Child Publications of the Seguin School, 1965. Pp. 171-196.

Bettman, J. W., Stern, E. L., Whitsell, L. J., & Gofman, H. F. Cerebral dominance in developmental dyslexia. **Arch. Ophthal.,** December 1967, **78,** 722.

Blau, H. Unusual measures for the spelling invalid. In **Building spelling skills in dyslexic children.** San Rafael, Calif.: Academic Therapy Pub., 1969. Pp. 1-3.

Blau, H., & Blau, H. A theory of learning how to read. **The Reading Teacher,** 1968, **22** (2), 126-129.

Blau, H., & Blau, H. Some multi-sensory approaches for the severely disabled reader. **Reading** (official organ of the United Kingdom Reading Assn.), 1968, **2** (1), 5-10.

Brain, L. **Speech disorders, aphasia, apraxia, agnosia.** (2nd ed.) London: Butterworth, 1965.

Carroll, L. **Programmed phonics,** Book I, Book II, and Tape. Cambridge, Mass.: Educators Publishing Service, Inc., 1967.

Clements, S. **Minimal brain dysfunction in children.** Washington, D.C.: U.S. Dept. of Health, Education & Welfare, 1966.

Cohen, R. Dyscalculia. **AMA Arch. Neurol.,** 1961, **4,** 301-307.

Critchley, M. **Developmental dyslexia.** London: Heinemann, 1964.

English & English. **A comprehensive dictionary of psychological and psychoanalytical terms.** New York: Longmans Green & Co., 1958.

Fernald, G. M. **Remedial techniques in basic school subjects.** New York: McGraw-Hill, 1943.

Glaser, K., & Clement, R. L. School failure. **Peds.,** 1965, **35,** 128. (Word Recognition Test)

Hermann, R. **Reading disability.** Springfield, Illinois: Thomas, 1959.

Houston independent school district informal reading inventory, 1961-62. Curriculum Bulletin 61CBM43244.

Johnson, D. J., & Myklebust, H. R. **Learning disabilities.** New York: Grune and Stratton, 1967.

Kellaway, P. In Baylor University Pediatric Grand Rounds, Russell Blattner, Chairman, May 21, 1965.

Luchsinger, R., & Arnold, G. **Voice-speech language clinical communicology: Its physiology and pathology.** Constable & Co., Ltd., 1959.

McDermott, R. P. City University of New York. Unpublished paper and personal communication.

Money, J. The laws of constancy and learning to read. **Selected Conference Papers,** Third International Conference, Assn. for Children with Learning Disabilities, Tulsa, Oklahoma, 1966. Pp. 80-87.

Myklebust, H. R. Psychoneurological disturbances in childhood. **Rehabilitation Literature,** 1964, **25** (12), 12-15.

Myklebust, H. R., & Johnson, D. Developmental dyslexia in children. **Exceptional Child.,** 1962, **29** (1), 14-25.

Orton, J. L. The Orton-Gillingham approach. In J. Money (Ed.), **The disabled reader.** Baltimore: Johns Hopkins Press, 1966. P. 119.

Schwalb, E. Clinical considerations of cerebral dysfunction in children. **New York State J. Med.,** September 1, 1967, **67,** 2320.

Schwalb, E., & Blau, H. Approach to the differential diagnosis of dyslexia. Presented at the XII International Congress of Pediatrics, December 1-7, 1968, Mexico City, Mexico.

Schwalb, E., Blau, H., & Blau, H. Child with brain dysfunction. **J. Learning Disabilities,** April 1969, **2** (4).

Schwalb, E., Blau, H., & Zanger, E. Developmental dyslexia: Diagnosis and remediation by modality blocking. **New York State J. Med.,** 1968, **68** (14), 1931-36.

Silberberg, N. E., & Silberberg, M. D. The bookless curriculum: An educational alternative. **J. Learning Disabilities,** 1969, **2** (16), 9-14.

Talking Books, Washington, D.C.: Library of Congress.

Tansley, A. E. **Reading and remedial reading.** London: Routledge & Kegan Paul, 1967.

Wallace, A., & Atkins, J. The meaning of kinship terms. **Amer. Anthropol.,** Feb. 1960, **62,** 58-79.

PART IV. THE FUTURE

Editor's Introduction

The decade of the 70's may be recorded in reading history as the era of educational accountability and of the "Right to Read". Already private enterprise (e.g., the Open Court Publishing Co.) is leading the way in initiating reading instruction which is guaranteed to do what it purports to do—teach children to read. The next few years will surely see more of this. As Cohen pointed out in Part II we will also come to recognize that how children are taught is indeed a critical variable in how well they learn. One of the puzzles of the last 30 years of reading instruction is how we could ever have confused what the teacher did in teaching reading with who she is! Somehow the "teacher variable" became the great cop-out which made us able to say that method really wasn't important. The severity of the reading problems of millions of school children is eloquent and tragic testimony to our inattention to how we taught. One of the real difficulties we face in our efforts to improve reading instruction is having few evaluation systems sensitive enough to provide data for daily instructional decisions. We have often waited an entire year for global achievement tests to tell us the child has been in difficulty in reading.

Precision Teaching, introduced in this section by Starlin, is one evaluation technique which could revolutionize research on the efficacy of group and individual reading instruction. Starlin presents the need and rationale for Precision Teaching techniques and describes in detail how to use these techniques. Some of the many possible applications of Precision Teaching to reading evaluation and teaching are presented. Reading teachers, remedial specialists, curriculum planners and researchers alike can demonstrably improve their teaching and evaluation skills by the use of Precision Teaching. The system is designed to be used by regular classroom teachers, which of course means that it can also be used by specialists who have fewer children at one time. The Precision Teaching system provides direct, daily, standardized, rate performance data on each child's reading. Few contributions have seemed any more needed or potentially valuable.

Penney and Adams provide a highly readable and interesting perspective on reading research. They point out that the first era was characterized by basic research. Beginning with World War I there was a shift toward measuring human abilities and instructional methodology. We are now entering a third era, somewhat disenchanted by the failure of the earlier emphases in improving reading achievement. The new emphases, they believe, will be on the reading process itself and on a multidisciplinary approach to studying reading pathology. We join Penney and Adams in hoping that the emphases they have projected, in which reading research will be guided by operationalized theory which includes attention to the reader, the material to be read, and the program, will truly be the emphases of the next few years. They also foresee a healthy trend toward direct observation of reading behavior. As suggested earlier, Precision Teaching techniques can be of great assistance in direct observation and daily decision-making about instructional procedures for each individual child.

"A view of the total situation regarding inner city education as a whole, and reading instruction in the specific, is bleak and as of this writing not very hopeful for future improvement," according to Ramsey's thoughtful and provocative study of the reading instruction programs of five of the nation's large inner city school systems. The status of reading instruction is placed, as it must be, in the perspective of de facto segregation, central control, teacher load, and lack of adequate financial support for education in the ghettos. Those who are concerned about the quality of education for all children, especially those being slighted by our present system, must give serious attention to the problems documented by Ramsey and to the possible future trends which might alleviate and eventually solve the problems of educational injustice.

The final paper of this volume might also have been the first. Frankel

386

looks honestly and penetratingly at a question that is beginning to be heard now and will probably be raised more frequently in the future, "Why teach all children to read?" Often the questioner points out that in this day and age information is readily available through media other than the printed page. MacLuhan is often invoked as support for the contention that reading is no longer important enough to justify extensive instructional efforts. Many educators are hard pressed to answer these sincere queries. Frankel's analysis of the role of reading in past and present societies makes it totally clear that reading performs functions which, as far as reasonable men can foresee, are essential and irreplaceable as long as men cherish physical and intellectual freedom.

Evaluating Progress Toward Reading Proficiency

Clay Starlin, Ph.D.
Assistant Professor
School of Education
Bemidji State University
Bemidji, Minnesota

This chapter[1] discusses the adaption of a standardized recording system, Precision Teaching, to the evaluation of those skills involved in oral reading. The information obtained in the oral reading area through the use of Precision Teaching tools and procedures provides objective quantitative data concerning a youngster's actual reading performance.

To give the reader the rationale for such an orientation to reading evaluation, it seems appropriate to discuss the reasons for having a data-based evaluation system in education and, in particular, why a *standardized* evaluation system such as Precision Teaching is deemed extremely important.

DATA VERSUS BELIEF IN EDUCATION

Using objective data as an aid in making educational decisions and to evaluate youngsters' educational performance is diametrically opposed to the common educational practice of making such decisions based on what we believe is the best method or material.

Faith in logic, authoritative opinion, and clinical experience accounts for much of the maintenance of belief systems in education. The problem with such faith is that there is a great deal of variation in different persons' logic, opinions and experience. Different persons do not have common referents for their opinions or logical conclusions. Consequently, many varying suggestions for educational diagnosis and remediation for one particular situation are obtained from different "logical" yet well meaning educators. Even if a suggestion based on logic, opinion, or experience proves to be appropriate for one youngster in one situation, this does not mean it will be appropriate for another child in another situation.

An excellent example of the pitfalls of logic occurred in the remedial reading clinic that the author has worked in for the past two years. An

[1]Portions of the work in this article are taken from the author's unpublished doctoral dissertation.

initial logical decision was made to work on reducing the remedial students' errors before any attention was given to accelerating correct performance. With this emphasis, a consistent pattern occurred of very little gain in reducing errors and almost no change in correct performance. However, with the reverse emphasis (not directly mentioning errors), the correct performance accelerated and the error performance decelerated slightly or stayed the same.[2]

If it is agreed that the primary responsibility of the educator is *to accelerate students' academic performance,* [3] then it must be asked whether "we should use the most precise and unbiased tools available to accomplish this task." If the question is answered affirmatively, then we have agreed to the use of a data-based evaluation system in education. The educator who responds to this question affirmatively ought to further add that it is our responsibility, not our choice, to use the most precise procedures and evaluation tools available. Furthermore, we need to make a commitment to take our direction from the data. Although our choice of what to do and what the data say often coincide, occasionally we may be directed to alter our "cherished" beliefs to do what is best for the youngster.

Just as the physician is obligated through professional responsibility to use the most refined techniques available to maintain the physical health of his patients, the educator's responsibility is to the intellectual health and growth of his students. As Harold Howe, U. S. Commissioner of Education (1968), stated, "In a civilized society, education is in a sense as much a matter of life saving as is medicine. . . ."

[2]The performance variation of the youngsters, due to the different emphases on reading errors, was detected because *daily* performance records were available on each child in the clinic. Having access to such unbiased information enabled the author to see the flaw in his logic. Sample projects demonstrating this performance variation may be obtained from the author.

[3]Academic performance is broadly conceived to include all areas that the educational institution is trying to teach—although we often get involved in trying to manage inappropriate behavior in the classroom which interferes with our main job of teaching academic subjects.

In medical training the medical student is taught those diagnostic, prescriptive, and operative procedures that the present body of accumulated research indicates are the most effective and efficient. There would be many more malpractice suits than there are today if these students as practicing physicians made decisions such as: "I don't like this operative procedure because it takes too much time "; "This diagnostic work-up is too complicated, therefore I will choose a different one "; "I never did like this technique because of the professor who taught it in medical school "; "I won't use this medication because I don't like the smell or I don't think the patient will like the taste of it." Physicians do not make such choices. They use standardized measurement instruments and standardized tests for diagnosing a patient and then prescribe the most appropriate remedial procedures based on the objective diagnostic information.

In contrast, too many educators persist in basing teaching techniques on beliefs and not data, saying, "I don't care what the evidence says, I believe this is a better procedure; therefore I am going to continue to use it," rejecting a method that has been proven to be a tremendous aid in facilitating academic progress because it takes too much time, or preferring to "love" children in deference to teaching them. The terms *love* and *teach* should coincide. As long as an educator looks upon his job as one of choice without responsibility and fails to use the precise evidence and tools at his disposal, the academic death rate (failures) will increase or remain at its already atrocious level and he will continue to retard the educational system and the youngsters in it rather than facilitate its progress.

Assuming the reader finds some basis for accepting a data-based system for approaching educational evaluation, the next question is why should we use the precision teaching system to obtain this information.

WHY PRECISION TEACHING EVALUATION?

Likely the single most important thing that Precision Teaching has and is contributing to education is a standardized recording system. Where the central focus of most educational systems is the modification of behavior, the central emphasis of Precision Teaching is the direct recording of behavior.

Performance Rate

Precision Teaching uses pupil performance rate as a standardized measurement unit. Pupil performance rates are used because, based on observation and thousands of rated projects (Behavior Research Company-Behavior Bank, 1969), this is the most legitimate measure of a youngster's academic performance. Performance rate refers to the frequency of responding (count) divided by the time (in minutes) during which the responses occurred (duration) ($\frac{count}{duration}$ = rate).

When the term *rate* is used, it should not be confused with speed as in racing or speed for the sake of speed. Rather the orientation is based on the equation of speed + accuracy = proficiency. That is, one needs to know both the accuracy of a response as well as the amount of time required to make a response(s) in order to determine whether a youngster has mastered the material on which he is working. Merely having knowledge of either working duration or count of tasks completed does not give adequate nor precise enough information. For example, two first grade youngsters may be given the same 1500 word book to read for a half-hour assignment. At the end of the half-hour, both may have finished the book. However, one youngster may have finished in 15 minutes (indicating a rate of 100 words per minute) and the other may have taken the full half-hour (indicating a reading rate of 50 words per minute). The precision information is lost by merely noting that both finished at the end of a half-hour or that both read the 1500 words.

Standardized Data

The system also uses a standardized behavior chart to represent all the performance rate information collected in the academic or management areas.[4] The performance rates are recorded on the chart using standardized charting conventions, vastly facilitating communication and the ability to cover large amounts of information in a short time.

What standardization has done for medicine is analogous to what a standardized system such as Precision Teaching can do for education. For example, we can go to an M. D. in New York or Wisconsin or Oregon and feel quite secure that each physician will check our blood pressure, pulse, eyes, ears, and throat with standardized measurement devices. Also, his laboratory results will be related to standardized information about acceptable regular limits. Although, even if a physician, using his standardized diagnostic tools and procedures, finds that two patients have an identical physical ailment, he may still prescribe a different medication or treatment because of individual body chemistry or clinical history. Similarly, in education we must individually tailor instruction for each student and use a standardized direct recording system (i.e., Precision Teaching) to determine if goals are being successfully achieved.

We would be somewhat concerned if a physician used his fingers to look in our mouth rather than use a sterilized tongue depressor. Unfortunately, education is still at the stage of having our fingers in students' mouths!

The crucial importance of standardization is also evident in all weight and length measures. It would be a disaster if someone in Los Angeles asked a manufacturer in Chicago to send one hundred 16" by 20" frames but the manufacturer had a different unit length for his inch and counted in base two! Because of the lack of standardization in

[4]Precision Teaching divides behavior into two main categories, academic behaviors (reading words, answering social studies questions) and management behaviors (inappropriate talking out, saying nice things, getting out of seat without permission).

educational measurement, a great deal of information is being lost resulting in erroneous statements about data, and exorbitant amounts of time being spent on interpretation of what data there is.

Descriptive Language

A second major contribution Precision Teaching has made to education is the introduction of a descriptive language that enables communication with all those persons directly or indirectly associated with education (parents, teachers, the public, teacher aides, specialists, administrators, psychologists, legislators, and most importantly the students themselves). The descriptive nature of the Precision Teaching terminology is illustrated by the identification of the two scales on the standardized chart. The left side is called "up-the-left" rather than vertical or ordinate and the bottom scale is called "across-the-bottom" instead of horizontal or abscissa. If the best possible job of educating youngsters is to be accomplished, information must be shared locally and nationally. This requires that everyone can understand each others' language.

Given the precise records and descriptive terminology of Precision Teaching, deciding what educational procedures should be used to achieve the desired changes in a youngster's academic or management performances remains in the hands of the teacher. The teacher has the most frequent and intensive educational contact with the pupil, thus he is best able to predict what instructional or motivational procedures might be most successful with each child. With the aid of the Precision Teaching records, field analysis techniques, and computer analysis, regular classroom teachers can determine if their predictions are correct; if not, they may try again to continue monitoring the students' performance records.

EXPLAINING PRECISION TEACHING
RECORDING AND CHARTING

So you, the reader, will have some background for interpreting the charts and a basis for the recording practices followed in keeping Precision Teaching records, this section briefly discusses the basics involved in Precision Teaching recording and charting.

Recording

Once the response categories to be used have been identified, we can then obtain time and frequency information and compute the students' performance rate. For example, in the reading area we would be concerned with response categories such as letter sounds, blending, and sight words.

Time sample. The period during which performance rates are recorded is called the time sample—the duration during which behavior is being sampled. The time sample should be distinguished from the program time which refers to all the time during which we are working on the behavior but not necessarily recording it. For example, you may plan a 20-minute lesson on reading but only collect performance data for two minutes of this period. The 20 minutes is the program time and two minutes of these 20 is the time sample.

The exact start and finish time for both the time sample and the program time should always be recorded. It may be that just the time of day when a lesson is presented and the data collected will influence the youngster's performance. However, without the start and finish times the influence of the time of day cannot be determined.

It is usually desirable to maintain a constant time sample particularly with projects in the reading area.

Daily record. There are three basic phases involved when Precision Teaching techniques are used to evaluate a youngster's performance. These three phases are the "before" phase, the "during" phase, and the "after" phase. The "before" phase refers to the period from the beginning of data collection in a project to the introduction of the first major educational change, so the "before" phase is the time *before* making an educational change. The "during" phase refers to the period *during* which some intervention has been introduced to change the behavior. Because first tries at changing a performance are not always wholly successful sometimes other procedures must be tried. Different tries (or "durings") are merely indicated by successive numbering such that there may be during 1, during 2, during 3, etc. The intervention procedures used are indicated in each "during" on the charts. The "after" phase is the period following (*after*) removal of all "during" intervention.

The time samples should be kept daily in order to show the daily fluctuation of the pupils' performance. It is extremely misleading to have a spot check sort of procedure like the popular pretest and posttest design from which conclusions may be drawn that distort the picture of the youngster's performance between the two checks. A project done during one term at the remedial clinic at the University of Oregon demonstrates the potential risks of such a spot check procedure (see Figure 1). If Mike's performance had merely been checked at the beginning of the term (the "before" phase) and at the end of the term

FIGURE 1

THE RISKS OF SPOT-CHECK DATA SAMPLING

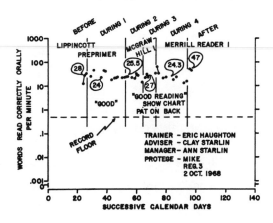

(the "after" phase), this spot check data would not have given any indication of his performance during the middle of the term.

Also, by having daily information, the teacher can make educational decisions on a daily or weekly basis. It is not necessary to wait for months to find out whether the intervention procedures he is using with a child are successful. The information is available a few days after intervention when there are daily records.

Permanent record. When obtaining the response frequency record in the academic areas it is necessary to have a record of the number of correct and error responses made during the time sample. It is therefore very important that some sort of permanent response record be obtained. The procedures for obtaining these records in the reading skill areas are represented in the section "Recording the Reading Skills."

Direct record. It is also extremely important to obtain a direct versus indirect measure of achievement. The count should be in close temporal proximity to the occurrence of the response, not remote (e.g., we should not have to think back over the day trying to remember how many words Hank read correctly during the time sample that was obtained in the morning and then derive the count from this reflection.) The direct record must involve our observation of the particular response of concern rather than recording a movement related to it and inferring a relationship. For example, the inference should not be made that because Richard hesitates a great deal in his reading he has a high error (mispronunciation) rate. Nor should the hesitation count be used as an error count. The hesitation problem may be a very legitimate project in itself but gross reading errors should not be inferred because Richard hesitates. If information is wanted about errors they must be directly counted.

With academic projects it is helpful to keep a copy of the materials being used (e.g., a xeroxed page from the reading book, a list of sight words which the student is working on) with the rate computation sheet and the chart. Then anyone who looks at the projects not only has the charted information but also an example of the material.

Charting

Central to Precision Teaching is the daily charting of the pupil performance rates. This procedure enables the teacher to have daily feedback from which to evaluate the success of her teaching techniques and provides her with information for making future tactical decisions.

The Precision Teaching chart enables charting of any and every human behavior (academic or management) that may occur in an average waking day and, for this reason, it is called a behavior chart.

The behavior chart is presented in Figure 2. The chart used in the classroom is identical to the one in Figure 2 except that the grid lines are blue and it is on standard 8½ x 11 erase resistant, translucent paper.

FIGURE 2

THE PRECISION TEACHING BEHAVIOR CHART

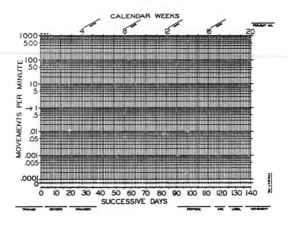

The four project team members of trainer, adviser, manager, and protege identified across the bottom of the chart are general terms that enable identification of a variety of people in these positions. Any position may be occupied by anyone, although characteristically in a classroom project the protege is a student; the manager is a teacher, teacher's aide or parent; the adviser may be a principal, counselor, resource teacher or similar person; and the trainer is often a university teacher trainer, school psychologist, social worker or someone in a similar position.

The team names were developed in an attempt to describe as precisely as possible the function that the various persons involved in a project may have. Very often the efforts of a number of persons are responsible for a youngster's improvement in any given area. Thus, by identifying all persons who functioned in some capacity on a project, all members of the team are credited.

The "age" space following "protege" refers to the age of the protege. In the "label" space, the protege's class placement (regular fourth, primary remedial reading) or occupation if not a student (teacher, counselor, plumber, parent) is entered. Finally, the "movement" category is where the movement that is being recorded on a particular chart is entered.

At the top right center of the chart is the address of the Behavior Research Company where the chart paper and the rate computation sheet can be purchased.

Across the bottom of the chart successive calendar days are indicated. Each heavy vertical line in the grid represents a Sunday line with Monday through Saturday lines occurring between the Sunday lines. In the upper left hand corner of the chart grid, the letters *M, W, F* represent a key for the days of the week. The numbers 4, 8, 12, 16 and 20 at the top of the grid indicate the number of elapsed weeks. Above the first four of these cumulative week indicators is a place to put the day, month and year of the Sunday on which the number is resting. So on each chart it is possible to record 140 successive calendar days which is 20 calendar weeks. Two charts will cover a full school year for one movement of one student.

Up-the-left side of the chart, labeled "movements per minute," is the grid for the performance rate. Remember,

$$\frac{\text{number of movements (responses)}^5}{\text{minutes recorded}} = \text{the rate.}$$

After computing the rates, directly transfer them to the chart placing them at the appropriate rate on the appropriate day. The range of the up-the-left side is from .001 per minute which means 1 count/1000 recorded minutes, to 1000 per minute which means 1000 counts/1 recorded minute. There are six basic sections to the chart. The rate to which the arrow is pointing refers to one movement per minute. The lines between 1 and 10 are counted by ones (2, 3, 4, 5, . . . 10). Lines between 10 and 100 represent steps by ten (20, 30, . . . 100), and from 100 to 1000 the lines are jumps by hundreds (200, 300, . . . 1000). Below 1 there are increments of tenths from .1 to 1, then hundredths from .01 to .1, and finally thousandths from .001 to .01. A useful way to remember how to convert the up-the-left rate statements to a movement/minute statement is represented below:

---

[5]The term *movement* or *movement cycle* is related to the term *response* but there is an important distinction that should be made between the terms at this point. Most persons are more familiar with the term response and its meaning, thus this term has been used in the first sections of the article to convey concern with an observable behavior of an individual. A behavior is called a movement cycle when merely discussing or describing it. The same behavior is referred to as a response only when it can be demonstrated that the behavior is performed at a designated rate and when it has been identified which events stimulate or consummate the behavior. Thus, the term movement cycle is a description of a behavior in the environment, whereas the term response indicates that a functional behavior is present in some persons' repertoire.

Place all rates above 1 over 1
$$1000 = 1000/1 = 1000 \text{ movements per minute}$$
$$50 = \quad 50/1 = 50 \text{ movements per minute}$$
$$2 = \quad 2/1 = 2 \text{ movements per minute}$$

Convert all rates below 1 to fractions
$$.5 \quad = 5/10 \quad = 5 \text{ movements in 10 minutes}$$
$$.03 \ = 3/100 \ = 3 \text{ movements in 100 minutes}$$
$$.005 = 5/1000 = 5 \text{ movements in 1000 minutes}$$

The rates below 1 can be converted to a "per minute" statement if it is wished. For example, 5 movements in 10 minutes would be equal to 1 movement every 2 minutes or .5 per minute which is less than once every minute. Five movements in 1000 minutes equals 1 movement every 200 minutes or .005 per minute.

The reason the horizontal rate lines squeeze up near the top of each of the six sections (i.e., (1) .001 to .01, (2) .01 to .1, (3) .1 to 1, (4) 1 to 10, (5) 10 to 100, (6) 100 to 1000) is because the up-the-left scale is a proportional scale on which equal academic gains are represented by equal visual distance. For example, the distance from 5 to 10 is the same distance as from 500 to 1000 because proportionally both gains represent a doubling of rate. Thus, a lower rate youngster gets as much credit for the same proportional gain as a higher rate youngster, which is not true on an arithmetic scale.

Based on classroom data and youngsters' comments, the progress (proportional) nature of the behavior chart may serve as a very strong motivational device itself. Children are very concerned about making their correct performance go up and incorrect performance go down. To keep their slope of acceleration or deceleration the same, they have to continue gaining by the same ratio.

The standardized up-the-left scale represents the range (in terms of rate) of all human behavior that could occur in an average waking day.[6] There are no human behaviors that occur at a rate of more than 1000 responses/minute, which is the upper end of the scale. The lowest possible rate a person could have in one day would be once in his waking day which is approximately 1 response in 1000 minutes or a rate of .001. And .001 is the lower end of the behavior chart scale. The behaviors characteristically of concern in the classroom distribute themselves over the range of the behavior chart in terms of their common rates. (Starlin and Starlin, 1969)

Lindsley (1969) has found that with the standardized behavior chart, as opposed to a nonstandardized graph, it is possible to obtain 10 times the amount of information in the same period. For example, using the behavior chart, with the standardized charting conventions a teacher may look through 30 projects in the same time it would take a teacher using nonstandardized techniques to look through three.

It also allows comparisons *within* youngsters on different performances as well as between youngsters on the same and different areas.

Charting conventions. There are a number of conventions to follow in recording data on the chart. So that the reader will have at least a summary of these conventions, Figure 3 has been included. For more elaboration of these conventions, see Starlin and Starlin, 1969.

A charting check list[7] developed by Dr. Eric Haughton (1968b) is presented for those persons interested in starting Precision Teaching projects.

---

[6]Based on data collected by Dr. Eric Haughton (1968a), an average waking day was determined to be around 16 and one-half hours or approximately 1000 minutes.

[7]This check list may be xeroxed and used as an actual check list for any projects you may wish to start.

Charting Project Check List

Projects

1 2 3 4 5

All performance measures are in terms of rate (i.e., movements/minute). _____

Daily records have been entered daily on the rate computation sheet. _____

Rates have been plotted on the behavior chart. _____

Charts are being kept daily. _____

If there is a frequency of correct and error movements, both correct and error should be charted and on separate charts. _____

Have record floor indicated. _____

Have record ceiling indicated. _____

Have distinguished between *ignored* and *no chance* days. _____

Have a chart for each rated movement. _____

Have included samples of protege performance (e.g., worksheets, photographs, tape recordings, etc.) with charts. _____

Have executed and indicated phases—before, during, after. _____

Have identified intervention procedures in each phase on the chart. _____

Have indicated middle rates for each phase. _____

Have identified all project team members on chart. _____

Have calendar synchronized charts and entered Sunday dates. _____

Have followed all charting conventions (see Figure 3). _____

FIGURE 3

A SUMMARY OF CHARTING CONVENTIONS

Term	Definition	Charting Conventions
RATED DAY	A day in which the movement could have occurred and was recorded.	Chart point on daily chart. Connect points with lines. Skip all no chance and phase change space. Chart in pencil only, no colors. Use dot for acceleration target (e.g., .—.) and x's for deceleration target (e.g., x—x) *Each movement cycle on a separate chart.*
NO CHANCE DAY	A day in which the movement has no opportunity to occur.	Skip day on daily chart
IGNORED DAY	A day in which the movement could have occurred but was not recorded.	Draw line across day only chart.
PHASE CHANGE SPACE	The space following the last rated day of one phase and the first day of the next phase.	Draw a vertical line on the chart in the phase change space. Don't connect data points.
RECORD CEILING	The highest measurable performance rate determined by the program or program events.	Draw dashed horizontal line on the chart at the maximum rate. Dashes should occur across Sunday lines, e.g., ———⟶
RECORD FLOOR	The lowest measurable performance rate, other than zero determined by length of time sample (i.e., 1/time sample = record floor).	Draw a horizontal dashed line on the chart at the record floor. Dashes should occur across week day lines, e.g., ———⟶

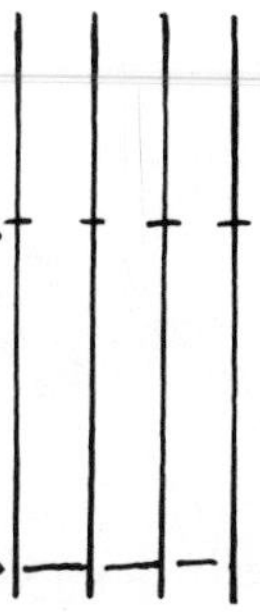

ZERO RATE	No movement cycle recorded within *the time sample.*	Chart point directly below record floor.
MIDDLE ACCELER- ATION RATE	Mid-point of rated days in each phase.	◯ tail of tear drop points at mid-point (middle), number inside tear drop.
MIDDLE DECELER- ATION RATE	Mid-point of rated days in each phase.	▽ tail of triangle apex points at mid-point (middle), number inside tri-angle.
CALENDAR SYNCHRONIZE	Standard time for starting all charts (i.e., the first day of school).	It requires two charts to cover a full school year. The first Monday of the first chart is the Monday of the first week of school. The first Monday of the second chart is the Monday of the 21st week.

READING DEFINED

Over the years there has been a good deal of confusion and disagree-ment on such points as how reading and comprehension are related, what skills are prerequisite to beginning reading, what precisely are the skills a youngster must master to be able to read and comprehend what he has read, or the order in which the tasks (if identified) should be pre-sented to him.

Two possible reasons for the confusion over such issues are failure to pinpoint precisely the movements comprising the reading and compre-hension areas with consequent imprecision in identifying what environ-mental events are related to what movements and failure to obtain di-rect daily pupil performance records even on those movements which have been identified.

Basic Segments of Language

Trying to pinpoint what is meant by reading brings unavoidable con-

406

cern with the science of language called linguistics, for reading involves an interpretation of written language. (Barnhart, 1960)

The many complexities underlying reading seem best understood by reviewing the three basic segments of language—phonology, grammar and semantics. (Gleason, 1961)

> *Phonology* involves the linguistic study of the speech sounds and sound system of a specific dialect or language during a particular period. (Lowry, 1968)
>
> *Grammar* involves the science or study of the system and structure of language. There are two basic components of grammar: *syntax* and *morphology.* Morphology deals with the grammar within words (the combination of roots and affixes) and may be contrasted with syntax which deals with the building of individual words into larger language structures (phrases, sentences). (Lowry, 1968)
>
> *Linguistic semantics* deals with the growth and modifications of word meanings. (Lowry, 1968)

Depending on the particular written language system encountered and the type of reading response made, all of these basic linguistic units are of concern to a greater or lesser degree.

As Hanna et al. (1966) point out, there may be different kinds of written language. There are alphabetic forms of language which, as the name suggests, are comprised of alphabetic letters. Other written languages may use pictures (hieroglyphics), numerals (mathematics), or some other linguistic unit other than alphabetic letters.

A numerical orthography would have an underlying phonology (sound system), but it would be primarily related to the morphology and syntax of the language. At the other end of the continuum, a purely alphabetic language would have its orthography determined primarily at the phonological level, with morphological and syntactical factors determining a small percentage of the alphabetic options. (Hanna, et al., 1966, p. 106)

Thus, in teaching persons to read an alphabetic written language, we are primarily concerned with teaching them the sounds the various alphabetic symbols represent. Whereas in teaching a person to read a written language more dependent on morphological or syntactical properties, the emphasis is on teaching the meaning represented by each symbol and what interpretation to make when these symbols are arranged in various ways.

One can start to see that the sounds which make up words in an alphabetic language are analogous to the components of, for instance, a mathematical formula in a numerically based language. In order to emit the correct response when confronted with the formula $5 + 7 =$ ☐ , it must be known what the symbols *5, +, 7* and = mean. Similarly, in order to emit the appropriate response when confronted with the word *cat,* it must be known what sounds are represented by the letters *c, a,* and *t.*

The preceding discussion in this section was presented with the hope of conveying to the reader the linguistic knowledge that must precede and underlie the understanding and subsequent teaching of reading. Drawing from this discussion, the definition of reading will be broadly viewed as the vocal or subvocal pronunciation of any written language. Thus the interpretation of a mathematical formula is reading as legitimately as is the pronunciation of a written word.

However, of particular concern in this chapter is reading the alphabetic language of American English. It will be this aspect of reading that will be inferred when the term "reading" is used.

The Alphabetic Nature of American English

The next question that arises is, if we are to treat American English as an alphabetic language rather than some other linguistic form, how closely does it in fact approximate the definition that a purely alphabetic language is one in which each graphic symbol (letter) represents only one phoneme (sound) of speech?

In the first phase of the scholarly study conducted by Hanna et al. (1966), it was found that of the 52 sound units (phonemes) they analyzed slightly greater than 73 percent demonstrated a consistent phoneme-grapheme (sound-symbol) correspondence in 17,000 commonly used English words. However, the 73 percent figure only represents a consideration of phoneme-grapheme correspondences in terms of phonological analysis. When both position in syllables and syllabic stress are considered, the 52 phonemes approximate the alphabetic principle slightly over 84 percent.

The criteria that Hanna and his associates used was, "if a given phoneme had one graphemic option which occurred 80% or more of the time in the entire (17,000 word) corpus, that particular phoneme-grapheme relationship was considered to exhibit a satisfactory approximation of the alphabetic principle."

Although there are a few reservations to bear in mind when considering phonemic position in syllables and the syllabic stress variations in an alphabetic analysis (Hanna, et al., 1966, p. 99), the conclusion of the authors was that "phase I. . .seems to have demonstrated satisfactorily the basic hypothesis that American English is primarily an alphabetic language."

The more sophisticated traditional[8] research studies support the teach-

---

[8]Traditional refers to the fact that most of these studies used a pre- post-achievement test design rather than obtain actual reading performance data.

ing of reading following phonic (alphabetic) regularity principles (Chall, 1967). It also appears from preliminary Precision Teaching data that the results of these traditional studies will be confirmed in terms of actual student reading performance.

Because of this large amount of information, for purposes of this chapter the teaching of reading written American English is viewed as necessarily approached from a phonic, or alphabetic, orientation.

Oral Reading

The potential stimulus events for *beginning* reading are words and the desired response is the saying of these words. So that we are assured that a youngster learning to read is consistently pronouncing the words correctly and fluently (i.e., with appropriate punctuational inflection, no repetitions, no hesitations), initially he should read orally. It is only through listening to a youngster reading that those areas that are in need of reading remediation can be identified. Once it is certain that a youngster has mastered the reading of words, he can then move toward reading silently.

Reading Distinguished from Comprehension

To further refine the definition of reading used in this chapter, a brief statement of the features that distinguish it from comprehension are discussed below.

Reading involves the saying of words whereas comprehension involves the understanding of what is read. This understanding may be demonstrated through any number of different movements (writing an answer, saying an answer, performing some activity) depending on the question asked. The illustration below differentiates reading and comprehension on two dimensions.

	Characteristic events present:	Characteristic desired movement:
oral reading:	words on a page	saying the words
comprehension:	a written question	writing the answer to the question

Summary

In short, the refined definition of reading as will be used in the remainder of the article involves 1) the assumption that American English is primarily an alphabetic language, which means that the teaching of reading is approached through the matching of speech sounds with the letter forms that represent them, 2) an oral reading approach is emphasized because the concern is in determining the correct and fluent word pronunciation of beginning or remedial readers, and 3) reading and comprehension are distinguished because of the different events and movements present when these skills are performed.

After pinpointing how reading is to be defined, the next task, as stated in the second paragraph of this section, is to collect some precise performance data on the skills that make up reading. Consequently, the remainder of the article is concerned with applying the Precision Teaching recording system to the evaluation of oral reading skills, with the reading instruction emphasis involving a phonic regularity (alphabetic) orientation.

PRECISION TEACHING AND READING

When using the Precision Teaching recording system to evaluate reading, we no longer use traditional testing procedures but completely rely on performance rate data for diagnostic and remedial success information. Traditionally and presently the main means of evaluating a pupil's academic progress or potential has been in terms of intelligence tests and spot check diagnostic and achievement tests. However, these assessment procedures seldom evaluate the actual performance. For example, the actual performance assessment of a youngster in oral reading involves determining how many words he can read accurately in a given period over so many days in a particular material. Unfortunately, such daily classroom performance of pupils has been overshadowed by their achievement test scores. These intermittent tests usually do not give precise performance data. Performance from the test scores obtained must be inferred. Nancy Johnson (1966) found that "pupils do not perform the same on an arithmetic achievement test as they do on their daily arithmetic assignments. . .and that teachers were more influenced in their ratings of superior students by their IQ and achievement test score than by their daily performance."

It must be known how many words a youngster can read and how many and what kinds of errors he makes in a designated period in the book or books that are available for him to read in. This oral reading is an accurate index of his reading performance, not that he has a 2.5 grade level score on a reading achievement test.

READING PROJECT PINPOINTS

Pinpointing refers to identifying a movement cycle (response) precisely enough to obtain a record of the movement. Thus, what is identified must be observable and countable.

There are three basic response skills involved in learning how to read phonically regular words. These skills include 1) knowing the letter sounds (knowledge of the relationship between letter forms and their sounds), 2) ability to blend these sounds together to make a word $\overset{\frown}{c}\overset{\frown}{a}\overset{\frown}{t}$, and 3) ability to blend the letter sounds fast enough for the student to be saying the word as a sight unit—that is, reading the words.

One other project that would be most helpful in aiding oral reading fluency is one on phonically irregular sight words (was, are, shoe). A

412

sight word is any word that the reader knows as a unit. There can be phonically regular or phonically irregular sight words. The reason for an emphasis on an irregular sight word project is because of the assumption that, if a student has been taught the regular sound-symbol relationships, he can sound out phonically regular words independently.

To assist in evaluating a student's progress towards the goal of oral reading mastery, there are four basic recommended projects. It is important to make a statement concerning both correct and error performance when identifying the pinpoints for the four project areas. Generally, the project pinpoints are as follows:
1. a) letter sounds said correctly
   b) letter sounds said incorrectly (errors)
2. a) letters blended correctly in sequence
   b) letters blended incorrectly in sequence (errors)
3. a) (irregular) sight words said correctly
   b) (irregular) sight words said incorrectly (errors)
4. a) words read correctly orally
   b) words read incorrectly orally (errors)

Reading Movements Handled by Instruction

There are also abilities such as moving from left to right in reading, discriminating between letters and words and appropriate inflectional emphasis in response to punctuation that should be considered in establishing oral reading mastery. However, attention in these areas is frequently handled by instruction without a project on the recordable movement. For example, a youngster may be instructed on how to move from left to right within words, phrases or sentences; but it is rather difficult to evaluate "a left to right movement" unless eye movement photography is used to obtain a record of fixations and regressions. Such a procedure is not very feasible and definitely not practical in terms of classroom projects. The discrimination area provides another good example of the distinction between a reading response category and instructional procedures aimed at teaching these various responses. There is not a discrimination response as such, but in reading a discrimination between letter forms and sounds and words. Thus, a discrimination error (saying /b/ for /d/) would show up as an error in a letter sound, blending, or oral reading project. Correct performance in these project areas would indicate correct discriminative ability at least for one given time sample. No specific project would be necessary on discrimination because both correct and incorrect discrimination performance would be picked up in the projects that require this ability.

The instructional intervention necessary to teach such skills as left to right and discrimination would be part of, or a complete "during" phase in one of the four project areas (see Figure 4).

FIGURE 4

AN EXAMPLE OF INSTRUCTIONAL INTERVENTION IN A BLENDING PROJECT

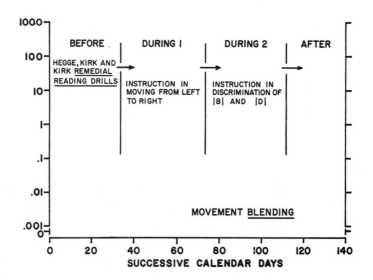

Refined Pinpointing

Although given the basic project pinpoints there are possible variations that should be kept in mind, an understanding of two fundamental dimensions of pinpointing enables more specific identity of a variation in a basic project that may be individually relevant to particular needs.

Calibration. One of the pinpointing dimensions is that of calibration. Calibrating involves assuring that the standard units of measurement are the same. We must be sure that the response unit conveys as precisely as possible the amount of information covered and the approximate length of time necessary to emit each response. The oral reading area is probably the most prone to potential calibrating difficulties. Figure 5 presents a range of refined pinpoints in the oral reading area from books at the top of the scale to letters scanned at the bottom.[9] As indicated in Figure 5, there are nonfunctional units for eval-

FIGURE 5

CALIBRATING IN ORAL READING

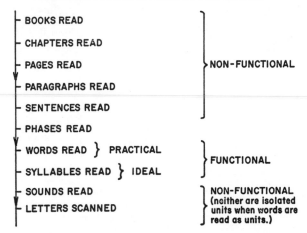

[9]Dr. Eric Haughton was most helpful in elaborating and refining this figure.

uating oral reading such as books, chapters, pages, sentences, phrases, letter sounds and letter forms; and there are two identified functional units (words and syllables). If oral reading were assessed in terms of books read, only an extremely gross indication of how many responses a youngster emitted would be obtained;and there would be almost no indication of the number of oral reading errors. The same situation exists with chapters, pages, paragraphs and sentences, though the degree of grossness decreases. Even when counting oral words read, which is one of the suggested project pinpoints, the measurement has not been refined as precisely as it should. For, if we concede that time spent performing is indeed an important element of mastery (almost all traditional testing procedures do concede this by the incorporation of time limits), then we must guarantee that the measurement unit identified does not require differing amounts of time to emit (i.e., one second or more variation). For example, if a youngster is reading a book with mostly three, four and five syllable words in it, instead of one with only one syllable words, there will be a significant difference in the amount of time spent pronouncing the different words. A five syllable word like *interpretation* takes at least four times as long to say as a single syllable word like *in* which is in fact one of the five syllables of *interpretation.* The number of prerequisite skills necessary to pronounce *interpretation* are greater than those needed to pronounce *in.* Thus *interpretation* is not only a more time-consuming word to read but also requires more knowledge to pronounce. It appears that the most functional and ideal unit of measurement in reading is a syllable count.[10] Even with the variation in the number of letters in such single syllable words as *a* and *shake,* the difference in the pronunciation time is almost nonexistent if they are read as sight units. However, the only practical and most functional unit at the

---

[10]Both "sounds read" and "letters scanned" are nonfunctional criteria for reading evaluation because, as indicated on Figure 5, they are not isolated response units separated by a closure in articulation as is the case with syllables. For instance, the emitted response that is made when the one syllable word *cat* is said as a whole is exactly *cat.* If the word is blended (c̆ăt), then it is possible to record a sound count, but these sounds are not isolated response units when the word is read as a whole.

present time is the word count. It is not feasible for a teacher to count the number of words read in a two minute time sample for 25 youngsters every day. Thus, it is necessary to have the student himself or some helper (teacher aide, mother, advanced student) do the counting. Because of the variation in breaking polysyllabic words and the amount of time involved in determining the number of syllables in each word, it is not feasible to ask a student or a helper to accurately and efficiently accomplish this task. However, words are easily visible and countable in books because of the spacing between them and thus are reasonable units for students and helpers to record.

Description. Once the unit of measurement that is to be used in a project has been determined, we must then be sure that the movement has been described as precisely as is desirable for our needs. The degree to which the movement is described involves the second major dimension of pinpointing. For each unit on the calibration scale there is a continuum of how precisely to describe the movement. An example of such a continuum has been added to the "words read" area of Figure 5 to give Figure 6.

FIGURE 6

THE TWO DIMENSIONS OF PINPOINTING

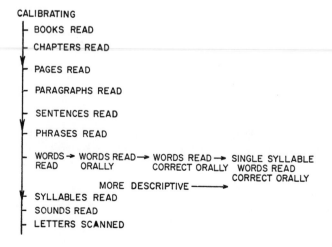

If a teacher plans to work with a student on a pinpointed movement that is more precise and descriptive than are the basic project pinpoints already listed, then the pinpoint should include this information. For instance, as in Figure 6, if a pupil will only be working on single syllable words, it would be more precise to make this youngster's project pinpoint "single syllable words read correctly orally" and "single syllable words read incorrectly orally" that just *words* read correctly and incorrectly orally. Of course, the latter basic pinpoint will cover reading of both single and multiple syllable words.

There are other examples of more descriptive pinpoints in the other basic project areas as well. For instance, in the letter sound area, a decision might be made to specifically do a project on short vowels, long vowels, or consonants. In the blending area one may wish to differentiate between isolated blending (enunciating each letter sound in sequence) and continuous blending (continuing one sound into the next in sequence) as different, more specific project pinpoints. In the sight word area there may be situations when projects involving regular sight words or a combination of regular and irregular sight words would be more appropriate—for example, a youngster becomes over-analytic in his blending. As in the oral reading area, one could also be more specific and indicate two-syllable sight words, medial short vowel sight words and so on.

Pinpointing of reading errors. All the error categories of the basic projects are in need of more precise and descriptive pinpointing. Rather than merely identifying "words read incorrectly orally," it should be specified that the error was an omitted word, a word substitution (*a* for *the*), a word reversed (*saw* for *was*), and so forth. However, again the problem of ideal versus practical arises. Practically, it is not feasible to have a classroom teacher keep one chart for each type of reading error a student makes. As more help is available for the classroom teacher in the form of parent helpers,

interested volunteers and teacher aides, this further degree of pre-
ciseness will become more feasible.

Even with the present more global pinpoints such as "words read
incorrectly," if we listen and watch carefully when evaluating a
pupil's daily performance, it is possible to identify specifically the
type of errors being made. With this information it is possible to
precisely tailor the remedial intervention for each specific error,
although still having a grouped error record.

There are some "error type" projects that should not be grouped
with a mispronunciation error project. Such things as long hesitations, repetitions, and "I don't know" responses should be separate
projects and distinguished from mispronunciations. There have been
projects done in these areas that will be discussed briefly in the next
section.

One final comment related to errors concerns "carelessness." Often
a teacher will infer that a youngster is being careless when he responds
correctly one day and incorrectly the next day to the same item, or
when he does not "attend" and makes mistakes such as saying *a* for
the.

Part of the difficulty with attaching the label "carelessness" to such
behaviors is that this term gives very few leads for what might be an
appropriate remedial procedure. On the other hand, to stay with a
descriptive statement such as, "June read the word 'horse' Friday
but on Monday she did not," requires a very precise statement of
June's performance.

It is likely that the pattern that many remedial youngsters display
of "knowing" a skill one day and not the next is explainable by noting the distinction between a behavior being a movement cycle or a
response. That is, because of a lack of practice, of systematic instruction or of appropriate motivation, a youngster may not have mastered

a skill to the extent that it is a functional response in his behavioral repertoire.

Whatever the pupil behaviors are that stimulate the use of the term "carelessness," the term takes us at least one step away from a precise description of the youngster's actual disturbing behavior and further suggests that it is the fault of the student, when the existence of such behavior usually indicates a faulty educational environment.

In summary, one should strive to calibrate and describe the reading response areas as precisely as is practical yet still functional. As is evident from the discussion in this section, there is considerable variation in what specific reading movements could be most relevant for a person to record in a given situation; although, after reading the "Recording the Reading Skills" section, the reader should understand how the four basic project pinpoints will enable obtaining most of the information necessary to efficiently and effectively establish oral reading proficiency in students.

PROFICIENCY

As is the purpose of most academic evaluation, the reason for evaluating student reading performance in terms of rated information is to determine the present level of performance mastery. Given such rated performance data, the question then arises: what performance criteria or standard should be used to determine how well or poorly a youngster is performing? That is, what does a proficient sounder, blender or reader look like in terms of performance rates? It is precisely the answering of these questions that is and has been a major concern of the author. Thus, before discussing any specific data or rated proficiency levels for the various project areas, it would be helpful to specifically delineate what the term "proficiency" is attempting to convey.

Components of Reading Proficiency

There are four factors which combine to determine proficiency levels in the reading skill areas.

Since correct and error performance rates are used as standard measures of evaluation, it follows that both response *speed* and *accuracy* (the two components of rate) are two factors involved in determining proficiency levels.

A third factor involved in the proficiency statement is *fluency.* Maintaining accuracy and moving fairly rapidly through the material, whether it is sounds, sight words or running words in a book, enables very little repeating, inappropriate hesitations or inattentiveness; for such nonfluent behavior would result in failure to reach proficiency. Although it is somewhat more difficult to obtain records of the fluency dimensions, fluency is always directly or indirectly part of the proficiency picture.

Not only should the performer achieve the designated standard in terms of speed, accuracy and fluency, but he must demonstrate the proficiency rates *consistently over time.* It should not be assumed that because a proficiency level is achieved on one day that the student is in fact proficient. *At least* a middle[11] performance rate for one or two weeks at or above the correct standard and at or below the error standard should be obtained. It is crucial that the definition of proficiency include both a statement concerning correct *and* error performance simultaneously. Otherwise, we might know that 40 letter sounds said correctly in a minute is proficiency and find that a student in fact achieved this, only to find out later he also had 15 errors per minute.

[11]The term "middle" is equivalent to the nonparametric median statistic. However, "middle" is more descriptive of the point (in a ranked distribution of data) which is being referred to than is the term "median."

Proficiency: A Minimum Statement

The proficiency statement refers to the minimum fluency, consistency, speed and accuracy performance levels necessary to demonstrate mastery of the material. For example, what are the fewest number of words read correctly orally and the largest number of errors that a youngster could emit with the least amount of fluency over the shortest length of time and still be considered a masterful reader? A youngster below the minimum correct standard is either not fluent or making too many errors. Above the minimum error standard the reader is inaccurate because of the many errors he makes. Confusing letter sounds, repeating words, and continuing to blend words that should be known by sight are but a few examples of some of the factors that may be interfering with a student reaching proficiency in one or more of the project areas.

The minimum nature of the proficiency statement says that a youngster must at least achieve this performance level if he is to efficiently and in many cases effectively work on the next task.

Ceiling Levels

There are likely physiological ceiling rates for the oral production of sounds and words. However, the proficiency performance rates, which will be suggested for the various basic project pinpoints in the next major section, do not approach the highest possible rates in these areas.

An approximation of the ceiling performance rates in the various reading areas has been obtained by screening adults who have mastered the reading skills very well. These ceiling estimates will be presented along with the proficiency standards. The discrepancy evident between the rate proficiency statement and the ceiling rate estimates, emphasizes rate not as speed for the sake of speed but rather the guarantee of enough speed to ensure mastery and fluency.

422

It would, of course, be possible to attempt to accelerate a youngster beyond the proficiency level in correct performance in a given area in an attempt to more closely approximate the ceiling performance rate. However, a question of educational efficiency then enters in: how much time should be invested in putting a little more frosting on the cake when it has been established by the proficiency standard that a child has mastered the material? Just because proficiency is achieved does not mean that a pupil cannot be encouraged to strive for a higher rate by continuing the project independently on his own time.

Independence of Age or Material

An interesting and unanticipated development of the proficiency picture, particularly relevant to oral reading, is that the proficiency standards appear to be the same regardless of the age or label (retarded, remedial, regular, gifted) of the pupil or the material being used. This might be explained first by recognizing that if indeed certain responses are prerequisite to other responses in various skill areas, such as reading, then regardless of the age or label of the student they must acquire minimum proficiency in the prerequisite skill before they can proceed to the next one. The suggestion that proficiency should not change even though the material does recall the definition of proficiency as a minimum criterion level. Any performance below this minimum would indicate some breakdown in the reader's mastery or fluency. Above the proficiency level there is still plenty of room— up to the ceiling level (for instance in the oral reading area)—for rates to fluctuate when reading a technical textbook as opposed to a light novel.

What the pupil performance rate data allow is the establishment of some normative information in terms of actual reading proficiency. Consequently, when it is determined that a protege who is supposed to be reading orally at 100 words correct/minute with 2 or less errors/minute is in fact reading at 20 words correct/minute and 10 errors/

minute, there is immediate and precise information regarding the discrepancy between where he is and where he should be. By maintaining daily records, it is then possible to determine on a daily basis the success of efforts to reduce or eliminate this discrepancy.

WHAT THE DATA SAY

The large majority of the reading performance data [12] available to the author falls into the four basic project areas of letter sounds, blending, sight words and oral reading. It is these four categories that will constitute four of the subsections of this section. Under each broad category where the information is available, some discussion of the pinpoint variations (e.g., a consonant or vowel project versus a letter sound project) mentioned in a previous section will be included. The fifth subsection includes a summary of a few projects related to reading fluency.

Letter Sounds

Information from seven adult projects, including a self-project of the author, indicate that with a flash presentation adults are capable of a middle performance of just greater than 100 sounds correct/minute with a middle of one or zero errors. By laying all the flash cards out on the table and going through them in this manner, it is possible to add approximately another 50 sounds correct with no loss in error performance. This information should give the reader some idea of the optimum performance level in the letter sound area.

---

[12]The data presented and referred to in this section have been collected by practicum students in the University of Oregon remedial reading clinic and by school teachers in the public schools in and around Eugene, Oregon, under the supervision of the author. The conclusions presented concerning these data have been arrived at through a hand tabulation of the data. A thorough statistical analysis has not yet been completed. Therefore, the conclusions drawn are of a tentative nature. When a more extensive analysis has been completed, it will be possible to make range and median statements about *large* groups of projects in the various areas.

Most of the student letter sound projects that have been supervised by the author have involved presentation of both upper and lower case letters by means of flash cards. The youngster is asked to give the sound of each letter presented.

At the time of this writing 66 youngsters' letter sound projects had been screened, 42 from the remedial reading clinic and 24 from a first grade classroom. A middle correct and error performance rate for the last five days of both completed and ongoing projects was taken for each of the 66 projects. The range of these "last five day middles" was from 17 to 89 sounds/minute correct and 0 to 9 errors/minute. The interquartile range was from 35 to 52 sounds correct and 0 to 2 errors. The middle of the ranked "last five day middles" was 43.5 sounds/minute correct and 1 error/minute.

Based on this information, a tentative letter sound proficiency standard of 40 sounds correct per minute and 2 or less errors per minute is recommended.

Figure 7 is representative of the 24 letter sound projects that are being recorded in the first grade room.[13]   During the before phase, Janet was in the middle of the class in terms of both correct rate (0 correct/minute) and error rate (19 errors/minute). Janet's correct chart indicates that it took her 19 days or four weeks to reach the proficiency standard of 40 sounds correct/minute for the first time. The middle number of days to reach proficiency for the whole class was 29. The median (middle) number of errors that a student was making when he achieved proficiency in the sounds was two per minute. The acceleration in correct performance and deceleration in error performance evident on Janet's sound charts was achieved by presenting (in the "during" phases) the sounds with a brief demonstration of how to say them, and then allowing the youngsters to practice.

[13]For assistance in interpreting this and the following charts, the reader might benefit from restudying the chart in Figure 2 and the charting conventions in Figure 3.

FIGURE 7

JANET MOVES FROM THE MIDDLE
OF HER FIRST GRADE CLASS IN THE "BEFORE" PHASE
TO LETTER SOUND PROFICIENCY IN 19 DAYS

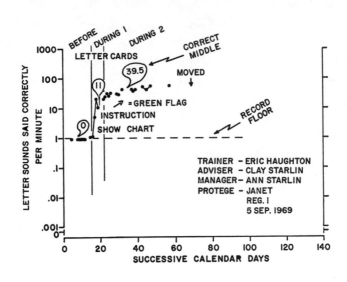

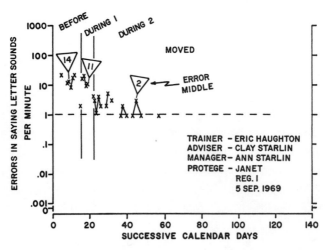

FIGURE 8

GENE REPRESENTS THE CLASS "BEFORE" PHASE PERFORMANCE IN ORAL READING, AFTER YOUNGSTERS HAVE BEEN MOVED TO ORAL READING, UPON ACHIEVING A PROFICIENCY LEVEL OF 40 SOUNDS/MINUTE CORRECT

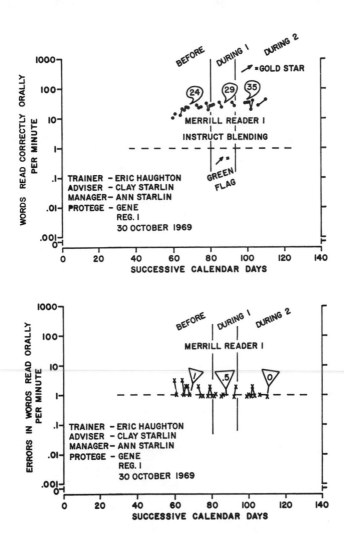

427

The projects from the first grade class are most likely influenced by the fact that the proficiency standard of 40 sounds/minute correct and 2 or less errors had been established on a trial basis at the beginning of the year, based on public school and remedial clinic data from the previous year. Consequently, both the teacher and the youngsters were aiming for these proficiency levels. However, all youngsters in the class did achieve these proficiency levels, even a little girl who had been "IQ tested" retarded before entering the first grade. The "last five day middles" interquartile range for the 24 youngsters was from 41 to 50 sounds/minute correct indicating that 40 sounds correct/minute was by no means unreasonably high.

To have the greatest confidence in recommended letter sound proficiency levels, large groups of youngsters are needed who have achieved various levels of correct letter sound performance (10, 20, 30, 40, 50 sounds/minute correct) with a low error rate, and then move these various groups on to blending and oral reading and see which youngsters achieve proficiency in the next skill the quickest.

For example, those youngsters who achieved the letter sound proficiency levels of 40 sounds/minute correct and 2 or less errors were then given some instruction in blending and were started in an oral reading project. Gene's performance presented in Figure 8 represents the class middle in terms of words read correctly/minute in the before phase of the oral reading projects, although Gene's middle oral reading error rate of 1 per minute was one less than the class error middle of 2 per minute.

The performance picture of these first grade youngsters as they move toward oral reading proficiency should be monitored and compared with other groups of youngsters who moved on to oral reading projects at different letter sound proficiency levels.

As more and varied types of proficiency related data are collected, it is also quite possible that we may run into situations such as: finding

428

that youngsters who were moved to blending projects after achieving 40 sounds/minute correct achieved blending proficiency a week sooner than a group of youngsters who moved to blending from 30 sounds/minute correct, yet the 30 sounds/minute group spent two weeks less on letter sounds, thus totally they reached proficiency in blending a week earlier than the 40 sound/minute group.

There are many questions such as the ones raised above that are in need of very refined and controlled investigation. It is the author's hope to undertake some of these investigations in the very near future.

The proficiency levels for projects that only concentrate on one portion of the letter sound area (e.g., digraphs, vowels, or consonants) appear to be approximately the same as those recommended for the inclusive letter sound projects. For example, Figures 9 and 10 present projects done in the remedial reading clinic, where only short vowels were recorded (Figure 9) and only consonant sounds were recorded (Figure 10).

Blending

Initially, a good deal of indecision existed on the author's part concerning what the most practical and functional project pinpoint should be for the blending area. Thus there is a considerable amount of variation in the types of blending related movements that have been recorded. For example, Figure 11 presents a project using words from the Hegge, Kirk and Kirk Remedial Reading Drills (1965) with the recorded movement being "words" blended correctly and incorrectly.

Other blending dimensions besides whether the basic pinpoint should involve words blended or sounds blended also developed. For instance, there is a difference between requiring a youngster to blend the sounds as isolated units and continuing one sound into the beginning of the

429

FIGURE 9

EXAMPLES OF MORE REFINED PINPOINTS
IN THE LETTER SOUND AREA

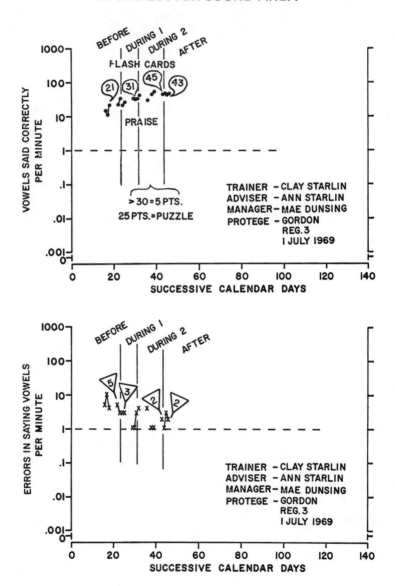

430

FIGURE 10

EXAMPLES OF MORE REFINED PINPOINTS
IN THE LETTER SOUND AREA

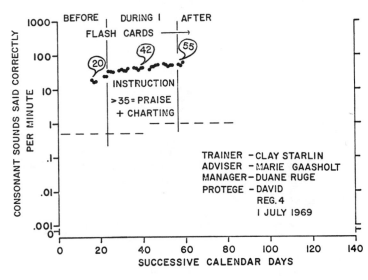

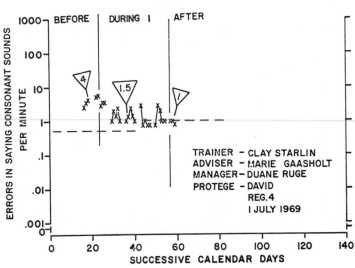

FIGURE 11

PINPOINTING "WORDS" READ IN THE BLENDING AREA

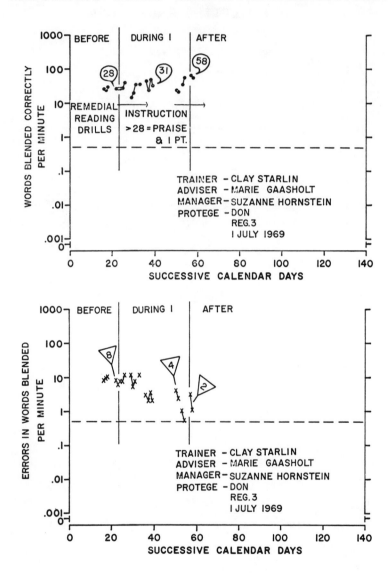

432

FIGURE 12

IDENTIFYING LETTER SOUNDS BLENDED IN SEQUENCE AS A BLENDING PROJECT PINPOINT

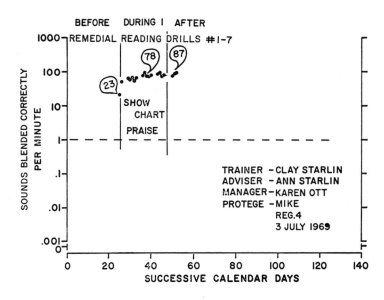

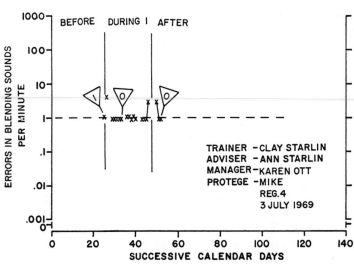

next sound. Since the youngster has learned the sounds in isolation some persons might assume that isolated blending is a logical intermediary between practicing sounds in isolation and continuous blending. [14] Engelmann (1969) adds another dimension when discussing fast and slow blending as variations of continuous blending. However, it appears that these blending dimensions can be handled through instructing (Engelmann, 1969) without the necessity of separate charted projects.

The reason for the basic project pinpoint in the blending area (letter sounds blended correctly and incorrectly in sequence) is to ascertain that in fact a pupil does blend the sounds in the correct sequence, and to ensure that the specific sound errors—if any—the youngster is making while blending, are identified. Such specificity enables better tailoring of the remedial instruction to the particular needs of individual students. Thus, if a youngster blends *p-ĭ-t* for *p-ă-t* the count would be two correct and one wrong. If sounding short i for short a in blending is a common error pattern, this knowledge provides some precise diagnostic information.

Because of the experimentation involved in trying to identify a precise blending project pinpoint, only five projects with the designated project pinpoint were available. The range of the "last five day middles" for these projects is from 37.5 to 136 letters blended correctly in sequence/minute and from 0 to 4 errors/minute. The middle correct performance was 85, for errors it was 3.

Three adult projects very tentatively suggest that optimum performance in the basic project area is between 180-200 sounds blended correctly in sequence per minute and two or less errors per minute.

To obtain a rough estimate of what student performance in the blend-

---

[14]The answer to this assumption will have to await more performance data than are available at the present time.

ing area should be, the ceiling adult correct performance was divided by two giving 90-100 sounds blended. It is the combination of this estimate and the middle of the student data discussed above that underlies the recommended proficiency levels of 90 letter sounds blended correctly in sequence per minute and 2 or less errors per minute.

The project done with Mike (presented in Figure 12) is representative of the five student projects to which the author had access. Mike's middle correct performance in the "after" was 87 sounds blended in sequence and the middle error rate in the "after" was 0.

As in moving from letter sounds to blending, the assumption is that a youngster should achieve and maintain a level of proficiency in blending before being moved on to oral reading. However, again analogous to the letter sound area, information is needed concerning what performance level of reading words orally youngsters achieve and how quickly they achieve them when they move to the oral reading area from different blending achievement levels (e.g., 20 sounds blended in sequence correctly, 30, 40, 50, 60, 70, 80, 90, 100).

Oral Reading

Two hundred and eighty public school oral reading projects were available to be analyzed. Again the procedure of taking the middle of the last five days of both completed and ongoing projects was incorporated. The correct performance range of these middles was from 35 to 224 with an interquartile range from 98 to 149. The error range varied from 0 to 13 with an interquartile range of 1 to 4. The middles of the correct and error distributions were correct 124 words read/minute and 2 errors/minute.

Combining the above information with that from five adult oral reading projects which suggest oral reading ceiling levels to be between 300 to 350 words correct per minute (depending on technicality of material) and a bottom level of one error per minute, the recommended oral reading proficiency levels are 100 to 120 words per minute correct and 2 or less errors.

Fairly consistent reading patterns have appeared in the collected oral reading data. One common pattern is the youngster whose correct performance falls between 15 and 30 words correct per minute and whose error rate is in the vicinity of 4-8 per minute or higher. (For example, note the correct and error performance of Mike in Figure 13.) This performance is very much of a remedial nature. Such students characteristically have not mastered some of the prerequisite reading skills or need some systematic instruction on reading from left to right, discriminating letters, and so forth.

A second common pattern is the pupil who hovers around 50 words correct per minute and whose error rate is frequently around 2 to 4 per minute. Such a performance picture is illustrated in Figure 14. Youngsters with this type of pattern seem to be on the launching pad needing the ignition to break through what seems to be a type of barrier between being an ineffective remedial reader and progressing on the way to be remediated. The error rate is typically not too serious with this performance pattern, the main difficulty being that the youngster for some reason (e.g., slow blending, hesitating on words, or repeating words) still finds attack of words in context tedious.

In terms of the correct performance picture, breaking through 50 words correct/minute appears to be a very difficult task. However, once this has been accomplished with some consistency, it is often only a matter of motivation and practice until the protege reaches an oral reading proficiency of 100 words correct/minute. There are, of course, individual differences in the rapidity (i.e., the steepness of the acceleration slope) with which different pupils move from 50 to 100, but the slope most often seems to be on an upward incline. Figure 15 demonstrates one pattern of such progress, although David had not quite reached 100 words per minute correct by the time the school term, and thus the project, ended.

Figure 16 represents the performance of David, a fourth grader who was proficient in both oral reading correct and error performance from the beginning of the project in November until the last four data points were collected in June. It is this type of performance that public school youngsters should be exhibiting in their grade level reading material.

The maintaining of oral reading proficiency for a period of one to three weeks in a given material is often a very appropriate criterion for moving a student up to more difficult reading material. As can be seen by David's chart, three such material change decisions were made by the teacher with no appreciable drop in correct performance or rise in errors.

Once intermediate grade level (fourth, fifth, and sixth) youngsters have demonstrated consistent, proficient oral reading for a reasonable length of time (a month) in grade level material or above, this might legitimately serve as a criterion for moving the emphasis from oral to silent reading, although it is probably desirable to make periodic oral reading checks even through the twelfth grade. With such checks it would then be possible to assure that a youngster's word attack skills were not breaking down as the vocabulary and content of their reading material became more sophisticated.

Sight Words

As briefly mentioned in the project pinpoint section, it is probably most efficient to have an irregular sight word project if the protege has been provided with the skills to sound out regular words. Although to facilitate greater speed, practice on regular words as part of a sight word project may be most helpful.

FIGURE 13

A COMMON PATTERN
OF A VERY REMEDIAL READER

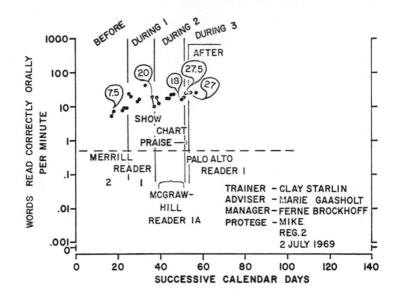

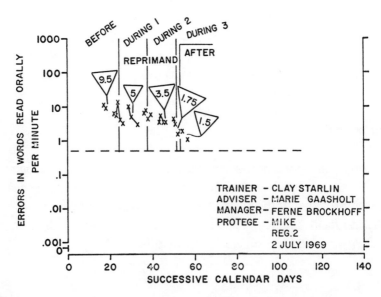

438

FIGURE 14

THE READING PERFORMANCE PICTURE
OF THE YOUNGSTER WHO LACKS
PRIMARILY SPEED AND FLUENCY

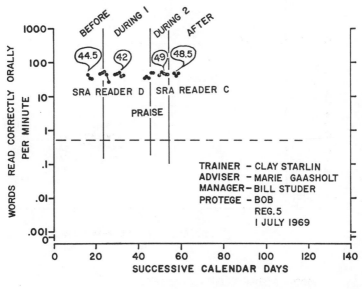

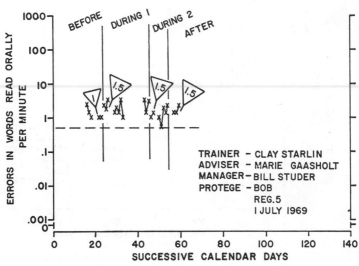

FIGURE 15

DAVID NEARS PROFICIENCY
IN MERRILL READER 3

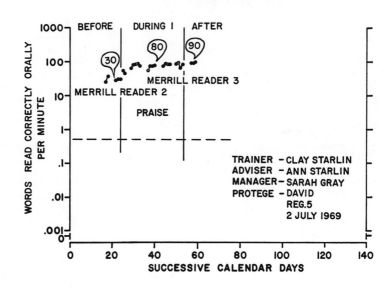

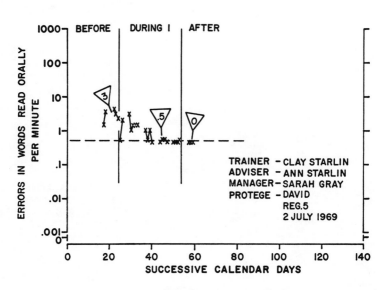

440

FIGURE 16

A PICTURE OF A PROFICIENT ORAL READER

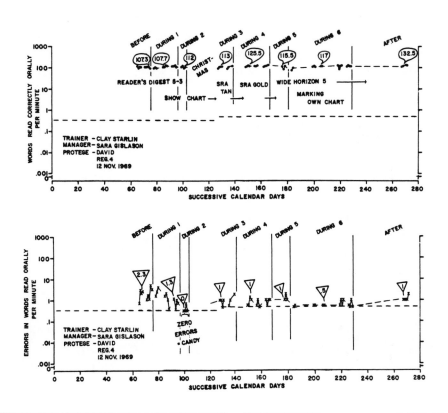

441

The ceiling and bottom adult performances with a flash card presentation using something like the 220 Dolch basic sight cards (Dolch, 1949) appears to be very close to the adult ceiling in letter sounds, a little better than 100 words per minute correct and one or no errors. Also, as in the sound area, it is possible to increase the correct performance by approximately 50 per minute by placing the cards on a table or listing them on a sheet of paper. This relation between the sight words and sounds might be explained by the fact that most of the words in the basic Dolch list are single syllable words. As pointed out earlier, the amount of time to say an isolated letter sound or a single syllable word is nearly the same. No data has been collected by the author yet, but it is very likely that the ceiling level will lower slightly as the sight words used move from one syllable words to two syllable to three syllable and so on.

Fifty-three student sight word projects ranged from 7.5 to 89 words said correctly per minute with a 0 to 13 error per minute range. The interquartile range for correct was 25 to 61, while the error interquartile was 0 to 3. A middle of the "last five day middles" was computed to be 40 words said correctly per minute and 2 word errors/minute.

Unfortunately, all 53 of these projects are from the remedial reading clinic. This means that the distribution of "last five day middles" and descriptive summary is likely biased toward lower performance.

Taking into account the fact that all the student projects available were the performance of remedial youngsters, and using the rule of thumb of dividing the adult ceiling performances by two to approximate student proficiency performance, a recommended figure for sight word proficiency levels is 50 or more words said correct per minute with 2 or less errors per minute.

Figure 17 is a representative sight word chart showing Bob moving from a middle of 35.5 Dolch words correct in the before phase to a middle of 50.5 in the after phase. Bob's error chart indicates that he maintained his errors at or below the recommended proficiency level throughout the project. Figure 18 shows Jeff's performance in a somewhat more refined pinpoint within the general sight word area. As in Bob's case, Jeff did not achieve correct proficiency until near the end of the project; however, in many cases reaching and maintaining a proficiency level are the criteria for ending a project in an area and moving on to another task or skill.

Proficiency Summary for Basic Project Pinpoints

Directly below is a summary of the recommended correct and error proficiency levels for the four basic project pinpoints.

Pinpoint	Correct	Error
letter sounds said	40/minute	2 or less/minute
letter sounds blended in sequence	90/minute	2 or less/minute
words read orally	100-120/minute	2 or less/minute
(irregular) sight words said	50 or more/minute	2 or less/minute

In Figure 19 the estimated ceiling, bottom, and proficiency levels for the four areas are presented on the behavior chart grid to give a summary picture of what the data say. This information can provide guidelines in setting reading goals with students.

Fluency

The third dimension of reading proficiency, fluency, merits a brief discussion in terms of some of the possible project pinpoints that will enable having some index of this dimension.

Repetitions. Most of the fluency related projects are of the deceleration type, noticing that a protege is doing something that interferes with his fluency which needs to be eliminated. As an example, the word repeti-

FIGURE 17

BOB ACHIEVES PROFICIENCY
IN SAYING ISOLATED SIGHT WORDS

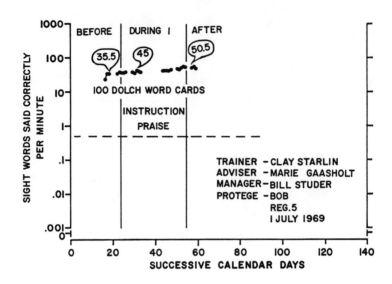

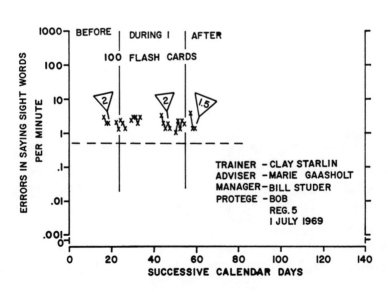

FIGURE 18

REFINING A PINPOINT IN A SIGHT WORD PROJECT

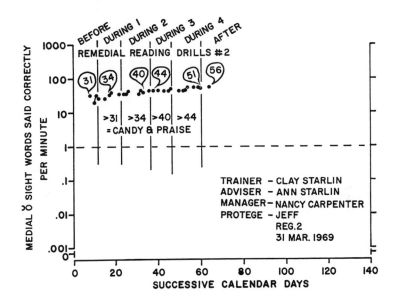

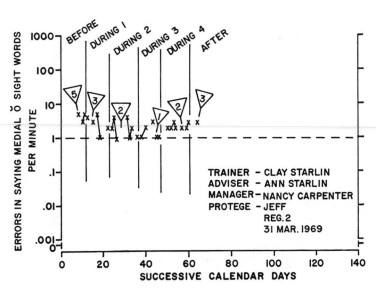

FIGURE 19

A SUMMARY PICTURE
OF THE BASIC READING PROJECT
AND PROFICIENCY LEVELS

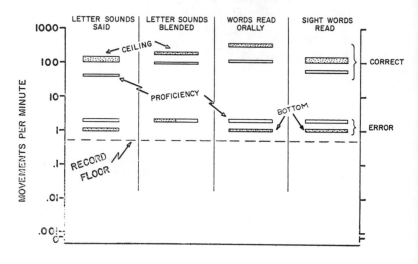

CEILING, BOTTOM AND PROFICIENCY LEVELS

tion project presented in Figure 20 demonstrates an interesting relationship between oral reading without repetitions and the repetition rate itself. Chris was repeating words at a rate of three per minute in his oral reading in the "before" phase. As his repetitions decreased (to zero) his oral reading rate (without repetitions) increased to a proficiency level.

Hesitations. Another fluency related project on hesitations is presented in Figure 21. The hesitation dimension is tricky for two reasons. One is because a hesitation is not a response but rather the ab-

446

FIGURE 20

A RELATIONSHIP BETWEEN ORAL READING FLUENCY AND REPEATING WORDS

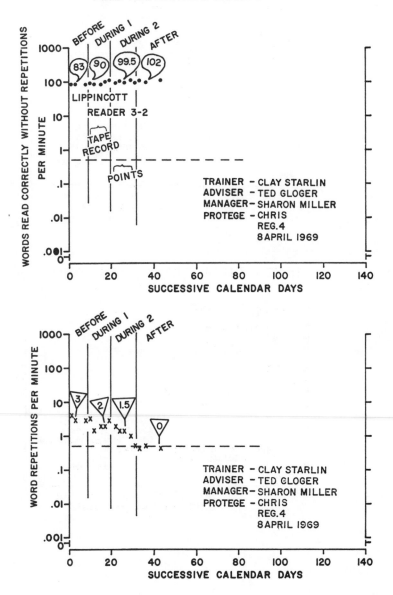

447

FIGURE 21

AN EXAMPLE OF RECORDING ORAL READING HESITATIONS

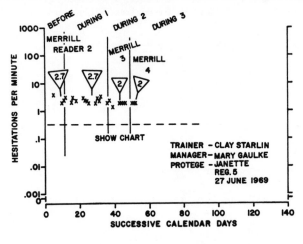

FIGURE 22

IF SCOTT DIDN'T KNOW, HE SAID SO

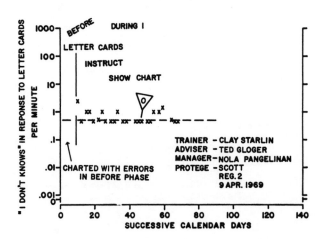

sence of a response for a certain length of time. Second, it is necessary to make somewhat of an imprecise judgment as to how many seconds of delay constitute a hesitation and then to consistently get a count when a hesitation occurs. With these cautions in mind in interpreting such projects, it can be seen that Janette dropped from three hesitations a minute to two and then remained stuck at two per minute for the rest of the project. There will always be a per minute ceiling on all hesitation projects because, for instance, the greatest number of five second hesitations a youngster can have in a minute is 12.

"I don't know." Finally, Figure 22 presents a record of Scott's "I don't know" responses. When Scott encountered a letter for which he did not know the sound, he said "I don't know." It is important to distinguish an "I don't know" response from an error response for these are very definitely different movements and in a number of cases suggest different remedial tactics. If a youngster is making "I don't know" related comments, this will influence his fluency as well as his speed.

RECORDING THE READING SKILLS

The recording plan and suggestions presented in this section enable us to achieve the greatest general application and practicality and still be as functionally precise as possible.

General Recording Suggestions

There are some general points concerning obtaining records in the reading skill areas that are important to keep in mind. These general points are listed immediately below. Following this general list are some specific suggestions for recording in each basic project area.

Do not let a close approximation of a correct response pass for a correct response. This is not a favor to the youngster for the responses as correct may decelerate the introduction of needed practice or instruction.

Do not let a youngster practice on exactly the same material he will be performing on in the time sample just before the time sample. This is like taking the test just before taking the test.

If a youngster exhibits a good deal of unusual behavior when being timed, offer a simple explanation of why time is an important segment of mastery. Then possibly try timing everything to help the youngster adjust to being timed. Let him time you on some things so he knows it is a two-way street.

Try not to become terribly upset if something interrupts a time sample. It is, of course, desirable that no interruptions occur. But, if the youngster drops part of the material necessary for him to perform the movement being recorded, or someone enters the room unexpectedly, the time sample can always be started over again.

If the protege is distracted for a few seconds when individual reading data are being collected and if a cumulative stop watch is being used, the watch can be stopped while the student is distracted and then resume the timing when he is attending.

Do not stop the record before the time sample is completed or 10 or 15 seconds after the planned sample is over just because a youngster happened to finish a sentence in his reading or got through the flash cards once. All the responses must be counted in *only* the specified time sample to maintain reliable records for making educational decisions.

There should always be more material present than a pupil will be able to finish during the time sample. This guarantees that a performance ceiling is not imposed on the student's performance by the fact that he finished all the material available before the time sample was over. In projects that involve such things as flash cards, if the youngster finishes the set once, he can just start over again.

If a time sample finishes in the middle of a story or in the middle of a page of sight words, it is of course permissible and in many cases desirable to let the youngster finish the page or story where the time sample ended is marked.

The achievement and maintenance of the proficiency standards in each area should be used as criteria for moving from one skill to the next on the skill ladder (e.g., from sounds to blending) or moving from Dolch set I to Dolch set II or moving from one book to the next most difficult book.

Remember to have a "before" and "after" for each project and as many "durings" as are necessary to reach proficiency. Five or seven days are usually the minimum number of days necessary in the "before" and "after" to obtain an accurate picture of the performance in these periods. Fifteen days is often the maximum number necessary in a "before" or "after" phase. The number of "durings" and the number of days in each "during" will of course depend on what types of educational decisions are being made based on the collected data.

Since the time sample is an attempt to obtain an indication of a pupil's independent performance, it is usually desirable not to introduce instructional or motivational procedures during the time sample. Educational intervention in the project area should occur during the other program time that is reserved for work in the area.

It is desirable to have a one minute time sample whenever possible for this eliminates the necessity of dividing to get the per minute rate statement. In the letter sound and sight word projects, a one minute time sample has proved to be quite satisfactory. In many cases a one minute sample may also be sufficient for the blending and oral reading areas, but other times a youngster needs a little longer to respond.

A sweep hand on a wrist watch or wall clock, a direct reading clock or a stop watch are a few of the devices available to assure an accurate time sample.

Letter Sounds

Characteristically the presentation procedure for the letter sound objects has been through flash cards. The letter forms (upper and lower case) are placed on flash cards and the protege is asked to respond when each card is presented. Those that are responded to correctly are placed in one pile while those responded to incorrectly are placed in a separate pile. After the one minute time sample is over, the number correct and the number of errors are determined and the per minute rates are placed on the chart.

It is also possible to have a sheet with the letter forms on it and to point to each letter and request the sound. If a separate identical sheet is kept by the recorder, the start and finish place can be marked on this sheet and errors can be indicated by placing a small *e* over them.

A suggested procedure for introducing the letter sounds is presented on the next page in terms of the first eight phases.

Blending

The author has found that one of the best materials to use for a blending project is the Hegge, Kirk and Kirk Remedial Reading Drills (1965). These drills actually have the words separated at the top of each drill to encourage blending. The drills range from those containing regular three letter medial short vowel words (cat, sit, cut) to the introduction

452

Before	During 1	During 2	During 3	During 4	During 5	During 6	During 7
common consonants B,b,C,c, D,d,F,f, G,g,H,h, J,j,K,k, L,l,M,m, N,n,P,p, R,r,S,s, T,t,V,v, W,w,Z,z.	common consonants	introduce short Ă, a	introduce X, x	introduce short Ĭ, i	introduce Y, y, Qu, qu	introduce short Ŭ, u	introduce short Ŏ, o

Movement: letter sounds

---

of more difficult sound combinations (sion, aught, ook). Of course, any list of regular words can be used as the material for a blending project. The youngster should blend the word rows from left to right to give him practice in the motion necessary for reading, rather than allowing him to go up and down a list. Having a duplicate drill book or word list again enables the recorder to mark where the youngster began and ended and indicate what letters he blended incorrectly. The error count is then subtracted from the total number of letters covered in the time sample to get a correct and error count. If the time sample was two minutes, divide the correct and error counts by two. If it was a one minute sample, it is not necessary to divide.

A suggested plan for the first seven phases in a blending project is indicated below.

Before	During 1	During 2	During 3	During 4	During 5	During 6
three letter short ă words (cat)	short ă words	short ĭ words (sit)	short ŭ words (cut)	short ŏ words (not)	regular words with digraphs (when)	short ĕ words (fed)

Movement: letters blended

453

Oral Reading

Again, if the person obtaining the record in the oral reading area has a duplicate book, he can keep track of the start and finish time and the word errors and also maintain a permanent record. It is considerably more efficient in obtaining the word count if a class member, aide or mother helper has previously gone through the books and lightly written in a cumulative word count for each sentence as well as a total count per page.

Because publishers are not standardized in their criteria for grading the various reading series, it is difficult to know what book of what particular series would be most appropriate for a given youngster. Even knowing a grade level from the nonperformance-based achievement tests does not help, for the 2-2 book in one series may be considerably more difficult than the 2-2 book in another series. The best solution to this problem is to make the best estimate of a youngster's reading grade level and then screen him on one or two available books at this level and on two or three books a half or full year below this estimate. This screening should continue throughout the "before" phase. The book in which the youngster attains the highest middle correct rate and lowest middle error rate is the one that should be continued into the first "during." An example of this record keeping procedure is shown in Table 1. The circled correct and error rates on Table 1 indicate the middle performances for the four readers over the five-day "before." Based on these "middles," Sherri performed the best in LET'S READ, Book 1, although her performance was very remedial in all the books.

Once the book to be used in the first "during" has been determined, work to establish and maintain oral reading proficiency in this book. Once this has been accomplished, move to the next most difficult book, establish proficiency in this book, move on to the next, and so on.

TABLE 1

A RECORD OF SCREENING AVAILABLE BOOKS IN THE "BEFORE" PHASE TO DETERMINE THE MOST APPROPRIATE ONE FOR SHERRI

Correct and Error reading rates for 5 days on 4 readers.
Manager: Faye Hammarback
Protege: Sherri, 6 years old
Time Sample: 2 minutes

Reader	Correct		Error	
	Count	Rate	Count	Rate
Let's Read 1	18	9.	2	1.
	17	8.5	3	1.5
	19	9.5	4	2.
	6	3.	6	3.
	14	7.	5	2.5
SRA				
A Pig Can Jig	19	9.5	7	3.5
	11	5.5	9	4.5
	1	.5	19	9.5
	2	1.	11	5.5
	8	4.	8	4.
Singer 1A				
A Fat Cat	20	10.	3	1.5
	11	5.5	14	7.
	10	5.	19	9.5
	13	6.5	7	3.5
	16	8.	9	4.5
Lippincott				
Preprimer	21	10.5	6	3.
	4	2.	20	10.
	3	1.5	11	5.5
	3	1.5	10	5.
	10	5.	6	3.

Following is an example of what the phases might look like in terms of material used in an oral reading project.

Before	During 1	During 2	During 3	During 4	During 5
Screened:	Merrill 1	Merrill 2	Merrill 3	Merrill 4	Merrill 5

Let's Read 1
Palo Alto 1
Merrill 1
Lippincott
 Preprimer
Behavior
 Res. Company
 Reader 1A

Movement: oral reading

Sight Words

As in the letter sound area, the sight words can either be presented by means of flash cards or on a sheet of paper. The recording procedures for obtaining the correct and error count are the same as discussed in the letter sounds area. It is suggested that the "before" phase and first "during" involve one-, two-, and three-letter irregular words such as *I, we, are.* The second "during" might involve three- and four-letter single syllable irregular words (own, tree, pony). The third "during" could include two-syllable irregular words (into, table), and the fourth "during" can extend to three- and four-syllable words.

Recording Summary

Even with some of the practical short cuts suggested, it is obvious that there is potentially a tremendous amount of time that can be invested by a teacher in obtaining the precise information that is necessary to evaluate and individually tailor a program for each youngster in the oral reading areas.

It is because of this time factor, as well as other reasons, that it is ex-

456

tremely important that the children be taught to record and chart their own performance rates. There is neither time nor space in which to go into the details of how this can be accomplished. However, there is a mimeographed handbook available from the author (Starlin and Starlin, 1969) that explains how the charting and recording can be taught to young children. First grade youngsters have learned (Starlin, C., in press) and are learning (Starlin, A., 1969) to use and record on the behavior chart. Therefore, if first graders can record and chart their own performance rates, all public school youngsters from first through twelfth grades should be keeping their own precise records.

YOUNGSTERS COMMENT ABOUT PRECISE READING

As with many educational innovations, there has been some controversy over the appropriateness and goodness of using Precision Teaching procedures to evaluate youngsters' performance and the feasibility of youngsters doing their own recording and charting.

Unfortunately, we as adults (as teachers particularly in this case) have certain histories which have created attitudes, beliefs, and assumptions about the appropriateness or difficulty of some material or procedure for school age children. By the very fact that these expectations of childrens' reactions are so frequently based on beliefs, it is difficult to collect qualitative data such as students' comments on how the students themselves react to the material or procedure. That is, the procedure may prove to be very helpful to the student regardless of how it was "thought" he would react.

The concern about "kids won't be able to read the charts," "youngsters will get upset when they are timed" and "kids will get upset if they don't see progress on the chart every day" has not been substantiated by either the youngsters' comments or by their actual performance.

As a matter of fact, the appropriateness of including reading in the school curriculum, which is usually not even subject to debate, was questioned by first grader Dean in a conversation he had with his teacher.

Teacher: "You know, Dean, you're almost to forty sounds a minute and, as soon as you get there, you can start to read."

Dean: "I don't want to learn to read."

Teacher: "Well, what did you come to school for?"

Dean: "Learn about the chart."

Another comment made by Dean when he moved from 20 to 30 sounds per minute from one day to the next was "Gee, going fast is really fun."

All the youngsters in a fourth grade room were asked to state their reactions to and describe the precise reading program they were involved in during their fourth grade year. The description and reactions of David, one of the class members, is presented below.

November 12, 1968 was the first day the fourth grade class at Ida Patterson in Eugene, Ore. did thier "Timed Reading" where you read to a helper for 3 minutes and the helper counts the errors and words then divides it by 3 to find how many words or errors per minute.

We the fourth grade class had fifth and sixth grade helpers. 7 peoples from our room went at one time because there were 7 helpers.

Some of us were reading in about fourth or fifth grade readers.

But a few of us were reading in Readers Digest at IRI (Informal Reading Inventory) level.

The week before Christmas Vacation the teacher (Mrs. Gislason) offered everyone who made zero errors a small piece of candy. That week of reading I noticed a big change in our reading, every-one started being more cautous in there reading and realy tried hard to get zero errors. Our teacher said she was seeing how many could make less errors but still stay <u>close</u> to thier average of words.

After Chrstmas Vacation the Teacher asinged 8 helpers from our own room. Each helper helped two people then two helpers got together and one helper read to the other helper then the other helper reads to the one who read before, it works pretty well. Also after Chistmas Vacation we decreased our reading time to two minutes instead of three.

Some of my feelings about this are: I feel that this useful and that we all have made <u>much</u> progress.

By a fourth grade helper and reader, David

One of the fourth grade helpers referred to in David's description made a number of interesting comments also.

Melora: "When we changed to a 2-minute time and after Christ-mas Vacation, some of my students' errors went up and words went down. But they soon recovered."

"I learned to use decimals and now I find it very fun to use them. I also learned how to use a chart; (and the chart was quite complicated) it was fun."

"I think this can tell the teacher who needs help on

oral reading and who doesn't."

Other comments by some other classmates were:

Dennis: "I think it improved my reading a hunderd persent."

Keith: "I have enjoyed filling out the chart and I have went up in my reading and down in my errors."

Deanne: "I think the 5th and 6th graders had something to be proud of. They now know how good the 4th grade class can read."

"I felt that this reading is good for me. Well I think it is good. Well I learned to be careful with my reading. Yes I think it is important to improve our reading."

Belinda: "At first to learn to chart it was hard but I cought on any way. And that's how it all happend."

Since all comments that have been accumulated from various youngsters could not be included, there was a selection bias operating in attempting to convey to the reader the variety of comments made, the humor in many, and the excitement and involvement that the youngsters begin to experience because they are such an integral part of their own education. In none of the 43 accumulated comments did a youngster say "I don't like" something about precise reading.

CONCLUSIONS AND IMPLICATIONS

The long range implications of using a standardized recording system, such as Precision Teaching, to look at reading and other curriculum areas is difficult to comprehend. Presently, all projects done using Precision Teaching procedures can be submitted to a national computer behavior bank in Kansas City, Kansas. There are presently over 3,500 projects stored in the bank (Linsley, 1969). Because of the standardized data and manner of submitting to the bank, the bank is able to, with increasing efficiency, store and retrieve more than 300 bits of information on each submitted project.

Because there have been relatively few studies done using pupil performance rates as the measure of reading performance, there are almost unlimited implications for future research. Following are examples of but a few researchable questions: 1) curriculum evaluation—what reading materials have proved to be most successful in achieving rapid acceleration in youngsters' correct reading performance rates; 2) have students achieved and maintained reading proficiency more rapidly by requiring letter sound, blending, and oral reading project; 3) what motivational procedures have been most effective in decelerating errors in letter sound projects; and 4) what instructional procedures have been most effective in eliminating a *b* and *d* reversal problem. There are many projects directed toward answering these and hundreds of other questions which need to be completed. Once these projects are completed and submitted to the bank, some highly sophisticated normative statements can be made about what instructional and motivational procedures have been most effective and efficient with what types and ages of youngsters in what situations in achieving reading performance proficiency, although we must still always be prepared to individually tailor for a given youngster in a given situation. Just because the bank said that in the 1000 projects in the sight word area, free time was found to motivate the most effectively, this is not a guarantee that this will be effective with every youngster, although this may be the first thing to try. The implications of Precision Teaching data in terms of communication are also very exciting. Having the same type of performance measure presented in visual form on a standardized chart enables teachers to share with each other those procedures that they have found successful and those that have been unsuccessful. All teachers can communicate to the principal or a department head using a standard framework to evaluate teacher effectiveness. Given the performance rate data and the proficiency level information, teachers are able to make precise statements to parents in terms of report cards and parent conferences about where a student is in reading in relation to where he should be. Possibly most important, the system enables communication to the general public who support the schools. The general public is increasingly demanding some objective evidence of teacher effectiveness. Using the Precision Teaching chart, the teacher can show the public where a youngster was upon entering the teacher's classroom (the "before" phase), what things were done, x ("during" 1), y ("during" 2), z ("during" 3), and that the student achieved proficiency in the third "during" and maintained this after instruction was terminated (the "after" phase).

The recording and charting of pupils' performance rates should continue to serve, as it does presently, to decelerate excuses for youngsters not learning (e.g., blaming the home, labeling the child). With the precise performance information, the teacher knows exactly where a youngster is in relation to where he should be. With the resource of his own powers of observation and the benefit of information in the behavior bank, a decision on what educational procedures to use to reduce any discrepancy can be made. By continuing to collect the performance data, the results of the decision can be seen. If the first procedure was not successful, another can be tried until there is success. Thus, youngsters are no longer slow, fast, dumb, smart, mentally retarded, dyslexic or gifted, but rather have varying performance pictures in various areas, some of which are satisfactory, some of which are not. Those performance pictures that are unsatisfactory require accelerated remedial assistance, not excuses for not teaching the youngsters.

If education is to progress and become more of a science and less of a belief-based system, it is essential that educators incorporate the use of objective performance data to evaluate curriculum and teaching techniques and make changes in these areas in accord with the data collected. Striving for this goal, one should remember that good data are those which describe the performance of a student, not necessarily the data that demonstrate the type of acceleration or deceleration desired. It is, of course, preferable that the desired effect and the data coincide but it is crucial that one remains astutely aware of the difference, not letting concern for the desired effect influence the quality of the data collected.

What has been presented in this chapter is a system for recording reading skill performance. Very little mention has been made of how one might go about remediating a reading problem. Rather, the reader has been given some information about what tentative proficiency standards may be in the reading skill areas and then given the tools to determine where in relation to these standards a given pupil or group of youngsters may fall. Part of the assumption upon which such an orientation is based is that in many cases half the battle of remediation is involved in knowing precisely and immediately that a particular remedial procedure did not work so something else may be tried. Teachers have known what to teach and how to teach in many cases for a good many years. What they have not come close to knowing is how to evaluate precisely whether what they have taught had an effect, or in fact what their aim was, in terms of actual reading performance. However, this recording system combined with the present abundance of remedial procedures enables success and having data to prove it or, if no success, to know how to try again.

My interest, training and inspiration in the area of reading is attributable to Dr. Barbara Bateman, while my involvement and training in the Precision Teaching system is due to my work with Dr. Eric Haughton. To these knowledgeable and competent educators I express my indebtedness and thanks. To my wife Ann, whose comments and precise records in her first grade class have provided much of the data and a good deal of the stimulation for the article, my devotion and thanks. A particular note of appreciation to all the youngsters whose reading performance made it possible to write such an article. I am also most grateful to the practicum students and public school teachers who were responsible for collecting the vast majority of the data referred to in the paper. Dr. Haughton was also most generous in giving of his time and energy in the editing of the manuscript. Miss Merrie Dinteman was responsible for the typing of the manuscript. Her secretarial skill and patience is particularly appreciated. For additional information concerning Precision Teaching and Reading, contact: Clay Starlin, College of Education, University of Oregon, Eugene, Oregon, 97403.

REFERENCES

Barnhart, C. L. (Ed.). **The American college dictionary.** New York: Random House, 1960.

Bateman, B. Reading. A controversial view research and rationale. **University of Oregon curriculum bulletin.** Eugene, Oregon: University of Oregon Press, May 1967, **23** (278).

Behavior Research Company - Behavior Bank; information concerning projects presently stored in the bank can be obtained by writing the Company at Box 3351, Kansas City, Kansas 66103.

Chall, J. **Learning to read: The great debate.** New York: McGraw-Hill, 1967.

Dolch, E. W. **Basic sight vocabulary cards.** Champaign, Illinois: Garrard Publishing Company, 1949.

Engelmann, S. **Preventing failure in the primary grades.** Chicago: Science Research Associates, Inc., 1969.

Gleason, H. A. **An introduction to descriptive linguistics.** New York: Holt, Rinehart, and Winston, 1961.

Hanna, P., et al. **Phoneme-grapheme correspondences as cues to spelling improvement.** Washington, D. C.: U. S. Government Printing Office, 1966.

Haughton, E. Personal communication, 1968. (a)

Haughton, E. Materials prepared for practicum in Precision Teaching, University of Oregon, 1968. (b)

Hegge, T, Kirk, S., & Kirk, W. **Remedial reading drills.** Ann Arbor, Michigan: George Wahr Publishing Company, 1965.

Howe, Harold. **Hello world.** Washington, D. C.: U. S. government printing office publication for the President's Committee on Mental Retardation, 1968.

Johnson, N. Daily arithmetic performance compared with teacher ratings, IQ and achievement tests. Unpublished manuscript, Univ. of Kansas Medical Center, 1966.

Lindsley, O. R. Personal communication, 1969.

Lowry, H. A glossary of terms: Linguistics. **The Reading Teacher, 22,** 1968, 136-44.

Starlin, C., & Starlin, A. The first 15 days: Introducing precision teaching into the elementary classroom. Unpublished manuscript, Precision Teaching Techniques, Eugene, Oregon, 1969.

Starlin, A. Personal communication, 1969.

Starlin, C. Peers and precision. **Educational Technology,** in press.

465

Forecasts of Future Reading Research

Monte Penney
Research Associate
National Center for Educational
    Research and Development
U.S. Office of Education
Washington, D.C.

Richard B. Adams
Consultant in the Behavioral Sciences
Wallingford, Connecticut

Predictions on the future of an area of research are analogous to hypotheses: they are statements which specify possible relationships, serve to stimulate thought and discussion, and then submit to the tests of experimentation or passing time. Like hypotheses, predictions must have one foot planted in present reality while the other gropes for solid ground beyond present reality. Like hypotheses, predictions must be capable of disproof. But here the analogy ends. Predictions are made not to develop new knowledge but to increase awareness of the potency of current factors which may influence the future. Once aware of such factors, we may act to enhance or repress their potency so that the future will tend to become the kind of future we want. Predictions, then, are most valuable when they allow us to assume an active rather than a reactive posture.

No developing discipline is entirely satisfied with its past. Progress is assured, though, when known errors are not repeated and when new directions are chosen responsibly. It was George Santayana who warned that, by ignoring the past, we are condemned to repeat it.

TWO ERAS IN THE HISTORY OF READING RESEARCH

Reading was not one of the first subjects of scientific research. Traditionally the Age of Enlightenment is credited with the development of the scientific method, but not until the late nineteenth century can inductive studies of reading based upon empirical observation be detected. A healthy balance of curiosity between reading itself and the teaching of reading characterizes the pre-World War I studies, which initiated the phonics versus look-and-say debate and built the foundations for studies of eye movements, reading speed, subvocal speech, and readability of materials. George Romanes, a Darwinian psychologist at Oxford University, found that contrary to popular belief, reading speed and "power of assimilation" are unrelated. (Romanes, 1891) Independent studies by Abell (1894) and Quantz (1897) appear to support Romanes on this point; but, for a broad overview of research during this formative era, one should see Edmund B. Huey's THE PSYCHOLOGY AND PEDAGOGY OF READING.[1] (Huey, 1908)

World War I brought a demand for measurement instruments which would discriminate one soldier's abilities from another's. Development of the Army Alpha, the first large-scale paper and pencil IQ test, heightened educators' interest in producing instruments for the measurement of academic progress and the effectiveness of instructional materials and practices. For nearly fifty years, the predominant research questions continued to be, "What methods of instruction are most successful?"; "What teaching materials produce the best results?"; "What remedial techniques correct reading failure?" and "What skills are prerequisite to success in learning to read?" The more fundamental question, "What is reading?" received attention from a dozen or more dedicated theorists, but even these few felt continuing pressure to produce information that could find immediate application in the classroom. The First Grade Reading Studies supported by the U.S. Office of Education may well have marked the end of the second era of reading research. These twenty-seven separate projects were begun in 1964, each attempting to compare two to seven approaches[2] to first grade reading instruction. In all, 78 approaches were studied, using a total population of over 22,000 children. Thirteen of the 27 projects followed their original subjects through grade two, and ten of these thirteen were continued through grade three with most of the original samples intact. Although the same pretests and posttests were used in all studies to insure comparability of data, these studies attempted to maintain little control over such factors as teacher behavior, socioeconomic

[1]To the delight of many, M.I.T. press has recently reissued Huey's book with introductory chapters by John B. Carroll and Paul Kolers.

[2]The word "method" is avoided here because it suggests a replicable, transportable, systematic procedure. "Approach," instead, suggests a mutable collection of generalizations that cannot be consistently actualized by different teachers.

status of the children, and the administrative climates of participating elementary schools. Greater control over such factors, however, would only have detracted from apparent differences among approaches and ascribed more variance in achievement to factors other than the instructional approaches. No single approach emerged as the "best" way to teach reading; in fact, the evidence strongly suggests that the effectiveness of a given approach to instruction is powerfully mediated by the community, school, and classroom setting in which it is used. (Bond and Dykstra, 1967) To many, the First Grade Reading Studies have demonstrated rather conclusively that reading instruction is not likely to be significantly improved by manipulation of approaches to teaching. The question, "What is reading?" must be more fully answered before instruction can be tailored to the realities which hide behind that question.

THE LAST FEW YEARS—A RETURN TO SCIENCE

Two major emphases in reading research have become quite visible since about 1960. One emphasis is concerned with the "pathological" states of reading and the other with reading in its healthy state. The goal of the first group is the elimination of reading problems through discovering their nature and causes. The second group seeks successful reading instruction through understanding the reading process. Although individual scientists and theories may be primarily identified with one of these two groups, there is considerable sharing of membership and ideas.[3] We are viewing, then, the marshalling of two armies that are not antagonistic, but complementary. The "pathology" group has attracted investigators from the medical and biological sciences to the study of reading. The "process" group, with its longer history of concentrated financial support, has provided findings which are useful to both groups. Thumbnail sketches of some

[3]The existing cooperation between the ERIC Clearinghouse on Reading at Indiana University and the University of Pennsylvania Library on Dyslexia offers a concrete example of liaison between the two groups.

470

activities of each group may serve to characterize their concerns and to indicate their combined effect upon future research on reading.

Reading Pathology

Although concern with reading pathology dates back at least to 1888 (Broca, 1888) and although a number of scientists have systematically pursued this problem for periods of ten years or so, it may still be asserted that this branch of investigation is in its infancy. The diffusion of the literature on reading pathology through many disciplines and the volatile nature of public opinion in this area have militated against the formulation of clear-cut policy in the various funding agencies. These factors and others have produced a series of conferences and task forces for which the main themes are "Where are we?" and "Where should we go?"

The Interdisciplinary Committee on Reading Problems, supported by the Ford Foundation through the Center for Applied Linguistics in Washington, D.C., began in September, 1967, an eighteen month effort aimed at a) facilitating communication and collaboration among researchers in many disciplines; b) rendering a comprehensive state-of-the-art report; and c) developing a comprehensive R & D blueprint for use by Federal and private funding agencies. Dr. Doris V. Gunderson, the Committee's Executive Director, coordinated the work of seven task forces composed of 64 leading scientists in the areas of definition and etiology, diagnosis, early prediction, incidence and implications, treatment configurations in educational settings, treatment configurations in other settings, and administrative aspects of school programs.

In May of 1967, a Southwest Texas State College research conference recommended that "a commission be established at the highest possible national level" (Zedler, 1967) to study the problem of dyslexia and related reading disorders. The 25 member group, directed by Dr. Empress Y. Zedler and supported by the U.S. Office of Education, produced policy recommendations for national efforts in research, diagnosis, treatment, and teacher training. As a direct result of this conference's recommendations, former HEW Secretary Wilbur Cohen convened the Secretary's National Advisory Committee on Dyslexia and Related Reading Disorders on August 23, 1968. By August of 1969, this group of 21 scientists, chaired by Dr. Arleigh B. Templeton, were to have structured a plan for continuing action in each of the four areas specified by the Southwest Texas State College group. A parallel committee of 20 Federal employees representing 13 agencies were to provide liaison and communication between the Secretary's Committee and ongoing work in the agencies.

The Interdisciplinary Committee on Reading Problems and the Secretary's National Advisory Committee on Dyslexia and Related Reading Disorders are both attempting to map courses of action for eliminating—or at least reducing—reading pathology. There are probably other efforts that should be cited, but these two are the most likely to initiate large-scale programs because their findings are awaited, respectively, by the Ford Foundation and the Department of Health, Education, and Welfare.

At least three ad hoc groups have met to exchange views on reading pathology. Their proceedings, which are either available or will shortly become available, contain papers which show the range of current theoretical approaches to the problem. (Keeny and Keeny, 1968; Money, 1962; Money, 1966; Young and Lindsley) Although these three groups made no attempt at mapping a research strategy, their reports are cited in acknowledgment of their contributions to the literature.

Reading Process

If a concern with instructional methodology has indeed dominated the field of reading research for the past forty or fifty years, it is because people expected studies of this sort to produce lasting benefit.

472

Clearly, work in this area is at a plateau—and the plateau is not high enough to satisfy popular expectation and demand. Over the past year, achievement test scores have been released by several major cities under headlines like, "Northern City Children Read Below National Norms." Suggested remedies for the reading problems in "Northern City" (or Los Angeles or Washington, D.C.) now center on more and better classrooms, more and better teachers, or the espousal of materials and methods that have ostensibly produced good results in other cities. Public interest in reading achievement, then, is urging support of activities which are perhaps worthwhile in themselves but insufficient for achieving the goal of highly successful reading instruction. It appears that the past cycle of disillusionment will be repeated—very expensively—unless the energy of public interest can be channelled towards support for research on the reading process.

One important influence upon public opinion and support for research is Jeanne Chall's book, LEARNING TO READ: THE GREAT DEBATE. (Chall, 1967) Former HEW Secretary John Gardner called it "the most important book about education in ten years" in an October, 1967, address to the Education Writers' Association. Dr. Chall has sifted the evidence with great care, often reanalyzing the data of individual studies, and presented an elaborately qualified group of recommendations. Where present methods are obtaining acceptable results, she argues, it would be undesirable to tamper with instruction. In changing methods that are not satisfying the needs of particular school systems, she suggests that curriculum planners pay appropriate attention to the slight margin of superiority she found for "code-emphasis" approaches over "meaning-emphasis" approaches in grades 1-3. These two suggestions seem to constitute a holding action against nonproductive, random juggling of instruction and the consequent dissipation of resources. This view of Dr. Chall's recommendations on reading instruction is helpful in understanding her recommendations for future research. Research is a cumulative endeavor that only occasionally produces information of concrete usefulness to instruction. Its long-range goal is to extend the knowledge base upon which instruction rests by building "a unified theory about the reading process." (Chall, 1967) During the long intervals between scientific breakthroughs, dedicated and astute synthesizers of research findings must provide the schools with intelligible, valid state-of-the-art information. This is not to say that all major improvements await further research. Dr. Chall's recommendations on the content of reading texts, for example, appear able to be implemented now.

A major philosophical position regarding research on the reading process is exemplified in Project Literacy, a consortium directed by Harry Levin of Cornell University. The consortium members generally agree that a "new science" for reading research is not necessary. Studies that increase understanding of the reading process will come from psychology, psycholinguistics, sociology, and other related disciplines and will have significance for their parent sciences as well as for reading. The aim of Project Literacy is to stimulate and perform such research and to build curriculum materials upon the research findings. Office of Education support has been provided for 16 separate projects and for the activities of the coordinating project at Cornell. The directors of the individual projects, and other investigators invited by Dr. Levin, met eight times over the past four years to present findings and discuss problems. Nine interim reports, containing 86 research reports on widely diversified topics related to reading, are the products of these meetings. Project Literacy's final report, which is now in preparation, will contain an overview of the entire research program, discussions of selected projects, and the new reading curriculum materials for kindergarten and first grade. Dr. Levin and Dr. Joanna Williams (1970) have edited a book entitled BASIC STUDIES ON READING which illustrates Project Literacy's basic research approach to the problems of reading and presents detailed findings from some of the projects. (Levin, no date) Two other products of this five-year effort cannot be thoroughly assessed at this time: the impact of talented young investigators whose work was made visible through the spirit of teamwork which characterized the entire program and the "generalizability" of the research management techniques developed by Dr. Levin and his staff in the first large-scale research program on the reading process.

Office of Education's Targeted Research and Development Program on Reading. In the fall of 1967, the Office of Education's Bureau of Research, now called the National Center for Educational Research and Development, began to review recent work on reading pathology and on the reading process. It had become increasingly clear that findings from the First Grade Reading Studies would suggest future research concentration upon teacher and learner characteristics rather than upon the effectiveness of various approaches to instruction. Project Literacy and other studies (Goodman, 1968; Kavanagh, 1968) were demonstrating that baseline information on the reading process was useful and obtainable. Jeanne Chall's book built a convincing case for studies aimed at the development of theory on the reading process. In short, the Bureau of Research staff decided that these events, plus the establishment of the Secretary's National Advisory Committee on Dyslexia and the Interdisciplinary Committee on Reading Problems, created a favorable climate for a new program of basic research on the reading process. The next step was to choose a program planning technique for use in initiating the program.

The search for a program planning strategy that was sufficiently flexible for use with research proceeded rather swiftly through conventional, networking systems to the concept of *strong inference* advanced by J. R. Platt:

> *Strong inference consists of applying the following steps to every problem in science, formally and explicitly and regularly: (1) Devising alternative hypotheses; (2) Devising a crucial experiment (or several of them), with alternative possible outcomes, each of which will, as nearly as possible, exclude one or more of the hypotheses; (3) Carrying out the experiment so as to get a clean result; (1')* [sic] *Recycling the procedure, making subhypotheses*

475

*or sequential hypotheses to refine the possibilities that remain;
and so on.* (Platt, 1964)

Continuing, Platt's article reacts to some real and serious problems
in science ("we measure, we define, we compute, we analyze, but
we do not exclude") by reminding us of the rigorous exercises in
logical thinking that gave us some early scientific breakthroughs in
the work of Bacon, Pasteur, and Newton. His argument is well summarized in this passage:

> *Or to say it another way, you can catch phenomena in a logical
> box or in a mathematical box. The logical box is coarse but
> strong, the mathematical box is fine-grained but flimsy. The
> mathematical box is a beautiful way of wrapping up a problem,
> but it will not hold the phenomena unless they have been caught
> in a logical box to begin with.* (Platt, 1964)

In rebuttal of Platt, E. M. Hafner and Susan Presswood wrote an account of the complex, 29-year evolution of the universal Fermi interaction in nuclear physics to show that theory and experiment cannot
always be as simply related to each other as Platt asserts:

> *We suggest that the notion of strong inference is an idealized
> scheme to which scientific developments seldom conform. . . .
> It is only an excellent model which, in complex circumstances,
> frequently breaks down.* (Hafner and Presswood, 1965)

Platt's ideas on strong inference, then, fit some sequences of investigation, but not others. Further, strong inference is a retrospective
approach to theory building. (Gephart, 1969) Because its focus is
upon the existing literature and upon the very next experiment to
be conducted, it can be of little assistance in predicting longer range
research needs.

The search for a planning system focused next on *convergence tech-*

nique (Carrese and Baker, 1967), a strategy developed by Louis M. Carrese and Carl G. Baker specifically for planning the research programs of the National Cancer Institute. It draws upon over 50 planning, scheduling, control, and costing techniques developed since World War II, but avoids the problems common to tight networking systems by substituting *logical* sequence for *time* sequence. In developing the program plan, or matrix, planners attempt to specify research tasks which, if accomplished, would logically contribute to progress towards a final goal:

> *If the research logic used for the construction of the matrix represents a valid model of the scientific content of the program to be conducted, and if the sequential ordering of the program elements is accomplished on the basis of this logic, then in reality, as research performance moves in the matrix from left to right in time, the intermediate objectives of each step and phase will be achieved and the scientific scope of the program will become narrower until all efforts* converge *on the end point which has been established as the over-all program goal.* (Carrese and Baker, 1967)

Application of the convergence technique begins with the selection of a planning team of four or five persons, each of whom has a clearly defined area of substantive responsibility with as little overlap as possible. One team member should have broad, general knowledge of the problem under study, but other members are chosen for their knowledge of separate subfacets of the problem. One member, who must have experience in systems analysis, acts as a catalyst by pressing the others towards clarity and specificity. The planning team's first task is usually to specify an overall program goal. Next, they attempt to phase the entire program according to logically derived intermediate goals. Criteria are specified for the achievement of each intermediate goal, so that progress can be objectively monitored. Individual research projects, then, are included in the program on the probability that each will contribute to the satisfaction of criteria for progress towards a goal.

A series of discussions with Louis Carrese further convinced several members of the Bureau of Research staff that the convergence technique was theoretically sound and that it was functioning quite well for the National Cancer Institute. It has not been tested outside of the bio-medical setting, however, despite its potential usefulness in any scientific endeavor. Application of the technique in the Targeted Research and Development Program on Reading would provide such a test *and* help to structure the new program. Under the terms of a contract from the Office of Education, William J. Gephart, Director of Research Services for Phi Delta Kappa, Inc., proceeded to make arrangements to conduct a convergence technique planning session in the summer of 1968. His planning team, which met from August 12 to September 20, was composed of an educational psychologist, a reading expert, a language psychologist, a cyberneticist, and a research management person. Dr. Gephart, a generalist whose main interest is the philosophy of science, functioned as a team member and as project director. His research associate and seven consultants also made important contributions to the effort.

This initial planning session identified the need for a multidimensional definition of reading and tentatively specified such a definition. The definition statement will be reviewed by experts in a score of disciplines, and then a second planning team will attempt to develop a detailed program plan. Because Dr. Gephart's report on the entire planning effort (Gephart, in process) will reflect several hundred man-days of disciplined effort, and because nothing less than a careful reading of the report would serve to expose its full implications, no attempt is made here to present a detailed discussion of the planning session. Instead, certain problems and ideas which commanded the first team's keenest attention are presented as major factors in the future of reading research.

478

Anticipating the future. Because no research has yet been conducted in direct response to the Phi Delta Kappa planning team's recommendations, the validity of its overall research strategy cannot be assessed. The team's deliberations, considered here as examples of inescapable concerns in future research, may be arranged in three categories: theoretical bases, research priorities, and support patterns.

Theory

A single theory of reading, when all the hypothesized facets of reading are considered, begins to appear as unobtainable as a single theory of human behavior or a single theory of politics. The planning team is indebted to John Lilly, a general scientist whose pioneering work in dolphin communication is widely respected, for his discussion of an approach to generating new theory. Dr. Lilly coined the word "metatheory" after Carnap's (Carnap, 1947) use of the word "metalanguage," a language created for the purpose of discussing languages —and therefore neither restricted nor contaminated by them. Metatheory is a formal, logical term which means theory about the derivation and operation of theories. In one sense, metatheory can be a "stepwise prescription" (Lilly, 1968a) for deriving new theories; in another sense, perhaps not expressly intended by Dr. Lilly, it can be a logical framework which connects theories in order to pursue explanation of some complicated phenomenon. Holding that a theory is a model of a real system, Dr. Lilly proposed a six-step metatheory for generating a theory of reading:

> Specify the real system. (The system may be the interlock of a human and a nonhuman intelligence; it may be a phenomenon in any realm of nature; it may be reading.) Specify how it operates, its current observables as far as possible.
>
> Specify the model, its elements, processes, and programs. (The model may be cybernetic, mathematical, conceptual, or mechanical.)

Operate the model.

Determine whether operation of the model generates observables that exist in relations and quantities similar to those of the real system.

Determine whether operation of the model generates new relations which can be determined by new experiments on the real system.

If the answer to the preceding two is no, then recycle to the beginning. (Lilly, 1968a)

Dr. Lilly's conceptualization of theory building had an immediate impact upon the planning team's work: a theory of reading must provide for the integration of all the currently observable elements and dimensions of reading. Thus, a theory of visual perception is not a theory of reading, nor is a theory of psycholinguistcs a theory of reading. Since variance is observed in the time required for different persons to assimilate a given passage, a theory of reading must have a temporal dimension. Because reading cannot take place without a) material to be read, b) a reader, and c) his "programs" (in the computer sense) for receiving and processing written language, these three elements must invariably be present in a theory of reading. All humans are born incapable of reading; some develop reading ability that approaches the limits of human capability to read swiftly, insightfully, and critically. A theory of reading must cover this spectrum and challenge even the hypothesized "limits" of human ability for processing language information. Solution of the reading problems identified elsewhere in this book, however, does not demand ultimate explication of reading. What is more immediately needed is a heuristic explication of reading that is "good enough" to provide a basis for instruction that is successful with nearly all learners. Viewing the need for a theory of reading and the need for practical advances in instruction, the planning team proposed a final program goal which responds to both of these needs.

The goal set by Dr. Gephart's planning team ("Proven ability to educate 95% of all ten-year-old school children to a criterion measure of literate behavior") (Gephart, in process) has six points of engagement.

First, it should be said that the practical flavor of this statement is not at variance with the widely shared view that a practical breakthrough in reading instruction awaits a conceptual breakthrough in basic research. This goal statement is meant to provide a test for insuring that new knowledge on reading does in fact provide a basis for successful instruction.

Second, the phrase "to educate" carries the argument that instruction must produce the desired changes in behavior. Developmental changes in behavior are not viewed as different in *kind* from learned changes. The changes in behavior must occur as a predictable result of instruction, not in spite of instruction.

Third, the 95% figure is based upon a guess that about 5% of all humans are in some way—through blindness, gross central nervous system damage, or genetic accident—utterly crippled in their ability to learn to read through the visual modality. Responsibility for teaching the remaining 95% to read cannot be waived.

Fourth, ten-year-old school children represent a relatively meaningful point on the continuum from no reading ability to ultimate reading ability. Consensus indicates that, by age ten, many children have acquired a basis for developing further reading proficiency without further formal instruction. This point on the continuum, then, is considered an appropriate point for testing the effectiveness of instruction. The assumption is made that the research logic which satisfies the goal statement can be systematically extended to higher and higher levels of ability.

Fifth, the criterion measure is expected to be a score on a test of literate behavior. Developing such a test may be the most difficult task in the entire research program. Its validity depends upon a more functional understanding of reading than we now possess.

Sixth, the term "literate behavior" is used to indicate that reading probably does not stand alone without its sister abilities of writing, speaking, and listening.

It should be noted that the goal statement satisfies the requirement that the goal of a program planned through convergence technique must be sufficiently precise to provide a basis for research action. (Carrese, 1967) Each of the six points of engagement discussed above suggests one or more research questions.

Major Emphases of Future Research

Granted that theories of reading will evolve in "umbrella" form as described, there are a number of predictions that can be made about the nature of the research to be conducted in affirmation or rejection of the theories. Once investigators accept the idea that the latest and best information can be expressed in a few, ever-developing models of reading, little research should have to be called atheoretical.

Returning to John Lilly's six-step metatheory, some expected kinds of research aimed at the first two steps can be cited. (The last four steps are so dependent upon the first two that no predictions regarding steps 3-6 are offered here.)

Specify the real system (reading). The targets of inquiry directed at step 1 are familiar. The literature abounds with good studies of eye movements, subvocal speech, readability of materials, and other factors believed to be parts of the real system. While the topics of research and research methodologies for this task are not new, a rising determination to integrate the findings of such efforts is relatively new and is judged a potent influence on progress. The result of this determination should be a proliferation of models of reading against

482

which a scientist interested, say, in visual perception can examine his findings to see if there is a fit. The kinds of studies expected to "specify the real system" will be largely observational; i.e., reading behavior will be examined at many stages of development, but the external manipulation of reading behavior through instruction or conditioning would probably not play a major role here. Observational techniques will cover a wide range, from ethological methodologies (Timbergen, 1968) through electromyographic and electroencephalographic techniques for monitoring muscle and brain activity. Some of these observations might be called phenomenological, because they would concentrate upon phenomena that occur during reading rather than upon the total interaction of materials, the reader, and his programs. Phenomena which accompany reading may facilitate reading, inhibit reading, or neither. The phenomena observed in this step are therefore given tentative places in the next (modelling) step.

Specify the model. No type of modelling is inherently good or bad; appropriateness is the only criterion. Pauling's (Pauling, Corey, and Branson, 1951) and later, Watson's (Watson and Crick, 1953) tinkertoy molecules proved to be entirely appropriate and quite useful in one sort of inquiry. Computer models may duplicate or parallel certain human functions. Mathematical models have demonstrated their general usefulness. Models are also built conceptually and expressed by using combinations of words, geometric figures, and lines. Future reading research may make use of all of these types of models, but a strategy proposed by the planning team in response to Dr. Lilly's metatheory is to draft a model conceptually, test its underlying assumptions and the hypotheses it generates, and then translate the conceptual model into a computer model. This strategy allows use of familiar, flexible, conceptual modelling techniques for model generation, but demands enough detail and accuracy to allow one to program a computer so that the computer actually operates in the way predicted by the conceptual model.

One test of the conceptual model of reading, then, is to create reading behavior in a computer. Realizing that computer technology does not now permit such a test and realizing that less than perfect explication of reading may be a basis for highly successful instruction, the planning team also recommended that conceptual models be tested in an operational setting. If a conceptual model can be translated into instructional materials and practices that satisfy the objective (criterion performance by 95%), then a heuristic explication of reading has been achieved. The computer modelling activity, however, stands as a safeguard against the eventuality that no less rigorous test will suffice and as a challenge to the growing computer technology.

After examining a number of conceptual models of reading, the planning team decided to explore in depth a partial model advanced by Kenneth Goodman, a psycholinguist who worked with the team as a consultant. It is a sequential, task analysis model which shows the interaction of ten perceptual and cognitive activities with each other and with the reader's memory. (Goodman, 1968) Dr. Goodman's model is clearly based upon the widely accepted belief that reading is a *sampling* activity. Two logical deficiencies in the model, lack of specific inclusion of materials to be read and lack of provision for developmental changes in reading, are being resolved by Dr. Goodman and Dr. Gephart.

Support for Future Research

Some rather extensive changes are forecast regarding patterns of support for future research on reading, but no major changes are expected in the near future regarding sources or levels of support. The Office of Education and the National Institute of Child Health and Human Development will continue to be the major sources of support.

The funds available to Federal agencies will have to be allocated with more care than ever, either through insisting upon increased excellence of proposal design or through insisting upon excellence *plus* relevance to program goals. The Office of Education has clearly chosen the latter alternative, as indicated by its announced intention to support reading research aimed at tasks delineated in the Phi Delta Kappa research strategy. (American Educational Research Association Newsletter, Nos. 7 & 8, 1968) The decision of other agencies to follow suit will depend largely upon their philosophies of research management and upon the success of the Office of Education's program.

Three additional factors, however, indicate that programmed support patterns for reading research will be adopted by most Federal agencies. The factors are the need for theory that coherently treats reading at all levels of ability, the multidisciplinary nature of the research actually needed, and the pressure on Federal agencies to engage in program planning that results in a tangible impact on the people they serve. Inferences regarding the potency of the first two of these factors may be drawn from one's experiences and from the earlier parts of this chapter. The last factor, program planning, probably needs some explanation, however.

The Program Planning and Budgeting System (PPBS), formalized under Robert McNamara's leadership at the Department of Defense, is grounded upon principles which have been around for a long time— since the Epicureans, according to some. Briefly, the attempt is to specify defensible goals and then to allocate manpower, facilities and funds to each task judged necessary to goal attainment. Some observers note that PPBS has proved effective in all but two areas: 1) getting all branches of the armed forces to use the same buckle and 2) planning research.

Program Evaluation and Review Technique (PERT) is an integral part of most PPB systems, but has been widely applied in other settings. Like PPBS, PERT is not new in concept. Its principles for systematic scheduling of component tasks must have been available to the Egyptians when they built the pyramids. PERT, too, and its variations fail as research planning strategies because their temporal frameworks cannot tolerate negative findings and because all component tasks in a research program cannot be specified at a high level of confidence. (Carrese and Baker, 1967) Widespread use of PPBS and PERT strategies in Federal agencies has, however, created a pressure on research managers to plan the unplannable and to schedule the inscrutable. While some expected responses to this pressure might include regression, withdrawal, or aggression, the development of the convergence technique provides a constructive alternative. The pressure to make specific plans for research and the availability of a technique for doing so are expected to fulfill the prediction that Federal agencies will program future research efforts towards goals which are expressed in terms of impact upon a target group. Resistance on the part of scientists to such "programmed" support is expected to wax and then wane when it becomes clear that convergence planning is essentially a recasting of the bench scientist's rigorous project or *tactical* planning techniques at the program or *strategic* level.

The pressure to develop strategic plans for research is expected to produce, in the long run, a change in the dynamics of Federal research support. If the forces which now influence research support are public interest, the state-of-the-art, legislation, appropriation, and authorization of funds, then the system looks like this:

FIGURE 1

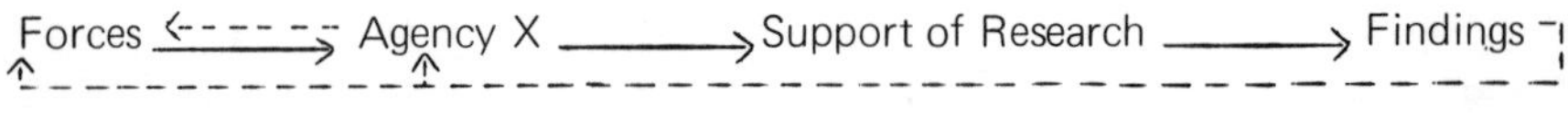

Forces ← - - - → Agency X ⟶ Support of Research ⟶ Findings

Solid lines indicate communication that is relatively more direct and decisive than communication indicated by dotted lines.

The paradigm that is expected to emerge as a result of agency research planning may be expressed as follows:

FIGURE 2

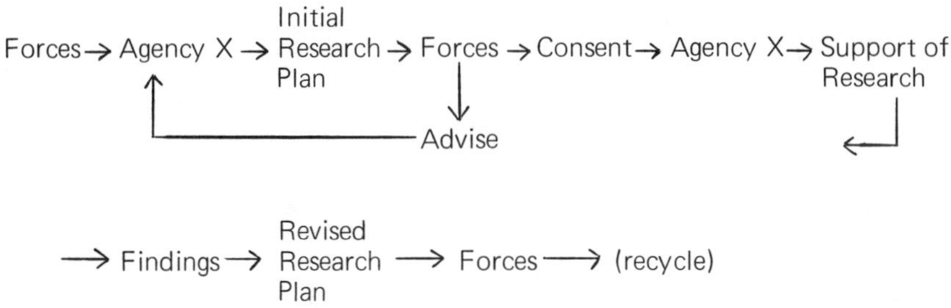

```
                    Initial
Forces→ Agency X → Research → Forces → Consent→ Agency X→ Support of
           ↑        Plan          |                        Research
           |                      ↓
           └──────────────────── Advise                    ←┘


                    Revised
    → Findings→ Research ──→ Forces ──→ (recycle)
                    Plan
```

SUMMARY

We are at the beginning of the third era of research in reading. The
first era, characterized by an appropriately heavy emphasis upon
basic research, ended when World War I engendered in the educa-
tionists a fascination with the measurement of human abilities.
From World War I to about 1960, fundamental studies were largely deferred in favor of research on instructional methodology. The
present era, marked by disillusionment with the second era's impact
upon reading achievement, places heavy reliance upon multidisciplinary research on reading pathology and on the reading process.

Recent events have persuaded the U.S. Office of Education that the
present climate is favorable for beginning a programmed research effort on the reading process. Phi Delta Kappa, in its application of
the convergence technique to the development of a strategy for
future reading research, specified certain problems and ideas which
will influence future theory, topics, and support patterns for reading research.

Theory

Future reading research, we believe, will be guided by theory which is operationalized in a model or models which treat material to be read, the reader, and his "programs" as three elements that exist in reading at all stages of development. Heuristically placed checkpoints (age 10, for example) will allow testing of the idea that new knowledge on reading can systematically improve instruction. When the evolving theory and model(s) have caught up with civilization's needs for better reading instruction, they will offer a framework for investigation of other phenomena (e.g., memory, information processing, learning) that are set in motion by reading behavior.

Research topics will tend to center upon observation of reading behavior at many levels of development and upon phenomena which are judged to be parts of the real system. Conceptual models of reading will be validated through translation to computer models and through actualization in instructional settings.

Support Patterns

Research planning built upon collaboration of the scientific community with the many funding agencies will create programs which respond more directly to the nature of scientific inquiry. The research plan for a given program will be a major medium for communication and decision-making regarding that program.

The authors wish to express their most sincere gratitude to Dr. Jeanne Chall, Dr. William J. Gephart, Dr. Kenneth Goodman, Dr. Thomas E. Moorefield, and Mrs. Lanora G. Lewis for the intellectual generosity they displayed in criticizing earlier drafts of this chapter. We hope that they will not be blamed for its remaining inadequacies.

REFERENCES

Abell, Adelaid M. Rapid reading: Advantages and methods. **Educ. Rev.,** Oct. 1894, **VIII.**

American Educational Research Association Newsletter. **Educ. researcher,** No. 7, 1968.

American Educational Research Association Newsletter, **Educ. researcher,** No. 8, 1968.

Bond, Guy, & Dykstra, Robert. **Coordinating center for first grade reading instruction programs.** University of Minnesota, 1967. (Final report of USOE Project 5-0341.)

Broca, Paul. **Memoires sur le Cerveau de l'Homme.** Paris: C. Reinwald, 1888.

Carnap, Rudolf. **Meaning and necessity.** Chicago: University of Chicago Press, 1947.

Carrese, Louis M., & Baker, Carl G. The convergence technique: A method for the planning and programming of research efforts. **Mgmt Sci.,** April 1967, **13** (8).

Chall, Jeanne. **Learning to read: The great debate.** New York: McGraw-Hill, 1967.

Gephart, William J. Application of the convergence technique to basic studies of the reading process. Bloomington, Indiana: Phi Delta Kappa, Inc. (Final report of USOE Project 8-0737, in process.)

Gephart, William J. Personal communication, February 26, 1969.

Goodman, Kenneth. (Ed.) **Psycholinguistic nature of the reading process.** Detroit: Wayne State University Press, 1968.

Goodman, Kenneth. Personal communication, September 11, 1968.

Hafner, E. M., & Presswood, Susan. Strong inference and weak interactions. **Sci.,** 1965, **149.**

Huey, Edmund B. **The psychology and pedagogy of reading.** New York: Macmillan Co., 1908.

Kavanagh, James F. (Ed.) **The reading process.** Washington: U.S. Government Printing Office, 1968.

Keeney, Arthur H., & Keeney, Virginia T. (Eds.) **Dyslexia: Diagnosis and treatment of reading disorders.** St. Louis: C. V. Mosby Co., 1968.

Levin, Harry. Personal communication and interim reports of USOE Project 5-0537.

Levin, Harry, & Williams, Joanna. (Eds.) **Basic studies on reading.** New York: Basic Books, 1970.

Lilly, John C. Personal communication, August 22, 1968.

Lilly, John C. Personal communication, November 20, 1968.

Money, John. (Ed.) **Reading disability: Progress and research needs in dyslexia.** Baltimore: Johns Hopkins Press, 1962.

Money, John. (Ed.) **The disabled reader: Education of the dyslexic child.** Baltimore: Johns Hopkins Press, 1966.

Pauling, Linus, Corey, R. B., & Branson, H. R. Structure of proteins: Two hydrogen bonded helical configurations. **Proceedings** of the U.S. National Academy of Sciences, 1951, **37.**

Platt, J. R. Strong inference. **Sci.,** 1964, **146.**

Quantz, J. O. Problems in the psychology of reading. **Psychol. Rev. Monogr. Suppl.,** 1897, **VII.**

Romanes, George John. **Mental evolution in animals.** New York: D. Appleton and Co., 1891.

Tinbergen, N. On war and peace in animals and man. **Sci.,** 1968, **160.**

Watson, J. D., & Crick, H. C. Genetical implications of the structure of deoxyribonucleic acid. **Nature,** 1953, **171.**

Young, Francis A., & Lindsley, Donald B. The influence of early experience on visual information processing: A conference on underlying factors in perceptual and reading disorders. (In preparation.)

Zedler, Empress Y. Research conference on the problem of dyslexia and related disorders in the public schools of the United States. Southwest Texas State College, 1967. (Final report of USOE Project 7-8270.)

Inner City Reading:
Status and Prognostication

Wallace Ramsey, Ed.D.
Professor of Education and
Consultant to the Reading Clinic
University of Missouri
Columbia, Missouri

The problem of the education of children in the inner city is one of the greatest of our time. Clustered around the heart of many cities are huge numbers of black children disadvantaged in many ways—socially, economically, and educationally. Many of the natural conditions that help more advantaged children in learning to read are missing—there is an absence of reading material in the home, experience backgrounds are poor, there is a lack of parental stimulation to read, a nonstandard dialect is spoken, and a strong desire to learn to read is not present. In addition to these factors, certain others contribute to a backwardness in reading development: loose family organization (frequently without a father), poor dietary habits, emotional insecurity, insufficient rest, and the presence of a greater-than-normal number of physical defects.

In the various cities across the nation, school officials are trying to cope with the problems of greater literacy for these neglected people. The conditions under which inner city reading programs are being operated are not conducive to success. School buildings are old and their arrangement is suited to a more formal type of program. The materials of instruction do not meet the needs of the situation. Teachers who have not followed the white trek to the suburbs are too often those of senior status who have neither the stamina, confidence, or imagination that moving to a new situation requires. They are those whose seniority makes them immovable—they are too old to move and too young to retire. They were not trained for the situation in which they find themselves. Very often they have neither the compassion for, nor understanding of, the children they teach.

There is, of course, a core of dedicated and capable people who stay on in the city schools because they want to help the black disadvantaged. These people frequently have more sympathy for the children than they have understanding, more determination than imagination, and more true grit than vision. When the paragon exists, possessing all of the needed characteristics, he frequently lives out his years of tenure frustrated by the system of bureaucracy, sightless central control, a routine-bound tradition, and overwhelming conditions of poverty and public indifference.

With a somewhat limited understanding of these conditions, the writer naively set out to study the reading instruction programs of five of the nation's larger inner city school systems. A grant from the small contract branch of the U.S. Office of Education[1] enabled him to study published documents, use questionnaires to get additional information and conduct telephone interviews with school officials in New York, Washington, Los Angeles, Detroit, and St. Louis. The writer also did on-site visits of schools and school officials in all except New York City.

The findings of the study were certainly not all encompassing since the writer was operating with such limited resources. However, the study yielded many impressions about the present status of inner city reading instruction and have led the writer to draw some conclusions about future development. These impressions and conclusions are outlined in this chapter for possible value to others interested in inner city reading instruction.

PRESENT STATUS—GENERAL PRINCIPLES

The following important general principles concerning the systems studied emerged:

All have substantial de facto segregation of schools.

Strong central control of schools is the rule, with some feeble attempts at neighborhood control emerging.

---

[1]The final report of the study contains more details than can be given here. Readers who wish to get a copy of the final report should contact the writer.

There is a tremendous shortage of certified teachers for work in inner city schools and many substandard teaching personnel are used in order to keep schools open.

The teaching unit is generally 30-35 pupils per one adult, usually a certified teacher, usually unassisted by an aide, and working in a self-contained situation.

The general approach to reading is basal instruction following an "adopted" series (or multiple series) most generally written for white, suburban children.

The most widely used method of caring for individual differences is in-class grouping according to reading ability.

There is very little use of teaching technology—the available hardware and technological aids are rarely in evidence nor are they employed.

There is very small scale experimentation with newer methods of teaching reading and little evidence of anything approaching extensive use of them.

The approach to first grade reading is, in the main, very formal and traditional with extended readiness being the rule for many children. The possibilities of using the children's own natural dialect as a natural introit into reading are not being taken advantage of—usually the natural dialect is ignored or (more commonly) attempts are being made to obliterate it.

In short, the inner city child is being subjected to the methods, materials, time schedules and organizational patterns that have been only modestly successful with white, suburban children.

The writer lists the above generalizations in full realization that generalization is always dangerous and subject to misunderstanding and dispute. It would be unfair to imply that there are not important and extensive exceptions to each of the generalizations but they constitute a just and valid general description of present inner city reading programs.

Examples illustrating most of them are given in the following sections. The exceptions give strong clues concerning future programs, which is the topic of the final section of this chapter.

DE FACTO SEGREGATION

A combination of segregated housing and the neighborhood school concept serve to keep schools segregated. In most of the cities, segregated neighborhoods would make school integration through bussing almost a practical impossibility even if there was public support for it.

For example, 93% of Washington's school children are black and live in crowded ghettos. In 1967 Judge Skelly Wright, in rendering his decision in the Hobson versus Hanson case, pointed out that de facto segregation existed in Washington and ordered an end to it. In 1969, when the writer visited Washington schools, he noted attempts to reduce segregation in the teaching staff in some schools. One junior high principal (a Negro in a school with 95% Negro student body) proudly pointed out the two young white teachers on his staff and described how well they fitted in. He pointed out, rather sadly, that both were leaving Washington the next year for jobs in white suburban schools.

Negro school officials in Washington also described how the bussing of blacks into the schools west of Rock Creek Park caused them to encounter a program much more academic in nature than they were accustomed to. They also missed out on established Title I programs and an enriched curriculum operating in their neighborhood schools. Their parents had to go substantial distances to P.T.A. meetings.

Even though about one-third of the school children in St. Louis are white, four of the systems six districts enroll over 99% black children. In May 1969 parents in a predominantly white south St. Louis district publicly objected to Negroes being bussed into local schools. When a school official agreed with the stand of white parents, there was a general wave of protest which resulted in his dismissal. School officials experimenting with integration find that segregation dies hard even in the enlightened north.

CENTRAL CONTROL

In all of the systems visited, strong central control was very obvious. Large central office staffs were housed in several floors of office buildings or complexes with titles plainly designating all-district responsibility.

New York City's experimentation with local control, and its accompanying difficulties like those in the Ocean Hill-Brownsville section, have been well publicized. The system is divided into eleven field districts with a superintendent for each. There evidently is substantial latitude within which each district may operate and extensive freedom of individual schools and teachers in selecting teaching materials, for example.

Real local control is missing in New York City, as the controversy of 1968-69 aptly illustrated. The other cities in the study probably have far less local control. Such control was certainly not evident in Washington except to a minor degree in enclaves like Logan School and in some schools in The Model Schools Division. The latter consisted of 25 building units, housing 20,000 children, described as "an education subsystem. . .a model school subsystem in the inner city area. . .to provide a wide range of programs and services. . .improved educational opportunities for low income families." The division could only properly be described as a semiautonomous one in terms of control. It had many other interesting features, which will be discussed later.

Los Angeles, St. Louis, and Detroit are all also very evidently centrally controlled. Teachers in all three cities complained to the writer about the bigness of the district and its bureaucracy. They told of long delays of getting teaching supplies, which must come from a "central office." They spoke of the inability to get help from the central office supervisory staff. It was evident, as the writer conferred with central office staff in some cities, that they were almost completely out of direct touch with teachers, children, and the realities of the classroom. This was repeated over and over again during the study.

One of the most serious indictments that can be made against bigness when the control is central is the difficulty of communication within the hierarchy. The implementation of school policy becomes exceedingly difficult. No matter how sound may be the ideas of a central staff, local implementation may frequently produce an ineffectual distortion due simply to administrative distance.

Central control of a large system may also be a deterrent to progress simply because diversity prevents the formulation of a common policy of value to all parts of the system—or when a common policy is promulgated it is ill-suited to the whole system.

The greatest indictment of bigness is that control seems so remote to a group of patrons of a specific school. Patrons come to feel that central office people do not know the problems of a specific neighborhood nor do they care what they are. Too often this is really the case—when the specific school is in a disadvantaged neighborhood. It is a well-known fact that ghetto schools frequently get older textbooks, equipment of lower quality, and frequently less of it, than do schools in areas where patrons are more prosperous, pay more taxes, and are more vociferous about their children's education.

TEACHER SHORTAGE AND LOAD

Every system the writer investigated suffered from a severe teacher shortage. In the year of investigation only 72% of New York City's teachers were fully certified, it was reported. No figures were made available from Washington but it was evident that a similar situation prevailed. In Los Angeles the turnover of teachers and growth of the district forced the employing of about 3,000 new teachers each year, requiring a prodigious effort of orientation on the part of district supervisory staff. About three-fourths of the system's teachers had permanent certification, the writer was told. This was due, in part, to the requirement of five years of training for such certification.

During the writer's visit to Detroit he attended an orientation session for young adults seeking to become probationary teachers in the city. The director of new teacher orientation indicated that the recruiting and orientation of new teachers was a major personnel problem.

During the time of investigation, 420 of St. Louis' 4,200 teachers were substitutes. In one of the almost all-black districts, in which the writer observed, sixteen percent of the teachers were substitutes. It was reported that, under pressure from the St. Louis School System, the State Department of Education had recently extended from sixty to ninety days the period during the school year which a substitute might teach. Many classrooms were staffed for a whole school year by a succession of substitutes, each working for a ninety-day period.

The shortage of teachers in the big city is partially symptomatic of the whole nation's teacher shortage. However, it is obvious that teachers follow the trek of the white middle-class children to the suburbs. The threats (and the realization) of violence towards teachers make many of them fearful for their own safety and cause them to flee the ghettos. It is not surprising that white teachers leave but so do many more capable Negro teachers.

In all probability one cause of the teacher shortage in the ghetto is the heavy per-pupil load. At a time when the national pupil-teacher ratio had fallen well below 30, it remained above that in several cities.

For example, in St. Louis it was 34 in 1968-69. It sank to 33 in 1969-70 due to a decline in enrollment; but, since the high school ratio was only 24, the size of the average elementary class was well above the overall district average. A similar situation undoubtedly prevailed in the other cities in the study, although the writer was not successful in obtaining figures to confirm this.

Taking some edge off large enrollments was the increased use of teacher aides, often supported by Title I E. S. E. A. funds or other federal funds. New York City reported that teaching aides were utilized by fifty-four percent of the system's classrooms. No figures confirmed the amount of money spent for such purposes so the figure of fifty-four percent probably includes many classrooms in which aides worked only a short time each day or occasionally.

In Washington the writer was told that the use of teacher aides was growing and in 1969-70 was likely to exceed the 1,000 being used in 1968-69.

Each of the other cities indicated aides were employed. St. Louis reported that about 300 paid aides worked in the schools with teachers and in school offices. An additional 110 were labeled "elementary teacher assistants," 31 functioned as school-home aides, and an additional 150 volunteers supplemented the work of teachers in art, music, elementary libraries, and in remedial reading. This was an average of one aide for every 195 children, a very small proportion to be of significant assistance. The writer would estimate the conditions were not greatly different in the other three cities studied—based on impressions received in his visits to classrooms.

DEVELOPMENTAL READING PROGRAMS

The general system of organization followed in ghetto schools is self-contained classrooms in grades K-6 and departmentalization in grades above. The incidence of nongradedness and team teaching remains very low in all of the systems studied. Los Angeles reported that five percent of its primary grade classrooms were nongraded. St. Louis employed a levels program through the third grade—a program similar to nongradedness in the area of reading. The kindergarten and the first three grades were divided into eight levels designated A-1, A-2, B-1, B-2, C-1, and so forth, largely corresponding to the levels in the reading series being used. Mastery of skills at each level was largely determined by standardized group achievement tests with all of their weaknesses in designating the status of *individual* children. Had the writer not been told that the primary was nongraded, he could not have distinguished the classes from the typically graded ones.

New York reported that in-class grouping was the only provision made for individual differences in reading in the first four grades. A similar situation appeared to prevail in the other cities. The assigning of children to classrooms according to IQ or some other ability or achievement measure existed to some extent in every system but did not appear to be predominant in any.

The basal reader was the core of instruction in every system studied. New York City had a multiple listing of textbooks and an individual school might select and purchase any textbook on the approved list. The research office indicated no systematic accounting of specific books but it was their observation that three or four series made up the bulk of those used. In Washington there was fairly free choice of materials among schools but it was obvious teachers were clinging to the use of basals.

In Los Angeles the system used state-adopted textbooks. The state-adopted textbook system was very thorough and offered schools many options. For 1969-70 Los Angeles schools could choose between the Macmillan and Harper-Row series as a regular basal and for disadvantaged groups would use a combination of the BANK STREET READERS and the Scott, Foresman OPEN HIGHWAYS series.

An interesting and unusual feature of the Detroit developmental reading program was the development of the CITY SCHOOLS READING PROGRAM, a series of primary-grade reading materials designed to be more appropriate to the needs of inner city children than were the typical basals. Beginning in 1959, and under the leadership of Gertrude Whipple, supervisor of reading, the first steps were taken to complete a textbook series to meet the needs of pupils in multicultural areas. The oral language of Detroit six-year-olds, half of whom were white and half black, was studied to determine typical vocabulary, sentence types, and other patterns. Interviews were also conducted to determine the interests of inner city primary children.

A series of three pre-primers was written, using the information gathered in the study. These were tried out in a study that compared children's responses to them with responses to a typical series. Results were so good that plans were made to complete the series through grade three by fall, 1969.

The series had previously been published by the Follett Publishing Company and made available for sale all over the country. Since its inception, other companies have begun to publish series appropriate for the inner city and the publishers of the major series of readers have brought out their regular series in multiethnic editions.

The Detroit system continued to make the CITY SCHOOLS READING PROGRAM available for experimentation in the city from 1960 to 1969. In the fall of 1969 the series was, for the first time, the adopted series for the primary grades.

In 1968-69, and for three or four years previous, the adopted basal reading series for St. Louis schools was the McKee Reading Series published by Houghton-Mifflin. At level A-2, GETTING READY TO READ, which taught the sounds of consonants and their corresponding letters, was used. (At level A-1, or kindergarten, the Ginn Reading Readiness materials were used.) Other books in the McKee series were used in levels A-3 to E-2. In the intermediate grades the Scott-Foresman series, chiefly the Open Highways track, was used.

Testing was very important in the system. The California Achievement Tests were used in primary grades and the Iowa Test of Basic Skills was used above that level. The tests, according to some teachers enrolled in the writers' university classes, were used as the chief basis for promotion, retention, and graduation of pupils and for the rating and promotion of teachers. It is not known if, and to what extent, these practices were really followed.

Multiethnic materials were being used to a widely varied extent. New York City reported that about half of its classrooms were using multiethnic materials. Washington reported that the use of such materials was very limited. Detroit had its own multiethnic series but it did not become the adopted series until autumn of 1969. Los Angeles began to use the BANK STREET READERS for disadvantaged primary grade children as an adopted series in the 1969-70 school year. Multiethnic materials were being used in St. Louis in only a very few classrooms.

All of the systems studied had conducted or were conducting small scale experiments with approaches to reading other than the conventional basals.

New York City had allocated substantial funds for this purpose and although the number of children involved was large, the proportion to the total school population was small.

When asked to indicate the number of children involved in research or innovative programs the following figures were given:

Special alphabets: 2,000 in grades one and two.
Language experience approach: 25,000 in grades one through six.
Linguistic materials: 40,000 in grades one through six.
Computer assisted instruction: 1,200.

In the space in which the numbers involved in programmed materials were to be listed on the questionnaire, no figures were entered. However, the press had reported several thousand New York City children had been involved in "Project Read," an experimental project involving the use of programmed reading materials published by Behavioral Research Laboratories of Palo Alto, California. All of the above information would suggest that over six percent of the elementary school children in New York City during 1968-69 were involved in research or innovative programs.

One of the most grandiose projects in the nation in research in various approaches to beginning reading was begun in New York City in September 1966 and continued until June 1969. Children in over one hundred thirty classes in primary grades (kindergarten, first and second grades) were exposed to one of several approaches or methodologies in learning to read, including the Initial Teaching Alphabet, linguistic materials, language-experience approach, a talking typewriter approach, and regular approaches. The program was under the direction of Dr. Miriam Goldberg of Teachers College, Columbia University, and experienced substantial difficulties, namely teacher turnover, differences with teachers over style and ideology, teacher strikes, parental pressures, and administrative revisions. By the time the experiment reached its halfway point, it had lost 1) one-half of its participating superintendents, 2) thirty percent of its school principals, 3) one-half of its original students, and 4) fewer than half of the original teachers. Pressure from parents to group first grade pupils homogeneously caused several of the schools to do so, despite original agreements to maintain heterogeneous grouping in the classes. Several schools pulled out of the project. What the findings will be concerning the relative value of different approaches, and whether they will be at all val-

505

id, remains to be seen.

In Washington various small-scale experiments with different approaches to reading had been tried. The most time and funds had been given to experiments involving linguistic approaches and programmed reading.

The Reading Center operation included experimentation with innovative practices for the last few years. During 1966-67 a program utilizing the MERRILL LINGUISTIC READERS was begun in one school. In September 1968 five additional schools were added. At present writing about 300 children, mostly in primary grades, were using the program. Tentative plans called for further expansion in 1969-70.

During 1968-69, 13,000 children in Washington were involved in Project Read, an experiment using programmed reading materials published by Behavioral Research Laboratories, a series very similar to McGraw-Hill's PROGRAMMED READING. The series was used as a basal program through grade six and as a corrective and remedial program in grades seven and eight. It was financed under Title I of E. S. E. A. and was being evaluated by George Washington University. No control group was used. The entire population used in the experiment was pretested in September 1968 and posttested in June 1969. A teacher attitude scale, determining teacher reactions to the program, was scheduled to be administered in July. Since the schools involved in the program had had a downward spiral in reading, it was felt that if the spiral was arrested while PROGRAMMED READING was being used, it would be regarded as successful.

The Model Schools Division in Washington (a subsystem involving 20,000 inner city children and their parents in a local control and neighborhood school experiment) carried on experiments of different kinds in different subject matter areas.

The part of the Model Schools Program of most pertinence to this study was the Language Arts innovation which existed as a part of it. All fourteen of the elementary schools used the BANK STREET READERS, seven utilized the Language-Experience Program in reading, three were involved in Project Read, and two had ITA experiments going. There was one Unifon project and one utilizing Words in Color. Nine elementary schools had heavy tutoring programs in reading. There were many other aspects of the Model Schools Program not related directly to reading but which affected it.

In Los Angeles the language-experience approach to beginning reading had moved from the experimental stage to the utilization stage. During the last five years there had been a concerted effort to get all first grade teachers oriented to the language experience approach to beginning reading and supervisory personnel indicated to the writer that the approach was being used in all kindergartens and first grades. About one-fourth of second grade teachers were said to be using it.

The reading supervisor informed the writer that the language experience program was instituted after an extensive in-service program that included many demonstrations and workshops. Videotaped demonstration lessons were scheduled to be used with new teachers in the fall of 1969 to orient them to the approach.

One of the great influencing factors on reading instruction since 1966 had been the Miller-Unruh law passed by the California legislature. It provided for state wide certification of reading specialists by examination, which was given annually by the Educational Testing Service. School officials contacted by the writer felt that many people who passed the examination were not really qualified by training and experience to be reading specialists. Therefore, Los Angeles schools insisted on other qualifications.

Under the Miller-Unruh law, statewide testing was done in reading in all school districts. The results obtained in February 1968 showed that Los Angeles pupils were relatively poor in reading. The State

Board of Education directed Los Angeles to take drastic action to improve reading. A massive program of in-service training and interschool visitation in 1968-69 was scheduled to be followed in 1969-70 by placing in the hands of all Los Angeles primary teachers the SPEECH-TO-PRINT PHONICS materials. All kindergarten teachers were to be given a copy of FOUNDATIONS FOR READING by Marian Monroe (Scott, Foresman Co.) and all first grade teachers were to receive a set of the Ideal Phonics Cards. All third grade classrooms were to receive Durrell's PHONIC PRACTICE PROGRAM. An outlay of $300,000 was scheduled to pay for the four-phase program.

Interest in approaches other than the basal were apparent in Detroit. The research office reported to the writer a project to evaluate six different methods of beginning reading including the Initial Teaching Alphabet, Programmed Reading, and other approaches. Their preliminary findings were that no method was superior and that the role of the teacher was more important than the method.

Some small-scale experimentation with innovations in teaching early reading was conducted in St. Louis in 1967-69, including tryouts of the Initial Teaching Alphabet, PROGRAMMED READING, the BANK STREET READERS, and other programs. In the Enright District, in which the writer observed classes, the BANK STREET READERS were being used in several primary grade classrooms on an experimental basis.

PROVISIONS FOR PROBLEM READERS

Attention to the needs of problem readers appeared in every system with the advent of Federal aid, and activity in that connection multiplied many times in the last few years. Each of the systems had provided for the problem reader before Federal aid, but such aid made it possible to provide in much greater fashion.

In New York City problem readers were helped in a variety of ways.

Small classes were used for 20% of them in grades two and three, for 30% in grades four through six, and for 10% in grades seven and eight. Some one percent of children enrolled in grades two through six, received reading clinic tutoring. About 10% of the children in grades two through six participated in classroom aide-assisted instruction. Fewer than one percent benefited from classroom reading instruction that was parent-assisted.

At the secondary levels, about five percent of junior high students (grades seven through nine) were involved in corrective reading programs and about three percent of those in grades ten and eleven were so involved. Fewer than one percent of secondary school students received remedial reading instruction in very small groups.

The extra programs, affecting much of the disadvantaged population, were numerous, varied, and complex in their makeup. The sheer size of the problem of studying the system was illustrated by the fact that there were over 500 Title I E. S. E. A. projects in operation during 1967-1968 and over fifty in reading alone in New York City.

In beginning reading, a twenty-one million dollar project for 130,000 pupils in grades one and two reduced class size to 15 in grade one and 20 in grade two. Extra materials were provided for children to take home and start their own libraries. A thrust to involve parents was made. Diagnostic services designed to determine at an early stage why children were not responding to reading instruction were provided. Teacher aides were provided for kindergarten teachers.

Nine special projects of an innovative or research nature were in existence during 1967-68 and several of these continued into the next year. Seven hundred children and adults were involved in a project utilizing talking typewriters. A computer-assisted instruction project had provided daily instruction in reading and math for 8,000 students and continued into 1970. A programmed reading project tested the McGraw-Hill materials and produced programs to improve reading comprehension. The Sullivan-McGraw-Hill Programmed Reading Series was tested in two kindergarten classes and its use was continued as the pupils progressed into first grade.

Eleven diagnostic reading centers had been operating in New York City, chiefly financed under Title I, and had striven for early identification of reading problems, had provided remedial instruction for children, and had conducted workshops and training sessions for teachers. The problems experienced in setting these in operation were the same as those encountered in other cities: late funding, shortage of personnel, finding space for operation, and so forth.

In Washington the Reading Center was the agent for implementing programs for problem readers. Of great impact was the spate of extra programs financed by federal legislation for the nation and overlying the regular school program in Washington, as elsewhere. Of primary importance was probably the role of the Reading Center and the influence of its director.

The Reading Center, housed in various places in the district during 1968-69, and at the time of this writing located in Phillips School Building in the Georgetown area in Washington, radiated its influence outward into every corner of the District but chiefly into those in which most of the disadvantaged children lived. The director's six assistants supervised the work of 172 reading specialists fulfilling various roles in the schools. About 140 of them were in instructional units in the schools, teaching small groups of problem readers in grades one through twelve. Some of the 140 also served as consultants to classroom teachers in the developmental program. Eighteen others were assigned to geographical areas as general reading specialists to aid teachers in the Reading Improvement Program.

Fifteen reading people worked as full-time diagnosticians, either in clinics established in schools or in mobile units especially equipped for the task and moved from school to school as needed. The eight mobile units, built on Ford Falcon chassis in 1965, operated for the last four years.

The reading program was strengthened in many ways by federal aid from N. D. E. A. and E. S. E. A. There was a growing number of teacher aides in the system. In 1969 they approximated 1000 in number, trained by the Reading Center, and employed by the system. In addition, there were at least 200 unpaid Urban Service Volunteers working in the schools. The director reported that there was no shortage of *qualified* reading specialists in the system. Several did not have full certification which required a master's degree plus twelve graduate hours, including a clinical reading course. Five years teaching experience were required before one could become a reading specialist.

Provisions for problem readers in Los Angeles included small classes for such readers, classroom aide-assisted instruction, parent-assisted instruction, late afternoon special reading classes, and summer reading classes. No figures were made available to the writer on the numbers involved in these programs. Unlike the other four cities involved in the study, Los Angeles had no system of reading clinics. The local teacher education institutions—University of Southern California; University of California, Los Angeles; California State University; Occidental College; and Pepperdine College were relied upon to provide clinical reading services for those children who needed it.

The Elementary and Secondary Education Act had been of great value to the disadvantaged children of Los Angeles. Supplemented by California Senate Bill 28 and the Miller-Unruh Bill, the act had brought many millions of dollars into the school system.

In 1968-69 the E. S. E. A. Title I program brought benefits to 117 elementary schools and 24 secondary schools. A total of 6.5 million dollars was expended on elementary programs and 4.8 million dollars on secondary programs. Because of changes in the guidelines for expenditure of E. S. E. A. funds, there were drastic changes scheduled in the Los Angeles program for 1969-70. The amount of money spent on secondary programs was to decline to 2.6 million dollars and the amount for elementary programs was to increase to 9.5 million dollars. The money was earmarked to be spent for early intervention programs designed to provide massive help for the most deprived children in an attempt to bring about marked improvement in their educational status.

The 1968-69 secondary E. S. E. A. program had included many aspects such as reading laboratories, small-group basic reading classes, the preparation of materials for instruction in the history and literature of black people, and a program to expose high school students to legitimate theater productions.

The supervisor of reading in the Office of Special Programs indicated that 16,000 students in 800 classes were being reached at the secondary level. He described workshops in which 130 content area teachers had learned to use techniques in teaching reading in content subjects. The project was in its second year and included a practicum segment in which participants applied what they had learned by teaching one child in the prescribed manner.

The writer visited reading classes in John Burroughs Junior High School, Gompers Junior High School, and Lincoln Senior High School. The latter two were deep in the ghetto. Both of these were part of the Student Achievement Center program serving 24 secondary schools and reaching 10% of the secondary school population. It provided special classes for readers with fairly intense problems. Small classes, in which teachers were aided by paid and volunteer help, utilized special materials and specially trained teachers. One aspect of the program trained minority teachers for administrative positions. There were many other aspects of the program including fine arts work, counseling services, and community-centered activities.

There were several other specially funded secondary programs. One had produced eight novelettes and four books of readings especially appropriate to inner city adolescents. It was reported to the writer that Los Angeles Schools had a contract with Scholastic Book Services to produce six mini-anthologies on black literature to mate with their regular literature anthologies for use in junior high school reading classes.

The Elementary Specially Funded projects were numerous in Los Angeles Schools. The Reading Specialist program, which began operation in September 1966 had provided for over 200 specialists and consultants in over 100 schools. They had worked with over 5000 pupils in the primary grades in small groups. Pupils having the greatest need were chosen and given instruction specifically designed to meet their needs.

The chief impact of Federal assistance in Detroit on reading had been to establish new programs to care for the needs of retarded readers.

During 1968-69 two hundred remedial reading teachers operated in Detroit's 232 elementary schools. Each teacher was restricted to classes of no larger than ten pupils and a total load of only fifty per week—if state reimbursement was to be retained. In Michigan the state could provide up to 75% of a remedial reading teacher's salary if state standards were met and certified personnel were employed. In 1968-1969 actual state support was only 40% because of revenue shortages.

Since approximately one-third of Detroit's 300,000 school children were in need of remedial reading, the 1968-69 program, which provided direct instruction for only 17,000, was woefully inadequate. Detroit school officials had formulated a plan whereby remedial reading teachers could become remedial reading consultants. Under the plan the specialists would continue to do diagnoses of pupils' reading problems but remediation would be done by classroom teachers. The remedial consultants would provide materials and assistance to teachers in implementing plans for remediation. To fully implement the program, and make available enough specialists so that each school could employ one such person half time, would have cost a million dollars. In the climate of economic squeeze in 1969, the chances for implementation of such a program appeared to be dim.

The need for clinical reading services was met in Detroit during 1965-1968 by six Centers for Communications Skills, financed under Title I of the Elementary and Secondary School Act. These centers functioned in a manner very similar to that of the St. Louis reading clinics. They provided careful diagnosis of reading problems by a diagnostician, a social worker, a psychologist, remedial reading therapists, and school service assistants. Remedial reading instruction was provided in the clinics for many children. For others recommendations for instruction were made to their classroom teachers, who were then expected to carry out the plans.

Due to the decline in federal funds, the number of clinics was gradually cut back. During 1967-68 only four operated and by May of 1969 the number in operation had dwindled to one. The latter was operated by the Neighborhood Education Community Project financed under Title III of E. S. E. A. It could be characterized as a demonstration project serving five schools: three elementary, one junior high, one senior high. The three-year cost of the project was six million dollars.

The apparent impending cutback in state and Federal aid in 1969 had Detroit School supervisory officials concerned. They expressed to the writer the fear that remedial reading programs would be among the first to suffer. They stated that over a million dollars needed to be spent in 1969-70 to provide each school with a half-time remedial reading consultant. Only about one-tenth of that amount appeared to be available, if budget plans in existence were implemented.

Federal financial assistance to St. Louis had been extensive since the onset of such aid five years before. In 1968-69, out of a total budget of sixty million dollars, more than six million came from Federal sources, mostly from Title I of the Elementary and Secondary Education Act. Out of a total of fifty-seven special projects carried on in the district (including twenty-five supported by E.S.E.A.), twelve were in reading or were related to reading.

Six programs which had been financed by E. S. E. A. funds and were directly related to reading improvements had expenditures over $500,000 in the years 1965-1969. The largest of these was the Elementary-Rooms-of-Twenty Project. This type of program had operated in St. Louis since 1953. It provided remedial instruction in basic skills for children in grades three through six who had failed to respond satisfactorily to regular classroom instruction.

Room-of-Twenty teachers worked with only twenty children in a self-contained classroom setting and utilized special equipment and materials in a great effort to improve language abilities, including reading, and basic arithmetic skills. School officials in St. Louis had been determined not to permit the rooms to be filled with mentally retarded or socially maladjusted children. (The system had its own extensive program of special education.)

In 1968-69 a total of ninety-nine of the Rooms-of-Twenty operated in the city, including forty-eight in the Enright District, the one in which the researcher did most of his observing and one of the most deprived areas in the city. The writer was told that the average gain in reading in the Rooms-of-Twenty was ten months per school year. This could certainly not be termed miraculous growth.

A Reading Center program, in which specially trained remedial teachers worked with small groups (six to eight) for 40-45 minutes per day, or two or three times per week, was also in operation. In the Enright District, enrolling about 10% of the system's children, the program operated in thirteen of twenty-nine elementary schools. In eight of these, it was supported by federal aid. The proportion of children served by this program was about 10% of the elementary school population in the district.

For children with more severe reading problems than could be cared for in the schools, work in one of St. Louis' six Reading Clinics was a possibility. In 1943 the first reading clinic, begun by the present superintendent, Dr. William Kottmeyer, was opened. Since that time the number has been expanded to six. Diagnosis for over 30,000 children had been performed in the years 1943-1969. Over 10,000 had been successfully taught to read in the clinics during those years, according to Reading Clinic directors.

When the report writer visited the headquarters of the St. Louis Reading Clinics in November 1968, the director of the complex indicated that in-service training was the primary purpose of the clinics and service to children was a secondary purpose. She also said that during recent years eighteen clinicians had been trained each year and had returned to their schools to become remedial reading teachers or teachers in Rooms-of-Twenty. The writer was also told that most recently appointed (during the last six to ten years) administrators in St. Louis had received training in the clinics.

The clinics had not always had an easy time staying open. During the second semester of 1967-68 they were forced to close because the personnel were needed as classroom teachers during a short-lived emergency.

A large outlay of E. S. E. A. funds (over one million dollars in 1966-69) was devoted to the support of the remedial reading program in elementary and secondary schools. Another sizable amount (over $800,000) was spent in the acquisition of school library resources during the same period. Two other programs cost more than $1,500,000 during 1965-69. One provided for summer school attendance of 12,000 elementary and over 5,000 secondary students. Another was a program for the training and employment of teacher aides.

A federal program that had gained much attention in the city and in some professional journals was the library program. In implementing it the hall space in several of the crowded ghetto schools had been converted into libraries. This was possible because so many of the ghetto school buildings were very old with spacious halls, actually larger than was needed. Teachers in the system were lavish in their praise of it and reported that it greatly increased leisure reading in the schools in which it was instituted.

SECONDARY READING PROGRAMS

Each city studied was devoting some time and resources to secondary school reading improvement. For various reasons not as much information about reading at the secondary level was obtained in this study as about reading at the elementary level.

In New York City systematic instruction in developmental reading for pupils in grades seven through twelve was evidently inconsequential when the system was viewed as a whole. The research office indicated that there was no time scheduled for it. When asked to indicate the percentage of total enrollment involved in developmental reading no figures were given, though such figures were given for corrective and remedial reading.

Little information concerning secondary reading in Washington was obtained. There was evidence of substantial activity to involve secondary content teachers in helping students use reading as a means of learning. The writer sat in on a two-hour session in one of Washington's ghetto junior high schools while various content teachers and a reading consultant planned activities to help students employ reading in content learning.

The writer was also especially impressed with certain aspects of the secondary reading program in Los Angeles schools. A three-phase program existed, with each phase adapted to the needs of the specific groups it served. The Reading Improvement Program, essentially "developmental" reading, was for average and above-average readers and enrolled over 5,500 secondary students in 1968-69.

The Basic Reading program, a corrective program for slow learners and retarded readers enrolled over 6,000 students. Power Reading was an accelerated course for above-average students who were reading at or above grade level. Power Reading enrolled over 2,300 students during 1968-69. Both Basic Reading and the Reading Improvement courses could substitute for required English for one or two semesters. These three programs reached only five percent of the secondary school population, however. School officials admitted that whatever reading instruction the other 95% received was in regular English classes. Extensive in-service opportunities for all secondary teachers to become informed about reading were made available and attendance was promoted in many ways, including allowing professional improvement points for attending.

It was obvious, however, that secondary reading instruction in the regular program was a voluntary matter for most students and actually reached only a small minority of them. Special state and federally funded programs, however, touched many more students.

In Detroit reading instruction in the junior high was embodied chiefly in a program entitled Reach, one which combined instruction in reading and speech. Senior high school reading instruction was confined to whatever instruction was given in English classes.

The St. Louis program was similar. School officials acknowledged that they had a great shortage of teachers in secondary reading and that the program suffered because of it. They felt very concerned but rather helpless in the face of such critical needs at the elementary level and the shortage of well-trained secondary reading teachers.

FINANCIAL DIFFICULTIES

At the root of many of the problems in the systems studied, was a lack of resources to carry out plans for sensible solutions to problems. In all of the states where systems studied were located, there were legislative fights in spring and summer 1969 for school appropriations.

A major problem in New York City schools, as with all larger inner city systems, was that of finances. In an annual school budget of about a billion dollars, around one hundred million in federal aid was included. New York City schools received over $12,000,000 under Title I of the Elementary and Secondary Act alone in 1968-69.

The state legislature had been more helpful than in most states. Governor Rockefeller used the power of his office to bring the second teacher's strike to an end and supported larger state appropriations for the schools of New York City. The Ocean Hill-Brownsville controversy was ended when the state took over the operation of the strife-torn independent district.

Money was no less of a problem in Washington schools than in any other city studied. The U. S. Congress acted on the system's budget and had been known to criticize it line by line. Being a showcase system because of its location probably caused it to get more money than it otherwise would have, but Washington's schools were not affluent, they were *poor.* One Model School Division administrator told the writer that the division's budget might be cut by as much as one-third in 1969-70.

Big school districts mean big financing and the proposed budget for Los Angeles schools for 1969-70 was $765.5 million. Unless legislation proposed in the state assembly was approved, well over half of the funds came from local sources. The district was forced to trim about forty million dollars from the budget, find new sources of revenue, or risk a deficit of the same amount if the legislation did not pass. The shortage of funds occurred because voters on April 1, 1969, rejected proposals for school bond and tax measures—a common occurrence in big cities across the country.

Like all of the other systems examined in this study, Detroit experienced difficulties in getting adequate state and local financing—even for the programs that existed before Federal aid came.

The common shortage of funds to support needed changes (or even continuation and extension of existing worthwhile programs) in inner city school systems was illustrated on May 6, 1969, during the writer's visit when Detroit's city school superintendent announced on television that, if the state legislature did not provide sufficient funds, there would be cutbacks in special services, possible double sessions, shortening the school day in the secondary schools, the layoff of scores of teachers, or even no opening of schools in Detroit in September. He pointed out that, while one-sixth of the state's revenue came from Detroit, less than that amount found its way back to the area.

By May 6, 1969, the Michigan senate had passed an 840 million dollar bill for state aid to education, the largest single appropriation bill ever passed in Michigan. This, according to state legislators speaking on Detroit's television channel 2, represented an increase of 11% over the previous allocation of funds to schools. The amount constituted over one-half of the state's budget. A parliamentary wrangle between Michigan's divided legislature and reform-minded governor threatened to delay full passage of the bill, however. The issue of state aid to parochial schools complicated the otherwise cloudy picture of state financing of Michigan education.

The Detroit picture was further darkened by the fact that Michigan's teachers were already the third highest paid in the nation and Detroit's Federation of Teachers presented demands in late April for salary increases costing thirty-two million dollars. The system had already piled up a thirty million dollar deficit over a two-year period. Increases in teachers' salaries could only be met, according to Superintendent Drachler (DETROIT NEWS, May 7, 1969), by laying off between 600 and 1300 teachers.

The financial problem of education in St. Louis was one shared with the other major cities in the nation. At a time when the nation as a whole was spending 40.3% of its state revenue on education, Missouri spent only 34.6% for schools. Under an outdated Foundation Program formula, annual state aid for each St. Louis pupil had been $103 less than the state-wide average (THE ST. LOUIS POST-DISPATCH, April 7, 1969). While school costs were climbing, the assessed value of property increased less than one percent. Since the major portion of school monies came from property taxes in St. Louis, the relative stability in assessments hurt badly. Revenue was cut even more by the fact that one-third of all the property in the city was tax-exempt.

PROGNOSTICATION FOR INNER CITY READING

A view of the total situation regarding inner city education as a whole and reading instruction in the specific, is bleak and as of this writing not very hopeful for future improvement. At the root of the problem lies weak financial support for ghetto education. It can almost be said that, unless this aspect changes, there is little hope for future improvement. Perhaps as the situation worsens and there is an increase in suffering, violence, and an increase of the activity of the leadership of the black community, more support from society's affluent element will be forthcoming. It is questionable if anything else short of revolution will produce the desired changes.

There are elements in the present situation which foreshadow some future developments. The subtle changes occurring among black leaders hold some promise. The last five years have seen a rise in the pride and self respect of many educated blacks, including teachers. The writer has noted, among black inner city teachers, a deepened desire to be of greater service to their pupils, a greater faith in their possibili-

521

ties for learning, and an increased level of activity to provide more effective instruction. The attempts to build a pride in being black, to promote an interest in black culture and heritage, are very obvious among black teachers. As this feeling grows in strength, and the means of imparting it to pupils become more obvious and available, the more powerful it becomes. The long-term effect of the subtle changes described here on education will be favorable. They will very favorably affect the ability of black children to profit from whatever educational opportunity exists. They will not be sufficient, by themselves, to reverse the present trend toward highly ineffective education in the ghetto.

A sheer need for more and better facilities in city schools is very evident in every city studied. Existing buildings are very frequently not suitable for the task. Some movement to windowless, more secure buildings is probably inevitable. Losses from vandalism are now tremendous. The ease with which outsiders can invade school privacy is probably unbearable. More flexible use of inner space is highly desirable and buildings can provide this if they are designed for it. While substantial sums of money will be needed to provide new facilities, some imaginative renovation of many existing buildings will make them much more usable.

Some movements to counteract the bigness of city districts is already under way. Every system is beginning to experiment with the smaller district or subsystem to overcome some of the difficulties of sheer size. The writer predicts that this trend will grow. It will probably not reach the stage where patrons will have direct control of their neighborhood school. There would be many problems connected with the latter situation. Schools might well become victims of neighborhood petty politics and subject to the ebb and flow of parents' whims of the moment with curriculum, teacher morale, and orderly operation suffering. The evolving of some intermediate-size units, with delegation of more power to local patrons than now exists, seems to be likely, with favorable effects on education being the result.

522

If the feeling can be built that schools belong to the parents and children attending them, vandalism will decline and motivation for learning will improve. Some attempts by local parents at curriculum improvement—with hopeful reductions on the stress on rote learning, education solely as preparation for higher education and emphasis on remote educational goals—would be effective changes. An increase in real stress on education as preparation for work and lucrative job opportunities might irritate classical educators but will stimulate ghetto pupils to learn. An actual increase in job opportunities must, of course, go hand in hand, and ghetto education must truly more nearly become *education for work.*

An increase in local control, coupled with a growing interest in education on the part of black parents, will cause parents to be more involved in education than they now are. The involvement will not only take the form of greater parent stimulation of their children to learn, but the use of parents in the schools will increase. The experience of the Los Angeles effort to stimulate this presages what can occur. Systems interested in greater parent involvement would do well to study the Los Angeles efforts.

In this writer's opinion the shortage of a sufficient number of well educated teachers will force two other changes: a trend to differentiation of staff function and a much greater use of technology in education. Federal programs like Head Start and Title I have demonstrated the feasibility of the effective use of teacher aides. The use of paraprofessionals in schools, as they are used in hospitals, has been long overdue in education in general and will be a requirement if ghetto education is to improve to any marked degree. There are many routine activities related to teaching and learning that can be carried out successfully by high school graduates or persons with less-than-baccalaureate preparation. Programs to recruit and train such personnel will result in even greater success in their use. Teachers themselves must learn to be receptive to such help and must be taught how to use them to raise the efficiency of education.

The large families of ghetto children, and the resultant lack of parental attention to individual children, make the need for a smaller ratio of pupils to concerned adults in ghetto schools much greater than in more conventional schools. Many younger ghetto children need a concerned adult to talk to and listen to in order to develop adequate language ability—this is their greatest need in the area of language development. The responses of ghetto children to tutoring by educated nonprofessionals in programs sponsored by student organizations show how effective such arrangements can be. The experiences with the rise of nonprofessionals in programmed approaches in language learning (such as the Bereiter-Engelmann program) or the programmed tutoring in reading carried on at Indiana University also show how effective nonprofessionals can be.

Militancy among teachers will help to force the growth of staff differentiation. The kinds of salary demands being made such as the 20-20 ratio the St. Louis teachers' union is espousing (each teacher teaching only twenty youngsters twenty hours per week), coupled with growing public pressure for increased efficiency and cost accounting on the part of education, makes differentiation of staff function inevitable.

The growing possibilities for the use of technology as the means (as in the case of computer or systems teaching) or as an effective aid (as in the case of greater use of audiovisual aids) will make the use of paraprofessionals very desirable and probably necessary unless the costs of education are to become prohibitive. We have the technical knowledge and capability, if put to work by a team of methods specialists, curriculum experts and educational hardware designers, to produce far better programs, systems and devices than those now in use. Some infusion of Federal funds would hasten this development but it will occur anyway. The trend to recent merging of publishers and teaching hardware companies (for example, Ginn and Xerox) foreshadow the kind of development visualized. When this occurs the pressures on state and federal legislatures for educational appropriations will rival those which initiated the federal highway building program.

The beginnings of early massive intervention, as viewed in Los Angeles' Ascot Elementary School, Detroit's Field School and Washington's Logan School, hopefully will spread. A very adequate Head Start Program followed by an elementary program utilizing large numbers of professional personnel, working in a well-equipped and well-supplied school, could well be the early push that will help ghetto children at least even their odds for academic success. The New York More Effective Schools Program and the St. Louis Rooms-of-Twenty Schools (despite the lack of spectacular success) are, in principle, very sound ideas and offer one promising blueprint for ghetto education.

The experiments with innovation in reading, occurring in every city studied, indicate some interest in discovering the methodology and materials more suitable for teaching reading to ghetto children. The use of urban-oriented readers like the BANKS STREET READERS, the CITY SCHOOLS READERS, and THE SKYLINE SERIES is to be lauded and encouragement given for it to increase. One hopes that ultimately the ghetto child can be taught to read using the combination of method and materials most suitable to his own special learning style, sensory potential, and special needs. The reduction of the ratio of children to educational staff and the increased use of technology may make this possible. If so, it will demand a cadre of highly trained reading diagnosticians who can discover the proper avenues for teaching each child. This need poses a mighty task for teacher education institutions.

The problems of inner city education and improving reading instruction in that setting demand the attention of many kinds of agencies and people if solutions are to be found. The situation is far from hopeless if all who are concerned approach the task with cooperation, energy and imagination. One day not too far away there may be a realization of the dream described so well by the fallen martyr, Martin Luther King:

> *I have a dream today . . . I have a dream that one day*
> *every valley shall be made low. The rough places will*
> *be made straight.*

John Gardner, in his eulogy to King, provides a fitting close to this paper:

> Teacher to man, he left a lesson to the world; so simple it could be read from a primer, so rigorous, educated men might ignore it. The hands of the poor ask a full measure of justice. If their cup is not filled, it will not disappear.

Why Teach Them to Read?

Herman M. Frankel, M.D.
Portland Public Schools
Portland, Oregon

"There's nothing that says he has to read by fourth grade!"

"Why should we make him suffer if he can't learn how to read?"

"Maybe some kids don't need reading."

"Why teach them to read?"

What begins as a recognition of individual differences can become transformed so easily into the setting up of groups! Dismay at the unsatisfactory results of our attempts to teach can trap us, so insidiously, into blaming a child for not learning; and then into finding explanations that will first excuse him for *his* failure and then excuse him from participating in the learning activity itself; then into establishing other, less demanding programs for him and others like him. When we haven't succeeded as well as we would have liked in teaching some of our children, and they have fallen behind while in our care, it is so tempting to seek a reason that will serve, ultimately, to justify expecting less from each of them. How tragic that this will also serve to insure that they will continue to fall further and further behind.

Why teach them to read? Why say, in S. Alan Cohen's (1966) words,
> *Rich or poor, black or white,*
> *Teach every kid to read and write?* (p. 62)

WHY DO WE TEACH AT ALL?

Before asking why a particular set of skills and behaviors should be taught, perhaps we might examine the question, "Why do we teach at all?" Surely many children—some authorities have said *most* children—learn "by anything you do"; many children learn *in spite* of us. Children learn from each other, from their parents, from other members of the community and from television. Why teach? Why have schools for all children?

528

Historical Background

The rise of industrial production in the United States in the nineteenth century set the stage for free public education by creating new problems that only public schools could solve. As the factory system grew, it drew men, women and children out of the home and workshop, changed the character of their work and created a paradox: production processes became increasingly complex and more intimately connected with the growth of scientific knowledge, but the activities of the individual worker, artisan, or craftsman became simpler and required less knowledge and skill.

The effect of urbanization and industrialization on the child was profound. As his environment was broadened by making him a participant in an increasingly complex system of production and market relations, the range and variety of things he needed to learn about was increased; but at the same time, he was deprived of the opportunity for the informal education of daily life on the farm or in an artisan's workshop. Direct observation of the social forces around him became increasingly difficult as social relations became more impersonal and remote. So at the very time when he needed to learn more about the increasingly complex world of which he was a part, his daily life gave him fewer opportunities to learn about them.

In this setting, newly organized trade unions and workingmen's parties of the 1820's and 1830's demanded free public education at the same time that they struggled for a shorter work day. Because of the abolition of economic qualifications for voting, unions were a political as well as an economic force. Irving Adler (1957) cites a demand of New York City workers describing public education as the "safeguard of liberty" which would "cut the root of aristocracy" with the "axe of knowledge."

> *The right of suffrage which we all enjoy cannot be understand-*
> *ingly exercised by those whose want of education deprives them*

*of the means of acquiring such information as is necessary for
a proper and correct discharge of this duty.*

There was initial opposition to these demands, not the least of which
came from those segments of the population which provided private education for their own children. In the same way, the previous
century had seen Jefferson's and Rush's and Webster's plans for a
national system of education opposed by Northern merchants and
Southern slave-owners. They were unwilling to pay taxes for the
education of other people's children and were unconvinced of the
need for formal education of the poor. However, with growth of fac-
tories and crowded cities, the 15-hour work day for men, women and
children, the disintegration of family life and the destructive effect
on health and morals of overwork, low pay and slum life, there developed a widening gap between what children needed and what they
could get from everyday experience alone. As industry continued to
grow during the nineteenth century, more and more Northern indus-
trialists were swayed by the arguments of such social reformers as
Horace Mann who stated that "education has a market value," and
thought that public education could produce efficient, literate, disciplined workers and that education would thus increase the value of
workers' labor.

By the middle of the nineteenth century, legislation for free public education had been established in the United States. It was to take another
hundred years to extend such legislation to all states, build the schools,
establish training schools for teachers, and get the children into the
schools—not only by curbing child labor and making education com-
pulsory, but by raising the earnings of adult workers so that families
would not be forced to depend on the labor of their children.

Historically, then, our schools are a product of the dynamic nature
of our democracy. Free public schools were created and extended in
the same context in which the right to petition the government for re-
dress of grievances was established, and in which the right to vote was

extended first to include landless free adult males and then ex-slaves and then women. At the same time that we regard our schools as a product of our democracy, we must view them as a major force to assure democracy's further progress. If democracy is defined as government based on popular sovereignty and used to promote the general welfare, and if this implies free choice of political ideas and representatives, then it follows that restriction of such freedom is contrary to the principle of democracy. Of even greater importance to educators is the corollary that people must have access to all knowledge and ideas, so that they may make their own free choices.

A Position

So why do we teach? We teach to develop the intellectual capacity of our children, to stimulate their intellectual curiosity and creative ability, to impart a knowledge of subject matter, to promote physical and mental health, to foster in each child an appreciation of others and a respect for himself, and to equip our children with skills and behaviors and attitudes that will enable them to participate effectively in the decision-making process as it affects them and their families and their communities and their country and their world. We teach our children to ask questions and to seek information and to separate fact from opinion and to examine conflicting ideas and to come to their own conclusions and to have confidence in their own thinking because we have learned that ignorance and apathy, like unbridled power and special privilege, are barriers to advances in democracy. We teach because there are things that each of our children needs to know and we accept the responsibility of insuring that he does come to know them as a result of his interaction with us.

SO WHY TEACH THEM TO READ?

Writing is a means of communication, a medium for the transmission of what some call *information* and B. F. Skinner called *stimuli*. Thus, for a person with the appropriate skills, a page of writing can serve as "input"; such a person can be affected by, or can make use of, a page of writing in ways unavailable to a nonreader.

On Media

Can a nonreader obtain the same input in some other way? If so, will the effect on him be the same and will he be able to make use of the input in the same ways that are available to the reader?

Marshall MacLuhan has written that media are extensions of man, that "all media are extensions of some human faculty." By altering our environment they change the way we perceive the world; they change *us.* "All media work us over completely. They are so pervasive in their personal, political, economic, aesthetic, psychological, moral, ethical, and social consequences that they leave no part of us untouched, unaffected, unaltered." (MacLuhan and Fiore, 1967) The medium does far more than transmit a message; it plays a significant role in determining what the message is to be and how the recipient will be able to respond to it.

Different media do not transmit identical messages. One's response to *identical details* of the Venus de Milo or of the destruction of My Lai hamlet or the Florida Everglades or Watts will depend in large part on whether those details are conveyed by a series of 8 x 10 glossy photographs or a silent film or a 40-second telecast or an editorial cartoon or a newspaper photo or a handwritten letter or a page from the Congressional Record. Can the needs of those children who have trouble learning how to read be met through cassettes and television?

Some of MacLuhan's arguments, although fragmentary and undisciplined in places, are very relevant to this question and deserve scrutiny. In UNDERSTANDING MEDIA, he characterizes media as "hot" or "cool": "hot" if they extend one single sense in high definition and intensity and are well-filled with data; "cool" if they are of low definition and intensity and give a relatively meager amount of data. Hot media of high definition or intensity do not leave much to be filled in or completed by the audience and participation is low, according to MacLuhan; in the case of cool media of low definition or intensity, participation is high. Any intense experience of high definition, he writes, must be reduced to a cool state if it can be assimilated or learned. He characterizes photographs as hot, cartoons as cool; a lecture is hot, a seminar is cool; books are hot, TV is cool. Assembly-line production, with "the old mechanical pattern of setting up operations in lineal sequence," is hot, as are concepts of synchronized order, sequential analysis, repeatability and the phonetic alphabet; electric technology and automation and the instant synchronization of numerous operations which they make possible, are cool. "The alphabet and print technology fostered. . .detachment; electric technology fosters involvement." In THE MEDIUM IS THE MASS-AGE, he goes on to say:

> *Ours is a brand-new world of allatonceness. "Time" has ceased, "space" has vanished. We now live in a global village. . .a simultaneous happening. We are back in acoustic space. We have begun again to structure the primordial feeling, the tribal emotions from which a few centuries of literacy divorced us.* (p. 63)

In spite of the inconsistencies and oversimplifications of some of his arguments, MacLuhan shows quite forcefully that one cannot simply replace one medium with another or expect that activities which can be carried out through the use of a given medium can be conducted as well, if at all, in another.

Printed Page vs. Electronic Media

Attempts to replace the printed page with electronic media are especially futile. The total emotional involvement which the tube elicits from its audience—how distractible are the children from the Saturday morning TV cartoons?—makes it exceedingly difficult for members of that audience to perform certain kinds of analysis and evaluation. The "detachment" fostered by the printed page, on the other hand, permits a kind of "involvement" which is impossible with television as a mass medium. It permits a reader to stop *at any point* and reexamine a particular passage and to place it in apposition with *any other information.* In this sense, it is the printed page and *not* an electronic medium like the television screen, which lends itself readily to instant synchronization and simultaneous examination of different contents. In this sense, it is the television screen which limits a member of the audience to receiving input *only* in the sequence in which the sender chooses to present it. Headlines and placement of a newspaper story in the right-hand column of page one give that story some prominence; but it allows the reader far more room for independent evaluation of the day's events than does the reminder, at the end of the eleven o'clock news, that "today's top story" dealt with "our flight to the moon" and not with the 567 villagers or our air raids inside Cambodia or the opening of international nuclear arms limitation talks or the papal denunciation of "scandalous spending, whether for luxuries or for war" or the decision of the Pentagon to postpone research on a new, synthetic disease-causing organism because of "growing criticism." Hearing an explanation and analysis of a senator's speech to the nation immediately following that speech—without even a pause for a commercial—provides a kind of input that is very different from reading the text of the speech and finding in the very next column— without even space for an advertisement—one man's analysis and explanation of that speech. Seeing and hearing Dr. Hayakawa explain on television that the film we have just seen of policemen beating striking students was not "real evidence" simply does not lend itself to the same kind of analysis and evaluation as does the appearance, on adjacent newspaper columns, of a photograph and of an interview denying the existence or validity of that photograph.

The very nature of media and of the printed page and electronic media in particular, make it impossible simply to substitute one for another; but this is not the only reason to teach every child to read and write. If, in a truly democratic society, people must have free access to all knowledge and ideas, then it becomes important to ask not only, "Can one do the same things with input received via TV as with input presented on printed pages?" but also, "Are the same inputs available to the nonreading member of the TV audience as are available to the reader?"

Television—A Mass Medium

Television is more than simply a means for the transmission of messages, and it is more than a corporate enterprise comprising an important growth sector of the total industrial economy. Television is a crucial service industry for the rest of the economy, as a marketer of goods as well as a manufacturer of consumer needs. Corporate industry, having mastered volume production technology, relies heavily on television; "the industrial system," writes Kenneth Galbraith, "is profoundly dependent on commercial television and could not exist in its present form without it." The food, beverage, tobacco, drug and cosmetic, soap and cleaner, and auto industries produce a great many boxes of Maypo and cartons of Kent and bottles of Mr. Kleen and Chevrolets; commercial television "penetrates" the household and produces consumers.

The marketing director for a nationally sold floor wax wrote:

> *Television is an attractive medium because it is a mass medium in quality and frequency. The medium is extremely well-suited to low-interest products because it is an intrusive medium. Products can be injected where they are not wanted—which doesn't sound very moral but it's a fact of life with television. . . . Television is the medium which depends least on consumer cooperation to develop a rich response to symbolic stimulation. . . . It provides* [the consumer] *with a response which he would otherwise have to contribute in a major part out of himself.*

Tom Seaver is paid to sell the idea of buying Maypo; television sells us on the idea of *buying.*

It is no secret that television, like other mass media, is employed to sell ideas as well as products. Fred Friendly (1967), former president of CBS, wrote the following:

> . . . *"See It Now"* . . . *saw the light of day* [in 1953] *primarily because of a sponsor, the Aluminum Company of America. After the antimonopoly decision of the federal courts, Alcoa had decided to embark on an advertising campaign designed more to improve its institutional image than its sales, and the idea of a Murrow television program interested the company.* (p. xix)

> [By 1955] *Alcoa's market was changing. The short supply of aluminum caused by the Korean War was ending; increased competition demanded more of a hard sell. The job that "See It Now" had been purchased to achieve had been done; for many the name Alcoa had become a symbol of enlightened corporate leadership.* (p. 75)

The relationship between the television industry and the sponsors, and the very role of television as a marketing industry, creates certain barriers to the free transmission of ideas. Frank Stanton, CBS president at the time of the 1954 "See It Now" program which attacked Senator Joseph McCarthy believed, according to Friendly, "that such controversy and widespread doubts were harmful to the company's business relationships." (p. 60) Later during the 1954-55 season when "See It Now" did a two-part report on cigarettes and lung cancer, "both CBS and Alcoa felt the pressures of the tobacco industry, which buys both air time and aluminum foil. The attitude at CBS was, 'Why does Murrow have to save the world every week?' " (p. 69)

536

Control

The very pervasiveness of television, its very effectiveness as a salesman, has resulted in its coming under a kind of control—self-imposed, perhaps—which limits its availability as a medium of communication. At the very time when "legitimate" theater, literature, music, film, magazines, and newspapers are being affected by the flourishing underground in those decentralized media, television, which reaches the greatest mass-cult audience of all, has demonstrated its artistic and intellectual integrity by cancelling the Smothers Brothers Comedy Hour for an alleged breach of contract.

As a corporate industry and especially as an advertising medium industry, television has been more concerned with broadcasting salable entertainment than public service messages, documentary presentations or unpopular opinions. In discussing the cancellation of "See It Now" as a weekly program, Friendly indicates that "the decision to change to irregular programming was primarily a business calculation to create more financial yield from the time period."

The "global (electronic) village" is not characterized by a free flow of communication, a ready availability of information, a free exchange of ideas. At the time of the cancellation of the popular but controversial Smothers Brothers Comedy Hour, many people noted the irony in the fact that Bob Hope could comment favorably on the U.S. involvement in Viet Nam and newsmen could criticize student protest while the Smothers brothers' nonestablishment views were silenced.

Mason Williams, a former writer for the show and an articulate poet and musician in his own right, had earlier responded to the network's weekly advance pre-viewings and frequent deletions with the observation that the censor sits with a "kindergarten arts and crafts concept of moral responsibility," deleting rough talk, unpopular opinion or "anything with teeth" and that the ultimate result is the rendering of a pattern of ideas full of holes, a doily for your mind." (Mason Williams, 1964)

537

In addition, then, to the inherent limitations of electronic media which become apparent when they are compared with the printed page, there are other reasons which make electronic media unsuitable substitutes for the printed page as vehicles for the free exchange of ideas and information in a democratic society. These reasons relate in large part to the fact that communication through written material can be conducted without complex and expensive physical equipment and is therefore less subject to control than is communication through electronic media.

Problems

One of the inherent limitations of television as a medium of mass communication becomes a potential advantage when television is used as an instructional medium. The television screen lends itself to simplifications of reality; there is little room for clutter or refinement or detail.

When such simplification is desired as part of an instructional program—particularly when it is desirable to have the student attend raptly without evaluating and analyzing the content or the presentation—then that part of the instructional program might be presented *more* effectively via television than by any other medium, including a live teacher.

The use of electronic media, however, simply as *substitutes* for a teacher or a book, are fraught with danger. It is one thing to use television, for example, to do a job for which it is particularly well-suited; it is quite another matter to use it as a substitute for something better. The reason is simple: when a child learns from a teacher or from peers or from his own experience or from his analysis of printed text, he learns *how* to learn from his interactions with those resources, he develops confidence in his ability to learn from those interactions and he learns how to decide when to trust those resources. He develops the skills and the habits he will need if he is to be an inde-

538

pendent learner after he leaves school. He acquires the competencies
he will need if he is to make his own free choices as a thinking adult,
if he is to be able to participate actively and rationally in decision-
making as it affects his future and his world. He develops the means
of acquiring such information as is necessary for a "proper and correct discharge of his duty" as a citizen in a democratic society.

If, instead, his learning experiences are limited largely to absorbing
the messages of the television screen, then he will be ill-equipped to
examine the ideas and information which will *not* be made available
to him through his television screen. More important, perhaps, he
will be ill-equipped to analyze and evaluate even those ideas and
data which do appear on his screen, except in the way that the pro-
grammer has planned. If the child must rely on television it will be
rather hard for him to learn to write his own answers; it will be even
harder for him to learn to write his own questions.

The test of democracy as a viable form of social organization comes
when problems need to be solved and decisions need to be made. A
measure of its viability is the degree to which all the people involved
participate in the problem-solving and decision making; the proof of
its viability comes when free people engage actively and successfully
in solving their own problems, governing themselves and promoting
the general welfare.

Surely we are faced with enough problems to solve: disease, poverty,
old age, hunger, unemployment, racism, violence, alienated youth,
drugs, environmental pollution, urban decay, war. The need to solve
our problems has never been greater. It is more urgent than ever that
ideas be contributed by the small as well as the great, by the young,
the elderly, the poor, the disenfranchised, the blacks, the silent, the
meek.

We must depend on the active participation of every member of each community in our society if our children and theirs are to live in better times than the present.

ONLY IF THEY KNOW

Why teach them to read? Not only so that they will be able to read to their children and appreciate Macbeth and study philosophy and get off at the right exit on the freeway and find the right door and follow an instruction manual and take the right bottle from the shelf and play a new children's game, and not only because written material lends itself to some kinds of information-processing more readily than does material presented through other media, and not only because communication through written material can be conducted without complex and expensive physical equipment and is therefore less subject to control than is communication through other mass media, but also because *only if they know how to read will they be able to write.*

If the ultimate physical weapon is a rock—or a brick—in the hand of a man who wants to be free, then the ultimate tool in a struggle of ideas may be a quill pen—or a mimeograph machine.

REFERENCES

Adler, Irving. **What we want of our schools.** New York: The John Day Co., 1967.

Cohen, S. Alan. Reading instruction: Beating the 50-year lag. In S. Gordon (Ed.), **Pressures that disorganize the schools.** Newark, N.J.: New Jersey Secondary Schools Principals Association, 1966.

Friendly, Fred. **Due to circumstances beyond our control.** New York: Random House, 1967.

MacLuhan, Marshall. **Understanding media: The extensions of man.**
New York: New American Library, 1964.

MacLuhan, Marshall, & Fiore, Quentin. **The medium is the massage.**
New York: Bantom Books, 1967.

Williams, Mason. **The Mason Williams reading matter.** Garden City,
N.Y.: Doubleday & Co., 1964.

INDEX